Carol Erting   U3L   BE

LANGUAGE AT HOME AND AT SCHOOL
Volume 2

Language development in the pre-school years

LANGUAGE AT HOME AND AT SCHOOL
Edited by Gordon Wells

Previously published

Learning through interaction: the study of language development
GORDON WELLS with contributions by ALLAYNE BRIDGES, PETER FRENCH, MARGARET MACLURE, CHRIS SINHA, VALERIE WALKERDINE and BENCIE WOLL

Forthcoming

Children learning to read and write BRIDIE RABAN

Language development
in the pre-school years

GORDON WELLS

Department of Curriculum
Ontario Institute for Studies in Education, Toronto
Formerly Centre for the Study of Language and Communication,
University of Bristol

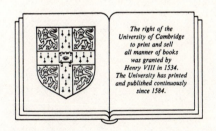

The right of the
University of Cambridge
to print and sell
all manner of books
was granted by
Henry VIII in 1534.
The University has printed
and published continuously
since 1584.

Cambridge University Press

Cambridge
London   New York   New Rochelle
Melbourne   Sydney

Published by the Press Syndicate of the University of Cambridge
The Pitt Building, Trumpington Street, Cambridge CB2 1RP
32 East 57th Street, New York, NY 10022, USA
10 Stamford Road, Oakleigh, Melbourne 3166, Australia

First published 1985

Printed in Great Britain at The Pitman Press, Bath

Library of Congress catalogue card number: 84–5527

British Library Cataloguing in Publication Data

Wells, Gordon
Language development in the pre-school years.—
(Language at home and at school; v.2)
1. Language acquisition
I. Title   II. Series
401'.9   p118

ISBN 0 521 26461 8 *hard covers*
ISBN 0 521 31905 6 *paperback*

Contents

Introduction

Having lived with a single piece of research for more than 13 years, either working on it or worrying about it, it is difficult to attain the objectivity which is expected of the writer of the traditional research report. In fact, during the last few years, as the moment approached when I could at last begin writing it up, I have given much thought to the question of how to present it. Should I aim at the traditional style of presentation, in which the results are shown to follow from the methodology without a glimpse being offered of the muddle and misadventure which I suspect is at least a part of the reality of every research project in the human sciences. Or, should I, like George Miller in *Spontaneous Apprentices* (1977), try to convey to the reader the actual experience of carrying out the research, with all the catastrophes and compromises as well as the achievements laid bare for all to see?

Neither solution seemed really satisfactory. To ignore the actuality, pretending that everything went smoothly according to the original plan, would be a serious distortion and, in any case, would lack credibility. For how could one gloss over the fact that a project that was intended to be completed in five years actually took over ten to reach a point at which the results were sufficiently comprehensive to justify their presentation. On the other hand, a history of the project in terms of the problems that had to be overcome would also be a distortion. They certainly influenced the kind of results that we were able to achieve, and for that reason alone must be mentioned. But they were only a part of the total experience, which, for much of the time, was far less dramatic: painstaking, laborious work of a routine kind that is familiar to every researcher. In the end, I have decided to approach the problem as follows. In the main body of the text, I shall endeavour to adopt the traditional, relatively impersonal approach, mentioning problems and the way in which they were resolved only where they are important for an evaluation of the results. In this introductory chapter, however, I shall give a personal account of the project, its history and major strengths and weaknesses, and I shall try to convey something of the day-by-day experience of carrying out the research, with its peaks and troughs of achievement and frustration, of excitement and despair.

The Bristol Language Development Study: the pre-school years

One very obvious characteristic of longitudinal research is that, inevitably, a long time elapses between drawing up the original plan and writing up results. During the intervening period, the discipline develops and questions that seemed of crucial importance at the planning stage may well be seen to be less important or will have been answered long before the research is completed. Equally probably, other questions, which the original plan did not address, will have become the focus of attention. This has certainly happened in the field of child language, and issues that were at the centre of debate at the very beginning of the research in 1971 are no longer so more than a decade later.

In the late 1960s and early 1970s, when the Bristol Study was still at the planning stage, research on language development was still heavily influenced by Chomsky's work, with its strong emphasis on syntactic rule-learning. However, the initial enthusiasm for this approach was already on the wane and other emphases were beginning to emerge. Although it had been shown that grammars written for individual children at successive points in development could yield important insights into regularities in what was being learned (Brown *et al.*, 1969; Klima and Bellugi, 1966) and, by appeal to cumulative syntactic complexity, offer tentative explanations for the order of learning (Brown and Hanlon, 1970), there was a growing feeling that the exclusive concentration on syntax was failing to do justice to the full richness of language in use. The complex relationship between the emerging formal system and the experiences and intentions of the moving, thinking and feeling child who was learning to use that system was largely being ignored.

As Brown himself subsequently recognized (Brown, 1973), in order to segment and classify the linguistic units which entered into the rules of the grammars written for successive points of development, the researcher found himself, inevitably, engaged in making a 'rich interpretation' of the child's utterances, drawing upon their assumed meaning intentions in context in order actually to 'hear' what the child said. However this was not just a temporary methodological embarrassment for child language researchers, which would eventually be overcome. It has since become clear that this is an essential characteristic of the way in which *all* human beings communicate through language and hence likely also to be central to any explanation of the way in which children acquire that system of communication. What became increasingly clear in the early 1970s, was that language is most fruitfully seen as a complex resource of lexical and morpho-syntactic systems which are used by members of a common culture to realize ideational and functional meaning intentions through conversational exchanges in specific situations. The acquisition of this resource can therefore only be adequately understood by studying it in its natural conversational context and by relating it to the child's simultaneous social and intellectual development.

Viewed from the vantage point of the 1980s, these statements may well appear self-evident, but they represent the outcome of a substantial number of individual research studies which were cumulatively bringing about a quite radical change in perspective from that which held sway in the early 1960s. In 1972, the paradigm shift was gaining momentum and it was against this background that the descriptive approach of the Bristol Study was gradually worked out. Crucial to this process was a period of collaboration, at the University of California at Berkeley, with Francesco Antinucci and Dan Slobin and his research group in the preparation of a semantic coding scheme which was to be used in the Berkeley Cross-Cultural Study as well as in the Bristol project. In August of the same year, the scheme was presented and discussed at the Second Child-Language Conference held in Florence.

At that same conference other novel, but now commonplace, ideas were being aired: the importance of non-verbal behaviour for an understanding of child utterances; the essential continuity of communicative functions from the pre-linguistic through to the fully linguistic stages of development; the value of accompanying recordings of communicative behaviour with careful assessment of the child's skills in the cognitive and social domains hypothesized to be the necessary foundations on which the edifice of language is later constructed; the importance of treating adult–child interaction as the object of investigation rather than the child's behaviour alone. Studies that have met at least some of these criteria have since been completed and reported (e.g. Bates *et al.*, 1976; Carter, 1979; Halliday, 1975; Ratner and Bruner, 1978; Snow, 1977), and in retrospect I wish we had been able to incorporate some of these approaches more fully into our own study. However, at that time they were still for the most part in an experimental stage and our limited resources were fully occupied in trying to attain our own chosen objectives.

First, we had to design a coding scheme that would enable us to carry out a comprehensive linguistic analysis of the speech of children learning English as their first language from the age of 15 months up to the point of school entry at the age of five years. As well as striking an appropriate balance between the description of the underlying meaning intentions of children's utterances and their formal realization in syntax and morphology, the scheme was also intended to capture the relationship between child utterances and their conversational context and to do so over the full age-range 15–60 months. The final version is described in chapter 2.

Secondly, we needed to obtain a corpus of data for description that was both longitudinal and representative. Longitudinal studies of language development are not new, of course. Indeed the majority of recent studies have had a longitudinal dimension, but the samples studied have been small and usually socially homogeneous. Large and representative samples have been studied before (McCarthy, 1930; Templin, 1957), but not in a longitudinal manner. However, in no study, to my knowledge, had a longitudinal design been combined with an attempt to ensure representativeness, of both the sample of children studied and the situations in which their speech was recorded.

As more attention has come to be focussed on the context in which language learning takes place and on the specific characteristics of the language that is addressed to young children, the representativeness of the data collected is an issue that has taken on particular importance. For, if some types of conversational experience particularly facilitate the child's development, and if these are more likely to occur in some situations rather than in others, it becomes of prime importance to ensure that naturally occurring variation between children in the quantity of such experiences is represented in the corpus of data to be investigated.

True representativeness can only be ensured, of course, when the parameters on which systematic variation occurs have been fully documented. Yet it was precisely such documentation that was lacking when the Bristol Study was being planned. We therefore took as representative a sample as possible within the constraints of what little knowledge was available, both about differences between speakers and about differences between situations. The precise methods used will be described in detail in chapter 1.

At this point, however, there is a further important issue that needs to be raised, namely that of ecological validity. If the aim is to discover what language children produce and understand at successive points in their development, and how that development is related to their experience of other people speaking with them, it is not sufficient to obtain a representative sample of families and to observe them in a representative variety of situations. It is also necessary to ensure that the interactions observed are those that are characteristic of the people concerned and not atypical performances artificially produced by the constraints of the research.

As is well understood by sociolinguists such as Labov (1972a), the style of speech adopted varies not only according to the activity engaged in but also according to the way in which the social context of the activity is perceived. Young children may not be particularly sensitive to changes in social setting, but it is difficult to believe that the mothers who are their most frequent conversational partners are not affected by the entry of relative strangers into their homes armed with recording equipment, notebooks and pencils, still more by the unfamiliarity of the social setting when they are requested to visit the researcher's laboratory and there to 'play naturally' with their child with the array of toys provided by the researcher. Until it has been proved to the contrary, therefore, I shall remain unconvinced by claims that the conversation recorded in such artificial situations does not differ in significant ways from that which typically occurs in the home when there is no observer present. Indeed our own recordings show that situations in which mother and child talk together while they play – the situation artificially set up by so many researchers – rarely occurs spontaneously in any home, and not at all in a substantial proportion.

To find a method of obtaining valid, representative samples of conversation between the child and his normal conversational partners was thus one of the major objectives of our study. Within the limits set by ethical considerations, we have come close, I believe, to attaining that objective – though not without difficulties, some of which will be recounted in the following section. However, insofar as we have been successful, I consider this to be one of the major achievements of the project.

Having recorded a sample of children much larger than had previously been studied in a longitudinal design, we decided to look first at the extent of the similarity that exists between children who are acquiring the same first language. As I shall argue in chapter 4, it is logically necessary to start by establishing a common base-line before one can begin to examine individual differences. Work to date, therefore, has been mainly concerned with the identification of the major common trends in development. These are described in chapters 4, 5 and 6. However, the same breadth of sampling also provides an excellent basis for the systematic investigation of individual differences, and it is to this that we shall be addressing ourselves in the next phase of our work. Until now, however, we have only been able to look at some of the more salient aspects of variation, such as variation in rate of development, and these are briefly introduced in chapter 3 and discussed more fully in chapter 8.

Since differences between children in rate of development may have quite a profound effect on their later ability to cope with the language demands of the classroom, we have also been concerned to identify environmental factors that contribute to this variation. Chief among these, I believe, is the quality of the conversational experience that the child enjoys with his parents and other care-takers. Whilst much of the work still remains to be done to discover precisely how this experience contributes to the child's learning, we have carried out one study that identifies certain features of the adult input that are associated with variation in the children's rate of development. This is reported in chapter 9. Finally, an interpretation of the main findings is presented in chapter 10 with reference to specific examples from the recorded conversational data.

Although the description of the sequence of development that forms the core of the book probably contains few surprises, we believe it is of value to have filled out and confirmed the picture sketched by previous researchers, and to have done so on the basis of a corpus of naturally occurring speech collected from a large and socially representative sample of children. The preliminary work on the contribution of the child's conversational experience to his language learning will, we hope, also prove of value. If the contribution of the parents to a child's language development is as important as I believe it to be, we need to understand precisely the nature of the relationship between input and development. Only then shall we be in a position to intervene effectively in contexts where help is needed.

The project: an insider's view
In the previous section, I emphasized two of the major aims of the project: representativeness in the sample and comprehensiveness in

its description. Both these aims require a project on a large scale and, as might be anticipated, this was the root cause of almost every one of the problems that beset us – from the scheduling and carrying out of the observations to the computer-assisted analysis of the data.

A few simple statistics will give some idea of the scale of the task. First of all the children: 128 of them plus a dozen 'reserves', each of whom had to be observed at three-monthly intervals over a 2¼-year period. This meant that more than 1280 recordings had to be arranged, carried out and transcribed within the space of three years. Each of these recordings then yielded an average of well over 100 child utterances, each of which had to be coded for some 100 linguistic categories, bringing the number of coding decisions to be made, checked, entered into the computer and finally analysed to a total in the order of 12½ million. Perhaps in the end it is more surprising that the task was completed at all than that it took twice as long as originally anticipated.

The troubles began with the recording equipment. Our aim was to produce a cheap but reliable programmable bugging device which would allow us to record short samples of naturally occurring conversation at predetermined times during the course of a normal day. Had we embarked on this task ten years later, we should have been able to reap the benefits of the microchip revolution, but in 1970 we had to make do with mechanical clock movements, electrical contacts and – at the heart of the apparatus – a synchronous motor. This motor, which was started by an electrical relay, completed a full cycle in 120 seconds, switching on the radio receiver and tape recorder, and switching them off again 90 seconds later. After several months' work we had assembled a prototype device that worked sufficiently reliably throughout the one-year pilot study to convince the Social Science Research Council that our speech-sampling design was feasible.

The grant for the main study was awarded in September 1972, with a planned starting date at the beginning of January 1973. As soon as the offer of the grant was received, the necessary components to make up nine recording devices were ordered and within several weeks all were received from the manufacturers – all, that is, except the synchronous motors. Several attempts to speed up delivery were made, but with no effect. On 22 December, I telephoned the suppliers in a desperate attempt to obtain them before the Christmas holiday, only to be told that there were none in stock and we should have to wait until further supplies were received from the manufacturers in France. I offered to go and collect them myself, but was informed that no purpose would be served by my journey, as the company was on strike.

The date for the first scheduled observations arrived, and, as there were only 16 recordings to be made during January, we were able to keep to schedule, using the pilot study prototype device. Meanwhile, the strike in the French company had come to an end and delivery of the motors was eagerly awaited. When they still had not arrived by mid-January, I telephoned again and received the stupefying answer that production of this particular motor had been discontinued and no further deliveries would take place.

Even at this late stage, however, the problem did not seem insoluble. Surely another source of supply could be found? It could not. So we next approached a local electrical engineering firm and asked them to design an electronic circuit to our specifications. The design engineer foresaw no problems and promised to produce a prototype in a couple of weeks. A month later, having heard nothing, we asked for a progress report and were told that they had 'hit a few snags, but should have it ready in ten days'. Two weeks later, the firm had to admit that they were unable to produce a circuit of the type we required.

By this time we were into March. Fortunately the schedule still only called for 16 recordings, which could be made using the prototype device. But April was coming closer, when 32 recordings would need to be made – a schedule quite impossible to meet with only one set of recording equipment.

At this point, my colleague, Dr Bernard Chapman, came to the rescue. He had already contributed many hours at the original planning stage demonstrating inventiveness and ingenuity in the overall design. These qualities were now called on to the full as he wrestled with the problem of achieving the precision of timing originally assured by the synchronous motor by different means. His solution to the problem is described in chapter 1. It was effective and cheap to produce, but difficult to make robust enough to stand up to almost constant use over a period of three years. For several weeks he and Ivan Colhoun, the technician, modified and adjusted the eight sets of components, each morning hoping that the over-night trials would have gone successfully. The beginning of April came and went, with each day seeing our hopes dashed yet again. By the end of the second week we had only made eight recordings and still had 24 to carry out before the end of the month. At that moment I almost abandoned hope and decided that if the equipment was not functioning reliably by the end of the following day, I should have to inform the SSRC of our inability to carry out the recording schedule as planned and offer to return or renegotiate the grant. It was a moment of deep despondency, and one which I should not like to have to live through again. Then the following morning, Bernard told me that the over-night trials had finally been successful. All the problems seemed to have been solved and the project would be able to go ahead after all.

Of course, the timing devices did not continue to work perfectly from that moment on. But they proved sufficiently reliable for us to be able to catch up with the planned schedule and carry it through to the end without any crisis of similar proportions.

This was not the only near disaster. Two arose during the long process of coding – the first because the families being studied were much more talkative than we had expected on the basis of the pilot study. The coding was carried out by part-time workers in their own homes, who were paid a fixed fee on the assumption that most transcripts would contain somewhere between 90 and 200 child utterances. In practice, quite a number of children produced upwards of 300 utterances in the set sampling period, and quite reasonably the coders felt the fee was too low. Since the total amount of money available to pay for the coding was fixed, some method of reducing the amount of work had to be found. First, we decided not to code the last two recordings of the older cohort, at five years three months and five years six months. These transcripts are still sitting in the filing cabinets, therefore, waiting for resources to become available enabling us to code and analyse them. Secondly, we decided to reduce the number of utterances to be coded in very long transcripts, by allowing the number of 90-second samples processed to be reduced as low as 12 out of the scheduled 18, provided (a) that the total number of utterances coded was in excess of 120 and (b) that the samples omitted were selected at random, and no more than two were dropped out of each block of four (see chapter 1 for more precise details).

Naturally, we were worried that this might distort the representativeness of the speech samples from these more talkative children and thus bias subsequent analyses, particularly those comparing children in terms of their rate of development. In the last resort, without actually coding all the recordings in full, we cannot know whether distortion has resulted or not, but as far as we can tell from the various statistical checks we have run, this does not seem to be the case. Although there is a significant relationship between rate of development and the amount of speech occurring in 18 90-second samples, there is no evidence of a systematic relationship between rate of development and the number of utterances actually coded.

The second crisis occurred right at the end of the period of coding, when the first statistical analyses were being run. The initial output from the computer, based on the first observation of the older children, contained some results that were rather surprising and one or two that were simply nonsensical. Having checked the analysis program itself, we looked next at the computer print-out of the codings and finally at the corresponding utterances in the transcripts. It immediately became clear that the bizarre results had been caused by coding errors. And in comparing the codings and transcripts of several children it was apparent that the errors were both many and serious.

For a short while it again seemed that we had suffered a disaster from which there could be no reprieve. However, we began to check the codings systematically and found that it was only the work of a few coders that was seriously in error. Even more fortunately, these unsatisfactory coders proved to have been amongst those who found the work uncongenial and who gave up after coding only a small number of transcripts. By fixing criteria of acceptability (described in chapter 1), we were able to identify all the transcripts that would have to be recoded and the number proved sufficiently small for the full-time staff, working many hours of overtime, to complete recoding in a matter of months. Once again, we were back in business.

Of all my experiences in carrying out this research programme, however, none has been so traumatic or as long-enduring as my love–hate relationship with 'the computer'. Let me admit at the outset that I have never succeeded in becoming one of that fortunate band of people who write FORTRAN as easily as they write English, can translate between binary and hexadecimal digits at a glance and can estimate accurately how many megabytes of data can be processed in a given time on a particular machine. However, over the years, perforce, I have come to understand a certain amount about both hardware and software and, in the process, have come to appreciate some of the difficulties faced by my programming colleagues, who have had the task of implementing the analysis of our coded data. But what I have still not learned to cope with is the inscrutability of the computer: its dumb insolence in refusing to tell me why it is not carrying out my intentions on this occasion when, only last week, it performed an almost identical task with such speed and efficiency.

Part of the problem, I now see with hindsight, was to design the coding scheme without knowing how the resulting coded data would subsequently be analysed by means of computer programs. At least some of the difficulties that had to be worked around by means of special-purpose modules of program could have been avoided if we had had a programmer as a member of the research team from the beginning. That is a lesson that I have learned the hard way. But for the remaining difficulties I think I can reasonably disclaim responsibility.

These began towards the end of 1978, as we were completing the first round of analysis of the coded data, using the Language Analysis Program (LAP) that Chris Amos had written for the purpose. By then most of the analyses of the semantic and pragmatic categories had been completed and we were embarking on the analysis of the strings of syntactic categories that made up the coding of the surface structure of each utterance. We already knew that the number of different string-types was too large to work with them as separate variables, and so we planned to group them and then to tabulate the frequencies of grouped categories at successive ages. In order to group strings into superordinate categories, however, LAP required a listing of the members of each group, so we first had to produce a complete list of all the string-types that occurred in the coded data. Before it had worked sequentially through more than about one third of the data, however, the university main-frame computer ran out of available memory and so the task could not be completed.

At this point two events occurred which together brought all analysis to a halt. First, Chris Amos left to take up a permanent full-time appointment in the Computer Centre of another university. Chris had written and implemented LAP both on our ARCTURUS mini-computer and on the main-frame ICL 4/75, and he understood the complexities of the various modules that had been necessary to cope with the format of the coded data. His successor, Frank Maddix, would clearly need some time to become familiar with the whole enterprise before he could be expected to tackle the problem that had arisen with the syntactic strings. But almost at the same time that Frank took up his appointment, Bristol University began to run down the facilities available on the 4/75 as part of the planned change-over to the new and more powerful Honeywell MULTICS configuration, which became operational in

1980. So, not only did he have to learn what the LAP program was intended to do and how it did it, but he also found himself immediately having to introduce modifications to the existing program in order to cope with the reduced capacity of the 4/75. Not surprisingly, the task proved impossible and no further progress was made using the 4/75.

As the change-over proceeded, we were advised to transfer the LAP program and the coded data files to the ICL 29/80 computer at the nearby regional computing centre at Bath. This involved writing programs to translate the data so that they could be read on this different machine, a task which was made exceptionally difficult by the fact that the 29/80 had no facility for interactive program development. In fact the task was never satisfactorily completed.

By the end of 1980 (two years after we had first hit the problem in the analysis of the syntactic strings), MULTICS was more or less fully operational and it was agreed with the Director of the Bristol Computer Centre that it would be sensible to transfer both program and data back to Bristol and to attempt to resolve our problems using the new computer. Once again, this involved translating the data and, because the machine had only recently been installed, this was not straightforward.

But that was only the beginning of a new series of difficulties. As on the 4/75, there was insufficient space in the core memory for program and data to be kept directly accessible and both had to be read in prior to each program run. As there was initially no private-volume disk facility, as there had been on the 4/75, the program and data had to be read from magnetic tape, which was extremely slow. But even when a dedicated disk did become available some months later, our problems were not solved, as the maximum amount of time allotted to any disk user, two hours, was insufficient to carry out a complete run. In spite of the fast operating speed of the powerful central processor in MULTICS, a full LAP analysis of one of the two data-bases (older cohort or younger cohort) required 40 minutes of Central Processing Unit time and, with the multiple-user system working to near its full capacity, this was impossible to achieve in the two-hour real-time slot during which our disk could be mounted. In spite of much hard work and the good will of all concerned, therefore, we still did not have a means of continuing with the straightforward analyses that still had to be carried out and we had made no tangible progress at all towards finding a solution to the problem of analysing the syntactic data.

At last, early in 1981, it was agreed to consider a radically different alternative, suggested by Frank Maddix. Rather than attempt to find a way of tailoring our need for relatively low-level batch processing of a large quantity of data to fit the operating procedures of a machine intended for high-level interactive data analysis, he proposed that we should transfer the work to a micro-processor-based mini-computer configuration, dedicated exclusively to the needs of the project. The University undertook to rent an LSI 11/23 configuration for six months until further support from the SSRC could be arranged. Ironically, this was the solution that we had proposed to the SSRC as long ago as 1975, but without success.

However, even this changeover was not without difficulties. By this stage, the data had been transferred backwards and forwards four times between computers, with translation from one format to another being required on each occasion. As a result, a small number of errors had been introduced, which had to be located and corrected. The supply of one essential component was also delayed by several months. Finally, at the beginning of August 1981, almost exactly three years after the last successful analysis had been carried out on the 4/75, it once again become possible to analyse the coded data and begin the program development necessary to group and analyse the syntactic strings. Three years of exasperating frustration. But I must hasten to add that since we have had our own mini-computer fully operational, we have also seen the other face of computing, as we have been able to develop and use the programs to investigate the sequence of language development on which the central chapters of this book are based. Without its capacity for rapid number-crunching, we should still have been tallying with pencil and paper and wrestling with the arithmetical calculations of the subsequent statistical analyses.

In fact, we were sufficiently optimistic throughout the long period of delay – or perhaps too cowardly – ever to attempt to carry out the analyses by hand. Instead, we concentrated on other aspects of the research programme: the first investigations of the relationship between input and development, which are reported in this volume, and the follow-up study which extended the original investigation into the years of primary education – a dimension of the research which will be reported in a subsequent volume.

If the project had its bad moments, it also had many good moments, not least when successive analyses produced results that began to add up to a coherent picture. It also had some extremely funny moments, of which one, at least, is worth recounting. Bugging families at home can be expected to yield some conversational gems. Some of the most amusing were the various accounts of the purpose of the project given by the mothers concerned to relatives and neighbours who asked about the hump that had suddenly appeared on the children's backs. But the incident I remember most vividly occurred on the very first recording of one of the younger children.

Between the selection of each child and the first of the ten observations, I visited each child's parents to explain once again the purpose of the project and to give the parents an opportunity to withdraw before we started the observations if they had any misgivings or reasons for believing they might not be able to see the project through to its conclusion. At this visit I assured the parents that they and their children would remain anonymous and undertook to erase any material recorded that they considered to be confidential. One family, however, was away from home every time I called, and it was on the morning following the first recording that I finally found the mother at home.

She was in a very excited state and immediately asked me to erase one of the samples from the previous day's recording. Apparently what had happened was that, during the day, while her husband had been out at work, a friend – the husband of her best friend – had called and stayed for a chat. While he was there the child we were recording had fallen and hurt himself and the mother had picked him up and kissed him better. The visitor had jokingly taken advantage of the situation and said he'd like one too and the ensuing kiss had been clearly overheard by the microphone bug.

However, this was not the full extent of her embarrassment. In the evening, the mother had invited her friend (the wife) to come and listen to the tape as it was played through (quite a number of families found the evening play-back more entertaining than watching television), and in front of both her husband and her friend, she had heard the whole episode replayed with full sound effects.

This is perhaps the most extreme example, but it is only one of many snatches of interaction which demonstrate the naturalness of the behaviour that we observed and give us grounds for believing that the families were, for the most part, forgetful of the fact that a microphone was in their midst, perhaps recording what they said at that very instant.

In the end, that is perhaps the most important achievement of the project: to have collected this rich and varied longitudinal record of the daily lives of 128 children in the early stages of their development. We have carried out an intensive study of these data from a linguistic point of view, but they also contain a wealth of information of other kinds that is still waiting to be explored. During the last few years, with financial assistance from the SSRC, the longitudinal records of 32 of the children – those who were the subjects in the follow-up study referred to above – have been typed into computer store and can now be reproduced either in hard copy or on disk or magnetic tape and made available to other researchers who wish to make use of this resource. Already, the studies for which they have provided data range from an investigation of mathematical experiences in the home, to two studies of the development of meta-linguistic awareness; from an investigation of children's quarrels to an exploration of the antecedents of personality disorder. After the effort that went into the making of these recordings of naturally occurring interaction, I am delighted that others should benefit from them too, and hope that they will continue to be used in the future.

For our own part, we have achieved *most* of what we originally intended, despite the many difficulties encountered and, looking back over the last ten years, it is not so much the difficulties that stand out in my memory as the efforts of all those who have been concerned in the research to make it a success. Many people, far too numerous to mention individually, have given generously of their time and energy to do their part, as interviewers, transcribers and coders in a team that over the years has numbered well over 100 part-time workers. Without their commitment to the research, which went far beyond simply doing the job for which they were paid, the whole project would have foundered when things failed to go according to plan.

To the children and their families we also owe an enormous debt of gratitude. With no benefit to themselves, and sometimes at the cost of considerable inconvenience, 128 families – the majority of the random sample who were initially approached – agreed to take part in the research and continued to cooperate over a period of several years, despite requests to repeat recordings that had failed and to make sometimes long and inconvenient journeys across the city to bring the children to the University for the regular programme of tests. I was warned before the study began to expect a 'drop-out' rate of at least one in three over a period of two to three years. Perhaps we have been unusually fortunate, but all but a small handful of the families continued to participate willingly and, almost ten years later, of the sub-sample of 32 families chosen for the follow-up study, every single one is still participating, even though several have moved house during that time, some to other parts of the country. To all of them I wish to express my thanks for their patience, their cooperation and their friendliness.

It is, of course, to the members of the central research team and to my colleagues in the School of Education that I owe the greatest debt. I have already mentioned Bernard Chapman and Ivan Colhoun. Bernard also gave generously of his time and expertise in the early stages of bringing the power of the computer to bear on the tasks of reading, checking and analysing the coded data. This role was subsequently taken over by Chris Amos, who wrote the Language Analysis Program and, on his departure, by Frank Maddix, who finally solved the problems of analysing the syntactic data.

At the heart of the project stands the Coding Scheme and to its design and use many people have contributed. The earliest outlines were sketched during the pre-pilot phase with the help of Kay Sandells. But it was during the pilot study proper that the scheme largely took on its present shape as a result of the very substantial contribution of Linda Ferrier in trying out successive versions, suggesting modifications, and finally working out the coding procedure. Chapter 2 of this volume is based on the paper in which we presented the main outline of the scheme at the Florence conference in 1972.

When Linda left the project, her place was taken by Bencie Woll, to whom fell the task of training the coders and supervising their work. During the early months of this task, she suggested a number of improvements to the coding scheme and, with her assistance, a revised version was prepared and published in 1975. It was Bencie, too, who bore the brunt of the task of recoding. Once the coding was completed, Bencie planned and carried out the first stage of the analysis of the data, some of the results of which she has written up and published.

During the same period the other full-time research worker on the project was Chris Sinha, who was responsible for the design of the maternal interview and for the administration of the various tests. An early version of the comprehension test was worked out with the help of Rosamund Platt but, as a result of experience during the pilot study, this was abandoned and the version actually used was designed by Valerie Walkerdine, who joined the team as an SSRC student. This test, and a test of imitation, were administered to all the children, at six-monthly intervals but, for various reasons discussed in the Final Report to the SSRC, the results were not considered to be sufficiently reliable to merit reporting in this volume. However, Valerie Walkerdine and Allayne Bridges, another SSRC student, were able to develop further tests, the results of which have been presented in their doctoral dissertations and published in a number of papers.

By 1980 none of these original members of the research team was left, and so, when we finally obtained our own mini-computer and were once more able to access the coded data, it was a different group of colleagues who helped to design and implement the method for establishing the sequence of development. Although I must take responsibility for the form in which the results are presented, the work on which they are based was largely carried out by Mary Gutfreund and Sally Barnes, with advice from David Satterly, who has been the co-director of this phase of the research.

As well as recognizing their contribution to this joint enterprise, I also wish to acknowledge my personal debt to them individually: to Sally Barnes for her untiring help in carrying out the data processing for the investigation of the role of the input reported in chapter 9; to Mary Gutfreund for her support and advice at all times and for her critical comments on chapters 4, 5 and 6; and to David Satterly for the benefit of his statistical expertise throughout all phases of the research.

Finally, I should like to thank Alan Brimer, formerly Head of the Research Unit of the School of Education, for initiating the research and giving me the opportunity to carry it out; Julie Bevan, and her successor as organizing secretary, Fran Child, for so ably keeping the whole enterprise together; and, not least, the funding bodies, the Nuffield Foundation (the pre-pilot phase) and the Social Science Research Council, who with their financial support made the project possible.

This book, then, is the outcome of many years of work by a large team of people with skills of many kinds. In presenting the results of their combined efforts, I wish to record my appreciation of their enthusiastic commitment and their unfailing support throughout the duration of the project. I should also like to thank Maureen Devoy and Margaret Binnie for their excellent work in typing and retyping the manuscript and in preparing the tables and figures.

1

Setting up the research

To what extent is there a common sequence of development amongst a representative sample of children learning English as their first language?

How great is the variation between individual children in such a sample in their route and rate of development?

What characteristics of the children or of their environment and experience can account for the observed variation?

These were the questions that the Bristol Study set out to answer. The background to the study has already been outlined in the Introduction and its theoretical orientation presented at some length in the first volume in this series (Wells, 1981). This chapter will move directly, therefore, to a description of the methodology that was devised to answer the questions posed above.

In designing the study, the major problems to which solutions had to be found were the following:

a) to select a representative sample of 'normal' children;
b) to obtain regular and representative samples of their speech in naturally occurring conversation with the people in their home environments;
c) to code the recorded speech samples in a form appropriate to discover developmental trends;
d) to devise a means of analysing the coded data with the aid of a computer.

In the remainder of this chapter and in chapter 2 each of these topics will be dealt with in detail. First, however, it is necessary to say something about the constraints under which the research was carried out.

1.1 Getting the balance right
Although independent in theory, the methodological questions involved in selecting the children, and in deciding on the best way

to record, code and analyse samples of their speech were, in practice, highly interdependent. From the beginning we knew that there was a ceiling on the amount of money that could be spent in carrying out the research. Consequently, a balance had to be struck between the number of children to be studied, the amount of speech to be recorded and the detail in which that speech could be coded and analysed. Getting this balance right was the problem that caused the greatest difficulty in designing the research. In essence, the larger the number of children, the less data it would be possible to analyse; conversely the greater the detail of the analysis, either the smaller could be the sample of speech obtained from each child, or the fewer the children who could be studied. As there was very little relevant information to draw upon from previously completed research, it was extremely difficult to predict what consequences would ultimately result from any particular decision, even though it was clear that whatever decisions were taken at this stage would significantly affect the scope and reliability of the final results.

The pilot study carried out in 1971–2 had allowed us to test the feasibility of certain aspects of the design. For example, it was during this period that the technique of speech sampling was worked out in detail and also the method to be used in sampling from the population. We also demonstrated during this period the feasibility of recruiting and training part-time staff to carry out the highly labour-intensive tasks of transcription and coding. However, the pilot study also showed up some serious inadequacies in the methods we had proposed to use, and so some fairly fundamental revisions were required before we embarked on the main study. And this, in turn, meant that the task–time estimates were no longer very accurate.

It cannot be claimed, therefore, that the balance that was finally struck was optimal. However, in general, it worked. Apart from the modification in the amount of speech coded, already described in the Introduction, the targets that were finally set were also ultimately attained. The description of the research design which follows, therefore, is also a reasonably accurate account of what actually took place.

1.2 Sampling from the population

The foremost objective in constructing a sample of children to be studied was that it should accurately represent the social diversity of the population. In spite of the arguments of Chomsky (1965) and Lenneberg (1967) for the relative unimportance of the contribution of the environment to the child's acquisition of language, it could not be assumed *a priori* that social differences between families have an insignificant effect on what is learned, still less on the rate at which learning progresses. Indeed at the time when the research was being planned, educationalists and sociolinguists were engaged in heated debate concerning the social antecedents of 'linguistic disadvantage' (e.g. Deutsch, 1965; Bernstein, 1971; Labov, 1970) and it seemed particularly important to investigate empirically the rival claims concerning variation in children's pre-school conversational experience.

At the same time, there were serious constraints on the total number of children that could be studied, if the description of their language development was to be anything other than superficial. Summary measures, such as Mean Length of Utterance (MLU), indices of sentence complexity (McCarthy, 1930; Templin, 1957) or test scores may be satisfactory for normative studies, but they are totally inadequate as a basis for the study of the fine detail of language development, as Brown *et al.*'s (1969) pioneering study of Adam, Eve and Sarah had shown.

From the beginning, therefore, a compromise could not be avoided. A sample of children small enough to permit the really fine-grained description of development that we saw as the ideal to be aimed at would not have begun to be socially representative. On the other hand, a sample large enough to have satisfied the assumptions on which parametric statistics are based would have precluded all but the most superficial linguistic analyses. Attempting to do the least injustice to these two rival sets of considerations, we settled on a target of between 100 and 150 children, equally divided amongst a number of social strata.

A further factor that had to be taken into account in carrying out a longitudinal study was the probability that the sample would be depleted as a result of family mobility, illness or unwillingness to accept the inconveniences caused by regular observations. The experience of other researchers who had attempted studies of similar duration suggested that wastage might be as high as 30% over the four- or five-year period, which would have meant that an unacceptably large proportion of the available resources might have been spent on collecting and processing data from children who eventually had to be dropped from analysis.

For this reason it was decided to adopt an overlapping longitudinal design, with two equivalent samples separated by two years in age, each being observed for only half the length of time that would have been necessary in a simple longitudinal study. The obvious disadvantage of this design is that the number of children observed at each age is reduced by half. However, the probability of retaining a high proportion of the sample for the total duration of the research was considered adequate compensation.[1] For reasons explained below, the ages selected were 15 and 39 months.

1.2.1 *Class of Family Background*
In their work at the Sociological Research Unit at the University of London Institute of Education, Bernstein and his colleagues had used an index of social class which combined information about the occupational status and terminal level of education of both parents. This was argued to be a more reliable index of social class than one based on father's occupation alone (Brandis and Henderson, 1970: appendix I).

A similar index was constructed during the pilot study for the Bristol research on the basis of interviews with the parents of a sample of 112 children, drawn at random from the notifications of births of children born in January and August between 1966 and 1970. The occupations of both parents were classified using the Registrar-General's five-point scale of occupational status. Since many of the mothers were no longer in paid employment, they were asked to list all previous occupations and the most highly rated was used in making the classification. With respect to terminal level of education, it was found that only a fairly small proportion of the sample of parents had continued beyond the year in which they reached the minimal leaving age. It was therefore decided to adopt a two-point scale, with the critical distinction being made between those who left at the minimal leaving age without gaining any examination qualifications and those who continued beyond this level. The correlations between the four variables are shown in table 1.1. When the data were submitted to a factor analysis, one general factor emerged, which accounted for 0.688 of the total

Table 1.1 *Correlations between family background variables (pilot study)*

		1	2	3	4
1	Father's occupation	—			
2	Mother's occupation	0.447	—		
3	Father's education	0.679	0.744	—	
4	Mother's education	0.527	0.638	0.632	—

variance. The loadings of the four variables on this factor and their relative weights (factor loading divided by standard deviation) are shown in table 1.2.

Table 1.2 *Factor loadings and weightings (pilot study)*

Variable	Factor loading	Weighting
Father's occupation	0.797	0.82
Mother's occupation	0.798	1.19
Father's education	0.875	1.91
Mother's education	0.846	1.86

On the basis of these results it was decided to use the formula: Family Background = F. Occ. + M. Occ. + 2 (F. Educ. + M. Educ.), which yields a scale in which children's scores can range from 6 to 18. Table 1.3 gives the actual distribution for the pilot sample of 112 children. The skewedness of this distribution owes something to the willingness of families in the initial random sample to be interviewed and to provide information on which the children's scores are based: only 69% of families initially contacted by post agreed to be visited and, from information available on father's occupation of those who did agree, it was established that the number of families interviewed was considerably higher for families where the father held a class I or II occupation and lower where he held a class IV or V occupation than would have been expected in a random sample from the population of Bristol. Nevertheless, it seems probable that in a truly random sample approximately 50% of the children might be expected to receive scores of 14 or 15.

Table 1.3 *Distribution of children in pilot study on the index of Family Background*

Score	6	7	8	9	10	11	12	13	14	15	16	17	18
N	1	10	9	3	2	3	13	6	31	26	7	1	0

Rather than use a sampling frame which attempted to represent the true distribution of the population on this index, with the problem of proportionally small numbers in many of the cells, it was decided, for the purposes of constructing the sample, to recast the index into four categories (table 1.4). These clearly correspond quite closely to what are often referred to as the middle, lower middle, working and lower working classes. However, since these labels are often used, as Wells and Robinson (1982) point out, in ways which fail to distinguish between class, status and power, it seemed preferable, in the present study, to coin a new term for the particular index being used, which is based only on occupational status and education. We shall refer throughout, therefore, to Class of Family Background, which is defined in terms of the score intervals on the index of Family Background shown in table 1.4.

Table 1.4 *Class of Family Background*

	Category			
	A	B	C	D
Index score	6–9	10–13	14–15	16–18

In order to facilitate statistical comparisons in the main study between these four classes of family background, it was decided to use the index to allocate all children drawn in an initial random sample to the four classes and then to draw an equal number of children at random from each class.

1.2.2 *Other stratifying variables*
Although a number of other social variables could be expected to influence a child's language development, such as size of family, position in the birth order, presence of both or only one parent, attendance at play-group or nursery, these had to be allowed to vary randomly since, whilst it might have been possible to control for them at the beginning of the study, it would certainly not have been possible to hold them constant throughout its duration.

On the other hand there were two other variables which were both amenable to control and likely, on the basis of previous research, to be associated with rate of development. These were sex of the child and month of birth. Initially, therefore, it was decided to stratify the population on these two variables and to select an equal number of children from each stratum.

However, the experience of the pilot study showed that a design in which children were selected with birthdays in every month of the year would be extremely difficult to organize. First, most families take their annual holiday in August and so it would have been almost impossible to carry out observations due in that month. Secondly, if in every month there had been some children who were due to be observed, there would have been no opportunity for members of the research team to have a holiday either. It was decided, therefore, not to select children whose birthdays fell in August or in any month that would have required them to be observed in August. Since the interval between observations was set at three months, this meant that no children were selected with birthdays in August, November, February and May.

With these four stratifying variables of age, sex, month of birth and Class of Family Background, the decision on the size of the target sample was rendered very straightforward. The four variables had, respectively, 2, 2, 8 and 4 values, yielding a four-dimensional matrix with a total of 128 cells. Assuming that month of birth was independent of the other variables and could be nested within Class of Family Background, this would yield a three-dimensional matrix with eight cases in each cell (see figure 1.1). With the addition of a further 10% to act as replacements for any withdrawals that might occur, this sampling frame was used in constructing the actual sample.

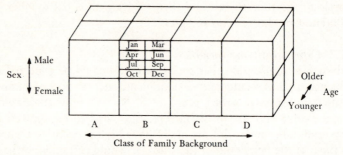

Figure 1.1 Structure of the sampling framework

1.2.3 *Constructing the sample*
Four steps were involved. These were repeated for each of the eight months in which the children were selected.

A) *Drawing the random sample*
Notification of birth was held by the Medical Officer of Health for every child born in the City of Bristol and for all children who had moved into the City since birth and who had been visited by a health visitor. Permission was granted for us to use these records, provided that officers of the Health Service made the first approach

to the families, thus safeguarding the confidentiality of the information contained in the records. Accordingly, an initial random sample of names of children, stratified by sex, was drawn from each of the eight selected months of birth for the years 1969–70 and 1971–2. Initially the size of the random sample for each age × sex × month was fixed at 20, but this proved insufficient and after the first months the number was increased to 30. In all, the names of 902 children were randomly drawn from the sample over eight months.

B) *Initial contact with the families*
The experience of the pilot study had shown that a low rate of response might be expected if the first contact was made by means of an official letter. When this was explained to the Medical Officer of Health, he offered to have the first contact made personally by members of the Health Visitor Service, who have a statutory duty to pay regular visits to the families of children under five years of age. This offer was gratefully accepted, and meetings were arranged with all health visitors involved to explain the purpose of the research and to discuss the way in which this initial approach was to be made.

It had already been decided that certain categories of children would be excluded from the study because they were likely to present special problems. The excluded categories were: (a) multiple births; (b) children with known handicaps; (c) children whose parents were not both native speakers of English; (d) children in institutional care or attending a day-nursery full time; (e) children whose families were likely to move out of the area in the near future; (f) siblings of children already selected for study.

(Categories (d), (e) and (f) were excluded because of the difficulties they would have posed in recording them rather than because of any problems that such children might be expected to experience in learning English.)

The procedure for making the first contact was agreed as follows. The names of the children were sorted according to geographical area and then allocated to the health visitor who already knew the families concerned. At the next visit the health visitor explained that the child's name had been picked at random for participation in a study of 'the language development of normal children' and a member of the research team would like to call to explain the study in more detail. The explanation was given in a way that assumed that the family would be willing to receive a visitor, but if a refusal was received at this point no further contact was made. However, in such cases, the health visitor was asked to let us know the occupational status of the head of the household so that an estimate could later be made of the social-class distribution of families refusing to take part in the study.

Although simple in theory, this part of the sampling procedure was not without difficulties. Some families proved extremely elusive and even after as many as six visits the health visitors were not able to make contact. Furthermore, some of the health visitors took it upon themselves to exclude a further category of children: those who 'would not be suitable subjects for the research'. No further reasons were given, so it must be assumed that such families were considered likely to be uncooperative or unreliable. Clearly, this introduced some bias into the sampling, but fortunately the number of such cases was extremely small (see table 1.5).

Table 1.5 *Distribution of children in random sample following health visitor contact*

Agreed to be inter- viewed	Handi- capped	In full- time care	Mul- tiple births	Parents not native speakers	Left Bristol	No contact	Health visitor 'unsuit- able'	Refused
63.4%	2.7%	1.2%	0.2%	4.2%	8.1%	8.4%	1.2%	10.6%

C) *Explanatory interview*
When the names of all the unwilling or unsuitable families had been removed from the list, the remaining names formed a pool of potential subjects from whom a selection had to be made in terms of the criteria already discussed. Thus, the families of about two-thirds of these children were visited by a member of the research team, drawn from a small team of part-time interviewers, who explained the research in detail.

The interview consisted of two parts: (1) an explanation of the purpose of the research and of what would be required of the family if they agreed to take part; (2) a number of standard questions to obtain the following information:

a) the age and sex of all children in the family;
b) whether the child attended a nursery school or playgroup and, if so, on which days;

c) whether any days were likely to be consistently inconvenient for recording or testing the child;

d) both parents' occupation and terminal level of education.

The reason given for carrying out the research was to find out more about how children learn to talk, in order to help those who have difficulties of various kinds. When the extent of the commitment that was being asked for – a series of regular observations involving recording in the home, followed by visits to the University – had been explained, the parents were asked whether they would be willing to take part. If they agreed, the interviewer proceeded to part 2 of the interview. However, even if the request to participate was refused, the questions concerning occupation and education were asked so that an estimate could be formed of the social distribution of refusals as compared with acceptances (see table 1.6).

Table 1.6 *Distribution of families agreeing and refusing to participate × Class of Family Background*

	A	B	C	D	Unknown	Proportion of total
Families agreeing	53	106	141	48		87.4%
Families refusing	5	1	18	10	14*	12.6%
Total interviewed	58	107	159	58	14	100%

* These parents refused to answer questions about their occupation and education

D) *Selecting the children*

The sampling frame required that, in each of the eight months, one child of each age and sex be selected from each of the four classes of family background. The principle adopted, therefore, was to fill each cell with the first child in the randomly drawn sample to meet the criteria for inclusion in that cell. However this principle was not adhered to in all cases as to have interviewed all families in the order in which names had been drawn would have been very wasteful of resources. Instead, interviews were carried out in a number of rounds, with the first round taking the first ten or so names in the random sample for each age-by-sex sub-sample. If all cells were not filled after the first round, the next group of families to be interviewed was selected from the names that followed, on the basis of addresses likely to yield subjects of the appropriate class of family background. Even this procedure was not successful in every case and in some months it proved impossible to fill particular cells. In such cases, the gap was filled at random by the first child meeting the criteria for that particular cell in either the preceding or following month.

Having selected the subjects, the Project Director then visited every one of the selected families personally. The object of this second visit was three-fold: to emphasize to the parents that their participation in the research was important and that their cooperation was fully appreciated; to clear up any misunderstandings that might have remained after the first interview; and to give any families who were not fully committed to participating the opportunity to withdraw before any observations had been made. A very small number of families withdrew at this stage; the children were replaced by the next child in the random sample who met the necessary criteria.

The pool of replacements

From the outset, it was expected that there would be a number of withdrawals from the study and so at steps C and D more families were interviewed and children selected than were needed to complete the target sample. Since there was no way of knowing which of these children would be called upon to replace withdrawals, they were treated from the beginning as full members of the sample.

As the study began to get under way, however, it became clear that withdrawals were not evenly distributed over the variables used in constructing the sample (see table 1.7). A greater number of

Table 1.7 *Distribution of withdrawals after at least one observation*

Age	Sex	Class of Family Background				Total
		A	B	C	D	
Older	Boys	2	0	4	7	13
	Girls	1	3	1	1	6
Younger	Boys	1	6	4	4	15
	Girls	0	2	2	3	7
Total		4	11	11	15	41

withdrawals from classes C and D than from A and B were to be expected for a variety of reasons: difficulty in travelling to the University from outlying housing estates, particularly when dependent on public transport; greater difficulty in making and keeping to arrangements necessary for carrying out the observations; less interest in participating in the research. However, none of these reasons would explain the much higher incidence of withdrawals amongst boys than amongst girls. This is particularly marked with respect to the older class D boys.

A partial explanation of this difference between the sexes may lie in the relatively greater importance that parents are believed to attach to the language development of their daughters compared with that of their sons (McCarthy, 1954). A different possibility is that the parents find their sons more difficult to control than their daughters. If family problems occurred during the course of the study, as they undoubtedly did in quite a number of families, the additional strains imposed by the research may have been greater where boys were concerned, thus leading to a higher rate of withdrawal amongst boys than girls. Since this pattern emerged fairly early in the process of sample construction, it proved possible to replace withdrawals by selecting additional children in the later months. This, of course, upset the distribution by month of birth. However, by combining adjacent months, it was possible to achieve a fairly balanced distribution in terms of season of birth: spring, summer, autumn and winter.

1.2.4 *The final sample*
Generally speaking, the various steps in the selection procedure were carried out according to plan. More families were 'lost' at the second stage than had been anticipated, either because they could not be contacted or because they were unwilling to be visited to be told more about the research. Since the social background information on these families is incomplete it is not possible to tell whether any systematic bias was introduced at this stage in the sampling procedure. However, on the basis of the information available from those who refused to be visited, this does not seem very likely. On the other hand, agreement to participate in the research, once it had been explained, was surprisingly high. Some families seemed to consider it a privilege to be asked and in no case did the lack of reward, financial or otherwise, seem to be a disincentive. Indeed the willing cooperation of the majority of families involved in the research was deeply appreciated by those who had the task of organizing the schedule of observations.

The uneven distribution of the withdrawals, however, was a source of considerable concern, since it meant that the final sample departed in certain respects from the ideal that had been proposed.

Nevertheless, although some of the individual cells were considerably depleted, the overall balance was not seriously distorted. At the end of the period of data collection, the sample consisted of 125 children distributed over the stratifying variables as shown in table 1.8. This total included a number of children for whom individual observations were missed due to ill-health or other family difficulties. Fortunately the number of such children was small and in no case did it involve more than one observation.

Table 1.8 *Distribution of the sample by age, Class of Family Background, sex and season of birth*

Age	Class of Family Background		Spring		Summer		Autumn		Winter		Total
	Sex		M	F	M	F	M	F	M	F	
Older	A		3	2	2	2	3	4	0	1	17
	B		2	2	2	2	3	2	2	1	16
	C		1	3	2	3	2	2	4	1	18
	D		2	5	1	0	2	2	0	2	14
	Total		8	12	7	7	10	10	6	5	65
Younger	A		3	2	1	3	2	3	2	1	17
	B		2	2	0	1	2	3	1	2	13
	C		0	2	4	1	3	1	2	3	16
	D		2	3	2	0	2	2	1	2	14
	Total		7	9	7	5	9	9	6	8	60
Total			36		26		38		25		125

1.3 Recording samples of speech

The major part of each observation was the recording of a sample of the child's speech. There are many ways in which this might be done so the choice that is made must depend on the aims of the investigator and the sophistication of the equipment available. In the present investigation the aim was to obtain representative samples of naturally occurring speech so as to make valid comparisons between different groups of children. To ensure naturalness, it is necessary: (a) that the child should be able to move freely around his home and its immediate vicinity; (b) that the people with whom the child interacts should not be inhibited by constant awareness that their conversation is being recorded.

To ensure representativeness it is necessary to sample from the full range of social situations and activities in which the child experiences language in use, and to do so in a way that takes account of their relative frequency. However, whilst it is possible to get close to fulfilling the requirements for naturalness, this is not the case for representativeness, since little is known about the range of activities in which children engage and still less about their relative frequency. Moreover, even if this information were available in a general form, it would clearly not be possible to predict how particular days would be spent by individual children.

The solution adopted, therefore, was to use, as the signal source, a radio-microphone worn by the child, and to link the radio-receiver to a tape recorder that was pre-programmed to sample at frequent but irregular intervals over the course of a whole day. In this way it was hoped that all activities of significant duration would be represented in the complete sample and that the speech that was recorded would be completely natural.

This specification, however, imposed a number of severe technical constraints on the design of the recording equipment. First, the microphone and transmitter had to be compact and light enough to be worn by a 15-month-old child without discomfort; secondly, the microphone had to be able to pick up clearly both the speech of the child who was wearing it and that of other people who addressed him from a distance of several feet; thirdly, the transmitter should be able to operate continuously for a period of at least nine and a half hours without attention. Finally, for the sake of safety and privacy with respect to the families taking part in the research, it was decided that the tape recorder and radio receiver should operate on a self-contained power supply and be enclosed in a sealed box inaccessible to investigation by anybody in the child's home.

The development of the equipment extended over a period of several years, during which a number of alternatives were tried and either modified or discarded. The constraints described in the previous paragraph were such that no existing package of equipment was found satisfactory – at least not one that was purchasable within the limited resources of the project – and so the final configuration, which was specially assembled for the purpose, made use of readily available components and modifications which could be undertaken with the limited workshop facilities at our disposal. The result, which is illustrated in figure 1.2, consisted of three principal components: a radio microphone in its carrying harness; a radio-receiver linked to a tape recorder; and an automatic timing mechanism. The radio microphone and receiver were based on a standard RMS 5 unit supplied by Audio Ltd of Shepherd's Bush, London. To reduce the bulk and weight of the transmitter, transmitters were purchased in circuit-board form and housed in home-made aluminium boxes. To reduce the overall size, the battery was separated from the transmitter and the deviation

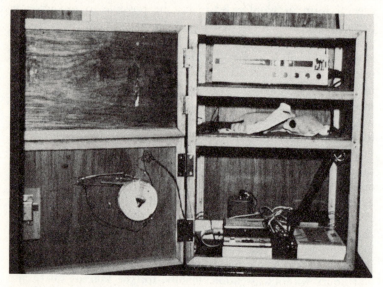

Figure 1.2

potentiometer was replaced by fixed resistors mounted on the main circuit board. The heavy screw-in DIN plug for the microphone, which acted as an on/off switch, was also removed and the two omni-directional AKG microphones were wired direct to the circuit board. One of these microphones, worn on the child's chest, was arranged to be attenuated 20 dB and to attenuate further at 12 dB per octave below 5 Kcs. This front microphone was chiefly intended to pick up the high frequencies of the child's speech, which experience had shown to be particularly important in facilitating accurate transcription. The second microphone, sited on the child's back, was intended to pick up the speech addressed to the child by other speakers.

The complete harness (illustrated in figure 1.3) weighed slightly less than 250 gm and the larger of the two pouches measured 12 × 12 cm. With a PP 3 battery the transmitter would operate for the required nine hours and, under optimal conditions, it had a range of more than 200 m. Unfortunately, however, conditions were rarely optimal, for both the removal of the transmitter's steel case and the unconventional positioning of the aerial led to the signal being likely to drift off frequency. Nevertheless, for most of the time, a range of 100 m was achieved with a signal free of all but intermittent distortion. After a period of two years or so, Audio introduced a much smaller capacitor microphone and several of the pairs of AKG microphones were replaced by a single capacitor microphone in the front pouch, with a significant improvement in the signal quality.

The Audio RMS 5 receiver and the open-reel Uher 4000 Report tape recorder were standard, except that their battery power supply was modified to allow it to be switched on remotely by the timing device. This was the invention of Dr Bernard Chapman and consisted of two parts: a spring-driven clock movement to determine the onset of each of the short sampling units during the course of the day, and a cassette tape recorder using a specially prepared tape with metallic sensing foil to determine the duration of each

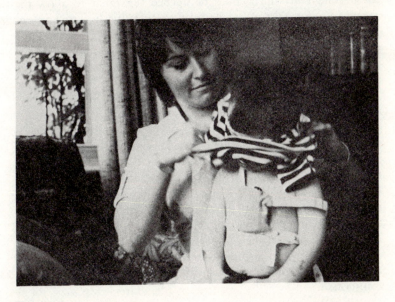

Figure 1.3

sample. The use of a Philips EL3302 cassette recorder offered a
cheap and effective method of timing the sample to within half a
second and at the same time allowed a series of marker tones to be
imposed on the speech sample recorded on the main recorder
without the use of additional equipment.

Switching on the cassette recorder and the radio-receiver and
Uher recorder was effected by closing two relays, which were
activated by the closure of a pair of contacts on the clock. Once
switched on, all three machines would run until one of the sections
of metallic sensing tape reached two copper contacts which were
attached to the erase head of the cassette recorder. Shorting out
these two contacts at the end of the timed sample released the relays
which caused the power supply to be switched off.

Control of the precise time of onset of each sample was achieved
by the spring-driven clock, to the hour spindle of which was
attached a continuous spiral of card, three inches in diameter. This
was constructed of 36 disks, each cut radially and joined to its
neighbour by adhesive tape. Each card was marked in minutes and
notches were cut at the points at which samples were to begin. At
each notch a trailing arm would fall, under gravity, and cause a pair
of contacts to close, thus activating the relays.

All components were housed in a lockable wooden box, one
compartment of which could be opened separately to allow the
parent to remove the microphone and transmitter in their harness.
When the harness was placed in the box, a miniature jack plug was
inserted into a socket on the side of the transmitter. Removal of the
jack plug when the harness was to be used completed the power
supply to the transmitter and switched it on.

Nine boxes of recording equipment were made up in this way.
The expectation was that eight boxes would be in use at any time,
the ninth being free for servicing or as a stand-by in case of
malfunction in one of the other boxes. In practice, the configuration
proved to be rather less reliable than we had hoped and there was
rarely a stand-by box in full working order. Several of the
microphones ceased to work as a result of damage when a child fell
or spilt his food. When this happened, they were replaced by
smaller capacitor microphones as described above. In spite of these
difficulties, however, the recording boxes worked well enough to
allow all the planned recordings to be made and almost all achieved
a sound quality of sufficient clarity for most of the speech to be
transcribed.

1.4 The speech-sampling programme

The arguments for maintaining as large a sample of children as possible have already been stated. Similar arguments also apply to the duration of the recording. Given that the purpose and content of conversation is dependent on the context and that this is likely to vary during the course of a typical day, it is clearly important to draw as many speech samples as possible. Given also that the number of utterances produced per unit of time varies from zero, for example, when the child is asleep, to as many as 50 or 60 per minute during very animated conversation, there are further grounds for wishing to draw as many samples as possible in order to obtain an overall corpus for the day that is representative of this variation. In addition, one might expect there to be considerable individual variation in talkativeness. Finally, given the fact that very many different utterance types can be produced even with very limited linguistic resources, it is clear that the larger the number of utterance tokens in the corpus, the greater will be the reliability of an estimate, based on that corpus, of the range of utterance types that the child is capable of producing.

No figures were available on the absolute size of speech corpus that would be required to meet this latter criterion; in any case, it would clearly depend both on the range of contexts that were sampled and on the stage of development of the child. In the absence of precise information about these various parameters of variation, decisions had to be somewhat arbitrary and so it was decided that 110 child utterances should be the minimum that would be aimed for, with 120 being the average number per corpus to be aimed for over all recordings. On the basis of the pilot study, we estimated that this target would be met by recording between 25 and 30 minutes of speech per occasion.

In deciding on the best pattern of sampling we were again in the dark. A young child's attention span is notoriously short, which suggested that activities would also be of short duration and therefore that a very large number of samples would be required. Furthermore, fairly lengthy periods when there was no speech to be recorded could be expected, because the child was either asleep or playing quietly alone. Frequent sampling would reduce the chance of such periods being over-represented in the day's corpus. However, any increase in frequency had to be bought at the price of a decrease in duration. Below a certain length, individual samples would be too short to capture complete sequences of conversation, and this would seriously reduce the possibility of studying the conversational context of individual utterances.

During the pilot study, various sample lengths from 30 seconds to two minutes were tried, and it was finally decided to use a sample length of 90 seconds. With shorter samples, it was felt, too much of the conversational structure was lost; on the other hand, longer samples required too great a reduction in the total number of samples drawn. The day's recording schedule, then, consisted finally of 24 samples of 90 seconds duration, distributed between 9 a.m. and 6 p.m. These two limits were set on grounds of practicality. Almost all families could be expected to be out of bed by 9 a.m. and to have had time to put the harness containing microphones and transmitter on the child. Shortly after 6 p.m. the transcriber would visit the family to replay the tape for the purpose of contextualization (see section 1.8.1). Furthermore, quite a number of fathers agreed to allow their children to take part in the research provided that the tape recorder was switched off in the evening so that they would be able to talk freely without risk of confidential or otherwise inappropriate matters being overheard.

In retrospect, it is clear that a very important segment of the child's day was lost to observation by the decision to stop recording after 6 p.m.: for many children the bedtime ritual includes a story-reading or story-telling session, during which some of the richest interaction between parent and child might be expected to occur. Against this has to be set, however, the advantage of having secured the agreement of such a high proportion of the families interviewed to participate in the study.

The period between 9 a.m. and 6 p.m. was divided into six periods of one and a half hours, and four samples were drawn from each of these 'time-of-day' units. Within each unit, the precise time of onset of each sample was selected at random within the constraint that no two samples should be further apart than 31 minutes nor closer than 13 minutes. The average interval between samples was 22 minutes. The purpose in randomizing the time of onset was to reduce the possibility that the families being observed would modify their behaviour as a result of their awareness of being recorded. To reduce the possibility of 'playing to the microphone' still further, six different recording programmes were constructed at random and different programmes were used on successive recordings of the same child.

From previous experience, we anticipated that some samples would be blank because the child was out of range of the receiver.

This was most likely to happen when the parent had to take a sibling to school, collect him at the end of the session, or make a brief expedition to the local shops. It might also occur if the child was playing out of doors and went beyond the range of the transmitter. The receiver was modified to identify samples in which the child was out of range by emitting a continuous hiss if the signal from the transmitter dropped below a certain minimal strength. By recording 24 samples, when only 18 were required to give a total of 27 minutes for the day's recording, an allowance was made for up to 25% of samples to be blank because the child was out of range. Where fewer blank samples were recorded, there was a set procedure (see below) for selecting the 18 required.

The typical schedule for one recording is shown in figure 1.4. With eight boxes of recording equipment, it was possible in theory to record four children each day and up to 80 children in the 20 working days in each month. As the total number to be recorded in any month, including reserves, never exceeded 75, this allowed for up to five unsuccessful recordings to be repeated. In practice, approximately 10% of recordings failed for one reason or another, and so some had to be postponed to the following month. Nevertheless, the vast majority of recordings were still completed within ten days of the date on which they should ideally have been made.

1.5 The programme of tests

Samples of spontaneous speech obviously have limitations as well as advantages as the basis for assessing a child's level of language development. First, although they provide a rich source of information about the child's production, they do not allow more than a very general estimate to be made of his comprehension; and secondly, although they can tell us what a child *does* say, that alone may yield a rather variable estimate of what he is *able* to say. As Ingram (1969) argues, a child's systematic knowledge of language at any stage can never be fully represented in the particular instances of behaviour that are called forth by the particular situations in which he finds himself, and Chomsky, as is well known, has made even stronger criticisms of the use of spontaneous speech to study language development, arguing that data collection 'must be carried out, in devious and clever ways if any serious result is to be obtained' (1964: 36).

Whilst not agreeing with Chomsky's dismissive attitude to naturalistic data – not least because it is a matter of very consider-

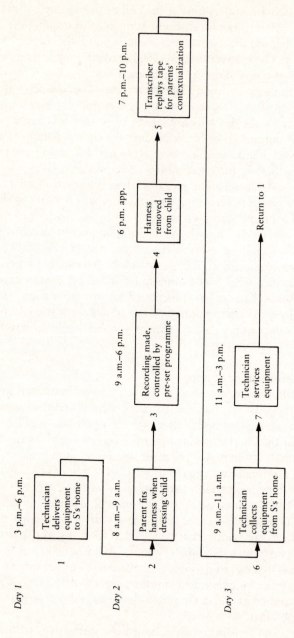

Figure 1.4 Sequence of steps in one observation of one child

Day 1

3 p.m.–6 p.m.

1 Technician delivers equipment to S's home

Day 2

8 a.m.–9 a.m.

2 Parent fits harness when dressing child

9 a.m.–6 p.m.

3 Recording made, controlled by pre-set programme

6 p.m. app.

4 Harness removed from child

7 p.m.–10 p.m.

5 Transcriber replays tape for parents' contextualization

Day 3

9 a.m.–11 a.m.

6 Technician collects equipment from S's home

11 a.m.–3 p.m.

7 Technician services equipment

Return to 1

able interest to find out what sorts of thing children say, to whom and on what occasions – it did seem advisable to attempt to complement naturalistic data with data obtained under more controlled conditions. This approach also has its limitations and these will be discussed in some detail in chapter 3, but we were sufficiently impressed by the results obtained by other researchers (e.g. Fraser *et al.*, 1963; Bever, 1970; Slobin and Welsh, 1973) to include a programme of testing alongside the programme of recordings.

The testing programme was divided into two distinct parts, comprising, respectively, those tests which were designed to monitor the general development of each child relative to all the other children, and those that were designed as experimental instruments to explore in greater depth certain specific developmental issues. The two groups of tests were administered, alternately, as part of each three-monthly observation.

The second group included a study of the development of comprehension of spatial and temporal relational terms carried out by Valerie Walkerdine and Chris Sinha, and two studies of influences on the comprehension process – maternal cues in the case of two-year-olds, and features of the task-context in three-year-olds – by Allayne Bridges. Since these studies have been reported in detail elsewhere (Walkerdine, 1975; Sinha and Walkerdine, 1978; Walkerdine and Sinha, 1981; Bridges, 1977, 1979, 1980; Bridges *et al.*, 1981) they will not be described further here.

In the first group were two tests designed specially for the research: a Test of General Language Comprehension and an Imitation Test. The former used the 'acting-out' technique and consisted of 63 items, which covered as wide a range of sentence types as possible. Items were arranged in order of increasing difficulty and only a sub-set were administered on any particular occasion. The imitation test also included a wide range of sentence types, but arranged so that they formed a story. This test was administered in full on each occasion of testing. Unfortunately, the effectiveness of the comprehension test as a measure of receptive language development was seriously compromised by a systematic failure to observe the instructions on the selection of items to be administered on each occasion. This was not discovered until it was too late to rectify the situation. As the results are unreliable, therefore, these two tests will not be further reported on in this volume.

In order to allow comparisons to be made between the sample of children under investigation and the wider population of pre-school children, two further standardized tests were selected: the English Picture Vocabulary Test (Brimer and Dunn, 1963) and the Morrisby Compound Series Test (Morrisby, 1955). The first of these is a test of listening comprehension of individual vocabulary items and the second is a test of non-verbal reasoning ability. These tests were administered to all the children when they were three and a quarter years old (the first observation for the older children and the penultimate observation for the younger children) and at the last observation of the older children when they were five and a half years old. Unfortunately, the Morrisby test did not yield usable data at three and a quarter years and so will not be reported on further.

After much debate it was decided not to include a test of intelligence on the grounds that, even though such tests purport to test non-verbal intelligence, it is doubtful whether a child's performance can really be considered to be independent of his verbal understanding. We were not convinced, therefore, that we should have been able to give a valid interpretation to the relationship between scores on such a test and scores derived from the more specifically linguistic aspects of the investigation. In addition, certain members of the research team had grave misgivings about the basis on which intelligence tests are constructed.

1.6 The maternal interview

Since there was evidence from earlier research of relationships between language development and attributes of the child's social environment (McCarthy, 1954; Templin, 1957), it was considered important that information should be obtained concerning the child's long-term social and intellectual environment by means of an interview with the child's chief caretaker (in most cases, the mother). At the time when we were planning the research, results of some of the studies carried out under the direction of Basil Bernstein at the Sociological Research Unit of the University of London Institute of Education were beginning to appear in monograph form, and these raised further, specific, topics for investigation. Professor Bernstein and Dr Peter Robinson, who had been Deputy Director of the SRU for some years, were kind enough to advise on the sort of questions that the interview might contain, and Bernstein made certain interview schedules available to us from his own investigations.

The interview was administered when each child was three and a half years old. Unlike the testing, which was carried out in a special suite of rooms in the Research Unit of the University, the interview took place in the child's home, though at a time when the child might be expected to be in bed. The schedule and the information obtained by means of it will be described in detail in chapter 7.

1.7 Overall programme of data collection

To summarize thus far, a sample of 128 children was selected, half at age 15 months and the other half at age 39 months, together with a small number of reserves for each group. Ten observations were to be made of each child, at three-monthly intervals, each observation involving a recording of spontaneous conversation in the child's home and the administration of tests at the University. An interview with the mother of each child was also to be carried out when the child was aged three and a half years.

Observations took place during two months out of every three, with approximately 75 observations being made in each. Planning the schedule of observations was thus a major task in itself. Not only did each observation have to be arranged within a few days of the child's birth-date, but several other factors had to be taken into account: the availability of recording equipment; regular commitments that made some days of the week inconvenient either for the family, or for the transcriber; the programme of testing, alternating between the two main types described above; and public or family holidays. Finally, there were inevitably arrangements that went wrong because of illness, sudden changes of plan or, in some cases, simple forgetfulness. The complete sequence of events involved in planning, carrying out and processing one observation of one child is shown in figure 1.5. Over a period of three and a half years this programme was carried out for more than 1350 observations.

1.8 Transcription of speech samples

In a study based on samples of conversation, the making of the recordings is only the first of a series of tasks that have to be carried out to produce the data that will ultimately be subjected to statistical analyses of various kinds. These tasks can be grouped into three main stages: contextualization, transcription and coding.

1.8.1 *Contextualization*

As already explained in section 1.3 above, the recordings were made without an observer present, in order to avoid the distorting effect of a stranger in the home. This meant, of course, that there

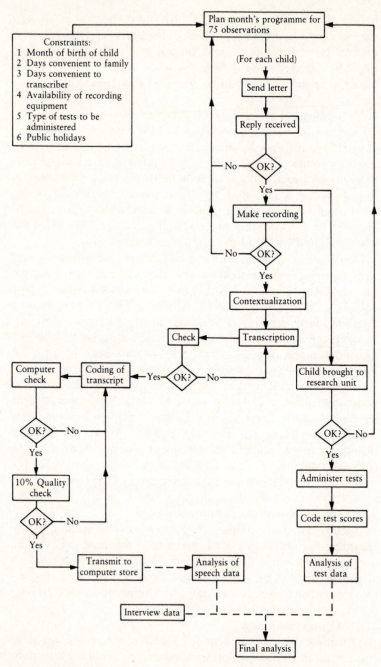

Figure 1.5 Steps involved in making one observation

was no on-the-spot record of the contexts in which the conversation occurred or of the non-verbal behaviour that accompanied it. To compensate for this as far as possible, the transcriber called at the family's home in the evening of the day of the recording in order to obtain as much information as possible relevant to making an accurate transcription. The procedure used was as follows: the tape was removed from the recording box and placed on a mains-powered reel-to-reel tape recorder and then played through from the beginning, one sample at a time. When each sample had been played through, the parents were told the precise time at which the sample had been recorded and asked: who had been present, what activity or activities had been going on during the 90 seconds and where the participants had been at the time. They were also asked if there was any background information that would help to make sense of the conversation. The tape was then rewound to the beginning of the sample, and it was replayed in small sections, so that the parents' interpretation or gloss could be obtained for any utterance that was difficult to understand. (A copy of the notes for transcribers is included as appendix 1A.)

The success of this method of contextualization was affected by a number of factors, most notably by whether either of the parents had been present during a particular sample and by their ability or willingness to reconstruct the events of the day in minute detail. It would have been possible to ask the parents to keep a continuous record of the child's activities throughout the day, but it was felt that this would have had an even more distorting effect on the spontaneity of events than the presence of an observer. For some recordings, then, there was very little information, particularly those of older children who spent much of the day playing outside in the garden or street with siblings or peers. On the other hand, recordings of the younger children, particularly those samples involving interaction between parent and child, were likely to be fully contextualized and we benefited a great deal from parental interpretation of utterances which to a stranger were almost unintelligible.

Naturally, there must remain some doubt about the sufficiency and reliability of recalled contextual information, but we have some evidence that transcripts prepared in this way are at least as complete as those prepared after an observer has been taking notes during the recording. As part of a radio programme about the Bristol Study for the Open University 'Cognitive Development' course, a comparison was made between the two methods of recording and contextualization. One of the families who had taken part in the research was contacted and asked whether they would be willing to allow us to make a recording of a younger sibling. The purpose of the recording was explained and the mother agreed to take part in the experiment. The equipment was prepared and delivered in the normal way and the recording went ahead, as before, with 90 second samples at irregular intervals. In addition, however, an observer was present in the home during the morning taking notes on what the child was doing. The observer was given details of the times at which the 90-second samples would be recorded so that she could take particularly full notes at those times.

The recording was terminated at midday and the observer was given a copy of the tape that had been recorded and asked to prepare a transcription, making full use of the notes that she had taken. In the afternoon, one of the regular team of transcribers called at the home and went through the standard contextualization procedure as described above. Using the notes obtained in this way, this transcriber also prepared a transcription of the recording.

Comparison of the two transcripts shows a clear advantage for the 'observer-present' mode as far as non-verbal activity is concerned, for example what the child was holding, where he was looking and so on. On the other hand, there were a number of episodes where the observer was unable to understand what the child was talking about because what he said depended for its interpretation on information about some previous experience. For example, when looking at a picture book containing a picture of Switzerland, which mother names, Robert says 'Jenny ge-got me jam.' Mother does not understand this at the time, but in answer to the transcriber's questions in the afternoon she recalled that a friend called Jenny had brought back some jam for them from Switzerland.

Each method has clear advantages – and limitations – therefore. But overall it is difficult to argue that either is clearly superior. For the majority of utterances, the results are equivalent, as can be seen from the two versions of the 90-second sample that are contained in appendix 1C. Of course it could be argued that this particular recording is not representative: mother was fully aware of why the recording was taking place and was probably giving more than usual attention to what Robert was doing. However, if this is the case, it tells equally, though in different ways, against both methods.

1.8.2 *Transcription*
Before commencing the transcription of the recording, surplus
samples, if any, had to be identified. At the top of the pro-forma
sheet used for contextualization (see appendix 1A), the 24 samples
were represented by a row of 24 boxes subdivided into six sets of
four, each set corresponding to a period of one and a half hours. As
the tape was played through, a tick was marked in the appropriate
box if the sample was within range and a cross if it was out of
range. The following rules were then applied:

a) If there were 18 or fewer in-range samples, all were to be
   transcribed.
b) If more than 18 in-range samples had been recorded, three out
   of the four in any one-and-a-half-hour period were to be
   selected at random for transcription.
c) If any one-and-a-half-hour period contained more than one
   out-of-range sample, the closest sample from one of the adjacent
   one-and-a-half-hour periods was to be substituted.
d) If, when all the 18 samples had been transcribed, there were less
   than 100 clear child utterances, further samples, designated as
   spare(s), were to be transcribed until that total was reached or
   there were no more untranscribed samples.

All recordings were transcribed in long-hand and in pencil, on
specially prepared ruled paper, from a Skrivrit reel-to-reel tape
recorder. This machine had the particularly useful characteristic of
emitting a signal on fast wind or rewind. This meant that sample
boundaries could be clearly identified in this mode, thus permitting
rapid location of particular samples.

The format for transcription was standardized according to the
conventions set out in appendix 1B. Briefly, the child's speech was
set out in the left-hand column, the speech of all other participants
in the centre column, with an identifying initial against each
utterance if more than one other participant was involved, and
notes on context, non-verbal activity and any other helpful information in the right-hand column, enclosed in square brackets.
Where the transcriber was in doubt about an utterance, or some
part of an utterance, it was enclosed in angle brackets ⟨ ⟩; where
an utterance was unintelligible, one asterisk was marked for each
word judged to have been uttered. Where the transcriber was aware
of responding to non-segmental features of the utterance, such as
intonation, or tone of voice, this information was included in
parentheses immediately after the utterance. Utterances for which

the orthographic transcription would not permit an unambiguous interpretation were glossed, and the gloss enclosed in parentheses. Utterances, or parts of utterances that were clear but uninterpretable were given a broad phonetic transcription using the symbols of the International Phonetic Alphabet. Otherwise all transcription was in Standard English orthography. (These and the other conventions are illustrated in the two versions of the same sample in appendix 1C.)

1.8.3 *Reliability of transcription*

When the recording and transcript were returned to the Research Unit, they were checked by one of two people employed almost exclusively for this task. In order to avoid arbitrary alterations by the checker, there were clearly specified rules as to what changes might be made. Briefly, the checker could only change the original by one degree of certainty. For example, if the transcriber had heard a child say 'Those my clogs', and had not indicated doubt about the interpretation, the checker could place ⟨ ⟩ round the utterance if she did not agree with this interpretation. Or, if she heard an alternative, she could add this, putting both versions in brackets: '⟨Those my clogs/Where's my socks?⟩'. Alternatively, if the transcriber had been doubtful about her interpretation and placed it in brackets, the checker could, if she agreed with the interpretation, remove the brackets. The checker was also required to check the timing of pauses and the marking of sample boundaries.

One surprising discovery that emerged during the checking of transcripts was the very considerable effect on what is heard of playing a tape on different machines. Because the checkers did not always use the same kind of tape recorder as had been used by the original transcriber, they were sometimes able to hear quite distinctly what had previously proved uninterpretable. The reverse seldom happened for, with the transcript in front of them, they were helped by being prepared to hear utterances which might otherwise have eluded them.

The procedure for checking just described raises the issue of reliability in transcription. Surprisingly, this is not an issue that is generally discussed in research reports and yet it is one of considerable theoretical as well as of methodological significance. Presumably, most researchers take their ability to produce accurate transcriptions for granted and, where only one person transcribes each recording, there is little opportunity for this assumption to be challenged. It is only when a recording is transcribed by several people independently that alternative interpretations are forced on one's attention and the true nature and size of the problem becomes apparent.

In an informal experiment carried out at the University of Melbourne, in which I was one of six participating child language researchers, the sound of a father interacting with a young child was copied from a video tape and each of us made an independent transcription of approximately five minutes of the sound track. Only about 30% of utterances were transcribed identically by all six transcribers; even after incorporating revisions made when viewing the video simultaneously with the sound, the versions did not show a significantly higher rate of agreement. Admittedly, a high proportion of the discrepancies were quite small, 'a' for 'the' or 'I'm going to' for 'I going to', but they occurred frequently. One particularly interesting discrepancy involved 'I'ld' which one transcriber heard consistently where all the others heard 'I'll'. It subsequently emerged that in the dialect that she spoke, this form was the more appropriate for the contexts in which she had heard it.

What this experiment shows is that the observer–transcriber is in no more privileged a position than the person to whom an utterance is addressed when it comes to producing a *verbatim* record of what was said. In order to transcribe one must draw on one's own past experience of similar situations as well as on the actual speech signal, to make the best possible guess as to what the speaker intended and, therefore, as to what he actually said. Since different people have different experience to draw on, it is inevitable that there should be discrepancies between them in what they hear.

In normal conversation most potential problems go unobserved and if the listener does become aware that his hearing of the speech signal does not match his expectations, he has a number of strategies which he can employ: he can simply hope that the meaning will become clear from subsequent utterances; he can ask for a repetition; or he can ask for clarification. The observer–transcriber can only employ the first of these strategies and it is only when several independent transcriptions are compared that it becomes apparent how much interpretation goes into the apparently objective task of converting speech signal to written record.

Since there is no possibility of determining the 'correct' version of any particular utterance it is not clear whether it is even appropriate to talk of 'reliability'. The ideal solution would seem to be to obtain, say, five independent versions of each transcript and to construct a final version from a comparison of all five. This, however, would have been quite impossible with the resources at our command. By having two people do all the checking, we aimed at least to achieve consistency.

1.8.4 *Selection and training of transcribers*

The transcribers were all mothers of young children who were selected from volunteers on the basis of an initial test and satisfactory performance while training. One recording was first transcribed by five people, who had gained considerable experience during the pilot study, and all five versions were written out in parallel. Volunteers were asked to transcribe the same tape and their versions were then compared with the parallel versions. Provided a volunteer's version was, for the most part, close to the majority opinion, the volunteer was accepted for training.

The training consisted of transcribing tapes which had been selected because they contained problematic material of various kinds. During training, a number of issues were focused on: the layout and conventions to be employed; attention to what was actually said, with particular attention to departures from what might be expected – dialect forms and omissions and substitutions of words and morphemes; division of the stream of speech into utterance units; the grounds on which an interpretation might be justified. The complete training programme involved them in some 30 hours of transcription and discussion spread over two or three weeks.

In principle, all the recordings of a particular child were transcribed by the same person. Although it was recognized that this might introduce a certain degree of bias, it was felt that such a possibility was more than compensated for by the benefit of the personal relationships that were established with the families by having the same person visit them each time. In practice, of course, it was not always possible to maintain this one-to-one relationship, but in general the procedure worked very satisfactorily.

Since the transcribers were all housewives rather than linguists, it is unlikely that they shared any particular theory of language development that might have affected the way they transcribed. At no stage were they given any idea of the theoretical leanings of the full-time staff and they were specifically instructed not to discuss the child's language development with the parents during their visits. There is little danger, therefore, that they introduced any particular bias into the speech data on which subsequent stages of the research were based.

1.9 Coding the transcripts

Once the transcript had been completed and checked, it was ready for coding. This next operation was carried out in a number of stages, again by part-time assistants working in their own homes.

The coding scheme, which will be described in detail in the following chapter, consisted of two major sections: the pragmatic and semantic analysis and the analysis of syntactic structure. For reasons that will be explained later these two parts of the coding were carried out sequentially by different groups of coders. All coding was entered directly on to specially designed 40-column computer cards. With each transcript, coders were given a cassette copy of the recording from which it had been prepared. This was to enable them to hear and make use of the prosodic features of speech as well as the purely lexico-grammatical information contained in the transcript in making their coding decisions.

Each child utterance was given a unique identification consisting of the code for the sample followed by a sequential number within the sample. This number was entered in the first columns of the first computer card for that utterance and also on the transcript in the left-most column. Next, the text of the utterance was written on the back of the first computer card used in coding that utterance. Entries were then made on the card, according to the codes set out in the manual, for the context, pragmatic function and semantic content.

Initially, all 18 samples were coded and, in the few cases where more than 18 samples had been transcribed to bring the number of child utterances up to the target of 100 (see 1.8.2), the spare samples were coded as well. As the work progressed and the children grew older, it became clear that in some cases 18 samples yielded far more than the 100–150 child utterances budgeted for. Since coders were being paid a flat-rate based on the average amount of time required to code a transcript of the expected length, they were unwilling to code transcripts that were very much longer. If there had been any money to spare in the grant, this problem could have been met by increasing the rate paid for longer transcripts. However, as there was not, the decision had to be taken to code fewer than 18 samples. Coders were therefore instructed to start by counting the number of utterances to be coded and, where it exceeded 150, to code first 12 samples, selecting at random two out of the three samples in each of the one-and-a-half-hour divisions. They were then to continue coding samples at random until the total number of child utterances coded was at least 120.

When this first stage of coding was completed, the coder would return the transcript, tape and stack of coded cards to the Research Unit and put the coded cards through a mark-sense card reader, which was attached to the Unit's ARCTURUS mini-computer. As the stack of coded cards was fed through the reader, a program in the computer inspected the codings, one at a time, and performed a feasibility check on them by comparing the actual code entered in each column or group of columns with the list of permitted codings. Cards containing errors were then printed out in full, with an indication as to which entries were in error. When these, essentially clerical, errors had been corrected, a further check was carried out by the full-time linguist on the project, who inspected 10% of the coded cards for each observation, selected to include one complete 90-second sample, for errors of a substantive kind. A list of errors found was returned to the coder who had to correct them and put the cards through the card-read-and-check program again before the stack was finally accepted. If consistent errors of a substantive kind were found during the 10% check, these were discussed with the coder, who was then required to check through the whole stack for possible errors of the same type.

The next stage of coding was similar to the first, except that the coding of syntactic structure was performed on the basis of the coding already carried out. That is to say, where the form of the utterance permitted alternative syntactic analyses, that analysis was to be entered which corresponded to the pragmatic and semantic interpretation of the utterance that had already been selected. For this reason, syntactic coders did not need to listen to the tape recording. The procedure for checking was identical to that used in the first stage, so when the cards had finally passed the 10% quality check and the last card-read-and-check inspection, the incidence of error should have been extremely low.

The final stage was the reading of the cards on to magnetic tape for transfer to the University main-frame computer, on which the analysis of the data was to be carried out. This was done in batches, when all the transcripts for one age-related occasion of recording had been coded and checked.

As with the transcribers, the coders were selected from volunteers on the basis of an initial test. No prior knowledge of linguistic theory was required, and in fact only one coder had had any formal training in linguistics, and that was as part of a degree in modern languages. Although no specific qualifications were required, in practice all those who were accepted for training proved to have had some form of higher education. To succeed they needed to have some 'feel' for linguistic analysis, and this was what the preliminary test attempted to assess. It took the form of half an hour's instruction in how to apply a simple version of case grammar followed by a fixed amount of time in which to analyse ten sentences in terms of the grammar just learned. Only those who achieved high scores on this test were accepted for training.

The training programme itself lasted about six weeks and involved a series of meetings in which the various sections of the coding scheme were explained, followed by periods of coding under supervision, then finally some independent coding of sample transcripts. Not all those who undertook training successfully completed the course and, of those who did, not all went on to become successful coders. In all, 80 people embarked on the training course and at least 50 did some actual coding. However the vast bulk of the coding was carried out by about nine people, several of whom were amongst the first group of coders to be recruited and trained during the pilot study 1971–2.

The complete coding operation extended over more than four years, between March 1973 and June 1977, and consumed nearly 500,000 cards. But even when all the coded data had been successfully transferred to the main computer, the task was not completed. When the first analyses were carried out, some of the results that emerged were so unexpected that we decided to go back to the transcripts involved to check that the results truly reflected the speech that had occurred. They did not. Certain transcripts had been so inaccurately coded (except for the 10% samples that had been systematically checked) that they had to be coded again in their entirety and others contained a level of error that we considered to be totally unacceptable. So we decided to carry out a systematic check of all the coding, using the following procedure.

Each coder's work was inspected in the order in which it had been done and all errors were marked and counted until the point at which the frequency of errors dropped below a certain criterion level. At that point, they were judged to have become reliable coders and all their subsequent work was assumed to be acceptably error-free. Fortunately, coders who had done a substantial amount of coding were found to have been quick to reach the criterion set, whilst those who had made the most errors were also likely to have given up after coding only one or a small number of transcripts. In all, about 7% of the transcripts were found to need recoding.

This procedure, which occupied the full-time staff of the project for a full three months, proved in the end to be very useful. Apart from leading to the correction of a large number of errors, it also allowed an estimate to be formed of the reliability with which the different coding categories had been applied. Equally importantly, it caused us to think in a very practical way about the level of error it would be reasonable to accept.

1.9.1 *Reliability of coding*
In any large-scale operation, where a large number of coders is involved, a certain incidence of error must be expected. The problem is to know what level of error to tolerate. Ideally, *all* errors should be corrected, but this would not have been feasible, partly because of the amount of time it would have taken (almost as long as the original coding) and partly because there will always remain a certain proportion of utterances about the coding of which it is impossible to reach complete agreement.

As with transcription, coding is a subject on which other research projects have tended to be extremely reticent. Where estimates of inter-observer reliability are quoted, they may apparently be as low as 80% and still be judged acceptable. If this means, as it appears to, that on one judgment in five there is disagreement, this seems to be extraordinarily high for any faith to be placed in subsequent statistical analyses of distributional trends. But a great deal depends on how the disagreement rate is calculated. Where each utterance is coded for a considerable number of different categories, each coding involving a relatively independent judgment, a quite different estimate of reliability will be obtained depending on whether disagreements are expressed in terms of the proportion of utterances containing one or more disagreements or in terms of the number of disagreements as a proportion of the total number of judgments made.

In deciding whether the coding of a transcript reached an acceptable level of accuracy, we used both types of calculation. The procedure used was as follows. Certain key categories were picked out for individual consideration, and the remainder divided into groups of not more than three categories. The number of errors occurring in the first 50 utterances coded was then calculated for each of the individual categories and for the groups of categories. Any transcript having more than four errors in any of these categories was rejected and was subsequently recoded. However, on this criterion alone it would have been possible for a transcript to contain the maximum number of permitted errors in each category and yet still be acceptable. Accordingly, a second criterion was applied which rejected any transcript that contained a total of more than 40 errors of any kind in the first 50 utterances. Given the average number of codings per utterance required by the scheme, this represented a criterion of less than two errors per 100 judgments.

In summary, therefore, coded transcripts were accepted with an error rate of up to 8% on individual categories, provided that the overall error rate was less than 2%. In practice, apart from those early transcripts that had to be recoded, the vast majority of transcripts examined had far less than this overall error rate and only occasionally did one reach the permitted maximum error rate on individual categories or groups of categories.

1.10 Computer assisted analysis of the data

When all the corrections had finally been edited into the coded data, which were stored in computer files, we were ready to begin the final and most demanding stage of the research.

From the initial planning stage it had been assumed that a computer would eventually be needed to assist with the numerical analysis of the coded data, but, at least initially, we were unaware that the requirement for subsequent computer processing of the data had important implications for the structure of the coding scheme itself. By the time that Chris Amos was appointed to the Research Unit and given the task of designing the computer program that would be used to tabulate the coded data, the basic structure of the coding scheme was already fixed in a form that was not ideally suited to the sort of operations that computers are designed to perform. Some of the difficulties that were later encountered could certainly have been reduced, if not completely avoided, had we recognized early enough that a research team needs to include someone with a clear understanding of computers and programming as well as others with a good grasp of linguistic theory, if the coding scheme that is produced is to yield data which are readily amenable to computer analysis.

As it was, the Language Analysis Program (LAP) had to be constructed to handle the data in the format that had already been determined by the coding scheme. Since this program will be described in greater detail in the following chapter only a bare outline will be given here. Essentially it had two functions: the first, which has already been described, was to carry out a column-by-column check on the acceptability of codings at the stage of initial coding; the second was to carry out cross-tabulations of the data with up to five variables at a time. The first of these functions was performed using the ARCTURUS mini-computer in conjunction with a Hewlett-Packard card-reader. The second function was performed on the ICL 4/75 main-frame, for which the full version of LAP was originally written. The coded data were stored in two files, one for the older children and one for the younger, each containing 15 Mbytes. Because of their size, these files could not be kept in permanent memory, but had to be stored on a private volume disk which was mounted on request. As a complete analysis of óne of the files required several hours of processing time, the disk was only mounted in the evening and so there was a delay of several hours between entering a job and obtaining the printed output. In order to facilitate development of new analysis programs, a small test-base of five coded transcripts was kept in permanent memory and trial runs were performed on this test-base prior to carrying out a full analysis.

Although somewhat unwieldy, this method of operating was employed reasonably satisfactorily for several months in 1977–8, and many routine two- and three-variable analyses were carried out on the pragmatic and semantic categories. When we came to attempt the analysis of syntactic structure, however, we found that, as implemented on the 4/75, LAP required more than the available amount of memory to handle the enormous range of utterance types that the children had produced over the course of the longitudinal observations.

The saga of difficulties that followed has already been described in the Introduction, so will not be repeated here. Suffice it to say that it was almost exactly three years before we were able, in August 1981, to recommence analyses of the data using our own LSI 11/23 mini-computer and to proceed to the stage of developing programs to group and tabulate the large variety of syntactic string-types present in the coded data. The method used will be described in chapter 2. The resulting syntactic analyses were finally completed early in 1983, allowing, at last, the integration of the various levels of linguistic analysis in one overall description.

1.10.1 *Evaluation of the computer-assisted data analysis*
At the root of the many and varied difficulties we encountered in trying to analyse the data with the help of a computer, lie two quite different problems. The first was the sheer quantity of the data and the demands this placed on memory space. This was something

over which we had little control, once the number of observations and the amount of detail required in coding them had been determined.

The second was one aspect of what Chomsky has drawn attention to under the rubric of 'linguistic creativity'. With a finite number of elements and rules of combination, there is a potentially infinite number of possible strings that can be generated, each of which differs at some level of delicacy from every other. In our coding scheme, we attempted to give scope for this creativity to manifest itself by using a free format, in which categories were coded in the actual order in which they occurred in the surface form of each utterance. However, systematic sequential searching of the data – the method employed by the computer as the basis for all forms of cross-tabulation – would have been rendered a great deal more straightforward if a fixed format had been employed throughout; that is to say, if, in the coding of each utterance, the same column had always contained information of the same kind. This was the solution ultimately adopted for the analysis of the syntactic data, as will be seen in chapter 2.

There is no doubt that the task of the coders was made a great deal simpler by the free-format mode actually employed, but, with the benefit of hindsight, it is now clear that the advantage was bought at too high a price. If we had the chance all over again to design a coding scheme and a computer program for analysing the coded data, we would plan the two components in an integrated fashion and would almost certainly employ a fixed-format mode throughout. Any future research of a similar kind would do well to take advantage of the lesson that we had to learn the hard way.

Describing child speech in its conversational context

As is immediately apparent from any longitudinal observation of a child in the familiar surroundings of his own home, his language occurs and develops through interaction with those around him. The roots of early speech, as Vygotsky pointed out many years ago (translated 1962), are social, the functions of early interaction being to maintain and develop the inter-personal relationship between the child and his immediate family circle and to organize and comment on the situations in which they find themselves and the activities in which they engage. From the earliest stages of pre-linguistic 'protoconversation' (Trevarthen, 1974), through the period of one-word utterances to the beginning of recognizably structured utterances and beyond, the child both initiates inter-action to achieve these purposes and responds to the initiations of others.

Although probably exclusively concerned with the inter-personal relationship to begin with, it is not long before the interactions between parent and child begin to incorporate objects and events in the immediate environment (Trevarthen and Hubley, 1978); gradually the child's language acquires a referential function and speech becomes linked to the cognitive representations of experi-ence that had been developing independently. From now on, the cognitive schemata the child possesses can be employed in the task of discovering the relationship between linguistic features in the utterances that are addressed to him and those aspects he already understands of the situations in which they occur (Slobin, 1973; Cromer, 1979). The same utterances can, however, also indicate the existence of new concepts to be grasped and suggest more powerful ways of inter-relating those already acquired (Brown, 1973).

If the child's early experience of language is essentially concerned with the exchange of meanings, both semantic and pragmatic, in the familiar and oft-repeated situations that make up his daily life, he is equally concerned with the acquisition of the formal system through which these meanings are expressed. Here too he needs the model provided by other, more mature speakers of the language he is learning. He also needs the opportunity to encode his own meanings in linguistic forms and to receive feedback on their appropriateness to guide his further learning.

Cross-cultural research on language acquisition (summarized, for example, in Brown (1973) and Slobin (1982)) suggests that, as a result of the basic similarity of the interactions available to the maturing infant between himself and the social and physical environment, there will be very great similarity in the meanings that the child understands and seeks to encode in his early utterances, whatever the culture in which he lives. However, the lexical items and grammatical structures in which these meanings are encoded will vary very considerably between one language community and another, as will the relative transparency of the relationships between meanings and lexico-grammatical realization (Slobin, 1979). Differences as well as similarities are to be expected, therefore, between children acquiring different languages.

Variation, both within and between language communities, is also to be found in the importance that the adult community attaches to children's language development, and in the function of language in family interaction and the topics which are considered worthy of discussion (Blount, 1977; Heath, 1983; Nelson, 1973, 1981). Differences in the quality and quantity of linguistic interaction experienced by a young child can be expected to have a substantial influence on the rate at which his language mastery develops and perhaps also on the route that that development takes.

2.1 Overall aims and organization of the coding scheme

This perspective on language development, which is developed in much more detail in volume 1 of this series (Wells, 1981), was the one that guided us in the development of the coding scheme for the Bristol Study. Clearly, it was necessary for the scheme to include a description of the 'surface' syntactic organization of children's utterances because that is the level of description which is both closest to the perceived form and most readily comparable with previous research. However it was considered equally important to attempt a description of the meanings, both ideational and interpersonal, expressed in children's utterances and of the activity or situational contexts in which the utterances occurred.

It was also decided to code the conversational context provided by the utterances addressed to the child. Ideally, of course, these utterances would be described in full in the same terms as the child's, so that all inter-utterance relationships could be examined. However, as explained in chapter 1, to code in such detail would have exceeded the resources available, so only utterances by other speakers that immediately preceded or followed a child utterance were coded, and even these received only a summary coding, as described below.

The scheme that was eventually used, and which is enshrined in the revised edition of the project *Coding Manual*,[1] was developed over a number of years on the basis of reading the available literature, converting the theoretical descriptions into sets of coding categories, trying them out on samples of data, and modifying them in the light of that experience. Certain aspects of the intended description were relatively straightforward to operationalize in coding categories, for example, the description of surface syntax. Others, such as utterance Functions or Sentence Meaning Relations, were much more problematic. This was partly because these were aspects of linguistic description which were only beginning to be investigated and there was therefore little guidance to be obtained from already published work. But they were also problematic in the more fundamental sense that it was not clear precisely how these domains should be described: how many distinctions should be made and which were the most important. These continue to be troubling questions, as is made clear by, for example, the debate on the appropriateness, or otherwise, of interpreting children's early utterances in terms of a fairly wide range of semantic relations (*Journal of Child Language* 8 : 2 (1981)) and by the very diverse sets of speech-act categories that are used by different researchers (see McShane, 1980). With the benefit of hindsight it is easy to see how some of the decisions that were taken then could be improved but, in general, the scheme has stood the test of use remarkably well.

The theoretical basis of the coding scheme is eclectic, deliberately avoiding the attempt to construct a description based solely on one of the competing theoretical models. Theoretical linguistics has been a particularly volatile discipline during the last two decades and of the theories that excited the most interest in 1972 there is not one that has remained active but unchanged over the intervening period. It would have been difficult not to have been influenced by transformational-generative grammar, in the version expounded in *Aspects of the Theory of Syntax* (Chomsky, 1965), for that work raises some fundamental questions about language acquisition that every researcher must be concerned with. There was also the example of Brown and his colleagues (Brown *et al.*, 1969; Klima and Bellugi, 1966), who successfully used a T-G model to write grammars for individual children at different stages of development, based on extensive corpora of spontaneous speech. Nevertheless T-G did not seem to us to be an appropriate choice, firstly because, within it, the relationship between meaning and surface structure is theoretically pre-determined, whereas we wished to treat it as a question for empirical investigation; secondly, to have carried out a full T-G description of all the speech samples we intended to collect would far have exceeded our resources.

Intellectually, we were, in fact, far more sympathetic to the ideas emerging in generative semantics and to the proposals for a case-grammatical deep structure (Fillmore, 1968; Chafe, 1970; Anderson, 1971), and their influence can be seen in the section of the scheme concerned with the semantic content of utterances. The newly emerging concern with speech acts (Searle, 1969) growing out of the pioneering work of Austin (1962) was also of help to us, as were the ideas of J. Sinclair and M. Coulthard. The framework that was to appear in *Towards an Analysis of Discourse* (Sinclair and Coulthard, 1975) was undergoing development contemporaneously with our attempt to find a way of describing the organization of parent–child conversation, and we benefited from a number of discussions with Sinclair and Coulthard, the results of which are again reflected in certain parts of the scheme.

The most important single influence, however, was undoubtedly that of Michael Halliday. We appreciated his open-minded empirical orientation to the task of linguistic description (see Halliday, 1964, 1977) and found that the overall structure of his systemic grammar, with its three macro-functions (Halliday, 1967a, 1967b, 1968), provided a most helpful theoretical framework for integrating various parts of our proposed description. We made our own use of some of his ideas, therefore, but for the same reasons that we rejected the T-G formalism, we decided not to attempt a full systemic description of our data. In spite of this cavalier attitude on our part, Halliday was kind enough to look at one of the preliminary versions of the coding scheme and to give encouragement and advice on some of the difficulties that we were encountering.

The final version of one section of the coding scheme was designed in collaboration with another major project. During the

Spring of 1972, I spent a few weeks at the Institute of Human Learning at the University of California, Berkeley, working with a group led by Dan Slobin and Francesco Antinucci, who were also constructing a coding scheme for the analysis of child speech to be collected in the Cross-Cultural Language Development Project based at Berkeley. Both groups had independently arrived at the decision to adopt a case-grammatical approach to the semantics of early utterances and the time together was spent in systematizing the categories to be used, and providing defining criteria together with examples. The end product was an agreed scheme for the description of Sentence Meaning Relations and the semantic modi-fications of Time, Aspect, Manner and Modality, which it was hoped would be appropriate for the description of adult–child conversation in a wide variety of languages.

2.2 Units of analysis

One of the first problems facing anyone attempting to describe samples of spontaneous speech is to decide on the units of analysis. Many candidates offer themselves: speaker turn, syntactic clause, tone-group, none of which are necessarily co-extensive. The root of the problem is that conversational acts, underlying propositions and units of expression do not stand in any simple one-to-one relationship. No one of the possible units can be said to be more correctly chosen as the basic unit of analysis; the choice must depend on the purposes for which the analysis is made. The solution adopted in this scheme is to use a hierarchy of units, different parts of the total description being made at the level of each unit. The units, in ascending order of scope are: Clause, Utterance, Sub-sequence and Sequence.

If any of these units is more basic than the others it is Utterance, for it is an utterance which is treated as the minimal conversational contribution, consisting of one or more clauses on the one hand and entering into larger units of discourse on the other. An utterance is defined as 'one independent unit of verbal communication together with any other units that are dependent on it' (Wells, 1975: 30).[2] Although by no means watertight as a criterion, when supported by the additional information yielded by pausing and intonation which was available to the coders, it proved to be adequate in practice and there were few problems of utterance segmentation. This is no doubt due to the fact that a very high proportion of child turns in conversation consist of no more than one independent clause and the adult speech that is addressed to them is syntactically well-formed and relatively simple.

In addition to the criterion quoted above, a number of rules were added for dealing with elliptical utterance segments and with paratactic and hypotactic sentences.

2.3 Utterances as conversational acts: the description of Inter-Personal Purpose

The description as a whole treats communication as one of many possible types of purposeful behaviour which are instrumental in the attainment of goals of various kinds, as in the model of hierarchical plans for behaviour proposed by Miller *et al.* (1960). Where the goal, or superordinate *plan*, requires collaboration between individuals, communication is an essential instrumental means. Speech is one, highly structured, type of communication, particularly well-suited to the exchange of ideational meanings. In interaction it may be accompanied by, or even partly replaced by, other forms of non-verbal communication. However, whilst recognizing the importance of non-verbal behaviour for a full account of communication which is predominantly carried on through speech, this scheme makes no attempt to describe such behaviour, on the grounds that in the recordings the evidence necessary for such a description was almost completely absent.

The plans in which linguistic communication serves as an instrumental means are too many to enumerate, but the ways in which speech enters into the execution of these plans can be more easily classified. There would probably be general agreement that the list should include at least the following: to control action, to seek and to give information, to express emotion and to establish and maintain social relations. In the normal course of events, individual contributions – conversational acts – occur within longer interchanges dominated by one of these purposes in the pursuance of some non-linguistic plan.

The communication of this plan, and the instrumental means to achieving it, is usually (but not invariably) the responsibility of the initiator of the interchange. If the other participant is willing at least temporarily to accept the plan and attendant decisions about means, the interchange develops smoothly and coherently. Sometimes, however, this is not the case because the second participant is either unaware of, or fails to agree with, the presuppositions of the initiator. In such cases the interchange may make frequent changes of direction or fail to reach any recognizable conclusion.

A conversational interchange usually also has a particular topic or theme, which can be recognized from a clustering of key lexical items in the succession of utterances of which it is constituted. The same problems apply in reaching agreement about topic, of course, as have already been discussed in relation to purpose. This is particularly true for what has been called 'phatic' communication, where almost any topic is suitable for discussion and where the constraints on topic-shift between adjacent contributions are considerably relaxed.

In the paradigm case, purpose and topic are mutually agreed and the interchange has a recognizable beginning and end. Such a unit with 'unitary topic and purpose' is defined as a conversational sequence. This is the highest and most inclusive unit within the descriptive hierarchy. The succession of sequences in a conversation is usually far from random (one topic leading to another, one purpose being followed by another; but both being related to some superordinate goal) but no attempt is made within the scheme to specify the patterning of sequences within longer stretches of conversation.

Sequences are classified according to the dominant purpose that they are taken to be designed to achieve:

Control: the control of the present or future behaviour of one or more of the participants.
Expressive: the expression of spontaneous feelings.
Representational: the requesting and giving of information.
Social: the establishment and maintenance of social relationships.
Tutorial: interaction where one of the participants has a deliberately didactic purpose.

It is important to stress that it is the dominant purpose of the sequence as a whole which is coded and not the purpose of any particular utterance, although the first substantive utterance in the sequence usually has particular importance in determining the dominant purpose of the whole sequence.

Within any sequence there may occur a series of smaller units of interaction, which are directed to the achievement of sub-plans within the larger plan. A Sub-sequence (or what in more recent work we call an Exchange) consists of an initiating utterance and all subsequent utterances dependent on it until the next initiating utterance. The categories of sub-sequence are the same as for sequences, with the addition of:

Procedural: management of the channel of communication and
rectification of break-downs due to mishearing or misunder-
standing.

Utterances which initiate sub-sequences have many of the same
characteristics as those which initiate sequences but, because they
are subordinate to a larger conversational plan, recognizing constraints set up by preceding utterances, they do not mark a change
of sequence.

A typical example of a sequence involving a number of sub-
sequences might be one in which the dominant purpose (Control) is
to get the child to shut the door on coming into the house. After an
initiating (Procedural) sub-sequence to gain the child's attention
there is a (Control) sub-sequence in which the actual request is
made. The child may then interject an account of where he has been
to get his hands so dirty (Representational) as an indirect justification for not complying. Mother next expresses her shocked reaction
(Expressive), before reverting to a repetition of her original
request with which the child finally complies (Control). The whole
sequence might look something like the following (invented)
example:

Mother: Stephen (v)⎫
⎬ Procedural Sub-s
Child: Yes ⎭

Mother: Shut the door when⎫
you come in please⎬ Control
⎭ Sub-s

Child: Well
I think I'd better not touch⎫
the handle ⎪
I've been cleaning my bike and⎬ Representational
my hands are very greasy ⎪ Sub-s
⎪
Mother: Are they?⎭
Child: Yes

Mother: Good heavens!⎫
You have got yourself filthy . . .⎬ Expressive
⎭ Sub-s

Anyway make sure you shut⎫
the door when you've ⎬ Control
washed your hands ⎭ Sub-s

Child: All right

The level below sub-sequence is that of Function, which is the
smallest unit in the analysis of Inter-Personal Purpose. The tax-

onomy of Function categories is very like the list of 'illocutionary acts' which Austin (1962) and Searle (1969) enumerate, except that the decisions as to which distinctions to make were taken from the perspective of children's conversation rather than that of philosophers. The complete list of Functions is organized in terms of the sub-sequence types: the range that is available for coding individual acts is dependent on a prior decision as to sub-sequence. So, within a Control sub-sequence, the permitted Functions include Command, Suggestion, Offer, Permit, etc., within Representational, Statement, Content Question, Response to Content Question, etc., and so on. Functions can be divided into two classes, as was stated above: initiating and non-initiating. Initiating Functions are specific to the type of sub-sequence in which they can occur: Command, for example, can only occur in a Control sub-sequence. Non-initiating functions are less restricted, so functions such as Request Justification or Condition are listed under several sub-sequences. However their precise significance is determined by the particular sub-sequence in which they occur. For the positive and negative responses 'Yes' and 'No' this is brought out by the Function labels: 'Yes' in a Control sub-sequence is classified as Assent, in a Representational sub-sequence as Affirm and in Expressive as Agree.

Assignment of utterance tokens to Function types is based mainly on form, including intonation, but experience shows that there is no simple one-to-one equivalence of Form and Function and, in the last resort, the total context is taken into account in reaching a decision. In the majority of cases one function is encoded by one utterance but it is possible to have more than one function realized in the same utterance as, for example, when a main and subordinate clause encode a Promise and the Contractual conditions that have to be met in order for the promise to be fulfilled, or when a Statement is followed by a Justification. Simultaneous codings of Function are not permitted, however: where more than one function is judged to be intended, it is the one judged to be dominant that is coded.

Although not theoretically at the same level of description, the category Mood was also included in the coding of inter-personal purpose. The relationship between Function and Mood is, of course, strictly one of realization, *Declarative* being the unmarked realization of the functions Statement, Promise etc., *Interrogative* of Question, *Imperative* of Command, and so on. However, as already pointed out, there is no simple one-to-one correspondence between Function and Mood choice, and, indeed, all forms of Indirect Request are marked in the sense that they are realized by choices from the Mood system other than Imperative. By linking the coding of Mood with that of Function the intention was to use Mood for making finer sub-categorizations of such Function categories as Command, Suggestion, Threat, etc. For example, the distinction between Direct and Indirect Request can be based on the criterion of Mood choice; Direct Request is defined as Command realized by the Mood choices of Imperative and Moodless and Indirect Request as Command realized by Declarative or Interrogative Mood.

2.3.1 *Utterance context*
Although the importance of the context of an utterance has long been recognized by linguists, particularly those concerned to make ethnographic descriptions of language use, there was no ready-made taxonomy of context that could be drawn upon in the construction of the present coding scheme. This is perhaps not surprising in view of the difficulty of determining what counts as the context on any particular occasion.

Speech always occurs in some situational context, but the relationship between utterance and context is neither simple nor constant. What is said both constitutes the context as being of a certain socially recognizable kind and, at one and the same time, is constrained by what that context is recognized as being. The relative importance of these two influences varies according to the nature of the physical environment as it is socially perceived, the previous shared interactional experience of the participants and their individual purposes on any particular occasion. This is equally true of adult–child interaction, even though most conversation involving young children is strongly tied to what is perceptually present.

Bearing these facts in mind, it was decided to be guided as much by what was said, in allocating sequences of conversation to contextual categories, as by the physical setting and activity in relation to which the conversation occurred. For example, a family might be eating a meal, but talking about a proposed outing for the afternoon. In this case, it seems appropriate to treat the discussion itself as the situational context of individual utterances rather than the activity of eating.

Much of the child's day is spent in play of various kinds. For this reason, an initial distinction is made, in classifying situational context, between Play and other activities. Within Play, two further independent distinctions are made: first, between Free Play, Rule-Governed Play, and Imaginary (Role-) Play; and, secondly, between Play Alone, with Other Children, and with Adult Participation. Other activities are divided into the following categories: Sleeping (in bed, but not actually asleep), Physical Comfort (being nursed or held), Dressing and Toileting, Meals and Snacks, Helping (where the child's intention is to help, although this may not be the adult's perception of the resulting activity), Reading (being read to or looking at a book), Watching TV, Non-Play Activity (where the child is interested in an ongoing, often domestic, activity, but may not necessarily be taking part) and Talking (where the talk is not dependent on the immediate situation).

The unit of analysis for context is the complete conversational sequence, on the grounds that if the socially perceived context changes there must also be a change in Purpose and/or Topic. Only one of the above categories is coded for each sequence of conversation.

Equally important in determining what is said and how it is understood is the context provided by preceding and following utterances in the sequence. Where the child being studied speaks two or more adjacent utterances in the same sequence each is coded in full, as already described. Where the utterance which precedes or follows the child utterance currently being described is spoken by another person, it is coded in terms of Sub-sequence, Function and Mood, using the same categories as for child utterances. Ideally, one would wish to be able to take into account all the utterances in a sequence, particularly preceding ones, when considering any individual utterance. However, the practical implementation of coding and analysis, to be described below, made this impossible. The coding of the Inter-Personal Purpose of immediately preceding and following utterances by other speakers was the most satisfactory compromise available in the circumstances.

Because conversation is a joint enterprise requiring collaboration by all the participants involved, it is possible to evaluate the appropriateness with which each utterance in a sequence meets the expectations set up by the immediately preceding utterance where (1) they are by different speakers and (2) the preceding utterance had a conventionally recognizable eliciting function. Utterances that meet this criteria are classified as either:

1 Semantically and syntactically appropriate (Appropriate).

2 Semantically appropriate but syntactically inappropriate (Side-step).
3 Semantically inappropriate but syntactically appropriate (Literal).
4 Semantically and syntactically inappropriate (Inappropriate).
5 Failure to respond altogether (Null).

Some eliciting utterances, such as commands, call for a non-verbal response. Where this response occurs unaccompanied by any verbal response, Non-Verbal is entered rather than Null.

2.3.2 *Speech for self*

Not all a child's utterances have a clearly interactional intention. Almost from the beginning it appears that speech is sometimes used exclusively for the speaker's benefit in the organization of his experience. Following Vygotsky (1962), we characterize such utterances as Speech for Self. Cutting across the speech-for-others/speech-for-self distinction is a further distinction between utterances where the child is playing the role of another and speech which does not involve role-play. Since role-playing speech can, and frequently does, occur in the absence of another conversational participant, we therefore have a four-way categorization of the status of the child's utterances:

1 *Social Speech:* addressed to another in his role as a child.
2 *Social Role-playing:* addressed to another, but in an adopted role.
3 *Speech for Self:* non-addressed, but in his role as child.
4 *Speech for Self* (role-play): addressed to or by an imaginary other.

Speech in the last category may involve quite an elaborate switching of roles, as the child plays the parts of the other imaginary participants as well as his own, or himself in an adopted role. Utterances in all but the status category Speech for Self (3 above) can be further classified in terms of the categories of Inter-Personal Purpose already described. Speech for Self, on the other hand, by definition does not have an inter-personal purpose. It nevertheless can serve a number of different functions for the speaker. The following distinctions are made:

Comment: descriptions of current activity or situation; self-addressed commands to plan and govern own activity.

Expressive: expression of affective response to situation, most frequently an exclamation.

Heuristic: verbalization of experience in order to increase understanding.

Practice: substitution routines, sound-play, etc.

Imitation: spontaneous imitation of another's utterance with no apparent communicative function.

The coding of speech from the perspective of conversational interaction is completed by the identification of the Initiator of each sequence and the identification of child utterances which are Dependent, in the sense that they either incorporate a segment of a preceding utterance (by self or another participant) in a more complex Build-Up, or imitate the whole or a part of an immediately preceding utterance by another speaker.

2.4 The analysis of semantic content

Topic, at the level of sequence and sub-sequence, has been left unanalysed. No satisfactory scheme could be found for the classification of the semantic properties shared by utterances that make up units at these levels. Indeed, this is also true for utterances consisting of more than one clause. The unit selected for the analyses of topic, therefore, corresponds to the underlying simple sentence, i.e. in most cases the syntactic clause.

2.4.1 *Sentence Meaning Relations*

Central to this analysis is a taxonomy of Sentence Meaning Relations (SMRs) based essentially on case grammar. Fillmore (1968) sees the semantic structure of a sentence as consisting of two components, 'modality' and 'proposition'. Much of what Fillmore would handle under modality has already been accounted for in our scheme under Inter-Personal Purpose. Proposition concerns the experiential content: what the sentence is about. From this point of view, the world of experience is conceived of as consisting of a large number of entities – persons and things – which can be in a finite number of states or relationships with each other. Fillmore likens this to actors in a play who take on varying roles in different scenes: each scene, or proposition, being characterized by the verb and an array of noun phrases in case–role relations to the verb. However a limitation of this characterization is that propositions with differing relations may still be described in terms of the same case-array. For example, in the following sentences:

(1) Harry painted the door.
(2) John moved the stone.
(3) The chairman postponed the meeting.

Agent and Patient would be the case-array for all of them, although the relationship between Agent and Patient is different in each example. In our coding scheme, distinctions of SMRs are made according to the type of state or relation the participant(s) are engaged in. The states that are distinguished are Existence, Attribution and Experience and the basic relations are those of Location in Space, Possession, Benefactive, Location in Time and Equivalence. Further distinctions are made in the Attributive and Experiential states: the attribute may be Physical, Quantitative, Evaluative, Dispositional, or concern Substance (e.g. 'wooden') or Classification; experience may be Physical, Affective, Cognitive (Perceptual), Cognitive (Mental), or concern Wanting.

Following Chafe (1970) we also describe the dynamics of the state or relation in which the participants are engaged, making a primary distinction between Static and Changing. Where change occurs, the cause may be specified as being either an Agent, an Instrument or an Agent using an Instrument, or the cause of change may be unspecified – simple Change.

These two dimensions taken together give a matrix which accounts for all but a small sub-set of the SMRs it was felt necessary to distinguish. Table 2.1 presents this matrix with invented examples and table 2.2 presents the sub-categories of the Attributive and Experiential states, together with the small set of SMRs that do not easily fit within this matrix: the intrinsic Functions of animate beings and certain inanimate objects and forces.

As talk about the location and change of location of objects is known to bulk large in the conversation of young children, it was decided to make further distinctions within the Locative Relation. There is only one form of Static Locative Relation, but if the relation is Changing, a variety of sub-types can be distinguished (see table 2.3). First there is Directional location, in which either source or goal or both are specified. Second, there is Movement, where it is the type of change of location that is in focus, rather than its direction, although often a movement from source to goal results. Third is the combination of these two types in Directional Movement, where both features are focused upon.

The fourth category, Target, is more problematic. From one point of view, actions such as 'touching', 'hitting', 'pushing', can be

Table 2.1 *Examples of main Sentence Meaning Relations*

Mode	Existence	Equivalence	States or relations				
			Attributive	Experiential	Locative	Possessive	Benefactive
Static	There are unicorns.	Herbert is the President.	The thread is long.	Eustace was sad.	The cork is in the bottle.	Miranda has two pennies.	The present is for Herbert.
Change of state	I was born.	Herbert became President.	The thread stretched.	Eustace grew more and more sad.	The cork is coming out of the bottle.	Miranda received a penny.	—
Agent cause change of state	The King declared war.	The people elected Herbert President.	Miranda broke the thread.	Miranda cheered Eustace up.	Herbert took the cork out of the bottle.	Miranda was given a penny by her father.	—
Instrument cause change of state	The death of the King caused a war of succession to break out.	The computer elected Herbert President.	The scissors cut the thread.	The letter cheered Eustace up.	The champagne forced the cork out of the bottle.	The loss of her purse left Miranda without a penny.	—
Agent cause change of state by means of Instrument	John made a hole with his finger.	The Queen knighted Herbert with a sword	Miranda cut the thread with a pair of scissors.	Miranda cheered Eustace up by writing him a letter.	Herbert used a corkscrew to get the cork out of the bottle.	Miranda's uncle left her a fortune by a bequest in his will.	—

Table 2.2 *Attributive and Experiential states and Functions*

	Attributive state				
Physical	Quantity	Class	Evaluative	Substance	Dispositional
The thread is long.	There are a dozen apples.	This poem is a sonnet.	The plan is excellent.	The boat is made of glass fibre.	Mr Brown is generous.

	Experiential state			
Physical	Affective	Cognitive (perceptual)	Cognitive (mental)	Wanting
Miranda is tired.	Miranda is happy.	Eustace can see Miranda.	Herbert knows the answer.	Eustace wants (Miranda to talk to him).

Functions			
Agent Function	Patient Function	Agent Function on Patient	Agent Function over Range
Herbert is whistling.	The bell rang.	The baby drank its milk	The old ladies are playing bridge.

Table 2.3 *Sub-categories of locative Sentence Meaning Relations*

	Movement	Directional	Directional Movement	Target	Directional Target
Static		The boulder is on the lawn. John is sitting in the chair. The houses stood well back from the road.	We live in Bristol. Mary is wearing a necklace. This bottle contains one pint.		—
Change	The boulder moved. The ball bounced.	The boulder fell into the ravine. The ball crossed the base-line.	The boulder rolled into the ravine. The ball bounced across the line.	—	
Agent cause change	John moved the boulder. Mary bounced the ball.	John threw the boulder into the ravine. Mary picked up the ball.	John rolled the boulder into the ravine. Mary bounced the ball across the line.	John hit his brother. Bill kicked the ball. The mother tickled her baby.	John pushed his brother into the river. Bill kicked the ball over the wall.

Instrument cause change	The flood moved the boulder. The testing machine bounced the ball.	The crane picked up the boulder. The racquet sent the ball into the net.	The flood rolled the boulder into the ravine. The racquet bounced the ball over the net.	The lorry bashed the car.	The lorry bashed the car into the ditch.
Agent with Instrument cause change	John moved the boulder with a pick. Mary bounced the ball with a racquet.	John picked up the boulder with a crane. Mary got the ball out of the tree with her racquet.	John rolled the boulder into the ravine with a pick. Mary bounced the ball over the net with her racquet.	John hit his brother with a club. The mother tickled her baby with a feather.	John pulled the cork out of the bottle with a corkscrew. Bill hit the ball over the wall with his racquet.
Agent cause co-referential change	John moved. Mary is dancing.	John went to the station. Mary remained at home. Our friends have arrived.	John walked to the station. Mary danced round the room. The birds flew away.	—	—
Agent with Instrument cause co-referential change	Mary is skating. John is swinging on a rope.	Mary travelled to London by train. John crossed the Atlantic in a boat.	Mary drove to London. John used a rope to swing across the ravine.	—	—

thought of as straightforward transitive relations in which an Agent acts on a Patient in rather the same way as with actions such as 'breaking', 'opening', etc. The main difference is that the former do not necessarily lead to a change of state in the Patient, whereas the latter certainly do. From an alternative point of view, the same actions of 'touching', etc. can be seen as one object changing location to come into contact with another object, rather as in the Directional location SMR exemplified by 'putting'. The difference here is that, in actions like 'touching', it is not clear whether the object that is the target of the action is best seen as Patient or as Location. The solution finally adopted was to treat such actions as a distinct sub-category of the Locative Relation.[3] Like Movement it can combine with Directional to yield the fifth category: Directional Target.

In certain types of relation, two participants may have the same referent. For example in

(4) Mary went to school.
(5) Mary danced.

'Mary' is both the Patient whose location changed and the Agent responsible for causing the change. Similarly in

(6) Mary washed herself.

'Mary' (Agent) and 'herself' (Patient) refer to the same entity. Such SMRs, which involve co-referential participants, are treated as distinct from those where Agent and Patient refer to separate entities.

A final distinction concerns embedding. Certain SMRs, by virtue of the type of state or relation involved, frequently have a second proposition embedded as the realization of one of the participants in the main proposition. This is particularly common for the Cognitive and Wanting experiential states, for example:

(7) Herbert knows *where the ball is*.
(8) The baby doesn't want *to drink its milk*.

As these sub-categories of experiential SMRs are both more complex than the corresponding items without embedding and also of high frequency, they have been treated as distinct SMRs in their own right.

Using this taxonomy, a coding is made of all clauses, finite and non-finite. Some utterances, however, do not contain sufficient lexical information for assignment to a SMR, for example, greetings, exclamations, polarity responses ('Yes', 'No'). Such utterances are assigned to the category Unstructured, which is itself further sub-categorized. Elliptical responses, on the other hand, are assigned on the basis of the full form which is recoverable from the conversational context: for example, 'To the shop', as a response to the question 'Where are you going?' would be assigned to the SMR Agent Cause Coreferential Change of Location: Directional.

2.4.2 *Semantic participants*

Each SMR involves one or more participants in specified case-roles selected from the following:

Agent: an animate being who causes a change of state in another participant or carries out a Function.

Experiencer: an animate being who experiences internal states or changes of state.

Patient: a physical object, animate or inanimate, an event or a mental or verbal representation of any of these, which is in a particular state or located in space or time or changes state or location.

Instrument: a physical object, natural force, event or mental representation of any of these, which serves as the immediate cause of a change of the state or location of another participant.

Locative: the location of a Patient in space, either at rest or in movement, or the source, goal or path of a change of a Patient's location.

Possessor: the location of a Patient, when this location is an animate being with ownership or temporary control of the Patient.

Benefactive: the animate being for whose benefit an object or event is intended.

Temporal: the location of a Patient in time.

Range: the patterned or conventional activity which results from or defines the Function of an Agent.

Purpose: the purpose for which a Patient is designed or intended.

Classifier: the participant in a Classification SMR which defines the class to which a Patient is assigned.

Only one instance of each participant case-role can occur in any clause, with the following exceptions. In Equivalence clauses, both participants are classified as Patients, e.g. '*Mr Smith* is *the manager*'. In Target Directional clauses, there are two Locatives. One of these is always combined with a Patient to form the Target; the other is the Source or Goal Location of the directional change of location, for example, 'He kicked *the ball* (P–L) *under the bed* (L)'. In Change of Location or Change of Possession clauses, both the Source *and* the Goal may be specified, e.g. '*He* (A-Poss. (source)) gave *to a deserving charity* (Poss. (goal))'.

This last example raises the issue of what we have called *obligatory* participants. These are the participants that are required for an utterance to be interpreted as the realization of a particular SMR. Change of Possession, for example, necessarily involves a Patient and at least the Source Possessor or the Goal Possessor. If the verb encodes an Agentively Caused Change of Possession an Agent is also necessarily involved. It may happen, however, that one or more of these obligatory participants is not actually present in the spoken realization of the clause. This may be because the speaker judges that this information is recoverable from the conversational context or from common knowledge. Or – as in the utterances of very young children – it may be omitted because of limitations on production ability. In such cases, obligatory case-roles are coded as being present in the underlying meaning intention; their non-realization is picked up in the coding of syntactic structure.

As well as lacking obligatory participants, utterances may also contain participants additional to those that are obligatory for the SMR in question. For example, in 'The children were playing in the garden yesterday', the SMR is Agent Function, for which Agent is the only obligatory participant. The Locative and Temporal participants are both *optional*; no change in the SMR would occur if either or both of them were omitted. Such participants are treated as deriving from superordinate clauses of the form 'X be in the garden' (Static Locative) or 'X be yesterday' (Static Temporal) and in coding they are marked as superordinate and optional.

The semantic participants in a clause may have their own internal structure and are described accordingly. The Headword itself is sub-categorized according to whether it refers to the Speaker, Addressee or a Third Party and, if the latter, whether the Third Party is Human, Animate, Inanimate, Abstract, Text or realized by an embedded clause. Third Party headwords may also be categorized as Deictic, Proper, Possessive or Interrogative. Where the participant is obligatory but unrealized, a coding to this effect is added to the coding for the sub-category selected.

Headwords may also be modified. The categories coded are Definiteness, Demonstrative, Interrogative, Number and General. General modifiers are further classified in terms of the SMR from which they are derived, irrespective of whether they are realized pre-nominally or post-nominally. The modifiers in 'my big, wooden hut on the beach', for example, are classified as being derived from clauses of Static Possession, Physical Attributive state, Substance Attributive state, and Static Location respectively. Modifiers may additionally be classified as Interrogative, Comparative or Superlative or realized as a qualifying clause.

2.4.3 *Clause modification*
If the SMR with its participants can be said to describe the nuclear meaning of the clause – the 'proposition' in Fillmore's terms – there are other aspects of the topic which would be included under what he termed 'modality'. These operate at the level of the clause, not as additional participants, but as modifications of the proposition as a whole.

The first of these is Polarity: whether the clause is positive or negative. Negative is the marked alternative and may apply to the clause as a whole, or to one particular category within it. Where a negative clause contains an optional participant, it is usually this which is negated, e.g. 'They are*n't* playing *in the garden*'. Contrastive stress may also pick out a particular element for negation. Otherwise it is the State or Change of State as a whole which is negated. Only categories of non-contrastive negation are handled by the coding scheme.

The second type of modification is Time. In English, Time seems to be perceived in terms of three theoretically organized oppositions. Now or Neutral v. Not-Now, with not-now encompassing Past v. Future and with both past and future less clearly divided into Immediate v. Remote. In practice, however, the latter distinction proved too difficult to draw and so was abandoned, leaving what amounts to a three-way division: Neutral, Past and Future. More detailed specification is possible through the addition of an optional temporal participant to the array of cases obligatorily required by the SMR. This participant may be realized by a word, phrase or clause. Seven sub-categories are recognized:

Point Time: e.g. 'now', 'at 2 o'clock'
Relative to Point: e.g. 'before it rains', 'next'
Duration: e.g. 'during the day', 'while it is light'
Time to: e.g. 'until we have finished'
Time from: e.g. 'since yesterday'
Extent: e.g. 'for a long time'
Frequency: e.g. 'often', 'once a week'

It will be noted that the temporal point of reference may be either deictic, that is, related to the time of speaking, or absolute. This further distinction was not included in the coding scheme, however, as such a high proportion of young children's conversation takes the present interests and activities of the participants as its point of reference.

Aspect is also concerned with time, but here it is the temporal status of the event or state which is focused upon rather than its location in time. One or more than one of the following sub-categories may be selected: Continuous, Perfect, Inceptive, Cessive, Durative, Iterative, Completive, Habitual. Clauses unmarked for aspect are coded as Neutral.

The term 'modal' is often used to refer to two different types of optional modification which happen, in English, to be most frequently realized by the modal auxiliaries. Halliday (1970), however, makes a clear distinction between them and it is this distinction which is employed here. Modality is concerned with the speaker's assessment of the probability of the state or event in the proposition. If no explicit assessment is made, the speaker implies that it is certain. He may, however, choose to make one of three explicit assessments: Certainty, where this is emphasized, for example, 'It is certainly true'; Possibility, for example, 'It may be true'; Inference, for example, 'It must be true, because . . .'. Modality may be realized by an auxiliary, or by an adverb or adverbial phrase or clause.

Modulation, by contrast, is concerned with the Ability or Willingness of the Agent to perform the actions specified in the proposition or with constraints on the state or event imposed by Permission, Obligation or Necessity. Modulation is realized in English by the modal auxiliaries or by quasi-auxiliaries such as 'have got to', 'be able to', 'be allowed to'. For convenience, two other types of modifications are included under Modulation: Try and Success. If not specified, it is normally assumed that an action involves the Agent in both trying to perform it and succeeding in doing so. Specifying either the attempt or the success is somewhat similar to specifying ability and, for that reason, they are included here.

The final type of clause modification is Manner. The most common type is the addition to a Change of State or Relation clause of an optional participant which describes how the change occurred (realized in English by an '-ly' adverb). There are, however, a number of other ways in which the manner of change can be specified, notably through conflation of the modification in the lexical verb, as in 'cheat', which means 'to take part in a rule-governed activity in a manner which contravenes the rules'. All such verbs are 'deconflated' and an entry made under one of the following categories:

Configuration: the stance or configuration in which a Patient is located, e.g. 'sitting in a chair'.

Extent: the extent of a state or change of state, e.g. 'The parcel weighs ten pounds'.

Recurrence: the recurrence of an event or return to an earlier state, e.g. 'again', 'He put it back'.

Convention: having reference to rules or social expectations, e.g. 'Henry disobeyed his teacher's command'.

Quality: a variety of dimensional attributes of change such as ±violence, ±speed, ±intensity.

Unintentional: the explicit qualification of an action as not deliberate or intentional.

Marked purpose: the explicit qualification of an action as deliberate or intentional.

General: the qualification of a change in terms of the manner in which it occurred or the state of mind in which the agent acted.

So far, the description of topic has been concerned only with single clauses, and with multi-clausal utterances in which one clause is embedded in another either as the realization of a semantic participant or as a modifier of one of the participants. Multi-clausal utterances also occur in which clauses at the same level are combined in some logical relationship. Traditional grammar recognizes two main types of logical relationship: parataxis and hypotaxis, giving rise to compound and complex sentences respectively. We have found it more satisfactory, however, to conceive of the logically related clauses as the terms of different types of Relational Predicate. The coding scheme distinguishes the following logical relationships: Conjunction, Temporal Succession, Adversative, Disjunction, Cause, Reason, Purpose, Hypothetical, Contractual, Concession. Also included here are Comparison and Reciprocity, the latter being coded for events which are by their nature reciprocal, such as 'colliding'. In keeping with the description of clauses related by a relational predicate being at the same level, each of the clauses involved is coded for the appropriate relational predicate.

2.5 Message orientation

Inter-Personal Purpose and Topic together account for most of the areas of substantive meaning that are drawn upon in the construction of messages. But there are also important decisions to be made about the Orientation of the meanings selected to fit them to the conversational context and to the information relevant to the topic that can be assumed to be already shared by the hearer. Young language learners, it is true, initially demonstrate very little skill in orientation but it is not long before they begin to use some of the systems available. The coding scheme includes three systems that are realized chiefly through syntactic means. Those that are realized chiefly by intonation are omitted, because the research team did not at that stage have the necessary expertise to carry out a coding of intonation.

The first two systems are concerned with information focus – the speaker's selection from the information that might be communicated, and its organization in terms of what he considers in context is most important. Voice is concerned with the decision as to whether to specify the Agent of an action and, if so, whether to give it prominence. The Active option specifies Agent but leaves it in the unmarked position before the verb. The Passive option also specifies the Agent, but in the marked and informationally more salient position after the verb. Truncated Passive leaves the Agent unspecified.

Thematization is another system which allows increased salience to be given to a particular element of the clause. The options here are the Preposing of an element that would occur in post-verbal position in the unmarked syntactic structure, Predication and Clefting. The organization of the message as a Topic–Comment structure is also included here.

The third system, Cohesion, is concerned with linking the message with previous contributions to the conversation. Of the types of cohesion discussed by Halliday and Hasan (1976), only those that are syntactically realized are coded. They comprise Anaphoric Reference, Substitution, Ellipsis and Conjunction. A further category, Nominal Transformation, is also included on the grounds that, although it is a type of lexical cohesion, it can be described in syntactic terms.

To summarize the description of meaning within the coding scheme, then, the utterance is treated as the pivotal level of description in a hierarchy which extends from sequence to clause participant. In making a contribution to conversation, a speaker is seen as selecting from two main areas of meaning: Inter-Personal Purpose and Topic. The description of Topic is made at the level of the clause and is organized around basic SMRs and their modification. The description of Purpose embraces all levels down to clause and provides one means of relating individual conversational acts to the larger units of discourse which make up an interaction. The third area of meaning, Orientation, may be thought of as having an enabling function in organizing the purpose and topic of the message to match the speaker's intentions to the demands of the context in which the utterance occurs. The actual form in which the message is realized is a result of an interaction between the choices that are made in the various areas of meaning and the lexical and syntactic resources that the speaker has available.

2.6 The analysis of syntactic structure

The final section of the coding scheme provides for the description of each utterance in terms of its syntactic and morphological structure. An Immediate Constituent analysis is adopted, represented by labelled bracketing. The four levels of the analysis – Utterance, Clause, Constituent, Element – form a rank scale (Halliday, 1961), in which a unit at a higher level consists of at least one unit at the level next below. Conversely, units at lower levels combine in structurally specifiable ways to form units at the level next above. Recursion is handled in terms of rank-shift: a unit from a higher level functioning in the structure of a unit at a lower level.

The unit Utterance is coterminous with the unit of the same name used in the analysis of Purpose and Topic. Since it is the highest level unit in the analysis, it is not sub-categorized. Each utterance consists of one or more Clauses, which may be either Main, Subordinate, Additioning or Tag. Tag clauses are further subdivided into Interrogative, Emphatic, Suppositional (e.g. 'He forgot it, *I suppose*') and Reporting (e.g. '"He forgot it," *she said*'). Although there is no limit in principle to the number of clauses that may be combined in an utterance, most utterances will contain a main clause. This is not obligatory, however, as some utterances consist only of a tag clause, or a subordinate or additioning clause which is heard as dependent on a main clause in the previous speaker's utterance.

Clauses consist of units at the next level down: Constituents. The constituents that are recognized in clause structure are: Subject, Complement, Indirect Object, Topic, Adjunct, Auxiliary, Main

Verb, Verbal Particle, Conjunction, Operator, Z-Nominal and Miscellaneous. Most of these are self-explanatory, but some need further explanation.

Complement includes both what is usually referred to as the Direct Object and also the Intensive Complement (Quirk *et al.*, 1973). The distinction between the two types is handled elsewhere in the description. Topic is used to describe topicalized subjects, as in 'Bananas, I love them!' It is also used for the nominal constituent in utterances such as 'All gone bus' or simply 'Teddy', where the precise function of the nominal is not known. Three main types of Conjunction are distinguished: Coordinating, Subordinating and Linking (e.g. 'however'), each is further sub-categorized into individual conjunctions. Also included as a sub-category are the items such as 'that' and 'whether' which introduce complement clauses, e.g. 'I think *that* we should go.' Operator includes two different types of item: negatives 'no' and 'not'; and the rather heterogenous class of items that can occur alone or combine with 'nominals' in early utterances, e.g. 'Thassa', 'all gone', 'more'. Z-Nominal is the term used by Sinclair (1972) for the constituent which functions simultaneously in a main and an embedded clause, as in 'They told *me* to go home'. Miscellaneous, as the name implies, is a rag-bag of items which are appended to clauses but do not enter into their structure. The category includes vocatives, terms of politeness and polarity responses. Miscellaneous items may also occur as complete utterances in themselves.

Although there are highly predictable sequences in which constituents appear in the structure of clauses of different kinds, no rules are prescribed in the coding scheme, as one of the aims of the study is to discover what syntactic patterns occur in children's speech as they develop. The implications of this decision will be considered below in the section dealing with the actual implementation of the coding scheme.

The constituents just described fall into two groups, those that are realized by single Elements, such as conjunctions, and those that are realized by structured groups of elements. Two kinds of structural groups are recognized, Noun Phrases and Verb Phrases.

Noun phrases function as the realization of the clause constituents Subject, Complement, Indirect Object, Topic, Adjunct and Z-Nominal. For economy of coding, prepositional phrases with the structure *Preposition + Noun Phrase* are included in the general description of the noun phrase, the preposition being treated as an optional element of structure. Unlike the clause, the nominal group does have predetermined structure of the elements which can occur. Headword is obligatory. The other elements, Preposition, Modifier and Qualifier are all optional, but if they occur it is in the order Preposition – Modifier – Head – Qualifier. More than one instance of each of the optional categories may occur in the structure of the noun phrase but there can be only one head, though this may have the coordinate structure Head *and* Head. All the elements in the noun phrase are further sub-categorized.

Prepositions, which may only occur in the realization of Adjunct constituents, are further distinguished as either Locative, Temporal, Metaphorical Locative/Temporal, Logical, Comparative, Case-Determined (e.g. 'for' – benefactive, 'with' – instrumental), and Other.

Modifiers are divided into Predeterminers, Articles, Demonstratives, Possessives, Interrogatives, Adjectivals, Comparative/ Superlatives, Nominals and Quantifiers, with listing of individual items for closed sets such as Demonstrative.

Headword is sub-categorized as Noun, Pronoun, Adverb (i.e. adverbial heads of adjuncts, such as 'here', 'today'), or Modifier (i.e. adjectival heads of intensive complements: 'that's *pretty*'). Within Pronoun there is further sub-categorization: Personal, Reflexive, Demonstrative, Possessive, Interrogative, Relative, Indefinite and Negative, with listing of individual items in all cases. Nouns are further classified as Count (singular, plural), Non-count or Proper.

Qualifiers are initially distinguished as either Simple or Complex, the latter class being realized by either a rank-shift phrase or clause. Both classes are further classified: simple qualifiers as Quantitative, Adjectival, Locative or Temporal, and Complex qualifiers according to function: Resultative, Condition, Non-Defining, Defining or Comparative.

The verb phrase functions as the realization of the constituents Auxiliary and Main Verb. In many grammatical descriptions auxiliary and main verb are both treated as constituents of the verb phrase, together with the negative. The decision to treat them here as separate clause constituents is motivated not by any theoretical consideration but by convenience of coding, in particular the marking of tense. By treating both auxiliary and main verbs as separate constituents, it is simpler to indicate where tense-marking actually occurs.

Verbal constituents have two obligatory elements: Verb and Tense. Verbs are classified as Lexical (the general category),

Compound-Lexical, Phrasal, Reporting or Auxiliary, the latter being further sub-categorized as Modal or as individual items 'be', 'have', etc. Tense distinguishes Non-Finite, Past and Neutral, with Past divided into Regular and Irregular. Non-Finite participial forms are classified as either Continuous, Perfect, Passive or Participial. Additional categories mark Person and Number, where appropriate.

From the foregoing it will be seen that the level Element is not theoretically pure. In principle, the items to be classified are morphemes and in the case of nouns and verbs this principle is very largely adhered to, with the separation of the morphemes of plural, possessive *s*, tense, etc. from the lexical stem. However, the morphemic structure of lexical items such as 'beauti-ful' is not described and there are a few categories, such as predeterminer, which are not further broken down according to their internal structure. The justification for this decision is one of expediency, supported by the consideration that these items are learned and used for some considerable time without awareness of their morphemic structure.

2.7 The coding scheme: an evaluation
Before going on to describe the manner in which the descriptive scheme was implemented as a procedure for coding, there are a number of issues of a theoretical nature that should be discussed. It must first be stressed, though, that the foregoing pages provide only a general plan of the scheme – an indication of its scope rather than a justification of its way of conceptualizing language. To give a full account, however, would far exceed the confines of this chapter and would, in any case, be inappropriate in a report of this kind. Those readers who wish to pursue these issues further are referred to volume 1 of this series (Wells, 1981, chapter 1).

2.7.1 *How much detail?*
In devising a coding scheme for the analysis of a large corpus of naturalistic data one finds oneself caught on the horns of several dilemmas, all arising from the enormous diversity of language in actual use. The first of these concerns the appropriate level of delicacy to adopt, that is, the number of distinctions to make in describing particular areas of meaning or form. As the range of texts examined increases, so does the number of distinctions one feels bound to draw to be faithful to the fine shades of social or conceptual meaning conveyed. However, the larger the number of

categories introduced, the more unwieldy the coding procedures become and the more difficult it is for coders to learn the scheme and to use it without making errors. Furthermore, the greater the degree of delicacy used in describing any particular system, the larger the amount of speech that needs to be coded for the differences in relative frequency of occurrence of the categories concerned to be treated as reliable.

On the other hand, where only a restricted number of distinctions is made, these are likely to be crude, and many utterance tokens will either have to be forced in order to fit the available categories or excluded from the analysis as uncodable. Equally seriously, the developmental picture that emerges from the study will be lacking in detail and, unless the criterial distinctions for plotting the sequence of development are known in advance, there will be long periods in which there appears to be no development at all.

Faced with this dilemma, we preferred to err on the side of too many rather than too few distinctions, since it is always possible to combine sub-categories at a later stage of analysis, whereas revision in the opposite direction is impossible without recoding. This, of course, meant that the initial coding was a very time-consuming and protracted exercise. Even so, there were some cases where it was insufficiently detailed, such as in the lack of discrimination among the modal auxiliaries. To rectify this for the younger children only required a subsequent recoding of 640 transcripts, a task which took several months.

Even more difficult than knowing which distinctions to build into the coding scheme, in many cases, is the task of selecting the defining criteria for the categories and constructing the rules which will guide the coders in reliably assigning tokens in the data to the appropriate category types. The utterances that occur in recordings of naturally occurring conversation are far more varied and 'messy' than the 'pure' examples that come to mind when one is sitting in an armchair devising theoretical categories. It was thus in the initial application of the scheme that we were faced most acutely by the second dilemma – that of the extent to which 'idealization' should be allowed in relation to the 'fuzziness' of meaning in what is actually said.

2.7.2 *Indeterminateness of meaning*
Ideally, from the point of view of subsequent statistical analysis, a coding scheme should provide sets of discrete, mutually exclusive

categories which, with the rules for their application, will enable every utterance encountered in a corpus of data to be fully and unambiguously classified. Conversely, for each distinct aspect of the coding, each utterance should be assignable to one and only one of the set of available categories. To achieve this goal, not only does the coding scheme have to be comprehensive and the categories clearly specified, but there also has to be a considerable degree of idealization of the data. Incomplete utterances have to be discarded, for example, and false starts and hesitations ignored. This, however, has been accepted as necessary by almost all those engaged in the grammatical description of naturalistic data, as without some idealization there is little hope of discovering regularities and formulating the rules to which speakers conform.

However, this practice, which is relatively uncontroversial in relation to phonological or syntactic analysis, becomes much more problematic where the analysis of meaning is involved. In phonology and syntax, categories *are* discrete and so it can be assumed that, whatever their actual performance, speakers are attempting to produce one or other of the permissible alternatives. Categories of meaning, by contrast, are much less clear-cut and indeed in some areas it is doubtful whether the categories with which speakers operate are either discrete or mutually exclusive.

This is particularly apparent in the case of utterance function in the description of Inter-Personal Purpose. Analysts have come to recognize something that, as conversational participants, they knew all along, namely that an utterance can be heard as simultaneously realizing more than one function and indeed can be so intended by the speaker. 'I've dropped my teddy', for example, said by a child sitting in a push-chair, can certainly be heard as a statement and will probably also be heard as an indirect request for someone to retrieve the fallen teddy on his behalf. Labov and Fanshel (1977) have shown that, in certain contexts, as many as nine different functions may be taken to be simultaneously intended. What is more, some functions seem to be more appropriately described in terms of continuous dimensions rather than as discrete categories which either are or are not realized. A requestive interpretation of the child's observation about his fallen teddy, for example, would be based on the presence of an accompanying paralinguistic feature such as 'whine', and this is clearly a continuous variable.

Where a speaker may intend his utterance to realize more than one function, there is clearly the possibility of the hearer's interpretation failing to match the speaker's intention, yet for both participants' accounts to be warranted by the form of the actual message. Indeed the fuzziness that is inherent in the many-to-one mapping between form and meaning is deliberately exploited by conversational participants from a very early age in the interests of exerting and evading control, face-saving and so on (McTear, 1981). For a variety of reasons, therefore, it is no longer possible to retain the coding principle that utterances should be assigned to one and only one of a set of mutually exclusive alternatives.

At the time when our coding scheme was being constructed, however, there had been almost no discussion of the theoretical problems posed by the essential indeterminacy of utterance meaning and we were insufficiently aware of the dilemma we faced. Our decision, both for utterance function and for longer stretches of conversation covered by sequences and sub-sequences, was to allow only one coding and, where there was doubt, to code what was described as the 'dominant' purpose. In retrospect, we recognize this to have been a mistake and in our current work we are trying to overcome this particular problem by working with a smaller and more precisely defined superordinate unit, exchange, and by coding utterance functions in terms of a number of simultaneous pragmatic features, somewhat along the lines of distinctive features in phonology. Alternative solutions have been proposed by Labov and Fanshel (1977) and by Davies (1979) but as yet it is too early to say which of the various approaches will prove the most satisfactory way out of the dilemma.

2.7.3 *The use of interpretative analysis*
The previous discussion of functional meaning raises the third dilemma that had to be faced: the length to which the analyst may go in interpreting utterance meaning as part of the task of coding. As participants in conversation, we are constantly involved in making interpretations, for that is an essential part of comprehending what we hear. Indeed it has been argued that the apparently simple perceptual activity of hearing necessarily involves the making and testing of hypotheses based on concurrent interpretation. We would argue, therefore, that the researcher should use the interpretative skills he has acquired as a participant in analysing his data, for a description that is restricted to an account of items and the rules of their combination is likely to be very superficial and possibly also misleading.

These arguments are particularly applicable when one is attempting to describe the utterances of immature speakers, who are restricted both by knowledge of the linguistic system and by limitations on the number of items they can combine in one structured utterance. The value of making a 'rich interpretation' (Brown, 1973) of early utterances was clearly demonstrated by the paucity of Pivot–Open descriptions when compared with the insights into children's productive ability which resulted from using context to disambiguate tokens of what was at one level of analysis the same utterance type (Bloom, 1970) and from extending this approach to children's utterances in general. Furthermore, the fact that most parents achieve a satisfactorily high success rate in communicating with their children on the basis of interpretations that go beyond the formal evidence available in their children's utterances should encourage us in our assumption that adults can arrive at accurate interpretations of children's meaning intentions.

However, if the need for rich interpretation is greatest when analysing the speech of young language learners, so also is the danger of attributing too great a sophistication to them. Because a parent interprets a child's utterance, for example, 'dolly bed' as a comment about a locative relationship holding between 'dolly' and 'bed', it does not necessarily follow that the child is expressing such a relationship. To be certain of the correctness of attributing a meaning intention couched in terms of case-roles to any particular utterance, Howe (1981a, b) argues, one needs independent evidence that the child understands that language encodes case-roles, including the ones in question. Without such evidence, a more parsimonious explanation would be that the child is expressing only the fact that a relationship holds between two named entities: it is the parent who, in interpreting the utterance in an adult framework, infers that a case-role relationship is intended.

There is obviously some force to this argument: parents do impute meaning intentions to children's utterances that are almost certainly unwarranted, particularly at the one-word stage. But equally, if the end-point of development includes the understanding and expression of case-role relations, there must be a point at which this development begins. Furthermore, it seems quite possible that the process of mastering the full range of case-roles available to be encoded in a particular language, and the possible relationships between them, extends over a considerable time, with certain case-roles and relations being understood and expressed before others. If this is the case, one might expect that the interpretations that parents – and researchers – put upon children's utterances would also show a developmental sequence and that this sequence would be substantially the same across a wide variety of families and even of languages. This would not, of course, provide the independent confirmation of the child's understanding of case-roles that Howe argues for but, in the absence of direct disconfirmation, it would certainly lend support to a position for which there are other developmental arguments (see Bloom *et al.*, 1981).

Our decision, therefore, was to use the context to arrive at an interpretation and to code children's utterances at the two-word stage and beyond in terms of these interpretations. Not to have done so would have been to ignore the interactional nature of conversation and of learning and to exclude from our study an important source of evidence on the child's development as a communicator. The correctness of this decision, we believe, is demonstrated by the results to be reported in subsequent chapters.

2.8 The coding procedure

Having constructed the descriptive framework, with its list of coding categories and defining criteria, there remains the task of deciding how the coding shall be implemented in a systematic manner to yield data that are amenable to various types of numerical analysis. Decisions have to be taken about the order in which coding judgments are made, how the results are represented and in what medium they are stored. Important factors to be considered at this stage are the amount of coded data to be generated and the procedures that will be used in the subsequent stage of analysis.

In the present case, it was clear from the start that the numerical analysis would require the use of a computer. It was therefore decided to make as much use of computer assistance in the earlier stages as was possible within the limits of our expertise. In principle, it would have been possible to develop a program to analyse text input in terms of at least some of the categories in the coding scheme, but we had neither the time nor the resources for such an undertaking. Nor did we believe that we could program all that was involved in making an interpretative analysis. We did, however, attempt to be as explicit and systematic as would be required in writing such a program. We were also influenced by computer technology, as in the decision to code directly on to computer cards, thereby cutting out the need for a stage at which codings are transferred from hand-written sheets to punched cards. This, too, required that the coding procedure be made as explicit as possible.

To achieve this, the categories of the coding scheme were arranged in a fixed order and rules written for the manner in which they were to be applied. One problem in particular exercised us a great deal at this stage. The speech data consisted of utterances of very variable length and complexity, some of them consisting of no more than a single word and others, by means of recursion at different points, consisting of several clauses. Within full clauses, too, some categories were 'optional', such as modal and manner or the selection of one of the options under thematization. Two possible solutions were available: to require a coding to be made for all possible categories with respect to every utterance, entering a coding of 'non-applicable' where the utterance contained no selection from the category in question, or to make a coding entry dependent on the presence of the category in the utterance.

The first solution had the attraction of mechanical systematicity and accorded well with the goal of computerization. The second was the solution preferred by the coders, partly because it came closer to their natural method of analysing utterances and partly because it reduced very considerably the number of coding entries that had to be made. But the deciding factor was the difficulty of converting the open-ended recursiveness of utterance structure into a finite number of coding entries in fixed order. In the end, therefore, a mixed solution was adopted. As much of the coding as possible was in *fixed format*, with *free format* being used for the coding of syntactic structure and a mixed system for the semantic analysis of the clause.

This, we subsequently discovered, was an unfortunate decision, with serious consequences for the computer analysis stage. At the time, however, nobody associated with the project was sufficiently familiar with the application of computer programming to the task of linguistic analysis to foresee what those consequences would be. In effect, by choosing to represent the open-ended variability of utterance organization directly in the format of the coding, we were simply postponing to a later stage the problems that these characteristics pose for a finite description of linguistic structure.

2.8.1 *The use of computer cards*
Computer cards consist of a fixed number of columns which are read sequentially. Information is represented in each of these columns by the number and position of the holes that are punched. Most frequently, the positions represent the digits 0–9 from top to bottom, with two further positions to carry additional information.

Numerical information is thus entered directly by punching the appropriate digit, numbers greater than 9 being spread over more than one column. The same system can be used for nominal data, by assigning a numerical value to each of the categories from which a single selection must be made in each column or group of columns. It is also possible, however, to use the positions in each column to represent letters and to assign a combination of letters to each of the possible coding categories. The advantage of this form of representation is that, with a small number of letters used singly or in combination, a very large number of alternatives can be represented in each column in codes that also have mnemonic significance.

This was the form of representation chosen in the present case and cards were printed to our own specification. The letters selected were A C E L N O P Q R S T Y. As the cards were to be marked by hand and subsequently read by a card reader, only 40 columns were printed on each card, to allow ample space for marking. Along the bottom of the card was a clock track to synchronize the operation of the card reader.

Using the 12 letters above, mnemonic codes were assigned to all categories in the coding scheme, including the various types of bracket used at different levels of analysis. The letters A to S were used to represent the digits 0 to 9 for those parts of the coding, such as utterance number and utterance length, that required numerical entries. Categories occurring in the fixed format part of the coding were given a number corresponding to the column on the card in which they should be entered. Categories in the semantic and syntactic sections, where the coding was in free or mixed format, were given rule numbers according to the order in which judgments were to be made as to whether they applied to the utterance being coded.

2.8.2 *The two stages of coding*
The coding of each transcript was carried out in two stages, and involved two different coders. The initial reason for this was that the construction of the section of the coding scheme dealing with the syntactic analysis was not complete by the time the first group of coders were trained and ready to use the sections covering the pragmatic and semantic coding. Rather than delay the start of the coding operation, it was decided to go ahead with the first stage, treating it as relatively self-contained, and to get the coders to carry out the second stage at a later time, when the scheme was complete

and had been given an adequate trial. In fact, by the time this point was reached, the first stage coders had become adept at coding the pragmatic and semantic categories and were reluctant to learn to use a completely new set of categories and procedures. In the event, therefore, the two stages remained separate throughout, and a second group of coders was engaged and trained to carry out the second stage.

This unintended separation had both advantages and disadvantages. The main disadvantage was that coders concerned with the second stage were not able to discuss the reasoning that lay behind the interpretations given to particular utterances and, although they added their coding of syntax to the cards that already contained the coding of the first-stage interpretations, their syntactic analysis was occasionally incompatible with the preceding pragmatic or semantic analysis. The advantage was that the codings entered in the first stage were systematically checked and, where necessary, corrected before the second stage was carried out, thus reducing the probability of compound errors occurring. To a very considerable extent, therefore, the advantages and disadvantages of two-stage coding offset each other.

The first-stage coder had the responsibility for segmenting the transcribed speech into units of analysis. Prior to coding each sample, the coder read it through as a whole and listened to the accompanying recording, and then marked sequence boundaries and, where necessary, made adjustments to the transcriber's judgments about utterance boundaries. Utterances in sequences of conversation involving the child being studied were then numbered sequentially from the beginning of each sample.

Coding was carried out for all child utterances, starting a new card for each utterance and continuing on further cards as necessary. Codings relating to preceding and following utterances by other speakers (if they occurred), were entered at fixed points in the coding of the child's utterance. At the second stage, the coding of syntactic structure was simply added on to the end of the first-stage coding.

2.8.3 *The coding format*

Utterance Identification and Inter-Personal Purpose
The first six columns of the coding of each utterance consisted of an utterance identification: (1) Age, Sex and Class Group; (2) Individual Child; (3) Number of Age-Related Occasion of Recording;

(4) Number of Sample; (5–6) Number of Utterance. Where a complete sample contained no conversation involving the child, a card was completed for that sample as far as column 4 and in column 5 an entry was made giving one of a set of alternative reasons for the lack of speech. In cases where a response was expected from the child, but no utterance occurred, the utterance number of the preceding utterance was entered in columns 5 and 6 and Y added to column 6.

Utterance Length was entered in columns 7–8. The rules for calculating utterance length, in morphemes, were those devised by Brown (1973) and previously published in Slobin (1967). Where utterances were interrupted or otherwise incomplete, an additional entry was made to this effect. Jargon ('rubbish') and uninterpretable utterances were identified as such in this column and no further codings made.

Columns 9–33 comprised the fixed format section of the coding. They included Context and Inter-Personal Purpose (columns 9–17). Columns 18–24 were reserved for a coding of the Speaker, Utterance Length, Sub-sequence, Function and Mood of the preceding utterance, where this was part of the current sequence and spoken by someone other than the child. With the exception of those for Speaker, codes for these categories were identical to those used in coding the child's utterance. Columns 26–30 were assigned to the following utterance, where spoken by someone other than the child, and again the same codes for Sub-sequence, Function and Mood were used. No coding was made of following utterance length.

Columns 32 and 33 were for Problems, Peculiarities and Errors and allowed a note to be made of the occurrence of unusual features or 'errors' in various categories of the child's or the preceding utterance. To some extent these columns served as a safety net for unanticipated problems that arose during the coding operation, when it was too late to make substantial changes in the rest of the coding scheme. Three of these deserve mention.

The unsatisfactoriness of not allowing simultaneous functions to be coded for individual utterances, discussed above (2.7.2), became apparent quite early on, but to have modified this principle would have called for a substantial revision of both coding scheme and procedure. However a small improvement was made by entering a coding in column 32 whenever the child's or the preceding or following utterance was judged to realize more than one function.

The meaning and form of the preceding utterance are likely to have a considerable influence on the child's utterance and it was for this reason that a coding of preceding utterance was included, albeit in summary form. As already mentioned, the coding included information about length and function; it also included information about sentence meaning relations and the occurrence and nature of the relationship involved in multi-clausal utterances. As coding proceeded, however, it was considered that the presence of an embedded clause and/or of negation in the preceding utterance might prove to be of significance. Once again, the simplest way to make these additions was to include them in column 32.

Children's utterances do not differ from those of mature speakers only in the omission of particular categories or the use of unusual word order. As is well known, they also contain irregularities such as the over-regularization of past tense and mismatch of form and referent, as when the child uses 'you' for self-reference. The first two types of irregularity – omission and word order – are recoverable from the syntactic analysis, which codes all the elements in the utterance in their order of occurrence. The other types are not recoverable, however, and so require specific entries to be made of their occurrence. All such 'errors' are noted in column 33.

A further type of irregularity was noted as the coding proceeded. Even when, from other utterances, it is clear that they have the necessary resources available, children frequently produce utterances that might be described as situationally elliptical; to a lesser degree, mature speakers produce similar utterances. Since we assume that the incompleteness of such utterances does not result from an inability to produce more grammatically complete utterances, it is important that their occurrence should not distort estimates of level of development attained. In order to allow them to be omitted from certain types of subsequent analyses, two categories of incomplete utterances were noted in column 33:

a) Situationally acceptable, but grammatically incomplete, e.g. 'Want a sweet?', ''m doing it'.
b) Although possibly interpretable in context, situationally unacceptable as well as grammatically incomplete, e.g. 'Put on the table', 'Coming soon'.

Topic and Orientation

From this point onwards, the coding was no longer in fixed format. Instead, brackets were used to mark the boundaries of units at different levels of analysis, whilst the codings within these units were entered in a fixed order. The procedure to be followed was set out in a form similar to Phrase Structure rules: italicized terms were not coded directly but were further expanded in subsequent rules.

1 *Utterance* → $S_1 \ldots S_n$ #

2 *S* → $\begin{cases} \textit{Clause + Text + Constituency} \\ \textit{Unstructured} \\ \textit{Uninterpretable/Non-Verbal} \end{cases}$

3 *Clause* → *Relational Predicate + SMR + Polarity + Time + Aspect + (Modal) + (Modulation) + (Manner)*

4 *Unstructured* → *Relational Predicate + SMR*

5 *Uninterpretable/ Non-Verbal* → No coding

6 *Text* → *Voice + Theme + Cohesion*

7 *Constituency* → */Participant$_1$ ... Participant$_n$ --*

8 *Participant* → *Participant Role + (Locative or Possessive Features) + (Head) + (Determiner and Number) + (Modification)*

{ = mutually exclusive   ( ) = optional

Subsequent rules expanded the 'terminal' categories from which a selection was made of the appropriate code to be entered on the card. The symbol # marked the end of the first stage of coding, that of Purpose, Topic and Orientation; / and -- marked the opening and closing of the smallest unit, clause constituent; ⟨ and ⟩ marked the beginning and end, within clause constituent, of embedded clauses, where these occurred. Instead of using a further type of bracket for boundaries between sentence units, these were marked by the presence of a Relational Predicate code.

Where there was a preceding utterance it was coded according to the following rules:

1P *Preceding utterance* → $\{ S_1^p \ldots S_n^p \}$

2P S^p → *Clause^p*

3P *Clause^p* → *Relational Predicate + SMR*

This, it will be seen, is a much reduced version of the coding for child utterances. Entries for the terminal categories of Relational Predicate and SMR were made from the same set as for child utterances. The complete coding was enclosed in brackets { }.

If the child utterance lacked internal structure (cf. 2.4.1), appropriate entries were made from Relational Predicate and the subset of SMR categories relevant to Unstructured utterances, then no further codings were made in this section and the first stage terminator (#) was entered. For those cases where a child utterance was called for but did not occur (marked Y in column 6), no coding at all was made in this section and # entered in column 34.

The remainder of the coding of Topic and Orientation was straightforward, proceeding according to the rules set out above and the categories discussed earlier in this chapter.

Syntactic structure

Essentially the same procedure as just described was used in the coding of syntactic structure, except that the order in which units were coded was determined entirely by their order of occurrence in the utterance. The relevant rules are as follows:

1 *Utterance* → *Clause*$_1$ . . . *Clause*$_n$;
2 *Clause* → *Clause status* {*Clause structure*}
3 *Clause Structure* → *Constituent*$_1$ . . . *Constituent*$_n$
4 *Constituent* → *Constituent label/Constituent structure* –
5 *Constituent Structure (Nominal)* → $\left\{ \begin{array}{l} (Preposition) + (Modifier) \\ + Head + (Qualifier) \\ \{Clause\ structure\} \end{array} \right.$
6 *Constituent Structure (Verbal)* → *Verb type + Tense + (Pers. & No.) + (Contraction)*
   ; = completion of coding

Although, from these rules, it may at first be difficult to see exactly how an utterance is coded, an example should quickly make matters clear. Instead of using actual codes, however, the category labels will be given in brackets as these are relatively transparent. The utterance to be coded is 'The boy in the park cried bitterly because he thought he had lost his new kite.' The coding is shown in figure 2.1. As will have been noted, this example contains two instances of units that have been rank-shifted to function in the structure of a unit lower on the rank-scale. Although 'he had lost his new kite' is a full clause, it functions here as the complement of the main verb 'thought' in the subordinate clause. This is shown by opening clause brackets immediately following the constituent label Complement, in the place where the opening bracket for constituent structure would normally occur. The other example of rank-shift occurs in the main clause: 'in the park' itself has constituent structure but functions as qualifier in the structure of the subject constituent. This is shown by opening constituent brackets following the coding of the element Qualifier.

				The		*boy*				*in*		*the*		*park*
Clause status	{	Constituent	/	Modifier	+	Head	+	Qualifier	/	Preposition	+	Modifier	+	Head – –
(main clause)		(Subject)		(Def. Art.)		(Noun + sing.)		(Defining)		(Locative)		(Def. Art.)		(Noun + sing.)

		cried		*bitterly*									*because*	
Constituent	/	Verb type + Tense	–	Constituent	/	Head	–	}	Clause status	{	Constituent	/	Subordinating	–
(main verb)		(Lexical) (Reg. Past)		(Adjunct)		(Adverb)			(Subordinate)		(Conjunction)			

		he				*thought*	
Constituent	/	Head	–	Constituent	/	Verb type + tense	–
(Subject)		(Pronoun–Personal) 3rd sing. masc.		(Main Verb)		(Lexical) (Irreg. Past)	

				he				*had*		
Constituent	{	Constituent	/	Head	–	Constituent	/	Verb type + Tense	–	Constituent
(Complement)		(Subject)		(Pronoun–Personal) 3rd sing. masc.		(Aux. Verb)		('have') (Irreg. Past)		(Main Verb)

	lost				*his*		*new*		*kite*			
/	Verb type + Tense	–	Constituent	/	Modifier	+	Modifier	+	Head	–	} }	;
	(Lexical) (Perfect)		(Complement)		(Possessive)		(Mod. Adj.)		(Noun + sing.)			

Figure 2.1 Example of syntactic coding

One feature of this section of the coding, deliberately omitted from the illustrative example, was the addition of codings which link the constituents in syntactic structure with the semantic participants that they realize. For all constituents except Conjunction, Operator, Z-Nominal and Miscellaneous, a coding of Semantic Derivation followed the constituent label. The list from which a selection was made includes all the Participant Roles (cf. 2.4.2) in the case of nominal constituents, and Clause Nucleus, Copula, Pro-verb, Aspectual and Suppositional/Modal/Modulation for the main-verb constituent. The relevant derivations were also coded for the auxiliary verb and verbal particle constituents.

This semantic derivation coding serves three purposes. First, it allows certain syntactic constituents to be more delicately subcategorized: complements, for example, can be divided into those that, as the direct object of the verb, realize a participant role (extensive complement) and those that are derived from the clause nucleus (intensive complement). Secondly, it allows a study to be made of the relationship between the characteristics of syntactic constituents and the semantic categories they serve to realize: for example, do complex nominal constituents more frequently realize Patient as opposed to Agent participants? Thirdly, it allows a more general study to be made of the relationship between the semantic categories that are judged to be intended in children's utterances and the syntactic structures through which those intentions are realized.

The syntactic coding section completed the coding applied to each utterance. Inevitably, some of the finer points of detail have had to be omitted from this account because of limitations of space. Readers who wish to obtain a complete account of the coding scheme and the procedures for using it are referred to the full version of the *Coding Manual* (Wells, 1975).

2.9 Computer data processing

Preparation of the data

Following coding, the cards were read by an optical card reader which scanned each column and registered which rows had been marked. At the checking stage, the image so produced was checked against a listing of possible entries for that column and, if no matching entry was found, the complete card image was printed with an error symbol against the column entry for which no match had been found. Only when no errors remained was the stack of cards coding a complete transcript read into the data file.

Computers work with information in binary form. Although letter codings can be converted into binary form each time the data file is accessed, we decided that it would be more convenient and economical to carry out a once-and-for-all translation into binary code. The twelve letters were given values corresponding to the powers of 2 from 0 to 11: $Y = 1$, $T = 2$, $S = 4$, $R = 8$, $Q = 16$, $P = 32$, $O = 64$, $N = 128$, $L = 256$, $E = 512$, $C = 1024$, $A = 2048$. In this code, each value can be represented by a single bit in a computer word. Furthermore, original codings involving combination of letters can be represented by the unique values that result from summing the values of the constituent letters, for example, $REQ = 8 + 512 + 16 = 536$.

Further to facilitate the process of searching through the coded data for particular entries, each of the superordinate categories in the coding scheme, for example, Context, Function, Aspect, Constituent, etc., was given an identifying numerical value. The appropriate category value was then appended to each code (the entry that had been made on the card) to form a category/code pair. With the data coded in this form, to count the frequency of utterances containing, for example, nouns functioning as modifiers, each utterance would be searched for an occurrence of category value 72 (= modifiers in syntactic structure) and the associated code value would be inspected to see if it was equal to 2176 (= AN, the code for modifying noun); if so, the counter would be incremented by one.

One additional modification was made at this stage, in order to safeguard against corruption of the data occurring without detection. The number of category/code pairs in the coding of each utterance was counted and the resulting value inserted as the code in a category/code pair which was added at the beginning of the utterance. Each time the data were read, this value was compared with the number of category/code pairs occurring in the utterance up to and including the code for utterance terminator and, if these values did not match, an error message was printed.

Once the data had been formatted in this way on the Research Unit's ARCTURUS computer, a copy was made on magnetic tape, which was then transferred to the University main-frame computer, at that stage an ICL 4/75. The data are stored on disks in the form of stacks, each stack containing the codings of all the utterances from one observation of one child. The stacks are arranged systematically: the largest division is an occasion, that is, one complete age-related observation of all the children in one of the two age cohorts. Within each occasion, the stacks are arranged by sex, within sex, by class of family background and within class by individual child. At the beginning of each file is an index, which lists the stacks in the order in which they are stored, together with the location of the first utterance in each stack. This allows rapid access to individual stacks in cases where the analysis to be carried out involves only a sub-set of the data.

Copies of these two files, complete with indexes, were subsequently transferred from the 4/75 to the computer which replaced it, and finally, after unsuccessful attempts to run analysis programs on these machines, back to the Research Unit for use on the LSI mini-computer (cf. 1.9).

2.9.1 *The Language Analysis Program*
The Language Analysis Program (LAP) is essentially a program for carrying out cross-tabulations of frequency data. The programming language used is FORTRAN.

LAP allows cross-tabulation of up to four variables in any analysis and can handle up to 25 tables on one run. The older and younger cohorts' files cannot both be accessed in the same run. The variables to be included in an analysis may be selected from the categories in terms of which the data are coded and the stratifying variables that are used in structuring the two files. For example, a two variable analysis might call for a cross-tabulation of context × occasion. This would yield a table in which each cell contained the total number of utterances produced by all the children in one type of context on one occasion of recording. Or a four variable analysis might call for a cross-tabulation of context × SMR × occasion × child. This would, in theory, yield a four-dimensional table, printed as 64 groups of tables (one for each child), each group containing ten tables (one for each occasion), each of which would have context and SMR as its two dimensions. In practice, there is a limit to the total number of cells that can be called for in an analysis. Where the variables concerned have many values, as for example do child and SMR, the analysis has to be carried out in several runs, each run accessing only a sub-set of the data.

To facilitate carrying out such part-analyses, the instructions for each run start with a number of sample definitions, which allow the user to specify which sex, class and occasion sub-sets of the data are to be included. If no specification is entered for any of these variables, the default value is automatically selected, which leads to all the sub-sets of that variable being included. By setting sex for male and class for A but making no entry for occasion, for example, one causes only the stacks of the class A boys from all ten occasions to be analysed on that run.

The sample definition also allows utterance type to be selected. The options available are those listed in columns 5 and 6 of the utterance identification. The default value for utterance type is the sub-set of complete, interpretable utterances.

The Tabulate statement, in which the user specifies which variables are to be included in the analysis, also calls for a statement of the number of values that each variable can take. This is supplied by counting the number of different codes that are possible for the category in question. In the Labels statement which follows, the code labels for each of the values may be specified so that, when the tables are printed, each row and column will be labelled appropriately in the margin. When labels are specified, rows and columns are arranged in the order in which the labels are entered. If labels are not specified, they are generated by the program as required and printed in the order in which they are generated. If only some of the codes in a category are to be included in an analysis, the number of such codes must be included in the Tabulate statement and the code labels entered in the Labels statement. Any occurrence of a code not specified will be registered in an Unknown Cell accumulator and the total in the cell printed at the beginning of the table.

A Print-On statement enables the user to call for tables to be printed at the end of any of the stratifications of the data, provided that the stratifying variable is not included in the Tabulate statement. Since the stratifications are nested, the specification of a deeply nested variable automatically leads to tables being printed at all higher-level boundaries. For example, if the Tabulate statement calls for a cross-tabulation of Sub-sequence × Time (and all the sample definition variables take their default values), the specification of class in the Print-On statement will lead to the first table of Sub-sequence × Time frequencies being printed when the stacks of all class A boys in Occasion 1 have been analysed. A second table will be printed after the stacks of class B boys have been analysed, a third after the stacks of class C boys and so on through all the classes of boys and then girls through all the occasions. The advantage of this use of the Print-On statement is that it allows the results of an analysis specified in the Tabulate statement to be printed in such a way that one or more of the stratifying variables is included in the analysis without taking up any cells in the tabulation matrix.

Also in the Print-On statement is the option to have cell totals calculated as percentages of either row or column totals and printed in the corner of the cell. Margin totals are automatically printed for each dimension. For analyses of more than two dimensions, this means that margin tables are printed in which the cell entries are margin values from the more deeply nested tables.

Certain categories contain a very large number of sub-categories. For example, the *Coding Manual* specifies more than 100 SMRs. As explained above (2.7.1), it was considered better to code in fine detail in the first instance, with the possibility of combining categories at a later stage, rather than risk failing to pick up important developmental distinctions. The Grouped Codes facility is included in the program to allow such combinations of categories. Superordinate groups are established, with labels, followed by a specification of the codes that are to be included in each group.

For certain analyses, it may be necessary to consider utterances only if they meet some particular criterion. For example, in an analysis of syntactic clause structure, one might wish to consider only utterances that are grammatically complete. This is achieved by introducing a Filter, which checks that the utterance meets the specification before allowing it to be included in the analysis. In the example above, this would require category 33 (Errors) to be inspected for the presence of either a T or Y code and category 50 (Cohesion) for the presence of E (Ellipsis). If any of these codes is found the utterance is not included. A number of frequently used filters are included in the program as options which may be selected in the Filter statement. New filters can be added by inserting an appropriate section of FORTRAN code.

2.9.2 *Using LAP: an example*

To illustrate the complete operation of LAP, an example will be described as a step by step procedure. The analysis to be exemplified is a relatively simple one, but is typical of the method used in constructing 'order of emergence' data (cf. chapter 4).

This example requires the cross-tabulation of Aspect × Occasion × Child, which is entered in the Tabulate statement in the form of category followed by the number of codes in the category, for each of the three variables. The actual codes are next entered in Labels statements, one for each variable, with the exception of Child, which is generated by the program as it reads the data. No filter or grouping is required for this analysis, and the Print-On statement is set to print at the end of the run. This will yield one table for each child in which the rows are the possible sub-categories of Aspect and the columns are the ten Occasions.

Let us suppose that there is some reason for wishing to keep the analyses of boys and girls separate. This means that, in Sample Definition, Sex will be set to girls (on a second run, Sex will be set to boys); all other variables in the sample definition will take their default value. The command file, containing sample definition, and Tabulate, Labels and Print-On statements, together with the name of the data file to be analysed and the version of LAP to be used, is composed on a VDU terminal. When the file is complete, the analysis is executed by typing the command RUN.

The program first sets up frequency matrices in computer memory equivalent to the tables called for by the command file and then proceeds to read the data, searching for the categories in question. Using the sample definition and the index, the program finds the beginning of the first stack to be included in the analysis – in our example, the first girl's stack in the data for occasion 1 – and checks the utterance identification of the first utterance against the information supplied in the index. If there is a match, it proceeds to the codings in categories 5 and 6 to check these against the utterance type specified in the sample definition in order to decide whether the utterance is to be included. If it is not, it moves on to the beginning of the next utterance. If it is to be included, the program reads through the utterance until it finds the first relevant category – in the case of our example, category 43 (Aspect) – and then having extracted the code in that category/code pair, it increments the counter for the appropriate cell in the frequency matrix of the first girl. As it is a category that can occur more than once in an utterance, the program then continues its search for further occurrences of the category until it reaches the end of the utterance, repeating the procedure described above for every further instance found. At the end of the utterance the program moves on to the next utterance, repeating the procedure described. It continues in this way until it reaches the end of the stack and then consults the index to find the next stack to be included. Finally, when all the stacks to be included have been searched, the resulting frequency matrices are stored in an output file, which may be printed immediately or at some later time.

2.10 Evaluation of computer analysis

For most types of analysis required by the research programme, LAP is straightforward and efficient. For analyses such as the example just described, the complete operation, including printing, can be carried out in a few hours and several analyses can be completed in one day.

However, because of the manner in which particular sections of the coding scheme were implemented in the coding procedure, analyses involving certain categories take much longer to complete. One example is the coding of Function. It will be recalled that Function was hierarchically linked to Sub-sequence, complete lists of functions being given independently for each type of sub-sequence (2.3). This principle was also adhered to in devising the coding procedure: codes are only mutually exclusive within sub-sequence types and the same letter code may be used to designate different categories in different types of sub-sequence. The consequence of this is that any analysis of Function has to be nested within an analysis of Sub-sequence. Or, to give a concrete example, to discover whether there is any development with age in the range of functions used, it is necessary to tabulate Sub-sequence × Function × Occasion instead of simply Function × Occasion. As there are six types of sub-sequence, this means that six times more computer store is required than would be the case if the simpler analysis were possible. In fact, the necessary amount of store is simply not available, and so the analysis has to be carried out in six runs, taking one Sub-sequence type at a time.

A second and more serious limitation, again resulting from the separation of programming and coding scheme construction, is the extreme difficulty of carrying out analyses which require the cross-tabulation of more than one category in the free-format sections of the coding. This follows from the fact that free-format categories can occur more than once in an utterance and, in such cases, it is impossible for the program to determine which instance of category X is related to which instance of category Y. If fixed-format coding had been adopted throughout, it would have been possible to specify the range of columns within which co-occurrences were to be sought. In principle, this limitation could be overcome by a recoding operation in which subscripts were added to categories according to the (numbered) clauses in which they occurred in both semantic and syntactic sections of the coding. However, although possible, this recoding has not yet been carried out.

The third problem is closely related to the preceding one, in that it also arose from the decision to employ free-format coding. As already mentioned in chapter 1, the coding of syntactic structure using a free format, in which the linear sequence of coding directly represented the structure of the utterance, gave rise to an extremely large number of unique string types. In order to establish whether there were any developmental trends in their frequency of occurrence, it was clearly necessary to reduce the number of types to be compared by grouping them in some way. However, the Grouped Codes facility in LAP requires that the string types to be combined in each group should be individually specified. Quite apart from the scale of the task (there were estimated to be nearly 4000 different strings), limitations of computer memory space made it impossible to arrive at a complete listing of all the string types to be considered for combination. What was required, therefore, was a procedure for recoding the strings in a fixed format that would allow groupings to be made without prior knowledge of what the membership of each group would ultimately be. This was achieved by two different programs, one for sentence/clause structure and one for the structure of the noun phrase. Since both are based on the same principles, only the first will be described in detail.

2.11 Clause constituency

The basic approach that was adopted assumes that any clause can be described in terms of a fixed number of ordered positions that may be filled or empty. For each position, therefore, a list was compiled of the categories or sequences of categories that might occur, and each combination was given a unique value. The positions recognized are shown in table 2.4, which also contains some examples to show how their constituent structure (in category terms) maps on to the labelled positions.

As will be seen, categories could occur more than once at a particular position (e.g. aux + aux + V at the position labelled Verb) and different orderings of the same set of categories were allowed for. As a result, the number of entries at each position varied considerably. Predicate had the largest number, with entries ranging from a simple constituent, such as Direct Object or Adjunct, to complex structures such as that shown in the last example in table 2.4, where, in addition to an Indirect Object, the Direct Object is qualified by a rank-shifted finite clause. In all, 122 different combinations were included in the table of possible entries for the Predicate position. Not all sentences consist of a simple clause, however, so some way had to be found to cope with multi-clause utterances. For the purposes of the present analysis, it was decided to describe compound and compound-complex sentences only at the level of the constituent clauses, rather than to

Table 2.4 *Position in the recoding of simple and complex sentences*

Sentence	1. Mood	2. Complexity	3. Clause status	4. Marked pre-verb	5. Fronted aux.	6. Subject	7. Verb	8. Predicate
The dog is excited.	declar.	simple	main	—	—	subject	copula	intens. comp.
Did the man give the dog a bone?	polar int.	simple	main	—	aux.	subject	lex. V.	ind. obj. + dir. obj.
Perhaps he didn't want it then.	declar.	simple	main	adjunct	—	subject	aux. + neg. + lex. V.	dir. obj. + adjunct
Who has been telling him stories he already knows?	*wh.* int.	complex	main	—	—	subject	aux. + aux. + lex. V.	ind. obj. + dir. obj. « finite clause »

carry out a full analysis, which would also have involved an analysis of the constituent clauses themselves. Accordingly, a list of nine types of compound sentence was specified in terms of combinations of Main, Subordinate, Embedded and Tag clauses. A final entry was included for any combination more complex than the nine listed. Complexity was entered at position 2. For complex sentences, that is to say simple main or subordinate clauses containing a single embedded clause, the simple clause was recoded in full and this coding showed whether the embedded clause was finite or non-finite. No further coding was made of the embedded clause. In order to allow sentence and clause structure to be considered separately for the different moods (Declarative, Polar Interrogative, etc.), position 1 in the fixed-format description was devoted to Mood choice, using the categories of mood already described earlier in the chapter.

Finally, a number of filters were set so that: (1) only fully coded utterances were read; (2) the following categories of utterances and constituents within utterances were omitted: (a) utterances ungrammatical at the level of clause structure (T or Y in category 33); (b) utterances elliptical because of discourse cohesion (E in category 50); (c) one-word questions and responses and miscellaneous forms, such as 'please', 'hello', 'ouch' (N in category 66).

The computer program required to implement this recoding typically involved two passes through the codings for each utterance. At the first pass the values for positions 1 and 2 were determined. As compound sentences and simple sentences containing more than one embedded clause were not analysed further, positions beyond the second were zero-marked and the next utterance accessed. For simple and complex utterances a second pass was made, which searched serially through the coding of syntactic structure. This involved the construction of a symbol-state table in which the possible codings at each position (including non-occurrence if permitted) were accompanied by instructions as to what action to take next.

When the search through the complete string of syntactic codings had been completed, the result was a numerical code corresponding to the values entered at each position. This was then compared with the appropriate array in the output (for an individual child, a particular occasion, etc., depending on the analysis called for), and, if a cell already existed for this unique numerical code, the counter was incremented by one, or a new cell was created and the counter incremented.

2.11.1 *Grouping of sentence structures*

At the first stage of the analysis, the frequency of occurrence of each unique code was printed for each occasion in the younger and older data-bases separately. On the basis of this information, decisions were taken: (a) to exclude a small number of infrequently occurring anomalous codes that were almost certainly the result of errors in coding; and (b) to combine codes that differed only in minor details, if the differences did not appear to have implications for the sequence of development.

The codes corresponding to the different mood types were considered separately. At the second stage, Imperative sentences were excluded (cf. chapter 5), as were Interrogatives realized by Intonation only. *Why*-interrogatives were combined with other *wh*-interrogatives and codes corresponding to elliptical sentences which had passed the initial filter were excluded. At the end of this stage, there remained grouped declarative sentence types, polar interrogatives and *wh*-interrogatives.

2.11.2 *Noun phrase structure*

A similar procedure was applied to the noun phrase. The positions in the structure of the noun phrase that were recognized for this analysis were: Preposition (position 5), Determiner (6), Modifier (7), Head (8) and Qualifier (9). Position 1 was used to indicate the status of the clause (Main, Subordinate, etc.) in which the NP occurred. Position 3 indicated the constituent (Subject, Adjunct, etc.) which the NP realized, and position 4, indicated the Semantic Derivation of that constituent (Agent, Patient, etc.). In the case of embedded clauses functioning as constituents of a matrix clause, all constituent NPs were described at position 2 in terms of the constituent status (Subject, Adjunct, etc.) of the clause in which they occurred. Where a qualifier was realized by a rank-shifted phrase or clause, this information was recorded at position 9, and the internal structure of the constituent NP(s) analysed in the same way as matrix NPs, but, in the case of NPs from rank-shifted qualifier clauses, with an entry at position 2 to indicate the function of the qualifier from which they were derived. Table 2.5 shows the full set of positions, together with the codings (in category terms) and their assignment to positions for each of the NPs in the sentence:

The old man told *my brother a story he* had *already* read *from a book.*
  (a)   (b)   (c) (d)   (e)   (f)

Table 2.5 *Position in the recoding of the noun phrase*

Noun phrase	1. Clause status	2. Constituent status of embedded clause	3. Constituent status of noun phrase	4. Semantic derivation of noun phrase	5. Preposition	6. Determiner	7. Modifier	8. Head	9. Qualifier
(a) The old man	Main		Subject	Agent		Definite article	General modifier	Noun singular	
(b) my brother	Main		Indirect object	Experiencer		Possessive adjective 1st singular		Noun singular	
(c) a story	Main		Direct object	Patient		Indefinite article		Noun singular	
(d) he	Main	Defining	Subject	Experiencer				Personal pronoun 3rd singular masculine	Defining clause
(e) already	Main	Defining	Adjunct	Temporal				Adverb	
(f) from a book	Main	Defining	Adjunct	Locative	Locative	Indefinite article		Noun singular	

2.12 Evaluation of the syntactic analysis

The establishment of the principles for the recoding just described was a reasonably straightforward process, involving a number of trials by hand until we were sure that all relevant coded information was being recoded appropriately. Writing the computer programs to implement the procedure was much more difficult, as no ready-made modules were available. Several versions were tried out and discarded before a satisfactory solution was achieved for each level of structure. The subsequent stage of grouping the tabulated frequency data was time-consuming, but straightforward. Once this had been done, routine analyses were carried out without difficulty. From beginning to end, the recoding operation took approximately 18 months.

Thus, although the results finally obtained were completely satisfactory, the time and effort required were out of all proportion to the nature of the original problem. This is the strongest argument, if such is needed, for the necessity of linguist and programmer working together from the beginning in designing a scheme of linguistic coding to be used in conjunction with computer analysis.

Some general characteristics of the data from the naturalistic observations

In this chapter we shall consider some general characteristics of the data and discuss some of the problems that arise in interpreting statistics derived from observations of naturally occurring conversation.

All the children in our study had relatively unrestricted opportunities to talk and to engage in conversation with others in a wide variety of contexts. There were no children who were seriously deprived in this respect and none who showed obvious reluctance to avail themselves of these opportunities. Nevertheless there was considerable variation both in the amount of speech that was actually produced and in the conversational contexts in which it occurred.

As will be recalled from chapter 1, the speech sampling was organized in such a way that, at each observation, 24 90-second samples were recorded at approximately 20 minute intervals between 9 a.m. and 6 p.m. although only 18 of these samples were subsequently transcribed and analysed. Thus, at each observation, each child's language experience at that age is represented by the same aggregated time-base of 18×90 seconds, that is, 27 minutes. It is possible, therefore, to make direct comparisons between children and between observations with respect to the amount and distribution of conversational experience.

3.1 Increase in conversation with age

Since vocal utterance is a form of behaviour which begins to emerge towards the end of the first year of life and systematic relationships between form and intention only become stabilized during the second year, there is initially considerable difficulty in determining which of the child's vocalizations should be treated as linguistic utterances. Some children were already clearly intelligible by 15 months but for others it was not until the observation at 21 months that the majority of vocalizations could be classified with confidence. This means that figures based on the first one or two observations must be treated with considerable caution.

Figure 3.1 shows that there is a relatively steep increase in the average number of utterances produced between the first observation at 15 months and the sixth at 30 months. Thereafter, although there is a continuing slight increase throughout the pre-school period, it is much less dramatic. Several points need to be made with respect to this finding. First, there is the issue discussed above: initially, at least, a proportion of the child's utterances may not be recognized as such because of the difficulty of distinguishing between non-linguistic vocalization and vocalizations that are linguistically organized. Secondly, these figures are affected by an increase in the actual time available for speech. At the age of 15 months, almost all of the children were still spending some part of the day asleep: in some cases as many as six of the 18 recorded samples contained no speech because the child was asleep or at least alone in his cot or pram just before or just after sleeping. By 30 months, however, most of the children no longer had a regular day-time nap and even those who did, did not sleep for very long.

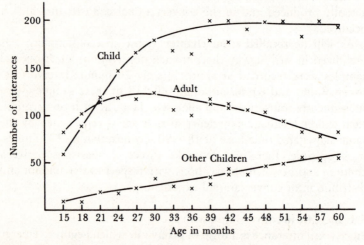

Figure 3.1 Mean amount of speech × age of child

Even when these facts have been taken into account, however, it is clear that there is a real increase in talkativeness during the latter part of the second and the first part of the third year of life. Furthermore, there is an increase in the proportion of the child's utterances that are recognizably socially directed.

With the increase in the amount of speech produced by the child goes an increase in the amount addressed to him. Correlations between the number of utterances produced by and addressed to the child are highly significant, for example, $r = 0.61$ ($p < 0.001$) for the three occasions centring around the occasion when the child's Mean Length of Utterance (MLU) was 1.5 morphemes (i.e. about age 24 months). Initially, most of the child's conversational experience is with adults (see figure 3.1), but there is a gradual increase, extending over the whole pre-school period, in the amount of conversation with other children. However this general trend obscures strong individual differences, largely resulting from position in birth order. Some of the children in the study were only children: most of these continued to have very little experience of conversation with peers throughout the period under investigation. Others were second or subsequent children, and they experienced conversation with older siblings and their friends throughout the period – although such opportunities were substantially reduced when the older siblings began to attend school. Still others were first-born children, for whom conversation with a sibling only became a possibility when they themselves were approaching school age. And there were yet others who had opportunities for conversation with both older and younger siblings to varying degrees throughout their pre-school years. But for almost all the children, the chief conversational partner throughout the period was an adult, usually the mother, but with father, grandparents, other relatives and friends of the parents playing a not inconsiderable role in many cases.

Given the high correlation between the number of utterances contributed respectively by the child and his conversational partner, it is of some interest to try to determine whether either of the partners is the more responsible for the general level of talkativeness that obtains. This might be investigated by identifying who initiates the higher proportion of sequences and who is the last speaker in each sequence. Although we are only just beginning to attempt to answer these questions in a systematic manner, it is clear that, overall, children initiate about two-thirds of the sequences of conversation in which they engage at home, though this proportion may be lower in the earliest observations.

3.2 Variation in the amount of speech by time of day
The 18 speech samples for transcription were selected as far as possible so that an equal number (three) were drawn from each of

six one-and-a-half-hour intervals starting at 9 a.m. The main aim in sampling in this way was to ensure that the total speech corpus at each observation was as representative as possible of the speech that actually occurred throughout the day. However, this stratified sampling design also allows us to ask whether there is a general trend for conversation to be more likely to occur at some times of day rather than at others. Figure 3.2 shows the results for all observations combined. It can be seen that the first period in which samples were recorded (9.00–10.30 a.m.) is by far the most productive. Thereafter, there is a general decline throughout the day, interrupted only by a slight rise in the early afternoon (1.30–3.00 p.m.).

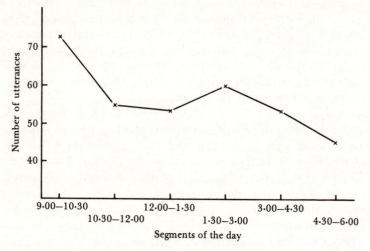

Figure 3.2 Mean amount of speech × time of day

Complicating interpretation of these results to some extent is the fact that the youngest children were more likely to have their daytime sleep either in the late morning or early afternoon rather than at the beginning or the end of the day. There is also the fact that, for those with older siblings, the last period, being after the end of school, was the one that offered the greatest opportunities for conversation with siblings.

Leaving these qualifications on one side, the most plausible interpretation of figure 3.2 is that the amount of conversation that occurs is chiefly a function of the energy level of the child – and perhaps also of that of his potential interlocutors. This interpretation is supported by the temporary reversal in the general decline in amount of speech that occurs in the period that immediately follows the midday meal. Perhaps the most surprising aspect of the time-based distribution of speech is the very low level at the end of the afternoon, particularly as this period usually contains a main meal-time and, as noted, it is also the period during which older siblings are most likely to be available for play. In practice, however, this is the time when, in most homes, the television is most likely to be switched on. Many of the recorded samples contained no speech at all as children and sometimes also parents sat watching the children's television programmes broadcast at this time of day.

Analysis of variance showed that the variation observed in amount of speech according to time of day was significant $(p < 0.01)$; there were no significant age, sex or class of family background effects, however, and no interaction effects. Although there was considerable variation between individual families in the amount of speech in total produced during the day, the pattern of waxing and waning speech activity occurring during the course of the day was found to be fairly constant across families, suggesting that it corresponds to natural rhythms in everyday life.

3.3 Distribution of speech by context
All conversations occur in relation to some context but the relationship between language and context is an interactive one: what is said both influences and is influenced by the context as it is perceived by the participants. Sometimes the context is one of physical action and the speech arises from the activity and plays an integral part in its organization. Such activities may already have a relatively predetermined pattern. In getting dressed for example, the talk is likely to be concerned with coordinating movements in such a way that clothes are put on or removed as efficiently as possible. Other activities, such as play with toys of various kinds, do not have a predictable structure: here the talk has a more creative role in defining and enacting the imagined events. In other cases, the context may not involve present action at all, but rather the recollection or anticipation of events or the discussion of real or imagined states of affairs that are independent of the current actions of the speaker. Here, what is said plays an important part in creating the context for the interpretation of individual utterances.

In classifying the context of sequences of conversation, it is thus necessary to take account both of what is said and of the situation

Table 3.1 *Percentage distribution of speech by context, sex and age*

		Age in months								All occasions
		18	24	30	36	42	48	54	60	
Physical care	B	2.3	5.4	4.6	0.7	2.8	1.4	2.3	1.6	2.6
	G	3.7	4.1	4.5	3.0	3.1	2.1	3.7	1.4	3.1
	All	3.0	4.8	4.6	1.9	2.9	1.8	3.1	1.5	2.9
Eating	B	7.1	7.7	4.7	5.5	5.7	4.6	7.4	3.8	5.6
	G	7.5	10.2	9.0	6.0	5.9	5.0	5.2	4.3	6.3
	All	7.3	8.6	6.9	5.8	5.8	4.8	6.2	4.0	6.0
Helping	B	0.3	1.9	2.1	1.7	4.0	1.5	3.3	1.8	2.4
	G	2.5	1.1	1.6	2.5	5.4	3.5	4.2	3.1	3.4
	All	1.5	1.5	1.9	2.1	4.7	2.6	3.8	2.5	3.0
General activity	B	33.1	19.9	19.8	34.2	16.8	18.6	17.0	26.5	21.6
	G	25.7	28.0	26.4	33.6	17.3	22.8	15.5	33.1	23.9
	All	29.3	24.0	23.2	33.9	17.0	20.8	16.2	29.9	22.8
Watch TV	B	1.8	4.4	4.9	2.8	4.5	2.7	4.8	4.2	4.0
	G	3.6	3.4	5.6	3.7	4.7	4.5	4.3	5.1	4.5
	All	2.7	3.9	5.2	3.3	4.6	3.7	4.5	4.7	4.2
Looking at books and reading	B	7.6	5.4	5.3	1.1	2.7	4.3	2.5	1.6	3.4
	G	5.5	4.2	4.8	1.2	1.9	1.2	3.4	2.2	2.7
	All	5.4	4.8	5.0	1.2	2.3	2.7	3.0	1.9	3.1
Talking	B	10.1	13.4	15.1	16.1	17.6	20.2	14.8	17.4	16.2
	G	9.0	15.5	15.1	14.9	20.8	19.6	21.9	13.1	17.4
	All	9.5	14.5	15.1	15.4	19.7	19.8	18.6	15.2	16.8
Play alone	B	18.4	21.4	16.6	19.5	19.4	21.0	17.7	17.5	19.0
	G	19.3	17.6	15.0	16.0	15.6	16.4	9.5	9.1	14.5
	All	18.9	19.5	15.8	17.7	17.4	18.5	13.3	13.2	16.6
Play with other children	B	5.5	9.7	12.5	8.7	15.8	15.3	19.1	17.3	14.0
	G	6.1	7.6	11.3	10.4	16.4	17.7	22.9	14.3	14.6
	All	5.8	8.6	11.9	9.5	16.1	16.6	21.2	15.8	14.3
Play with adult	B	8.1	7.1	8.5	6.8	6.1	3.9	3.6	3.3	5.7
	G	6.3	5.6	3.9	2.1	2.7	2.9	2.6	1.7	3.1
	All	7.2	6.3	6.2	4.3	4.4	3.4	3.0	2.5	4.4
Game with other children	B	0	0	0.2	0	0.2	0	1.7	1.9	0.5
	G	0	0	0.3	0.2	0.6	0.3	0.9	2.3	0.7
	All	0	0	0.3	0.1	0.4	0.2	1.2	2.1	0.6
Game with adult	B	0	0.2	0	0.4	0.1	0.4	0.9	0.7	0.4
	G	2.3	0.5	0.3	0.4	0.3	0.5	0.7	3.2	0.9
	All	1.2	0.4	0.2	0.4	0.2	0.5	0.8	2.0	0.6
Role-play alone/ with other children	B	0	0.9	3.8	0.7	2.5	4.0	3.5	1.6	2.3
	G	0.6	1.1	1.4	3.9	4.0	2.1	4.5	6.5	3.4
	All	0.3	1.0	2.6	2.4	3.3	2.9	4.1	4.1	2.9
Role-play with adult	B	0	0	0.6	1.6	1.3	2.0	1.4	0.7	1.1
	G	0.9	0.3	0	1.4	0.7	0.1	0.5	0.3	0.5
	All	0.5	0.2	0.3	1.5	1.0	1.0	0.9	0.5	0.8

in which the conversation occurs. In the present study, 16 categories of context were employed, as described in 2.3.1, and each
sequence of conversation, and all the utterances that constituted it,
were assigned to one or other of these categories. Table 3.1 gives
the proportion of utterances occurring in each of these contexts at
six-monthly intervals, for boys and girls separately and combined.
(Categories of Context containing less than 0.5% of utterances are
omitted.)

While on the whole there is little change with increasing age in
the relative proportions of speech occurring in the different contexts, there are one or two interesting changes in absolute proportions. Talking is the most notable. This is the category for
conversation which is not directly related to any activity occurring
in the here-and-now. As might be expected, there is rather little
such conversation in the early observations (only 5% at 15 months)
but the proportion increases sharply during the third and fourth
years to reach a peak of nearly 20% at 48 months, declining slightly
over the following 12 months. Play with Other Children is another
context in which there is an increasing amount of speech over the
period (cf. figure 3.1 which shows the corresponding increase in the
number of utterances addressed to the study subjects by other
children).

Contexts in which there is a decrease in proportional frequency
include Physical Care and Eating: presumably there is less need to
talk about these activities as the child becomes more able to manage
them for himself. Play with Adult also accounts for a decreasing
proportion of utterances over the period. However, this is balanced
by the increase, already noted, of talk in the context of Play with
Other Children.

There are two contexts, which show patterns of a rather different
kind: Helping and Looking at Books and Reading. Helping shows a
substantial peak at 42 months (confirmed by the three-monthly
observations immediately preceding and following) for which no
obvious explanation suggests itself. The rapid decline in the amount
of speech occurring in the context of Looking at Books and
Reading, on the other hand, has a fairly straightforward explanation. Examination of the transcripts of a sub-set of the children
(Wells, in press a) shows that in the early observations, looking at
books is a context that is widely used for the teaching of vocabulary
through the asking of display questions concerned with the names
and attributes of pictured objects (cf. Ninio and Bruner, 1978;
McShane, 1980). After the age of 30 months, however, this activity

is less frequent, and most of the talk that occurs is contributed by a minority of children who have stories read aloud to them.

There are some interesting sex differences in the distribution of speech across contexts. The most striking is in the amount of talk in the context of Play. Boys talk more when playing alone or with adult participation (an average of 24.7% of their utterances occur in the two contexts combined compared with only 17.6% of those of girls). Girls, by contrast, talk more in the contexts of Helping and General Activity – though less consistently so. This suggests that, from an early age, there are differences between the sexes in the activities in which they most frequently engage – or at least in the activity contexts in which they are most likely to converse. The question of sex differences will be discussed more fully in chapter 8.

3.4 Distribution of speech by Inter-Personal Purpose

The purposes that speech served in the child's interactions with others were analysed at three levels: Sequence, Sub-sequence and Function (cf. 2.3). The emergence of the different Functions in children's speech will be dealt with in chapter 4 and is too complex to present in an overview. Sequences, on the other hand, change so much in length over the period that a comparison at that level would run the risk of giving a distorted picture of the overall distribution of the purposes that utterances serve. However, Sub-sequence, being the basic unit of interaction, is ideally suited to this purpose. Furthermore, the number of different sub-sequence modes is sufficiently small for a fairly clear picture to emerge.

A typical sub-sequence consists of two turns: the initiation by one speaker and the response by another speaker. Although adult turns occasionally contained more than one utterance, this was rare for the children. In general, therefore, the child contributed one utterance to each sub-sequence, either as initiator or as respondent. A comparison of the number of child utterances occurring in each sub-sequence mode thus gives a good estimate of the way in which the children's experience of interaction was distributed across the different categories of purpose at successive ages.

Table 3.2 presents the data, at six-monthly intervals, in the form of percentages of total utterances occurring in each category for boys and girls separately and for both sexes combined. Almost all the categories show change over the period studied. The proportions of utterances occurring in Control and Representational sub-sequences both increase quite sharply up to the age of 30 months. (This is particularly marked in the case of Control, which only accounts for 12.4% of utterances at 15 months.) These increases are balanced by a decrease in the proportion of utterances in Expressive sub-sequences and in the proportion of utterances that are not socially addressed but rather have some function as Speech for Self. During this same period the proportion of utterances occurring in Procedural sub-sequences rises to a peak at 24 months and then declines quite sharply to the level at which it will remain for the rest of the pre-school period. The same is true of Tutorial sub-sequences, though these occur at a very much lower level.

During the second half of the period, from 36 to 60 months, the proportion of utterances in Control sub-sequences declines slightly whilst the proportion in Representational sub-sequences continues to increase. By the age of four years, the exchange of information

Table 3.2 *Distribution of speech by sub-sequence mode, sex and age*

		Age in months								All occasions
		18	24	30	36	42	48	54	60	
Control	B	18.9	24.6	28.9	30.0	27.3	23.8	27.1	24.7	26.1
	G	17.5	25.6	30.2	33.3	30.4	27.5	29.9	28.7	28.8
	All	18.2	25.3	29.5	31.7	28.9	25.8	28.6	26.7	27.5
Expressive	B	14.0	11.9	10.6	9.7	10.2	9.0	12.4	10.1	10.7
	G	16.7	11.3	10.7	9.9	10.6	14.1	11.8	10.9	11.7
	All	15.4	11.6	10.7	9.8	10.4	11.7	12.1	10.5	11.2
Representational	B	23.3	31.3	36.4	34.5	35.1	40.8	38.4	36.5	35.4
	G	26.4	27.5	34.4	32.4	33.6	34.1	34.6	37.9	33.3
	All	24.9	29.3	35.4	33.4	34.3	37.2	36.4	37.2	34.3
Social	B	4.7	3.8	2.1	2.4	1.3	1.2	0.4	1.9	1.9
	G	6.0	1.7	2.6	1.6	1.9	1.4	2.4	1.9	2.2
	All	5.4	2.7	2.4	2.0	1.6	1.3	1.5	1.9	2.1
Tutorial	B	4.6	3.2	2.6	0.9	2.1	0.7	1.0	1.3	1.9
	G	2.5	4.2	1.6	0.7	1.1	0.2	1.2	1.0	1.4
	All	3.5	3.7	2.1	0.8	1.6	0.4	1.1	1.2	1.6
Procedural	B	19.9	15.4	11.0	10.5	11.5	11.4	10.5	10.4	12.0
	G	14.9	21.6	15.1	12.4	11.9	13.8	13.3	10.5	13.4
	All	17.3	18.6	13.1	11.5	11.7	12.7	11.0	10.4	12.7
Speech for self	B	12.6	9.1	7.1	9.6	11.8	12.6	9.5	14.1	11.0
	G	14.8	6.5	5.0	8.6	9.7	8.1	8.1	7.8	8.3
	All	13.7	7.8	6.0	9.1	10.8	10.3	9.2	12.1	9.7
Unanalysable	B	2.0	0.6	1.3	2.3	0.6	0.4	0.7	1.0	1.0
	G	1.3	1.4	0.3	1.0	0.7	0.8	0.6	1.3	0.9
	All	1.6	1.0	0.8	1.6	0.7	0.6	0.6	1.2	0.9

has come to assume by far the greatest importance amongst the purposes for which language is used (37.2%) with the controlling of action, both present and future, being, as might be expected, second in order of importance (26.7%).

Sex differences are not so marked for purpose as they were found to be for context. There is a consistent trend for girls to produce a greater proportion of utterances in Control sub-sequences and for boys to produce more in Representational sub-sequences, but the differences are not very great. Boys also show a consistent tendency to produce a greater proportion of Speech for Self. These differences seem likely to be related to the differences already noted with respect to context. Boys spend more time playing alone, frequently talking to themselves while they do so and calling on bystanders, if any, to show an interest in what they are doing. Girls, on the other hand, being more engaged in household activities, tend to be drawn more into talk aimed at organizing the task in hand.

3.5 Development of control of linguistic resources
The preceding sections have concerned the social and pragmatic dimensions of language during the pre-school years – who children converse with, in what situation and for what broad types of purpose – and have shown that there is relatively little change with age. This may be taken as confirmation of the claims for functional continuity made by such writers as Dore (1974, 1975), Griffiths (1979) and Halliday (1975). This is not to say that there is no development. As we shall see in chapters 4 and 6, the change with age in the relative frequency of utterances in the different sub-sequence modes is related to an increasing differentiation of the functions that individual utterances perform and this, in turn, can be seen as being made possible by the child's increasing mastery of the grammatical and lexical resources of the language.

3.5.1 *Measures of increasing length*
As a very rough indication of the rate at which grammatical resources are acquired, we can consider an index such as Mean Length of Utterance (MLU), which capitalizes on the fact that, at least in the early stages, increases in grammatical mastery tend to result in utterances of increasing length. This measure, which is probably the most frequently cited in the literature on language development, was given particular significance by Brown and his colleagues (Brown *et al.*, 1969; Brown, 1973), who used it to define the bounds of their notional stages I–V of grammatical develop-

ment. Employed as an alternative to age for the purpose of grouping speech samples for further analysis, it has the advantage of being simple and quick to calculate and, as Brown has shown, it has considerable heuristic value.

However, it is equally true that it is a crude measure, in that it does not discriminate between the various types of linguistic development that give rise to an increase in number of words or morphemes and, more importantly, it is totally insensitive to other types of development that are not manifested in increasing length. Indeed, in the case of ellipsis, mastery of a new linguistic system can actually lead to a decrease in MLU, as is found when comparing consecutive three-monthly samples from several of the children in our study at about the age of four years. Furthermore, as cross-linguistic studies have demonstrated, MLU is a language-specific measure. For these and other reasons, Garman (1979) has rightly argued that 'stages' of development, defined qualitatively, are certainly to be preferred to those defined in terms of MLU, and Crystal (1974) has cast doubt on the propriety of using this measure at all. Despite these limitations, we nevertheless decided, prior to carrying out more detailed analyses of the speech samples, to use MLU as a heuristic device, to obtain a very rough indication of the level of grammatical development achieved by different children at particular age-related observations. And, as will be seen in chapter 8, we found that, until around the middle of the fourth year, the distribution of scores on this index correlated quite highly with more specifically linguistic measures of development.

The procedures used for calculating utterance length were those recommended by Brown (1973), the units counted being morphemes overtly realized in the surface form of the utterances. In calculating the mean for each observation, however, all recognizable utterances produced by the child in 18 90-second samples at a particular observation were considered, rather than a fixed number, such as 100. Repetitions were not omitted, as it was not possible to include a point-by-point comparison of utterances in the computer analysis program to identify those that were repetitious. A further departure from Brown's method was the omission, from the calculation of the mean, of all 'unstructured' utterances, that is to say of utterances such as 'Yes', 'Hello', 'Please', that do not have any internal grammatical structure. The reason for adopting this procedure was the very great variability in the relative frequency of such utterances, depending on features of the conversational context, such as the activity in progress, who the child was talking with, and the purpose of the interaction. However, MLU, as specified by Brown, was used initially to define the boundaries of the stage-related bands of MLUS that correspond to those given by Brown (1973).

As already mentioned, Mean Length of Structured Utterance (MLUS) ceases to be a very reliable measure after the age of about 42 months. However, it seemed possible that a measure based on the longest utterances produced might continue to have a reasonable degree of reliability for some time after that age. The reason for this expectation was that, whereas MLUS is affected by grammatical devices such as ellipsis, the Mean Length of Longest Utterances (MLUL) should reflect the continuing growth in use of embedded, dependent and relative clauses.

To test this expectation, MLUL was calculated for each child on each occasion, using the five longest utterances produced during the observation. (This use of MLUL is somewhat equivalent to Brown's 'upper bound' (1973:53).) In practice, however, MLUL yielded a curve almost exactly parallel to that for MLUS, with a marked levelling off after 42 months (see table 3.3). It seems, therefore, that although children do continue to produce progressively longer utterances with increasing age, drawing upon grammatical knowledge which continues to increase until well after five years, the occurrence of particularly long utterances is relatively rare and strongly context-dependent. The probability of actually observing such utterances in a sample of 100–150 is therefore too low for a measure based on 5 such utterances to be at all reliable. Furthermore, even in appropriate contexts, the constraints of normal conversation must place an upper bound on length which young conversationalists are unlikely to pass.

It is thus with severe reservations that we present the data on MLUS and MLUL, emphasizing the unreliability of these measures after about 42 months. Nevertheless, if we confine attention to the data up to that age, table 3.3 and the accompanying figure (figure 3.3) are a graphic indication of the variation that can be expected at any given age.

Remembering that the sample contained no children known to be handicapped in any way, the size of the difference in MLU between the highest and lowest scoring children at each age is very considerable. If an MLUS of greater than 1.0 morphemes is taken as an indication of the onset of the ability to express two or more elements of a relational meaning in a single utterance, the age at which this occurs varies from less than 15 months to 30 months or

Table 3.3 *Mean length of utterance × age*

		15	18	21	24	27	30	33	36	39	42	45	48	51	54	57	60
MLU (S)	Young mean	1.2	1.3	1.5	2.1	2.5	3.1	3.6	3.9	4.1	4.3	4.5	4.6	4.7	4.9	4.8	4.8
	Old mean									4.2	4.5						
	Young SD	0.34	0.36	0.55	0.68	0.92	0.95	0.90	0.76	0.80	0.75	0.74	0.69	0.70	0.77	0.73	0.64
	Old SD									0.85	0.71						
	Young range	1.0–2.2	1.0–2.4	1.0–3.6	1.0–3.9	1.0–4.6	1.2–5.3	1.4–5.5	1.8–5.6	1.8–6.0	2.0–5.7	2.4–6.3	3.0–6.6	2.8–7.4	2.4–6.9	2.8–6.9	3.0–6.0
	Old range									2.0–5.7	2.8–5.8						
MLU (L)	Young mean	1.5	2.0	2.5	3.9	4.5	6.1	7.2	7.9	8.5	9.2	9.4	9.9	10.1	10.6	10.5	11.6
	Old mean									9.0	9.6						
	Young SD	0.69	0.95	1.26	1.48	2.00	2.12	1.92	1.97	2.31	2.10	2.00	2.28	2.03	2.36	2.26	2.20
	Old SD									2.18	2.10						
	Young range	1.0–3.2	1.0–5.0	1.0–6.4	1.0–7.2	1.0–10.2	2.0–11.4	2.4–12.4	3.2–11.6	2.8–15.8	5.2–14.0	4.0–14.0	5.4–17.0	4.4–16.6	3.6–16.2	6.6–16.8	6.2–18.4
	Old range									3.2–14.6	4.4–14.2						
MLU (ALL)	Young mean	1.1	1.1	1.3	1.6	1.9	2.4	2.8	3.0	3.2	3.3	3.4	3.6	3.7	3.8	3.7	3.8
	Old mean									3.1	3.4						
	Young SD	0.18	0.16	0.34	0.54	0.65	0.74	0.68	0.69	0.69	0.61	0.64	0.59	0.66	0.65	0.69	0.61
	Old SD									0.74	0.66						
	Young range	1.0–1.8	1.0–1.9	1.0–3.0	1.0–3.2	1.0–3.5	1.1–4.0	1.4–4.1	1.4–4.3	1.2–4.7	1.7–4.9	1.8–5.2	2.2–5.0	2.2–6.4	2.0–6.0	2.2–5.8	2.2–5.0
	Old range									1.4–4.9	1.6–4.9						

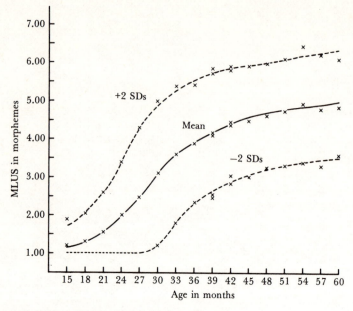

Figure 3.3 Mean length of structured utterances × age

later. Similarly, if we consider the range of MLUS scores observed at 42 months, we find that children scoring as high as two standard deviations (+2 SDs) above the mean have a score that is greater than the mean of the sample as a whole at the time of the last observation of the older children (18 months later), while those scoring as low as two SDs below the mean have a score equivalent to the mean observed for the sample as a whole as much as 15 months earlier. Insofar as these measures of MLU are at all reliable as indices of grammatical development, they suggest that rate of development varies very widely indeed within the population of children believed to be 'normal'.

A second important point that can be made by reference to these data is the very close match between the two age-based samples of children. The study was designed so that there would be an overlap of two observations between the two independent cohorts. The intention was to use the overlap to establish whether the two samples could be treated as having been drawn from the same population, thus allowing the developmental data to be combined as if it had been obtained from a single continuous longitudinal study. As can be seen, the distributions of scores at both observations (39 and 42 months) are very similar in the two samples; the differences that do occur are not statistically significant. On the basis of these data at least, therefore, there are no grounds for rejecting the assumption that the two samples are equivalent in terms of the populations from which they were drawn.

Looked at from another point of view, the fact that two independent samples of children, each observed on two separate occasions, yield score distributions that are so similar is an indication that, however crude they may be as indices of linguistic development, these two measures of MLU have a fairly high degree of reliability for children of this age.

3.6 Alternative indices of overall development

If measures of length are at best inadequate and at worst misleading, what is the alternative? Ideally, of course, what is required is an instrument which is based on a thorough understanding of the developmental process and which gives due weight, at each stage or level, to those systems or features of language which are at the cutting edge of development. It should also give adequate representation to the various dimensions of language on which development is simultaneously taking place. Unfortunately, in the present state of our knowledge, such an ideal is far from having been attained. Furthermore, it is based on an assumption that there is an invariant sequence of development within particular languages, but this has still to be established. What evidence there is about development on the syntactic dimension certainly tends to support such an assumption, but it is still far from adequately based on longitudinal studies of representative groups of children; the situation is still less clear for the semantic and pragmatic dimensions and the relationships between these various dimensions. However these are issues that will be addressed more fully in chapters 4 and 5.

In the absence of the ideal, multi-dimensional developmental measure, one possible solution is to attempt to create measures for individual linguistic systems and to bring these together in an overall profile. This certainly has an interim usefulness for diagnostic assessments of individual children and for researchers who are attempting to investigate the relationship between language and other aspects of the child's development or characteristics of his environment. Furthermore, information derived from the use of such measures, even though somewhat fragmentary and disjointed, can play a part in increasing understanding of the full developmental process on which the ideal measure will ultimately be based.

This, at least, is the rationale that lay behind the approach originally adopted in the present study (Wells, 1978).

More recently, however, we have begun to use a different approach. Whereas initially our measures were chiefly quantitative, with scores being given for the number of items mastered within a particular system, now we are able to use information which is more qualitative in nature, as we have established developmental sequences within and across the various systems studied. Currently, we are exploring ways of utilizing this information to construct a single integrated scale.

The data on which the scale will be based are presented in the following chapters. But before a definitive version can be prepared, it will be necessary to compare the use of spontaneous conversational data with other sources of information about children's linguistic ability, and to attempt to evaluate the strengths and limitations of the research method on which the greater part of the results in this report are based.

3.7 Naturalistic and experimental methods compared

The naturalism and authenticity which is the most obvious characteristic of data obtained by sampling spontaneously occurring conversation is at one and the same time the greatest strength and the most serious limitation of this research method. On the one hand, one can be certain that what is recorded is the 'real life' behaviour of the subjects studied and, provided that the researcher has succeeded in avoiding the 'observer paradox' (Labov, 1972a), that it is not an artefact of the research technique employed. On the other hand, the data obtained are liable to be unrepresentative in other ways, as a result of the biases introduced by a whole host of situational variables which are inadequately understood and impossible to control. Even when an attempt has been made to sample from as wide a range of contexts as possible, the corpus of recorded utterances is only a minute sample of the child's total output and even that, if recorded in full, would be only a – possibly biased – sample of what the child could say, given sufficient time and the appropriate eliciting contexts. The researcher's goal is to give an account of the child's linguistic resources, his ability, but this can never be achieved by observing only the particular instances of behaviour that are called forth by the contexts in which the child actually finds himself (Ingram, 1969).

The researcher is thus faced with the problem of how to make inferences about linguistic ability – that is, potential behaviour –

from the limited sample of actual behaviour that he is able to observe. In particular he runs the dangers of either over-estimating a child's ability, as when, for example, observed utterances are taken to be novel constructions when, in reality, they are imitations of utterances heard prior to the observational period. More experimental techniques, such as the use of verbal or non-verbal stimuli to elicit particular linguistic responses, appear at first sight to overcome these limitations. Certainly, with the use of such techniques, the context can be controlled, as can the linguistic domain within which the child's responses are most likely to occur. Where the researcher wishes to probe the limits of a child's mastery of a particular linguistic system, there is much to recommend this approach, but the price to be paid is uncertainty about the extent to which the behaviour observed in the 'test' situation can be generalized to naturally occurring settings and the very limited area of knowledge that can be investigated in this way on any occasion of testing.

The same evaluation must be made of tests of comprehension, whether the technique used is that of picture identification or that of 'acting out' the stimuli with dolls and other toys. Furthermore, although it is generally believed that comprehension and production draw upon the same linguistic resources, it is certainly not the case that the two processes are equivalent in the way they make use of those resources or that an estimate of linguistic ability derived from one of the two processes can be assumed to stand as proxy for an estimate derived from the other (Bloom, 1974; Huttenlocher, 1974).

Nor do the more experimental techniques entirely avoid the problems, already discussed, associated with inferring ability from observed behaviour, for a child's responses in test-like situations are just as much a sample of 'performance' as are the utterances spontaneously produced in naturally occurring settings. The fact that the researcher controls many of the external variables of situations and stimuli in the test setting but not in the naturalistic setting does not overcome the fact that the determinants of the child's behaviour – besides the availability of the particular response – are to be found in the total context *as the child construes it*. That is not under the researcher's control in either paradigm. It is no more likely to be available, therefore, to the tester than to the eavesdropping observer. Inferences from 'incorrect' or irrelevant responses are thus just as difficult to make from test as from spontaneous data (Walkerdine and Sinha, 1978). Furthermore, there are substantial differences between children, generally favouring those from the upper range of Family Background, in their ability to cope with the demands of the 'de-contextualized' test setting (Wells, 1982).

One must conclude, therefore, that no method has privileged access to a child's linguistic ability and that each has its strengths and limitations. With their different emphases, they are thus best seen as complementary: the naturalistic approach leading to hypotheses concerning specific aspects of development which may be tested by a more experimental approach, or supporting evidence being sought for findings obtained under experimental conditions in an investigation of naturally occurring situations in which similar behaviour is expected to occur.

Although the relationship between the two broad approaches is ideally cyclical, when both are employed within a single research design, it is more common for the experimental approach to be used to explore in greater detail areas opened up in a more diffuse way by the naturalistic approach. This was the intention in the present study, but in practice it proved too difficult to achieve within the constraints imposed by a longitudinal study of a relatively large number of children. Some data were collected under more experimental conditions, but we did not succeed in articulating the two approaches as we had intended, for the major part of our resources were taken up by the more labour-intensive collection and analysis of the samples of spontaneous conversation. Furthermore, the repeated administration of the General Linguistic Comprehension Test did not yield data in which we could place sufficient confidence to compare the results with those obtained from the naturalistic observations.

3.8 Problems in the analysis of naturalistic data

As already noted, the most serious problem in working with naturalistic data is that we are far from having an exhaustive list of contextual variables and further still from understanding their influence on what a speaker says on any particular occasion. If we knew what all these factors were and understood how they interacted, we should be able, at least in theory, to record a sample of speech that maximized the chances of obtaining an adequate representation of a speaker's repertoire. In the absence of this knowledge, the aim must be to sample as widely as possible from the population and to record as large a corpus from as wide a range of contexts as possible, having taken *a priori* decisions about the parameters to recognize in stratifying the population and the contexts in which recordings are made. In practice, however, even this aim is unattainable, for limited resources almost always force the researcher to trade off size and representativeness of the population sample against representativeness of contexts and size of the corpus of recorded utterances. The decision taken in the present study to study a relatively large number of children and to accept the consequent restriction on the amount of speech analysed from each child on each occasion led to a number of problems, the most important of which need to be discussed prior to reporting the results of the analyses.

The recorded samples of speech, when coded according to the scheme described in chapter 2, yielded data in the form of frequencies of occurrence of the various categories specified in the scheme. These frequencies range from zero to a theoretical ceiling which, for any particular category, is as high as the number of occurrences of the linguistic domain in which the category might have occurred. The researcher's problem is to know how to interpret an actually observed frequency in terms of acquisition of the category in question or, to put it differently, to know what minimum frequency to treat as evidence that the category has been acquired.

From one point of view the problem can be seen as hinging on the notion of probability. The difficulty is that different categories have differing probabilities of occurrence, depending on how many alternatives there are in the system to which the category belongs and on whether the system itself is obligatory or optional. This difficulty is still further compounded by the fact that, even when all the alternatives in a system are available, they do not have the same probability of occurrence. Some examples will help to clarify what is at issue. Compare the relative probabilities of observing an occurrence of the following categories in a sample of 100 utterances selected at random from continuous conversation: past tense, polar interrogative mood, the personal pronoun 'he' and the modal auxiliary 'may'. To begin with, past tense and polar interrogative are both categories belonging to systems from which a choice must obligatorily be made for each clause, whereas modal auxiliaries and pronouns are systems which are optional, in the sense that well-formed sentences can be constructed that do not require a selection to be made from either system. However, within the two obligatory systems there are differing numbers of options: Tense may be either past or not past, whereas the Mood system comprises five options:

Indicative, Imperative, Polar Interrogative, *Wh-* interrogative and Moodless. Theoretically, therefore, there is a one-in-two chance that any clause will contain an occurrence of past tense if each option is chosen with equal frequency, but only a one-in-five chance of it containing an occurrence of polar interrogative. The probability of observing an occurrence of a category belonging to an obligatory system can thus be calculated, at least in theory. But the same is not true for members of optional systems although, given the occurrence of a choice from an optional system, it is possible to calculate the theoretical probability of it being any particular category, just as in the case of tense or mood. However, the comparison of 'may' and 'he' introduces a further difficulty of a general kind. The domain within which the system of modal auxiliaries operates is the clause, whereas the domain for personal pronouns is the nominal group, of which there may be several within any clause. Thus the theoretical probability of observing an occurrence of 'he' is considerably greater than that of observing an occurrence of 'may'.

But this is not the end of the problem for, even within particular systems, some categories are selected far more frequently than others, both by speakers in general and by individual speakers. For example, in a sample of several thousand adult utterances addressed to the children in our study, 'he' was found to occur only a third as often as 'I' but nearly four times more often than 'him'. Similarly 'may' was found to occur only about a third as often as 'could'; furthermore, whereas 'could' occurred in the adult speech addressed to 57% of the children, 'may' occurred in that addressed to only 13% of them.

Finally, of course, there is the effect of context. For although it might be possible to calculate the theoretical probability of a particular category occurring a certain number of times in a sample of a certain size, whether it is actually observed depends very much on the context in which the talk occurs: who is speaking to whom, about what and for what purpose.

One solution to the problem, adopted by Brown (1973), is to set a criterion of correct use of a category in a certain proportion (e.g. 90%) of the linguistic contexts in which it is obligatorily required. This is reasonably satisfactory for categories such as grammatical morphemes but, as has been shown, the majority of categories which one might wish to describe do not have obligatory contexts in this sense and even for those that do, the criterion may be more appropriate for some dialects of English than for others.

A second solution might be to set a criterion in terms of a minimum proportional frequency, calculated with respect to the domain from which selection of the category in question is made, that is, x% of clauses in the case of 'may' or x% of nominal groups in the case of 'he'. But this still fails to take account of the differential probability of occurrence of items within their respective domains. Moreover, since a substantial proportion of items of interest occur with a frequency of less than once per 100 utterances (1%), even in the speech of adults talking with children, it is clear that one must either record a sample of several hundred utterances at each observation or accept a single occurrence as relevant evidence. As we were unable, because of limited resources, to adopt the first solution, we were forced to settle for a version of the second.

In practice, of course, once a category has appeared in a child's speech, it tends to appear on successive occasions, usually with increasing frequency. Thus, for most categories, the problem only poses itself in an acute form with respect to the decision on point of acquisition. Adopting the criterion of a single occurrence obviously increases the risk of making a false positive error. To reduce this possibility, in the case of all but the most rarely occurring items, a single occurrence of a category in a particular observation was only allowed to stand as positive evidence if there was at least one occurrence of the same category in one of the next two observations.

Even with the above safeguards, a single occurrence of a category is very weak evidence when considering children individually. However where a substantial number of individuals is being studied, the evidence is considerably strengthened if a very similar pattern is repeated across the sample as a whole, and this was indeed frequently the case. For certain purposes, therefore, data from individual children are combined and results reported in terms of central tendencies, such as the mean or median value for the group as a whole.

One further qualification needs to be made. The use of the term 'acquisition' suggests an instantaneous, all or nothing event. But for many categories this is an inappropriate way of conceptualizing the learning process, for a considerable period may be involved during which the child's control of the category develops from correct use in a single, limited context to full mastery across all relevant contexts. For evidence of the complexity of the developmental process to emerge, therefore, it may be necessary to make a fine-grained analysis of data collected at frequent intervals.

This is very clearly brought out by Fletcher's (1981) preliminary analysis of the development of perfect aspect, based on some of the Bristol data, which shows that, although all the children in the younger age-group were using this category by 42 months, if a simple morphosyntactic definition *have + Ven* is applied, this hid a much more variable state of affairs. In fact, for some of the children the *have + Ven* form only occurred in the constructions 'have got' or ''ve got' and none of the children whose transcripts he examined were using the form across the full range of constructions that he had identified in adult speech. On the basis of this evidence, therefore, he concludes that, although the mean age of first recorded use of perfect aspect was as early as 27 months, most of the children still had not completely mastered this category some 12 months later. As he himself recognizes, however, such a conclusion must be somewhat tentative as the frequencies on which it is based are very small.

In fact, his study clearly exemplifies all the problems that have been discussed above concerning the making of inferences about acquisition from frequencies derived from naturalistic data. To begin with, the present perfect is a member of an optional system, aspect, which itself has a probability of occurrence of considerably less than one per clause. When this category is further sub-divided into the 11 different constructions that Fletcher differentiates, it is clear that, if these have differential frequencies of occurrence in normal adult speech, the chances of observing even a single occurrence of the least frequent of them in a sample of some 120 utterances from a child is very small indeed. Thus, in attempting to avoid the error of over-estimating ability that can occur when occurrences of just one constructional use of a category are taken as evidence of acquisition, one runs the risk of making the opposite, false negative error – that of treating non-occurrence as evidence of non-acquisition.

There is no real solution to this problem. However, the danger of making erroneous inferences can be substantially reduced by increasing the amount of data analysed at each observation and by decreasing the interval between observations. It can also be reduced by taking due note of patterns of frequencies in successive observations both within individual children and across a sample of children at the same stage of development. As far as the present study is concerned, the first alternative was not available to us, and this inevitably puts a limit on the level of detail of analysis that can be undertaken since, beyond a certain point, the expected frequencies of categories are so low that no conclusions can be drawn from those actually observed. It also means that the study of the development of individual categories from first use to complete mastery across the full range of constructions and contexts, is in most cases not really possible. For this reason, we do not use the term 'acquisition' but prefer, instead, to speak of 'emergence', by which we mean the occasion in our longitudinal observations when a child was first observed to use a category correctly. On the other hand, by making full use of the longitudinal dimension in the records of individual children and of the size and representativeness of the sample of children studied, we can provide evidence about the broad outlines of development that can, we believe, be accepted with a considerable degree of confidence.

In the chapter which follows, developmental data will be presented for most of the linguistic systems that are included within the framework provided by the *Coding Manual*. In a few cases, however, the coded data were judged to be too unreliable to warrant a systematic longitudinal analysis. This was true of the systems of Cohesion and Thematization. Certain other judgments made in the coding of utterances are not amenable to the analytic approach described in the following chapter. These include the types of error that were noted and the identification of some utterances as imitations of immediately preceding utterances. Analysis of these aspects of the data, together with the investigation of patterns of cooccurrence of options from different linguistic systems, will, we hope, be carried out in subsequent phases of the research programme.

The sequence of emergence of certain semantic and pragmatic systems

To those who see language as unfolding from within the human organism – driven by an innate Language Acquisition Device or by the development of cognition, which follows its own universal sequence – it is natural to assume that the development of language will follow a universal sequence. This was the assumption that underlay much of the research on language acquisition carried out in the 1960s, and the results of that research on the whole confirmed the assumption. Then when results of studies of languages other than English began to be reported, it became apparent that there was some degree of variation in sequence from one language to another. However, this could largely be accounted for in terms of differences between languages in the relationships between underlying meanings and surface realizations (Slobin, 1973), and so the assumption of universality has continued more or less unchallenged.

To those who see language as a social as well as an individual accomplishment, on the other hand, the expectation of a universal sequence of development is less self-evident. Whilst the results of studies to date might seem to indicate a universal sequence, these results might be equally well accounted for by the similarity of the interactional experience of the children investigated, since, in almost all studies, the samples have been socially homogeneous. However, if a larger and more representative sample of children were studied, it might be argued, the results would be somewhat different. Although there might be evidence for a universal sequence at some very general level – simple sentences preceding complex sentences, for example – considerable variation might be expected in the order in which more specific meanings or structures were acquired, as a result of variation in the environmental conditions affecting children's everyday conversational experience.

To investigate this issue was one of the major objectives of the Bristol study. Hence the emphasis on the selection of a socially

representative sample of children and on the collection of spontaneously occurring conversational data from a wide range of
contexts found in children's homes.

Even under these conditions, however, the investigation of
universality has a built-in bias. In the unlikely event of no similarities being found there would be clear evidence against a universal
sequence, but little more could be said. However, the more likely
result is that there will be some similarities of sequence between at
least some of the children. In these circumstances, the most
satisfactory way of reporting the results is first to describe what is
common to all, or a majority, of the sample and then to report the
differences in terms of departures from the 'norm'. Thus the search
for universals precedes and provides the base-line for the study of
individual or group differences.

In the work to be reported in this chapter, the emphasis will be
on common patterns and it will be shown that the evidence strongly
favours the view that there is a broadly similar sequence of
development for this sample of children learning English as their
first language. Within this broad similarity, however, there is
certainly some individual variation. But because the study of
individual differences in this sample of children has only recently
begun, the question as to whether these differences are systematically related to differences in the children's experiences will have to
be left to a subsequent publication.

4.1 The nature of the evidence

As already explained in the previous chapter, we do not claim to be
able to report on the sequence of *acquisition* of the items under
investigation. We shall therefore speak only of *occasion of emergence*, by which we mean the occasion on which a child was first
observed correctly to produce a particular item. The actual first
production may, of course, have occurred on any day since the
previous observation, three months earlier − or earlier still if the
sampling procedure had failed to detect it on that previous occasion. Occasion of emergence is thus a very conservative estimate of
first productive use.

Data drawn from three-monthly observations also provide very
conservative evidence of items being ordered with respect to each
other. In the total production of any individual child, every item
must inevitably be ordered with respect to every other, simply by
virtue of the fact that a speaker can say only one thing at a time. To
some extent, of course, an order based on continuous observational

data would be spurious, since it would be unduly influenced by the chance occurrence of one item before another when the reverse order might equally well have occurred. With continuous data, too, there is no principled way of segmenting the continuous dimension of time such that items first occurring during a particular period of time could be said to cooccur, whilst items first occurring in adjacent periods could be said to be ordered. When samples of speech are recorded at intervals of several weeks, on the other hand, this difficulty is overcome, since all the items first observed in a particular sample clearly share the same occasion of emergence and are ordered with respect to those first observed on preceding and subsequent occasions. There is a price to pay, of course. Sampling at intervals inevitably leads to less precision in ordering, since some items will be observed to have the same occasion of emergence when in reality there was a real time difference in their entry into the child's production. And the longer the interval between samples, the greater the number of items that will fail to be observed as ordered.

To some degree the reduction in precision that results from sampling at intervals is compensated for by the greater generalizability that may attach to results obtained from the study of a large number of children. To the extent that the same pattern of emergence is found in a sizeable majority of children and is not contradicted by the data from the remainder, the evidence of there being a common sequence becomes stronger and more reliable. Nevertheless, it is to be expected that the evidence obtained from sampling at intervals rather than from continuous monitoring of children's speech will under-estimate the extent to which there is an invariant sequence of development. The evidence will be further weakened by the sensitivity of sampling to variability in item frequency that was discussed in the previous chapter.

4.2 The procedure for investigating sequence
The first stage was to investigate the evidence for sequence in the various linguistic systems considered individually. Matrices were constructed in which rows represented children and columns items within systems. The entry in each cell was the occasion number on which the item emerged in the speech of a particular child. (Occasions were numbered consecutively from 1 to 10 for the younger children and from 11 to 18 for the older children.) Where an item was not observed at all by the last observation of a particular child, an entry was made in the cell to that effect. Table

Table 4.1 *Occasion of emergence*
(hypothetical data)

Child \ Item	E	F	G	H
Z	3	5	5	6
Y	4	4	4	7
X	2	3	3	4
W	6	5	6	8
V	3	7	7	6
U	2	5	5	4
T	4	7	7	9
S	3	5	5	5
R	3	2	2	4
Q	3	6	6	5
P	4	4	4	7
O	5	7	7	6
N	3	5	4	7

4.1 provides hypothetical data for illustrative purposes: occasions of emergence of the four linguistic items E, F, G and H are shown for the 13 children Z to N. To establish whether the four items are ordered it is necessary to compare each item with every other item in a series of pairwise comparisons. For any such comparison there are four possible outcomes with respect to any pair of items i and j in the speech of any individual child. These are: i precedes j $(i \rightarrow j)$; j precedes i $(j \rightarrow i)$; i and j are coemergent $(i \Leftrightarrow j)$; neither i nor j is observed to emerge during the period under investigation $(\bar{i}, \bar{j})$. When data from a number of children are obtained, the comparisons will yield frequency values for each of these possible outcomes.

Ideally, a claim for order would be based on an identical outcome from all the children investigated. This is the case for items E and H in table 4.1: here $f(E \rightarrow H) = 13$, whilst $f(H \rightarrow E) = 0$ and $f(E \Leftrightarrow H) = 0$. However, when sampling from naturalistic data at relatively infrequent intervals such unequivocal results are likely to be rare. Much more probable is a distribution of the kind that is illustrated by the comparison of the items E and F. Here the majority of cases support the order $E \rightarrow F$, but there is a minority that supports the converse order $F \rightarrow E$ (see table 4.2). The problem is to know whether the number of cases for whom $E \rightarrow F$ exceeds the number for whom $F \rightarrow E$ by a sufficient margin to justify the claim that E is ordered with respect to F and precedes it.

Table 4.2 *Frequencies of the outcomes of the comparison of two hypothetical items*

E → F	F → E	E ⇔ E	Ē, F̄
9	2	2	0

In work on behavioural indices of development, Bart and Krus (1973) faced a similar problem. Their data were cross-sectional and consisted of judgments about the presence or absence of specific behaviours at a particular observation. Their problem was to know whether the observed behaviours were developmentally ordered. The method they used was one of pairwise comparisons, the results of which were cast in the form of a 2 × 2 contingency table. Table 4.3 shows one such table. Bart and Krus were only interested in two

Table 4.3 *Occurrence of items of behaviour (hypothetical data)*

of the cells: *a* which contains the frequency of cases showing only item A (14) and *d* which contains the frequency of cases showing only item B (5). Cells *b* and *c* which contain, respectively, the frequencies of cases showing both or neither of the items, were ignored. To test whether the difference between the frequencies in *a* and *d* was sufficiently large to claim that one item preceded the other, they used the procedure for testing the significance of differences between correlated proportions which is based on the Critical Ratio Test (McNemar quoted in Guilford and Fruchter, 1978: 161–3):

$$z = \frac{a - d}{\sqrt{(a + d)}}$$

Applied to the data in table 4.3, this gives a value of $z = 2.06$, which is significant between the $p = 0.05$ and $p = 0.01$ levels. This allowed

Table 4.4 *A 2 × contingency table (hypothetical data)*

a		b
E→F 9	E⇔F 2	
Ē F̄ 0	F→E 2	
c		d

them to claim that item A most probably does precede item B in development.

Our problem was sufficiently similar for us to consider it justifiable to use the same procedure as Bart and Krus, but it was necessary to adapt it to fit the rather different data that we were dealing with. Where Bart and Krus had observations of presence or absence of behaviours on a single occasion, we had data on the occasion *by which* a behaviour (i.e. linguistic item) was observed. The values in our 2×2 tables were therefore not frequencies of presence of either of the behaviours but frequencies of the four possible outcomes of the pairwise comparisons. Casting the data in table 4.2 in this form, for example, we have table 4.4. Applying the formula, this gives a z ratio of 2.11 which is significant between the 0.05 and 0.01 levels. As with the Bart and Krus example, this would allow us to conclude that E very probably does precede item F in development.

However, we were not entirely satisfied with this procedure for two reasons. First, from further trials on hypothetical data with a much larger value of N (for example, $N = 100$) we found that a significant value of z could be achieved even when a substantial number of cases supported the opposite order. With values of a and d respectively 65 and 35, for example the value of z is 3.0, which is significant at better than the 0.01 level. Whilst statistically speaking it may be correct to infer from these data that item i is likely to be earlier to emerge than j, this ignores the evidence in favour of an alternative interpretation, namely that there are actually two alternative developmental sequences and that each of the possible orders is favoured by a substantial proportion of children.

If it is to be argued that one order rather than the other represents the common sequence of development, it is necessary in our view to show not only that the distribution of outcomes from a comparison of the items in a pair significantly supports that order (i.e. that the value of z has an associated probability of $p < 0.05$) but also that the evidence in favour of alternative sequential possibilities is sufficiently small to be discounted. This means that all the relevant data must be taken into account. The calculation of the z ratio makes use only of cells a and d. However there are two other cells to be considered. Cell c contains the frequency of cases for whom neither item was observed. Since such cases contribute no information at all about the developmental sequence of the two items being compared, cell c can safely be ignored. Cell b, on the other hand, does contain information of relevance, and although cases who show i and j emerging simultaneously do not provide evidence in favour of either hypothesized order, they should be taken into account in deciding whether to reject either or both of the hypotheses. If, in fact, the majority of cases are found in cell b, the latter seems to be the most appropriate decision to take. Accordingly, following a positive outcome of the Critical Ratio Test, the value of cell b was compared with the combined values of $a + d$. Only in the case

$$(a + d) > b$$

was a hypothesis of order further entertained.

It is not sufficient, however, that the majority of cases should support one or other of the hypothesized orders. In our view, if one order, $i \rightarrow j$ for example, is to be accepted, the proportion of cases that show the reverse order (i.e. those that disconfirm the hypothesized order) should not be more than a small proportion of all the cases that provide relevant information (i.e. d should be a small proportion of $N - c$). Bart and Krus do, in fact, suggest a formula for calculating the proportion of disconfirmatory evidence. It is:

$$k = \frac{d}{a + d + b}$$

If this formula is applied to the data in table 4.4, the value obtained is $k = 15.4\%$. The question is: Is this too high a proportion of disconfirmation for the significant value of z to be accepted as evidence for the order $E \rightarrow F$? Unfortunately, there is no statistical test for evaluating the significance of k. Bart and Krus suggest that each researcher should select a criterion value in the light of all the conditions relevant to the investigation. How this advice was applied in the present investigation will be returned to after we have considered the second reason for dissatisfaction with the Critical Ratio Test as the only method of evaluating the sequential relationship between a pair of items.

As already stated, the calculation of z is only relevant to an evaluation of the evidence supporting a hypothesis of order. However there is a further possibility which is of equal interest when considering the sequence of emergence and that is that the items i and j are coemergent. This would be the most reasonable inference to draw if the value in cell b was equal to or close to N. To evaluate the evidence relevant to a hypothesis of coemergence we have used a formula that expresses the evidence for and against the hypothesis as a ratio.

$$\theta_1 = \frac{a + b/2}{d + b/2} \text{ where } a > d \text{ or } \theta_2 = \frac{d + b/2}{a + b/2} \text{ where } d > a$$

Values of θ may range from 0 to 1.0. The closer the value to 1.0, the stronger the evidence in favour of coemergence. The closer the value to 0 the weaker the evidence in favour of coemergence but, conversely, the more likely it is that the items are ordered.

As with k there is no statistical test of significance for θ so here again a criterion value had to be selected. In fact, since the aim was to ensure that no pair of items could meet the criterion for order *and* for coemergence simultaneously, the two values finally selected for k and for θ were set after an investigation of their interaction for a wide range of values in the three relevant cells of the 2×2 contingency table. These values were:

$$\text{CRIT}_k \leqslant 0.08 \qquad\qquad \text{CRIT}_\theta \geqslant 0.8$$

This criterion value for k is considerably more stringent than the necessary, but not sufficient, condition with which we started, that the critical z ratio should have an associated probability of $p < 0.05$. Indeed, it might be argued that the criterion is too stringent. A second criterion was therefore established which we shall refer to as the weak criterion of order:

$$\text{CRIT}_{k(\text{weak})} \leqslant 0.20$$

With θ there is a different sort of problem. For a pair of items to meet the criterion for θ, what is crucial is that the values in cells a and d should be close to equal. The value of b, on the other hand, may fall anywhere between 0 and $N - c$. A pair of items may thus be found to be coemergent with no counter evidence when two very different conditions obtain. In the first, where $a = d = 0$, all cases that contribute evidence show the items as emerging simultaneously. This is only likely to occur when the two items are in some way interdependent, as, for example, would be the case if the items to be compared were the I-P Function 'Request Permission' and the Modal Auxiliary 'can' (permission). At the other extreme, θ may have a value of 1.0 where $a = d$ and $b = 0$. In this case there are no cases that show the items emerging simultaneously; instead, the children who contribute evidence are equally divided between the two orders. There are two possible interpretations of such a result: either that the items in the pair, although not interdependent, are nevertheless truly coemergent, but sampling error has led to one or other being observed to emerge first by chance in individual cases; or that there are two equally favoured sequences of development with respect to this pair of items. Our method does not allow us to choose between these two interpretations. However, we can identify those pairs of items which, whilst meeting the criterion for coemergence, might equally well be described as showing both orders in parallel. This will be signalled i/j for any case where $(a + d) > b$.

The full procedure for evaluating the evidence for sequence of development with respect to any pair of items is shown in the form of a flow chart in figure 4.1. To illustrate how the procedure is used, we will apply it to the five remaining comparisons of the data first presented in table 4.1.

(i) E v G $a = 9$, $b = 3$, $c = 0$, $d = 1$
$z = 2.53$ $p < 0.05$
$(a + d) > b$
$k = 0.076$
Decision: $E \rightarrow G$

(ii) E v H $a = 13$, $b = 0$, $c = 0$, $d = 0$
$z = 0$
$(a + d) > b$
$k = 0$
Decision: $E \rightarrow H$

(iii) F v G $a = 1$, $b = 11$, $c = 0$, $d = 1$
$z = 0$
$\theta = 1.0$
$b > a + d$
Decision: $F \Leftrightarrow G$

(iv) F v H $\}$ $a = 8$, $b = 1$, $c = 0$, $d = 4$
     G v H $\int$ $z = 1.15$
$\theta = 0.53$
Decision: Insufficient evidence to decide the relationship between F and H, and G and H.

Having applied the procedure to all the pairwise comparisons, we can now draw the full hypothetical system (see figure 4.2) where the conventions of representation are: (1) a solid line denotes strong evidence of ordering ($\text{CRIT}_k \geq 0.08$); (2) a broken line denotes

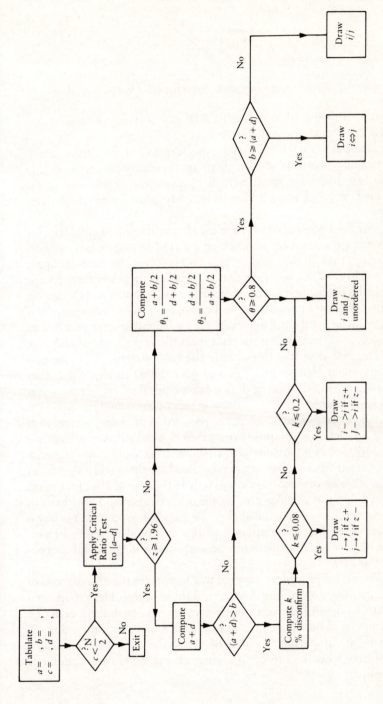

Figure 4.1 A flow chart of the procedure for evaluating sequence of development for any pair of linguistic items

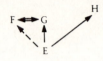

Figure 4.2 Sequence of emergence (hypothetical data)

weak evidence of ordering $(CRIT_k \geqslant 0.20)$; (3) a double line denotes coemergence $(CRIT_\theta \geqslant 0.8)$.

It appears therefore, that in the learning of the items in this imaginary linguistic system, there are two fairly distinct stages. In the first stage, the single item E emerges; this is followed in the with F and G having a high probability of emerging at the same time.

One final point needs to be made about the method employed for investigating sequence of development. The procedure just outlined assumes that all the children are observed over the same age-span. It will be recalled, however, that in this study there were two groups of children, the first observed from 15 to 42 months and the second from 39 to 60 months. If an account of sequence of emergence was to be given for the full age-range, 15–60 months, some way had to be found of articulating the data from the two groups of children.

The first step was to compare the two age-groups on the two overlapping observations (39 and 42 months) to check that they could be treated as being drawn from equivalent populations. For all items that had emerged in the speech of between 25% and 75% of the children being studied, the proportion of children using each item in each age-group was compared on both occasions. The vast majority of comparisons (88%) showed no significant difference between the two age-groups, and even where there was a significant difference on one occasion it was only in the case of 2% of the items tested that this was repeated on the other occasion. On the basis of these results we concluded that the two age-groups were drawn from equivalent populations and that it would therefore be permissible to combine them for the purposes of longitudinal analysis of the data.

The actual procedure adopted was to number the observations of the younger group from 1 to 10 and those of the older group from 11 to 18. Items that were not observed to emerge in the speech of a particular child were entered in the data matrix with the value 49. Then, in comparing any pair of items, the data from individual children were discarded if either of the following conditions applied:

(i) Both items were entered as emerging on occasion 49, that is to say, they were never observed in the speech of that child. Such cases provided no evidence of order of emergence for the pair of items under consideration.

(ii) Both items were entered as emerging on occasion 11. This could only happen in the case of older children, for whom occasion 11 was the first observation. Since it was very probable that one or both of the items had been occurring in the child's speech for some considerable time before the first observation, it was decided that to treat them as coemerging would seriously distort the evidence. The better alternative was to omit such data from the analysis.

Applying these restrictions meant that the number of children contributing data to any pairwise comparison was variable. In calculating the percentage of disconfirmatory cases, therefore, the denominator in each comparison was the number of children actually contributing relevant data.

The application of condition (ii) above led, in some comparisons, to a distortion of the true order of emergence, since there were undoubtedly cases where, for a pair of items that were both first observed on occasion 11, one truly emerged on that occasion whereas the other had been present in the child's speech for some months before the first observation was made. The result of discarding the data in such cases was to reduce the denominator for the comparison and hence to inflate the proportion of cases that yielded disconfirmatory evidence for $i \rightarrow j$. In order to avoid this distortion for those comparisons, *and only those comparisons*, where (a) 50% of the younger children were using both items in the pair and, (b) the order of emergence found in the younger children only was stronger than that found in both age-groups combined, the order found in the younger age-group was taken as definitive. (In no case did the data from the combined group suggest an order different from that found in the younger group alone.)

As a result of adopting this method of combining the data from both age-groups, it was no longer possible to relate the sequence of emergence directly to age. However, this was not seen as a disadvantage as it had been our intention to investigate sequence of emergence independently of age. For certain purposes, nevertheless, it may be important to know in general terms how the sequence maps on to age. This issue will be considered in chapter 6, where both the number of children using items and the relative frequency of items will be discussed in relation to increasing age.

Finally, before proceeding to report the results of the investigation of sequence of emergence, a proviso must be added concerning the linguistic description employed. The coding scheme designed for the project, like other linguistic descriptions, postulates systems of various kinds, the members of which enter into syntagmatic and paradigmatic relations with other members. The set of auxiliary verbs is such a system, as are the options, Declarative, Imperative, Interrogative, etc., which make up the system of Mood. From such a point of view, one can ask whether, from the evidence of the utterances that a child produces, a particular system forms part of his linguistic repertoire at any particular point and, if so, which options within the system are available to him.

This, however, is the perspective of an adult who has full command of the language and who has a systematic metalinguistic formalization of what he knows. Whilst there is occasional evidence from replacement routines, such as those reported by Weir (1962), and from puns and other chance remarks, that at least some children develop some degree of metalinguistic awareness at a remarkably early age, it remains a question for empirical investigation as to whether the systems utilized in linguistic description have a functional significance in the acquisition and development of language. And it is at least possible that the answer will vary from one child to another. However, hypotheses about development can only be tested if the speech data which provide the necessary evidence have been described in a systematic and consistent manner (Atkinson, 1982). At present, linguistic descriptions based on the speech and intuitions of mature language users provide the best hope of meeting these criteria, though it may ultimately be necessary to develop alternative transitional descriptions which are appropriate to particular stages of development. For the moment, though, we shall leave this question on one side, and continue to use the adult systems as a descriptive convenience for the presentation of the data on sequence of emergence. In keeping with this intention, we shall in this chapter concentrate on the observed sequence, leaving consideration of the possible reasons for this sequence until later.

4.3 Sentence Meaning Relations

As soon as children begin to produce utterances in which two or more words are combined, it is now generally agreed that the meanings they intend to communicate go beyond the meanings of the individual lexical items of which their utterances are composed.

Using the method of 'rich interpretation', in which both utterance form and utterance context are taken into account, the vast majority of early structured utterances can be assigned to one of a relatively small set of SMRs. The justifications for the method of rich interpretation have been carefully set out by Brown (1973): parents' ready and apparently appropriate assumption that children mean more than they are able to say, and that what they are judged to mean is usually relevant to the context of utterance; the evidence, in those languages such as English where word-order is informative, of a much greater than chance frequency of appropriate word-order for the meaning judged to be intended; and the apparent universality of the meanings attributed to early utterances by those adopting this approach to acquisition data from a wide variety of languages. However Brown also goes on to note that, whilst a number of researchers are agreed on the appropriateness of using the rich interpretation approach, they do not necessarily agree on the precise set of meaning relations to be recognized in describing early utterances. 'This is a very important fact because it makes clear that the relations or roles are abstract taxonomies applied to children's utterances. That it is not known how finely the abstraction should be sliced and that no proof exists that the semantic levels hit on by any theorist ... are psychologically functional' (Brown, 1973: 146). We certainly agree with Brown's reservation and would not wish to make any *a priori* psychological claims about the taxonomy of SMRs employed in the present investigation (described in detail in 2.4). It is intended, rather, as an instrument for exploring this aspect of language development, to be modified in the light both of the empirical evidence it generates and of theoretical developments in the understanding of infant cognition. For this reason its categories are finer-grained than those of most of the schemes discussed by Brown and it is certainly more comprehensive, in that it accounts for meaning relations that have not been observed until well after Brown's stage I. Where it is less fine-grained is in the inclusion, in the single category Operator + Nominal, of the various 'Operations' that Brown treats separately as Nomination, Recurrence and Non-existence. A further analysis in terms of these categories, of the utterances coded as Operator + Nominal, could be carried out by cross-tabulating them with the category Operator in the syntactic section of the coding, but this has not yet been carried out.

For the purposes of the present analysis, as for all those concerned with sequence of development, incomplete and uninterpretable utterances were omitted. All the remaining child utterances were analysed, each clause being assigned to one of the SMRs or to the category Unstructured. The SMRs were then grouped for the first stage of the analysis according to the type of meaning relation involved: Location and Possession, Attribution, Experiential, and Function. Order of emergence was then tested for each of these groups separately.

4.3.1 *Location and Possession*

As was the case for all the sub-systems, some of the categories of meaning relation had a very low frequency of occurrence, both in the speech produced by the children and in that addressed to them. Since the chances of observing tokens of rarely occurring categories in the speech of individual children are reduced relative to more frequently occurring categories, it was decided to combine certain pairs of categories where at least one of the pair had a low frequency of occurrence and where they differed in no more than one feature. On these grounds, all types of Locative meaning relation that included an embedded clause were combined; similarly all meaning relations involving Instrumental Cause of Change were included with their respective agentive cause of change types. With respect to Possession, since Change of Possession with Agent unspecified was relatively rare, it was combined with Agent Cause Change of Possession. Other categories not included in figure 4.2 failed to reach the criterion of emerging in the speech of at least 50% of the older group of children by the time of the last observation at five years.

Although not all items are significantly ordered with respect to all others, there are several clear trends. Firstly, Operator + Nominal precedes all other categories. Secondly, Locative relations generally precede Possessive relations. This, it might be argued, is a result of the ways in which these types of relation are typically realized syntactically. Locative relations almost always have a clausal realization (e.g. Static Location: 'Lorry out there', Gavin, 21 mths), whilst Static Possession is frequently realized through modification of the headword of a clause constituent (e.g. 'Bye-bye my box', Gavin, 24 mths). However, this does not substantially affect the general trends. For Static Possession, however expressed, tends to emerge after the expression of Static Location ($CRIT_k < 0.08$) and Change of Possession (e.g. 'Can I have one of these' (now that I've had my breakfast), Scott, 42 mths) emerges after Change of

Location (e.g. 'Where my choo-choo gone?' Gavin 24 mths) ($CRIT_k < 0.2$).

Finally, for both Location and Possession, there is a tendency for the first relation expressed to be static, followed closely by (but not coemergent with) agentively caused change. In the case of Location, Change of Location emphasizing manner of movement (e.g. 'jump', 'run', etc.) and Locative Action on a Target (e.g. 'push', 'hit', 'kiss') emerge significantly later than simple Agent cause Change of Location (e.g. 'put', 'take') ($CRIT_k < 0.08$). In the case of Possession, both Static Possession and (Agent cause) Change of Possession significantly precede the Benefactive Relation (e.g. 'That's for the doll', Theo, 42 mths) ($CRIT_k < 0.08$).

Locative meaning relations that specify the directional goal in addition to the manner of movement (e.g. 'We'll have to jump onto the fence', Jill, 42 mths) or the directional goal of an action on a target ('Now I can pull it back', Penny, 39 mths) are both late to emerge, as are those that specify the instrument involved in a change of location ('You can pick it up with your hand', Scott, 39 mths). Possessive or Benefactive Relations that include an embedded clause ('Our mum's going to make her a cardigan', Penny, 39 mths) (treated as '⟨Our mum's going to make a cardigan⟩ *be for* her') are also late to emerge. Finally, it is interesting to note that the Temporal Relation emerges at the same stage as this later group of Locative and Possessive categories.

The general picture for this sub-system can be represented as in figure 4.3. (The conventions are as explained for figure 4.2 with the addition of * = does not meet the criterion of emerging in the speech of 50% of the older cohort by the last observation.)

4.3.2 *Attribution*

The first point to note about this sub-system is the number of categories that failed to reach the criterion of emergence (see above). None of the SMRs involving Dispositional Attribution (e.g. 'The dog is friendly') or Substance Attribution (e.g. 'The box is made of wood') reached this criterion, neither did any of those involving Change of Attribution except Physical and Existence. Of the remainder, Equivalence, in which the two uniquely referring expressions are said to be equivalent (e.g. 'You're the Daddy') was considered to be so similar to Classification, where an entity is described as belonging to a class (e.g. 'He's a fireman') that the two categories were combined.

Classification clearly overlaps in intention with the operation of

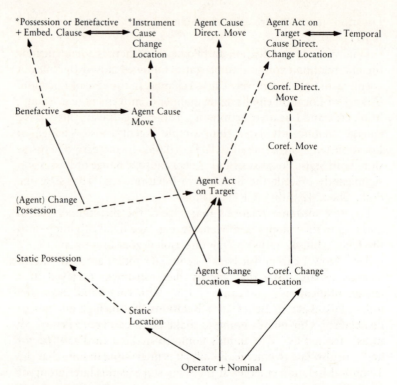

Figure 4.3 Sequence of emergence: Locative, Possessive and Temporal meaning relations

Nomination, separately treated by Brown, but here included within the overall category Operator + Nominal. For a clause to be coded as a token of the Classification meaning relation both nominal participants had to be realized (except in elliptical response to the question 'What's that?'). Not surprisingly, therefore, this meaning relation emerges significantly later than the more inclusive Operator + Nominal ($CRIT_k < 0.08$).

Both Physical Attribution (e.g. 'Is egg hot?' Christopher, 30 mths) and Evaluative Attribution (e.g. 'Teddy alright now', Christopher, 30 mths) emerge together with a trend for their emergence to follow that of Classification ($CRIT_k < 0.02$). (Agent) Change Physical Attribution (e.g. 'I won't mend it', Justin, 30 mths) also emerges at the same time. The attribution of Static Existence (e.g. 'There's got to be a tunnel', Oliver, 42 mths) emerges significantly later than Physical Attribution, reflecting perhaps its relative rarity in the language as a whole. Comparatively speaking, reference is made more frequently to Agent Change Existence (e.g. 'Can I make nests for birds?' Gerald, 42 mths) and this is reflected in its earlier emergence ($\text{CRIT}_k < 0.2$). The explanation of the late emergence of Quantitative Attribution (e.g. 'So it's three pounds' (in weight), Jill, 39 mths) is almost certainly to be found in the fact that this meaning relation is more frequently realized through modification within a nominal participant than through a clausal predicate. In fact, when both realizations of Quantitative Attribution are taken into account, this meaning relation emerges at approximately the same stage as Classification.

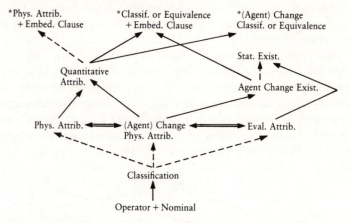

Figure 4.4 Sequence of emergence: Attributive meaning relations

4.3.3 *Experiential*
Before commenting on the order of items within this sub-system, two important points need to be made. Firstly, unlike many other child language researchers (particularly those studying American English), we have not made use of a catenative form 'wanna' either in transcription or in analysis. Thus, where others have analysed 'want to', in an utterance such as 'I *want to* play with that', as a form of auxiliary verb, we have preferred to treat 'to play with that' as the embedded clause complement to the full verb 'want'. Inevitably, this has meant that children have been credited with production of embedded clauses earlier than would otherwise have been the case, for it is as complement to 'want' or its equivalent that they first emerge, and almost always with the subject of both main and embedded clauses being coreferential, as in the above example.

Secondly, it is important to draw attention to the fact that SMRs involving speech are included within the category Agent Cause

Change of Cognitive Experience. Like 'want', verbs such as 'ask' and 'say', together with verbs that encode a Static Cognitive Experience, such as 'think' and 'know', frequently take a full clause as their complement (e.g. '(When I go round and round a lot) you see if the house moves', Jill, 42 mths). They form the second major context in which embedded clauses emerge in young children's speech.

In analysing this sub-system, certain categories were combined. For Cognitive Experience, where this was Agentively Caused, the distinction between Static (e.g. 'show', 'listen') and Changing (e.g. 'learn', 'tell') was collapsed. Additionally, all categories of Cognitive Experience followed by a clausal complement were combined in a single category.

Two main trends emerge from this analysis. Firstly, there is a trend for the various types of Experiential meaning to emerge in the order: Wanting – Cognitive – Physical/Affective. Secondly, for those meaning relations that may involve a clause complement, the form with a simple nominal complement (e.g. 'I know that') precedes the more complex form with a clause complement (e.g. 'I know it's hot'). The general picture for this sub-system is as figure 4.5.

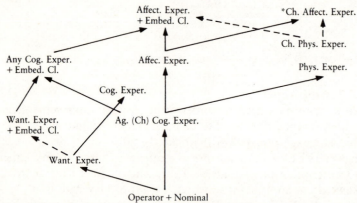

Figure 4.5 Sequence of emergence: Experiential meaning relations

4.3.4 *Function*

The Function categories form a rather heterogeneous group. What they have in common is the notion of actions which are intrinsic to the entities concerned. Thus, bells ring and kettles boil (Patient Function); dogs bark and children play, etc. (Agent Function). In some cases the function is carried out with respect to a Patient (e.g.

'He's eating the saucepan', Jill, 42 mths, referring to a guinea pig) or the Agent causes an object to perform its normal function (e.g. 'Mummy's put the light off', Jimmy, 39 mths). Not very different, and included with the Function sub-system for this analysis, are the Neutral, or unspecified action (e.g. 'I'll do it', 'What shall we do?'), the relation of Agent Cause Agent Act, where the second clause is realized as the embedded complement of the first (e.g. '(We thought) we could make the jeep go', Jimmy, 39 mths) and Happen (e.g. 'What happened?')

In this sub-system, the first categories to emerge are Unspecified Action and the group Agent Function, Patient Function and Agent Function on Patient. Agent Cause Patient to Function and Agent Function over Range (e.g. 'What's you playing, Jo?' Emma, 36 mths, to mother, who is playing snakes and ladders) emerge somewhat later ($CRIT_k < 0.2$) as do all meaning relations involving embedded clauses. In the last group to reach criterion are Happen and Purposive + Embedded Clause (e.g. 'Mummy, is that to make jelly?' Elspeth, 42 mths). (See figure 4.6.)

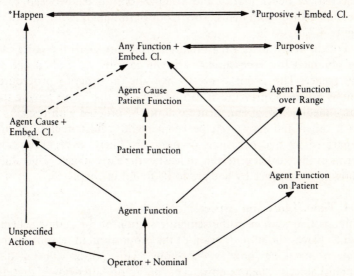

Figure 4.6 Sequence of emergence: Function meaning relations

4.3.5 *Sentence Meaning Relations: the full system*
Up to this point, the SMRs have been discussed as separate sub-systems. This was partly for convenience of presentation, since the number of categories is too great for a single table to be

intelligible. But there is also an important sense in which the items within sub-systems share features of meaning that they do not share with items in other sub-systems – at least from the point of view of the semantic theory that underlies the taxonomy. However, there are similarities of other kinds that cut across the sub-systems, as these have been semantically defined. For example, the category Agent Act on Target is in many respects similar to Agent Function with respect to Patient, in that both involve a simple transitive relationship between Agent and Patient, realized through the syntactic structure *S-V-O*. There are clearly also similarities between all categories in which the complement is realized by an embedded clause.

To explore these and other relationships between the various types of meaning relation, it is necessary to make comparisons between the different sub-systems. One way of doing this would be to extend the procedure for pairwise comparisons to all possible pairs of meaning relations. However, this would be extremely laborious. Instead, certain items within each sub-system have been selected as bench-marks and comparisons made between each possible pair of such items. The results of this analysis are shown in figure 4.7.

For the remainder, a reasonably satisfactory general picture can be obtained by representing each category by its median age of emergence. This is not as precise as using the ordering procedure, but as a general principle it can be assumed that items having the same median age of emergence will not be ordered with respect to each other and may even be coemergent, whilst items that are separated by two occasions or more are likely to be ordered in terms of the weaker criterion, at least in the early stages. (The tables showing emergence by age are to be found in chapter 6.)

4.4 Time, Tense and Aspect

Time is that system in the semantic section of the coding scheme which places the state or event of the proposition in relation to the time of speaking 'now' v. 'not-now', with 'not-now' being distinguishable as 'before-now', i.e. 'past', or 'after-now', that is, 'future'. Time is thus a 'notional' category (Lyons, 1968) and is independent, at least in theory, from the system of tense, through which it is syntactically realized. In practice, of course, once the child has the syntactic resources for marking tense, this becomes the chief clue to the intended time reference; but even before this is fully under control, the intended time reference of most utterances can

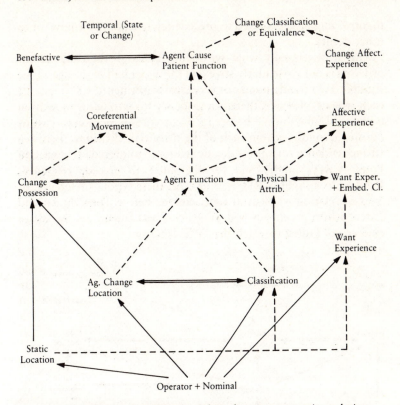

Figure 4.7 Sequence of emergence: Selected sentence meaning relations

be inferred by reference to the context and from temporal adverbial expressions, if they occur.

In addition to the notional three-term deictic contrast of now, before-now and after-now, time can be specified in relation to other events, e.g. 'when the volcano erupted' or to 'absolutes' such as 'in 1972', 'at 3 o'clock'. Both deictic and fixed points can then be used to make reference to times 'before', 'after', 'during', 'until', 'since' those points. The extent, or duration, of an event or its frequency may also be specified. Taking reference to the time-of-speaking as a neutral starting point, one might predict that the deictic contrasts of past and future would be the first to emerge both because they are conceptually simpler than 'secondary' reference to other events or to absolute times and because they have a less complex syntactic realization. Within the more specific types of reference, reference to a particular point in time might be expected to be the first to emerge, and both for this and for the secondary types, reference to 'now' might be expected to precede references to 'not-now' or to other events.

This was generally what we found, although the evidence for ordering is not particularly strong in the upper half of the age-range studied. Two trends stand out very clearly (see figure 4.8). First, for each type of reference, there is a tendency for it to occur in relation to Neutral time ('now') before its occurrence in relation to Past or Future. Secondly, within each of the three time divisions, there is a strong tendency for simple deictic reference to precede reference to Point ($CRIT_k < 0.08$) and for the latter to precede references Relative to a Point ($CRIT_k < 0.08$). All these types of reference, at least in relation to Neutral time, emerge before Time Up To and Extent whilst Frequency and Time From and During are the last to emerge, all failing to reach the 50% criterion.

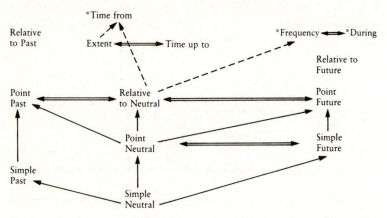

Figure 4.8 Sequence of emergence: Time

Finally, we have found, as would be expected, that where time was specified by reference to point of utterance or to another event, such specifications were first realized by means of a single adverb (e.g. 'now', 'later', 'yesterday') then by prepositional phrases (e.g. 'I want you to be my mummy for ever and ever', David, 39 mths) and finally by subordinate clauses (e.g. 'He's going to come out when he's eaten this', Geraldine, 42 mths, referring to her hamster which was chewing a toilet roll).

Aspect, as Lyons (1968) notes, is a category that includes a number of distinctions, most of which are not mutually exclusive. A clause, therefore, can express a number of aspectual modifications. What all these modifications have in common is that they are concerned with the temporal status of the event or state encoded in the proposition, rather than with its location in time.

As with the category Time, it is the syntactic form of the utterance that provides the strongest evidence that an aspectual modification is intended, but here too a decision does not depend solely on the full and correct syntactic realization of the distinction in question. This is particularly so for Continuous and Perfect Aspect, as the intention can be clear when either part of the discontinuous structure is present in the utterance. In fact, in the speech of most children, the first realization of Continuous Aspect to emerge lacks the auxiliary (e.g. 'I running') and the same is true of Perfect Aspect (e.g. 'I done it').

Both Continuous and Perfect Aspect emerge at the same time and significantly before any of the other aspectual distinctions ($CRIT_k < 0.08$). The next to emerge is Completive. This is perhaps to be expected, since its most frequent realization is 'have finished', which can be seen as a very specific type of perfect aspect.[1] Cessive ('stop'), Habitual ('used to', 'always'), Inceptive ('begin'), Iterative and Durative ('keep on') all have specific lexical realizations. This may account for the fact that they are both infrequent and not significantly ordered.

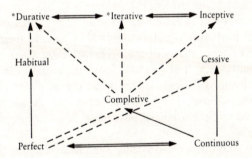

Figure 4.9 Sequence of emergence: Aspect

From what has already been said, it will come as no surprise that few generalizations can be made about the syntactic realizations of the categories of Time and Aspect. There are essentially three reasons for this. Firstly, with regard to tense, the picture is clouded by the strong possibility that children proceed to the mastery of 'regular' and 'irregular' past forms in different ways. In general, certain specific irregular forms are the first to emerge, quite possibly learned as unanalysed lexical items, followed somewhat later by one or two regular forms. What typically then happens is that the 'rule' for past tense is quickly generalized to many other regular verbs and, by many children, to irregular verbs as well, leading to a wide variety of 'over-regularizations' sometimes with more than one 'incorrect' form being used simultaneously for an irregular verb which, only a few weeks previously, had occurred in its 'correct' form.

A second problem area has already been hinted at with respect to continuous and perfect aspect. As Labov's (1972b) studies have shown for certain dialects of American English, the inclusion of the auxiliary element of these discontinuous forms is governed by quite complex variable rules. This also proves to be the case for at least some of the families in our study. Whilst the presence of the auxiliary seems to be obligatory for all adults in negative declarative and polar interrogative sentences, utterances such as 'Where you been?', 'What you doing?', 'Look what he done', 'I going to take you up the playschool', are sufficiently frequent in the speech addressed to some children for there to be doubt about the significance of such forms when they persist in the speech of children. Are they evidence of immaturity, that is to say that the child has not fully mastered the adult model, or are they evidence that the adult model that is being mastered is not as straightforward as speakers of Standard English believe it to be?

A third problem is raised by Fletcher (1981). All regular verbs have a past participle which is identical in form to their past tense. The same is true of many of the irregular verbs which children use very frequently (e.g. 'put', 'made', 'got'). If, as has been argued, the first realization of Perfect Aspect omits the auxiliary element, it is not always possible, in particular cases, to decide whether an utterance contains a token of past tense or of (incomplete) Perfect Aspect.

For these and other reasons, any attempt to describe the sequence of acquisition and of the syntactic rules for realizing the semantic distinctions of Time and Aspect in English would require observations made at much more frequent intervals than was the case in the present study. It would also be desirable to have more detailed information about the immediate context, so that ambiguities such as the one just referred to could be resolved. However it also seems likely that there will be considerable individual differences in the route that is taken from first correct use to full mastery of the organization of the verbal group in English. This, then, is a domain in which data based on 'emergence' are likely to be more misleading than informative.

4.5 Modal and Modulation

Although conceptually distinct, as Halliday (1970) makes clear, the categories of Modal and Modulation are best treated together, as they overlap very considerably in their realization through the system of auxiliary verbs. Treated within the context of the development of the auxiliary verb system as a whole, data on the emergence of the categories of Modal and Modulation up to the age of 42 months have already been reported elsewhere (Wells, 1979a). This section will therefore merely summarize the relevant sections of that report and extend the findings up to the age of five years.

First, however, a note of explanation. In the 'semantic' section of the *Coding Manual*, the category Modal is described as a system with three terms: Certain, Possible/Probable, Inference; and Modulation as a category with seven terms: Willing, Ability, Permission, Obligation, Necessity, Try and Success. In the syntactic section, where certain individual auxiliaries are distinguished by unique codings, the modal auxiliaries are treated as a group and not given separate codings. At the time when the *Coding Manual* was being constructed, this seemed a sensible economy of coding effort. Later, however, it became apparent that this had been a mistaken decision, as it precluded any detailed study of the development of the auxiliary verb system. When it was subsequently decided that such a study might be of considerable interest, both in its own right and for the opportunity that it provided for investigating the relative influence of a number of factors on order of emergence, a considerably more delicate analysis was carried out of all the relevant data from the younger sample of children. It is on these data that the report was based. Unfortunately, it has not been possible to extend this analysis to the recordings of the older sample and this has resulted, inevitably, in a certain disjunction between the two sets of results. The solution that will be adopted is to describe first the results for both age-groups that are derived from the two systems as defined in the *Coding Manual*. These will then be amplified by reference to the more delicate analysis of the data from the younger children only.

Of the two systems, the Modal system is later to emerge than at least the first of the options within Modulation. Possible is the first of the three options to emerge, with Certain next ($CRIT_k < 0.2$) and Inference last ($CRIT_k < 0.08$), although the latter pair are not significantly ordered with respect to each other. With Modulation, a group consisting of Ability, Permission, and Willing comes first, with the first two emerging significantly ($CRIT_k < 0.08$) before a second group consisting of Obligation and Necessity, which coemerge with Possible in the Modal system. Try and Success, which are arguably not true members of the Modulation system, are significantly later still ($CRIT_k < 0.08$), with Success tending to be later than Try, and coemergent with Inference in the Modal system. The inter-relationships among the two systems are shown in figure 4.10.

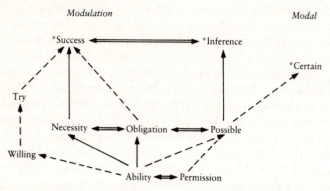

Figure 4.10 Sequence of emergence: Modal and Modulation

Turning now to the data from the younger children only, a further note of explanation must be added. In the earlier report (Wells, 1979a), order of emergence was based only on median occasion of emergence, as the procedure for testing the hypotheses of ordering and of coemergence had not been developed at that time. The results reported here will differ somewhat from that original report as the procedures outlined at the beginning of this chapter have the advantage of being both more stringent and independent of age. However the more delicate classification of Modal and Modulation meanings will be retained in the following discussion of the auxiliary verb forms of which they are the realizations.

In that report, a description of modal auxiliaries was proposed in terms of a matrix, the cells of which are defined by the two dimensions of Degrees and Types of modality. Four Degrees were proposed: Possible, Predictable, Necessary and Actual; and five Types: Inference, Likelihood, Constraint, Potential and Performative. On the dimension of Degree, the distinctions are self-explanatory; in the case of the strongest degree, Actual, there is no qualification and, typically, no modality is expressed. The most important distinction with respect to Type concerns the perspective adopted towards the event or state described in the proposition. In the case of Potential, the meaning of the modal verb concerns the Agent's potentiality (ability or intention to act) in relation to the event, and in the case of Constraint it concerns the presence or absence of constraints on the Agent's performance of the act. By contrast, in the Likelihood type, the modal meaning is concerned with the probability of the event being actualized (or, in the case of logical discourse, of the proposition being true), whilst in the Inference type, the probability of an event which is not directly known is inferred from other information which is available. Finally, by contrast with the other types, Performative meanings are concerned with the acts that are performed by virtue of uttering the sentences that contain them.

To make the distinctions between the Types of Modality clearer, consider the following examples:

Potential: 'I can swim five lengths now.'
Constraint: 'We can/may stay up till 10 o'clock tonight.' 'It's raining, so we can't go out.'
Likelihood: 'The forecast says there may/could/might be snow today.'
Inference: (Telephone rings) 'That will/must be my mother. She usually rings at about this time.'
Performative: 'You may/can have a sweet now you have finished your dinner.' 'You can't have that one.' (*prohibition*)

The full matrix (with the omission of the Actual degree) is set out in table 4.5 and the order of emergence in figure 4.11.

Of the various meaning–form pairs shown in figure 4.11, only nine reach criterion by the age of 42 months. Of these, three out of the first four fall within the Potential modality; 'can' (ability), 'will' (intention) and 'be going to' (intention). The fourth 'can' (request permission), belongs to the Performative type of modality. In the earlier report, 'can' (permission) was found to have a median age of emergence one occasion later than 'can' (ability). When evaluated by θ, however, the two meanings of 'can' are found to be coemergent. This suggests that the modal auxiliary form 'can' is one of the first two to emerge in the speech of almost every child, with a majority using it simultaneously to express both the Potential and the Performative meaning. With this exception, the order previously reported is confirmed here: the first modality meanings to be expressed have to do with the Agent's potentiality for action. These precede the first expression of Likelihood, 'will' (predict)

Table 4.5 *Meanings realized by modal auxiliaries (adapted from Wells, 1979a)*

	Inference	Likelihood	Constraint	Potential	Performative
Possible	*Tentative possible* might, could *Possible* may, can	*Tentative possible* might, could *Possible* may, can *+Contrafactual* could, would	*Lack of constraint:* *Permitted* can, may *Circumstantial* *possibility* can, could	*Ability* can, be able to *Intrinsic Potential* can, will	*Request/Grant permission* can, may, could might *Request/Offer Action* can, may, could will, shall, would would like
Predictable	*Probable* will	*Predict* will, shall, be V+ing, be going to *Habitual* will, would		*Intention/Volition* will, shall, be V+ing, be going to *Insistence* will, would	*Command* shall, will, can *Suggestion/Request* *Evaluate Intention* shall, would like
Necessary	*Tentative Conclusive* should, ought *Conclusive* must, have to, have got to		*Advisable* had better *Obligation* should, ought *Required* must, have got to, (will) have to *+Contrafactual* should, ought		*Formulation of* *Advisability* had better *Formulation of* *Obligation* should, ought *Formulation of* *Requirement* must, have got to, have to, be to

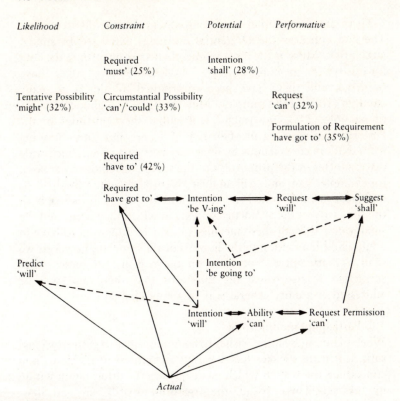

Figure 4.11 Sequence of emergence: Modal auxiliaries

$(\text{CRIT}_k < 0.2)$. They also precede the first expression of Constraint, 'have got to' (required) $(\text{CRIT}_k < 0.08)$ and – apart from 'can' (request permission) – the first two Performative meanings, 'will' (request) $(\text{CRIT}_k < 0.2)$ and 'shall' (suggest) $(\text{CRIT}_k < 0.08)$.

As no comparable data are available from the older group of children, there may be some value in reporting what evidence there is about those meanings that have emerged in the speech of at least some of the children but have failed to reach the 50% criterion. Since there is a general tendency for the age at which any particular item emerges to be correlated with the proportion of the sample to have used that item by any occasion within the period studied, we can take the differing proportions of users at 42 months as a rough indication of order of emergence after that age. Taking the arbitrary cut-off point of 25% of children showing use, the overall picture to emerge from the analysis of the younger children's data is as represented in the upper part of figure 4.11.

There are three rather surprising absences from this sequence. The first concerns the Inferential meanings expressed by modal auxiliaries. 'Must' is the most frequently occurring form in the data for this type of meaning, but by 42 months only seven tokens have occurred, and these have been contributed by almost as many children (10% of the sample). 'May' with the Likelihood meaning of possible (3%) and 'ought' with either the Constraint or the Performative meaning of obligation (3%) are also form–meaning pairs that are conspicuous by their very rare occurrence. Such wide discrepancies in the proportion of the sample using them between, for example, 'can' and 'will' in their Potential meanings (both 98%) and those just mentioned are all the more surprising in view of both the similarity of the syntactic contexts in which they occur and the significance that all these meanings might be supposed to have in adult–child interaction in the home. For the moment, however, we shall not attempt to speculate on the reasons for these rather surprising results, since the questions that they raise will be addressed in a more general way in a later chapter.

4.6 Participant modification

When planning what he wishes to communicate in a conversational turn, a mature speaker has a variety of options available to him concerning the way in which he distributes the information within his message. These include the organization of 'given' and 'new' information (Clark and Haviland, 1977), and of 'theme' and 'rheme' (Halliday, 1967b); he must also decide whether to disperse his information over a number of short, simple sentences or over a smaller number of more complex sentences, in which a substantial proportion of the information is contained in embedded or subordinate clauses or phrases. However, perhaps the simplest device available for increasing the density of a message is the inclusion of some of the information as a modification of one of the semantic participants in a simple proposition. Instead of saying 'I saw a woman. She was old. She had an umbrella', one can convey very much the same information in a more condensed manner by saying 'I saw an old woman with an umbrella'. From a syntactic point of view, some of the information that has been packed into the denser version of the message occurs as an adjectival modifier, 'old', preceding the headword 'woman', whilst the remainder occurs as a phrasal qualifier, 'with an umbrella', following the same headword. From a semantic point of view, however, both 'old' and 'with an umbrella' are modifications of the participant 'woman'.

According to Chomsky's (1965) model of transformational grammar, noun-phrase adjectival modification is derived by various transformations from a simple sentence containing a predicate adjective. Post-nominal qualifiers are similarly derived by transformations from simple sentences of other kinds. Whatever the psychological significance of this description for actual sentence production, it gives salience to the substantial similarity that exists between the various types of SMR considered above and the types of semantic modification that can occur in relation to the participants in simple sentences. That is to say, for most of the basic SMRs, there is a corresponding type of modification:

'The woman was old'	Static Physical Attribution SMR
'The old woman'	Physical Attributive Modification
'She had an umbrella'	Static Possession SMR
'with an umbrella'	Possessive Modification

Given the considerable correspondence between the two sets of categories, two questions are worthy of investigation: (1) Is the order in which the types of modification emerge similar to that observed for the SMRs? (2) Is there a systematic tendency for those meanings that are common to both systems to emerge first in propositional form and only later in modification, or vice versa?

Before attempting to answer either of these questions, however, it is necessary to review the evidence concerning the emergence of the different types of modification. Of the 16 categories for which there is a closely corresponding SMR, only ten reach criterion by the age of five. On the other hand, there are other categories of modification for which there is no straightforward equivalent. Instrumental modification, for example, is similar in some respects to the SMR Static Purpose (cf. 'carving knife', 'This knife is for carving the meat') but this latter category is too narrow to cover such other examples as 'laundry bag', 'dancing shoes'. (Also included in the classification of modification is sentential modification, which does not rightly belong in this system at all, since it describes the structural relationship of the modifier to the participant modified rather than the type of modification. It is included here to allow comparison between the semantic and the syntactic levels of description.)

Since modification can additionally be comparative or superlative, there is provision for these features to be added to each of the basic categories. One such combination, Comparative Quantity, reaches criterion within the period, but for this category, too, there is no equivalent SMR.

Amongst the categories that reach or almost reach criterion by the age of five, the evidence for order suggests that there are three broad stages, with at least some of the items emerging at each stage being significantly ordered ($CRIT_k < 0.08$) with respect to some of those emerging in the preceding or following stage. At the first stage are Possessive ('my', 'John's'), Quantity ('two') and Physical Attribute ('red', 'heavy'). Evaluative ('nice', 'naughty'), Equivalence ('same') and Instrumental all emerge together at the second stage, and the remainder fall into two groups of coemergent categories, which together make up the third stage. In the first group are Substance ('wooden'), Locative ('*kitchen* chair', 'pond *in the park*') and Comparative Quantity ('more'); in the second, Dispositional ('*friendly* dog'), Function ('broken'), Temporal ('next') and Ordinal ('first'). Sentential modification, where the modifier is realized as a relative clause, is coemergent with Instrumental Purpose at the

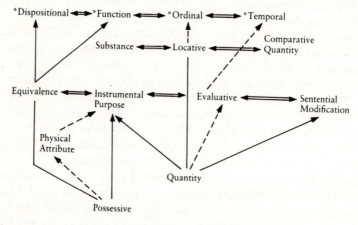

Figure 4.12 Sequence of emergence: Participant modification

second stage (see figure 4.12). With this information we are now in a position to attempt to answer the two questions posed above.

1. Is the order of emergence similar for both SMRs and types of modification? When the orders of emergence, based on median occasion of emergence for the two systems, are submitted to rank-order correlational analysis, the resulting coefficient is close to zero. This indicates that there is no relationship between the two orders.

2. Is there a tendency for meanings to emerge in one system earlier than in the other? Here the answer is variable. In the case of Locative, Evaluative and Equivalence, emergence is earlier in the system of SMRs. In the case of Quantity and Substance, on the other hand, the order is the reverse. And in the case of Possessive and Physical Attribution, the evidence does not support either order.

What the answers to these two questions suggest, therefore, is that, although at an abstract and theoretical level there may be a relationship between the two systems, this is not systematically exploited by children in the course of acquisition. The main reason for this seems to be that, although most SMRs can occur as participant modification, and vice versa, in many cases there is a 'preference' for encoding a particular type of meaning in one system rather than the other. Locative meanings, for example, are more readily expressed in the form of SMRs, whereas quantity occurs more readily in participant modification. There are, however, some types of meaning which are almost equally likely to occur in either system. Under these conditions, it appears, children are able to exploit the positional alternation, though it may still be the case that they show individual preferences for one position rather than the other in relation to particular lexical items.

4.7 Participant Headword

Within the case grammatical descriptive model on which much of the semantic coding is based, the propositional component of a sentence consists of the verb and the various participants that are in case relations to the verb. As explained in chapter 2, these participants may be obligatory or optional, the optional participants including manner, superordinate locatives, benefactives, etc. Participants are most typically realized syntactically through a noun phrase, with the addition of a preposition in some cases to mark the case relationship or to specify the type of locative. In some instances, however, the participant may be realized adverbially and, in our analysis, also adjectivally, as where the 'verb' of the proposition takes the form of copula + predicative adjective. In this case the adjective is treated as realizing a participant for the purposes of the syntactic analysis.

In analysing Headword, therefore, we are concerned with a syntactic system, but one whose scope is defined in relation to the realization of the participants in the (semantic) proposition. Typically, the headword is a noun or pronoun and, for this reason, we shall also refer to this system as that of the Nominal Headword. However, as explained, the system also includes adverbs and predicative adjectives and, to complicate matters still further, modifying adjectives which are elliptically functioning as headword (e.g. 'Pass me the red', 'I've got the biggest').

Within this system, pronouns are considered as classes only: Personal, Demonstrative, Indefinite, etc. Order of emergence within the classes of pronouns will be dealt with in the following section. One further addition is the Intensifier. All headwords may optionally be intensified (e.g. 'This is *very* big', '*Just* John came').

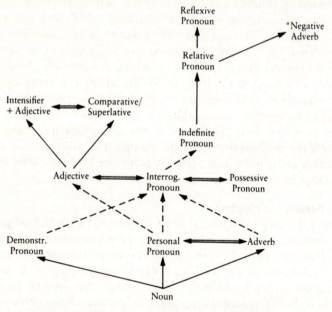

Figure 4.13 Sequence of emergence: Participant Headword

As will be seen from figure 4.13, the evidence shows a rather clear sequence of emergence for the Headword system, as just defined, with all the categories except Negative Adverb (e.g. 'never') reaching criterion by five years. It should be pointed out, however, that for the classes of pronoun, the claim for emergence is based on the occurrence of the first member of each class. The sequence seems to split very neatly into six stages, with items at each stage ordered with respect to items at each of the others, if the weaker criterion of ordering is adopted. Items within each stage also show a strong tendency to meet the criterion for coemergence.

4.8 Pronouns

Each of the classes of pronoun was treated as a separate sub-system for the purposes of coding. The intention was to test for order within each sub-system separately before considering the system as a whole. As will be seen from figure 4.14, however, only Personal and Demonstrative pronouns emerge in full by the age of five; in the other sub-systems only some of the options are being used at all widely. For example, the only reflexive pronoun to be used by most children is 'myself' and amongst the relative pronouns there is a very strong preference for 'what', whatever the syntactic relationship of the pronominalized constituent in the relative clause to its headword in the main clause (e.g. 'This is the ball *what* we bought at the Habitat', 'There's the boy *what's* in my class at school', David, 42 mths).

As already noted in the discussion of Headword, the first group of pronouns to emerge are all deictic and refer to two of the three points of the communication triangle: 'I' (the speaker) and 'it', 'that' (the spoken about). From this point of view, 'it' and 'that' might be described as being initially in free variation although subsequently, of course, they come to communicate differentiated meanings. The next group to emerge, which are also deictic in function, includes two coemergent pairs, 'you' and 'me', and the two interrogative words 'what?' and 'where?' Strictly speaking, 'where?' should not be included with the pronouns but, as one of the set of interrogative words that can occur as head of the noun phrase, it seems very probable that, for the learner, it forms part of the same system as 'what?' and 'who?' In any case as it is locative relationships which account for the largest part of the content of early utterances, it is not surprising to see the two interrogative words that correspond to the Patient and Location terms of such relationships emerging early and together.

At the third stage, the major development is seen in the personal pronoun sub-system, where 'he', 'she', 'we', 'they' and 'them' all emerge in a group with no significant internal ordering but with only 'they' and 'them' coemergent. At first sight it might appear that there is no clear pattern here, but systematic relationships become apparent if comparisons are made across as well as within stages. Looked at from this point of view, it is clear that for both the first and the third person there is a clear tendency for singular pronouns to emerge before plurals ('I' → 'we' ($\text{CRIT}_k < 0.08$), 'me' → 'us' ($\text{CRIT}_k < 0.08$), 'it' → 'they'/'them' ($\text{CRIT}_k < 0.08$)) and to a lesser extent for subjective forms to emerge before the corresponding objective forms (e.g. 'we' → 'us' (CRIT$_k$ < 0.08)). The singular before plural order is not disconfirmed by the close emergence of 'he' and 'she' with 'they', as 'they' can reasonably be seen as first emerging as the plural of 'it'. On the other hand, the coemergence of 'they' and 'them' certainly weakens the argument for subjective before objective forms.

There is also some indication that, amongst the animate third person singular forms, there is a tendency for masculine to precede feminine. A possible explanation for this rather intriguing pattern is to be found in the typical pattern of child-rearing – mother spending her day at home with the children while father is out at work. Under these conditions it would not be surprising if the absent parent were referred to more frequently, thus leading to the earlier emergence of 'he' and 'him'.

Also emerging at the third stage are 'this' (clearly later than 'that' at stage one (CRIT$_k$ < 0.08) and earlier than 'these' and 'those' at stage four (CRIT$_k$ < 0.08)), 'one', which is the first of the indefinite pronouns to emerge, and 'mine', which is the first of the possessive pronouns.

At stage four there is another large cluster of coemerging items which includes the last of the personal and demonstrative pronouns and the first of the relative pronouns. Thereafter the remaining pronouns to reach criterion by five years show little evidence of order and none of coemergence.

In summary, by five years of age, most children have some control over all the main classes of pronoun, but several individual pronouns still remain to emerge.

4.9 Clause coordination and subordination

In this section we are concerned with the relationships between clauses that are realized through coordination and subordination. These relationships will be considered from a syntactic point of view in the following chapter; here we shall be concerned with the type of relationships involved considered from a semantic point of view. Nevertheless, the items that we shall be examining are conjunctions, but with sub-categorization where necessary to mark semantic distinctions which are not apparent in the form of the conjunctions alone. For example, 'so' is sub-categorized as: Result (e.g. 'He didn't cough like that so he's not having any mixture is he Mummy?', Andrea, 60 mths); Purpose, that is, 'so that' (e.g. 'Put it on the bottom so she can be very nice and sleepy', Judith, 60 mths, referring to her dog, which she is pushing around in her doll's pram); and Linker (e.g. (I've finished eating) 'So can I take my microphone off?' Nicholas, 54 mths).

One of the consequences of using the evidence of the actual conjunctions is that emergence cannot be treated as evidence that the child has understood the full logical force of the relationship that a particular conjunction encodes in adult speech. From the syntactically appropriate use of 'because' in 'Don't spit on it 'cos it's made of paint' (Gary, 42 mths), for example, one might not wish to infer that Gary had a clear understanding of the reason why spitting was forbidden. On the other hand the considerably younger Gerald (27 mths) expresses a relationship of reason which is syntactically well formed and, as his mother indicates by her reply, situationally plausible as well:

Gerald: 'I didn't see many little worms 'cos they were hiding in the water'
Mother: 'Were they? They hide underneath the sand don't they?'

Emergence in this case, therefore, is restricted to the emergence of the different types of coordination and subordination as evidenced by the first occurrence of the relevant conjunctions in appropriate syntactic contexts.

With this proviso, the emergence of the types of relationship between clauses that reach criterion by five years can be described as occurring in four stages. 'And' is the first relationship to emerge and this significantly precedes all others ($CRIT_k < 0.08$). 'Because' is coemergent in the second stage with 'when', which is the only temporal subordinating item to reach criterion by five years. At the third stage 'but' and 'if' are coemergent, with the latter ordered later than 'because' ($CRIT_k < 0.2$). At the fourth stage there are two groups. In the first are narrative 'and then', 'or', 'in order to', realized simply as 'to' (e.g. 'I need them to hang this washing out', Stella, 60 mths, referring to clothes pegs) and 'so' utterance initial linker, all coemergent. 'That', as clause introducer (e.g. 'I'm sorry to say that the people that made it I think are a bit silly', Jonathan, 60 mths) also coemerges with this group. In the second group are three items which, although not ordered with respect to the first group, are distinct from them in that they all fail to reach criterion by five years. This group consists of 'so' (result) 'so/so that' (purpose) and 'if/whether' as clause introducer.

At first sight, it might seem surprising that the temporal relations that are realized by 'until', 'before', 'since', etc. do not reach criterion by five years, seeing that the temporal categories Time up

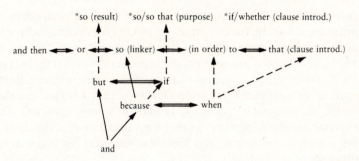

Figure 4.15 Sequence of emergence: Sentence conjoining

to, Time from and Relative to Past do reach criterion. The most probable explanation is that, in the majority of cases, these temporal relationships are phrasally (e.g. 'until tomorrow', 'before tea') rather than clausally realized.

4.10 Mood

Having considered the major systems in terms of which the propositional content of utterances is organized, we shall turn now to the other major dimension of meaning – the functions that utterances perform as communicative acts. As is generally recognized, there is no simple, one-to-one relationship between the function of an utterance and either its propositional content or its syntactic form. Nevertheless, it is equally clear that content and form together provide the linguistic evidence on which, in context, the functional interpretation of an utterance is based, and it is the choice of mood which gives the most important cue. Before proceeding to investigate the development of the functional repertoire, therefore, we shall look first at the sequence of emergence of the options in the mood system.

Sometimes described in terms of canonical form, the relationship between mood choice and functional meaning is one of probability. Sentences in the imperative mood have an extremely high probability of being intended and interpreted as commands; sentences in declarative and *wh-* interrogative mood have a high probability of association with, respectively, the giving and requesting of information; and polar interrogatives have a reasonably high probability of association with requests for confirmation or denial of the associated proposition, although in everyday conversation they probably have an equally strong association with requests concerned with the present or future actions of the conversational participants. Viewed from the somewhat different perspective of discourse structure, the options in the mood system can also be seen as being ranged on a dimension of prospectiveness (Wells *et al.*, 1981), according to the strength of the expectations that they set up for a response. The selection of imperative or interrogative mood leads to an utterance being strongly prospective: a response, either verbal or non-verbal or both, is very definitely expected. The expectation of a response is weaker for a declarative, particularly if the sentence is elliptical; and moodless sentences have almost no prospective force at all.

Fúll mastery of the subtleties of mood selection to achieve particular functional effects in context is not attained until well after the period covered by this study, but acquisition of the syntactic contrasts involved certainly takes place during the pre-school years, as does the development of some understanding of the functional and discourse potential of the different options. Indeed, as we shall see, the ability to communicate more than a very restricted set of functional intentions is dependent on this development.

The mood system, as defined in the *Coding Manual*, distinguishes the four major options – Declarative, Imperative, Interrogative and Moodless – and divides Interrogative into Polar and *Wh-*. A further distinction is made within *wh-* interrogatives, with 'why' interrogatives being coded separately. Tags are also coded separately, as are Declarative + Tag and Imperative + Tag. In order to avoid artificial inflation of the frequency of declaratives, utterances intended as Yes/No or Content Questions, but marked as such by a specific intonation contour rather than by the appropriate syntactic structure with subject–auxiliary inversion, were coded separately. Figure 4.16 gives the data on order of emergence.

Given the extremely limited syntactic resources of the child who is restricted to one- or two-word utterances, it is inevitable that his earliest utterances should be coded as Moodless, but, at this stage, it is hardly appropriate to treat this as an option from the mood system. The first real development comes with the emergence of the opposition between declarative and imperative. These two options coemerge and precede any of the forms of interrogative mood ($\text{CRIT}_k < 0.2$). However, this is a case of coemergence with both orders equally strongly supported. Within the interrogatives, there is a tendency for *wh-* interrogative to emerge before polar interrogative, with the 'why' sub-category being significantly later than other *wh-* forms ($\text{CRIT}_k < 0.08$). As Brown and Hanlon (1970)

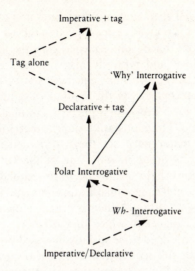

Figure 4.16 Sequence of emergence: Mood

predicted, tags do not emerge until after the emergence of polar interrogatives ($CRIT_k < 0.08$) and utterances consisting of a tag alone are later to emerge than those in which a tag is appended to a declarative. Interestingly, there is considerable individual variation in how soon tags are used, once the prerequisite components are present. In no child's speech are they used productively before polar interrogatives are widely used but, whilst some children begin to use them almost as soon as they have reached this stage, others do not do so until many months later.

4.11 Inter-Personal Purpose

As well as being 'about' some aspect of experience, conversation is a form of action. Utterances, therefore, both refer to some event or state of affairs (propositional content) and convey the speaker's intentions as to how the hearer should 'take' the information encoded in the proposition. These intentions are what is coded by Functions. Since utterances typically occur as part of a conversation, their functions also contribute to the turn-by-turn organization that is necessary for successful interaction.

As described in chapter 2, the taxonomy of functions was divided into a number of sub-systems according to the major purposes that sequences of conversation are intended to achieve: Control, Expressive, Representational, Tutorial and Social. However, although the purpose of a sequence may be apparent in retrospect, to participants as well as to analysts, the largest unit of conversational organization that is typically experienced in the act of conversing is the sub-sequence.[2] Each sub-sequence consists of an 'initiating' (prospective) move and typically also of one 'responding' (less strongly prospective) move. Sub-sequences may be initiated for any of the purposes recognized in the analysis of sequences; they may also be initiated for a Procedural purpose – to manage the channel of communication. Functions are grouped, therefore, according to which of these major purposes they are intended to serve. The initiating functions occur in only one of the six sub-sequences. However, functions that typically occur in responding moves such as Acknowledge or Request Justification, may be found in almost every sub-sequence, although their precise significance depends on the type of sub-sequence in which they occur.

Every utterance judged to be socially intended was coded according to the type of sub-sequence in which it occurred and, within sub-sequence, according to its function. Simultaneous codings were not permitted. Where an utterance was considered to be realizing two functions simultaneously, a decision had to be made as to which function was dominant, and only that function was coded. Secondary codings were permitted, however, for utterances that contained two or more clauses, where the second (or later) clause provided a Justification or some other form of modification of the intention realized by the primary function.

4.11.1 *Control functions*

One of the most commonly occurring functions within this sub-system is Request. In the *Coding Manual* the label used is Command, but as the category includes Indirect as well as Direct Requests, the label Request is a more accurate descriptor. The distinction between direct and indirect requests is made in terms of the mood selected in the utterance. Direct Requests are realized by the selection of imperative mood, Indirect Requests by the selection of interrogative or declarative mood. Other Control functions in which declarative mood occurs are Wanting (e.g. 'Want a polo', Benjamin, 18 mths), Intend (e.g. 'I'm going to get wood and chop', Benjamin, 27 mths) and Formulation (e.g. 'Mum, you've got to say help when you're in the water', Jill, 42 mths). The decision as to which Function category an utterance should be assigned to depends on the content, in particular that part encoded by the auxiliary or main verb. One category, Performance of Command to Verbalize, was omitted from the analysis on the grounds that, as it typically involves only the production of isolated words, such as 'please', 'thank you', it was not comparable with the other categories. Four other categories that typically only involve single word responses, Assent, Refuse, Reject and Acknowledge, were also omitted from the present analysis. Since these functions, or comparable ones, occur in all sub-systems, they will be considered later, in a separate section.

With the exceptions just mentioned, data on order of emergence for all Control functions reaching criterion by five years are shown in figure 4.17. The first function to emerge is Wanting, which is the least differentiated of the Control functions. Halliday (1975) found two Control functional categories, Instrumental and Regulatory, amongst the first to emerge in Nigel's protolanguage at the age of nine months, so it is to be expected that Wanting, which combines them, should emerge very early. Significantly later ($CRIT_k < 0.08$) comes Direct Request. For an utterance to be coded as such, there had to be some indication that the hearer was to provide the required object or carry out the required action.

The next group to emerge includes Intend, Request Permission and Prohibition (e.g. respectively 'I'm going to put some water in', 'Can I have my purse /ə/ put money in', and 'Oh don't smash mine cup', all produced by Mark at 30 months). The latter two of these categories are coemergent. The progression up to this point can be seen as a gradual differentiation of the initial unspecified Wanting – a progression that is made possible by the mastery of the imperative and interrogative options in the mood system.

Request Permission is the first in another progression, as the child becomes aware of the negotiability of control. On the one hand, he learns to take account of the desires and intentions of others and begins to produce a group of functions which includes Suggestion (e.g. 'Mel(v) shall we have the shop?' Penny, 36 mths), Offer (e.g. 'Do you want to try one on?' Penny, 36 mths offering a friend the chance to wear one of her father's boots), Query Want (e.g. 'Do you want these?', Betty, 42 mths), Query Intend (e.g. 'What you going to do?' Stella, 33 mths) and Indirect Request (e.g. 'Will you pour the drink out?' John, 42 mths). These functions emerge shortly after Request Permission. On the other hand, the child also begins to give Justification for his requests and intentions (e.g. 'I won't come because – because Robert's here', John, 42 mths) and to Request Justification for those made by others (e.g. 'Why not?' Lewis, 45 mths, in response to mother's refusal to let him walk on the soil). The first justifications that he himself offers are quite

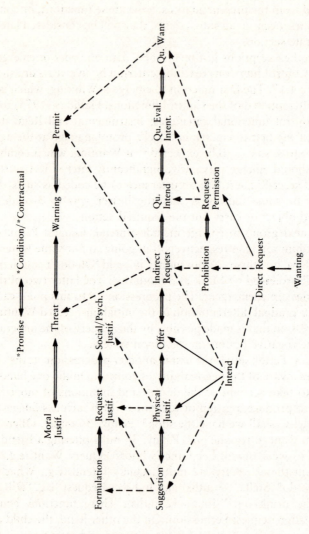

Figure 4.17 Sequence of emergence: Control functions

specific and limited to physical consequences, but by five years, Specific Social, Psychological and Moral Justifications have reached criterion. Very few children, however, are yet offering Universal Justifications. As in the example above, most justifications occur as secondary functions, in the same utterance as the Request or other function that they are intended to justify.

The last group of functions to emerge, Permit, Threat, Warning, Promise, Contractual and Condition (the latter three not quite reaching criterion), show the child beginning to use language to control behaviour at a distance. With the emergence of this group, the sub-system is more or less complete. Subsequent development will be largely a matter of learning to deploy these functions more appropriately in relation to the particular social context of interaction (cf. Ervin-Tripp, 1980).

4.11.2 *Expressive functions*
With the Expressive functions, too, there is a development from 'self orientation' to 'other-orientation'. The first function to emerge, Exclamation, is essentially a non-reflective affective response to the current situation, which may equally well be spoken in the absence of an addressee. Since utterances realizing this function typically consist of a single word or phrase, it is not surprising to find them emerging very early. The next pair are very different from each other. Verbal Accompaniment to Action is typically realized by a rote expression such as 'there we are', 'oops a daisy', while Express State or Attitude is a personal and more specific response to a situation (e.g. 'I'm hungry', Nancy, 36 mths). Both these functions are ordered with respect to Exclamation ($CRIT_k < 0.08$ and < 0.2, respectively) and to the succeeding pair, Query State/Attitude (e.g. 'Do you like this?' Nicholas, 45 mths) and Encourage ($CRIT_k < 0.2$ or better). Following these first other-oriented Expressive functions, which express an attitude of interest and cooperation, the majority of the remaining functions to emerge in this sub-system are more negative in content and reflect the competitive nature of much peer-group interaction in the later pre-school years. (See figure 4.18.)

4.11.3 *Representational functions*
Although the Representational sub-system is essentially concerned with the exchange of information, the concept of 'new' information is relatively slow to develop (cf. Halliday, 1975). Most early utterances with Representational functions are confined to com-

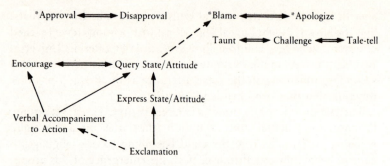

Figure 4.18 Sequence of emergence: Expressive functions

menting on known information about the current, shared situation. However, one might speculate that it is only through exchanging utterances about known information that the child discovers the general Representational function of language, which is a necessary prerequisite for the intention to convey information to his addressee which he believes to be unknown (Griffiths, 1979).

Ostension, the first representational function to emerge, has also been observed to occur very early by other researchers, although the labels used have not always been the same. Similar early functions noted by others include Labelling (Dore, 1975), drawing Attention to Object (Carter, 1974) and Personal/Interactional (Halliday, 1975). What all these labels together suggest is that in these early utterances, the child is sharing with an addressee his interest in, or his pleasure in being able to name an object in the shared environment or, alternatively, is using a reference to an object in the shared environment to establish or sustain interaction with an addressee. Following this 'protorepresentational' function (cf. Bates *et al.*, 1975), the first truly Representational functions to emerge are Statement, Content Question (e.g. 'What . . .?' and 'Where . . .?') and Response to Content Question. Statement and Content Question are both ordered with respect to Ostension ($CRIT_k < 0.08$) and Statement precedes Content Question ($CRIT_k < 0.2$). Response to Content Question is significantly ordered with respect to both Ostension ($CRIT_k < 0.08$) and to Statement ($CRIT_k < 0.2$).

Just as Polar Interrogative was significantly later to emerge than *Wh*- Interrogative in the Mood system, so Yes/No Questions are later to emerge than Content Questions ($CRIT_k < 0.2$), although Request Explanation (e.g. 'How do you get pastry out Mummy(v)?' John, 42 mths; 'Mummy(v) why didn't you put one rubber band at the front?' Nicholas, 51 mths) are significantly later still (CRIT$_k$ < 0.08).

All the specific types of Justification/Explanation emerge during the later pre-school period but, generally speaking, after they have emerged in the Control sub-system. None of the types of Universal Justification reach criterion by five years. (See figure 4.19.)

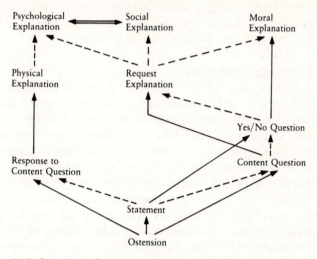

Figure 4.19 Sequence of emergence: Representational functions

4.11.4 *Tutorial and social functions*

Unlike those in the other sub-systems, the functions that the child masters in the Tutorial sub-system are essentially responses to adult initiations. Imitation of a proffered model form is the first to emerge and this is followed by Response to Display Question and the Supplying of Required Forms (e.g. 'Please', 'Thank you/ta'). Some children also supply Fillers to Frame Questions (e.g. 'Jack and Jill went up the —', 'hill'), but this function does not reach criterion, as not all parents adopt this particular tutorial strategy. None of the initiating functions reach criterion by five years; as they belong to the adult role in this type of interaction, this result is not at all surprising.

Only two Social functions are included in the taxonomy: Talk Routines and Greeting/Farewell. Both emerge very early and are perhaps best seen as extensions of the Personal/Interactional functions noted by Halliday (1975). The absence of further functions in the social sub-system should not be taken to suggest that, beyond this early stage, conversation ceases to have a significant 'social' function. On the contrary, much of the interaction that children engage in serves to sustain inter-personal relations but, because the utterances have a combination of propositional content and illocutionary force (realized by selection from the mood system), they are ostensibly realizing functions in other systems. Thus children will make requests or proffer comments on what is going on in order to engage adults in interaction, and the reverse is also true. Rather than double code such utterances, they have been analysed only in terms of their ostensible functions.

4.11.5 *Procedural functions*

Unlike exchanges in all the other modes, Procedural exchanges rarely form the 'point' of a sequence of talk. Concerned to open or repair the channel of communication, they are essentially supportive of the intended purpose of the interaction. It is in this sense that the term 'contingent query' (Garvey, 1977) has been used for what is called in the *Coding Manual* Request for Repetition or Request Identification. In the interests of standardization of terminology, we shall adopt Garvey's term in discussing these functions.

The channel-opening function is typically performed by an exchange containing an initiating Call and an Availability response. Call is the earliest of the functions to emerge in this sub-system, but the answering Availability response does not emerge until more than two years later. Presumably young children either do not recognize the expectation that they signal their availability or they do so in non-verbal ways, such as looking at the speaker or going to where the speaker is. However it may well be that availability responses are not required, as adults do not employ a call to initiate interaction with young children, preferring to use the characteristic exaggerated intonation and high pitch noted by Garnica (1977) instead.

The next functions to emerge, significantly later than Call ($\text{CRIT}_k < 0.08$), are the initiating and responding moves in the Contingent Query: Repetition exchange. Although adult contingent queries are usually genuinely motivated by a failure to understand, this is not necessarily true of the child's use of the same function. Quite a number of children seem to use them, as indeed they use the Call, simply to sustain the interaction: from the child's point of view, they may perhaps be thought of as 'discourse operators' (Homewood, 1983) which conveniently fill a slot in the sequential organization of the conversation whilst making minimal demands on his lexico-grammatical resources.

Check, the repetition of the previous utterance with rising tone, and Identification in response to a Contingent Query intended to secure more precise identification of an intended referent, coemerge significantly later ($CRIT_k < 0.2$), followed by Contingent Query: Identification and Availability Response, and still later by the function New Topic Marker. The total picture for Social, Tutorial and Procedural functions is as shown in figure 4.20.

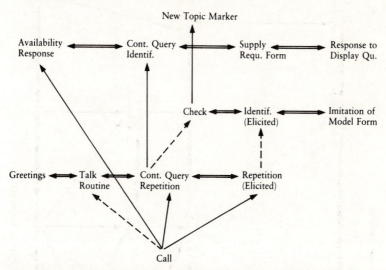

Figure 4.20 Sequence of emergence: Social, Tutorial and Procedural

4.11.6 *Inter-personal functions: the full system*

Having considered the various sub-systems individually, we can now attempt to get a more general overview by comparing selected items across the sub-systems. What is particularly interesting is the number of groups of coemerging functions, with significant ordering between the groups, at least at the weaker criterion level. In the first group are functions which may be considered to be undifferentiated prototypes of the major functional sub-systems: Wanting, Ostension, Exclamation and Call. Subsequent development may therefore be thought of as, to a considerable extent, the progressive differentiation of these prototypical categories. The first stage of this differentiation takes place with the emergence of the pair Direct Request and Statement.

As already suggested, the differentiation of the function system is quite closely tied to the emergence of the various options of the

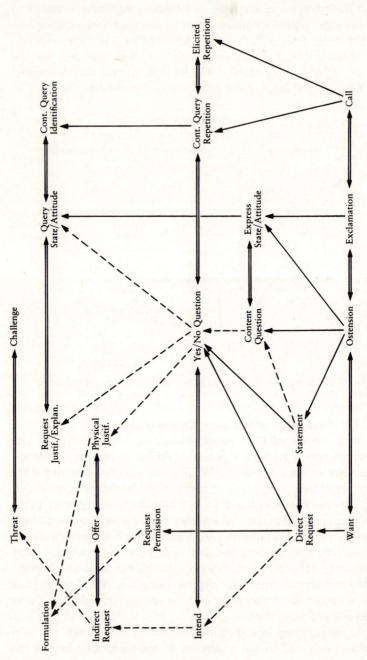

Figure 4.21 Sequence of emergence: Inter-Personal Function (selected)

Mood system. Most typically, Direct Request and Statement are realized respectively by Imperative and Declarative. With the emergence of *Wh-* and then Polar Interrogatives we find the related emergence of Content Questions, Yes/No Questions, and various Indirect Requests. Some of the patterns of coemergence in later groups may be fortuitous, but there are some general trends which find expression across sub-systems in a way that suggests that functional categories emerging in one system may be extended by some process of analogizing or generalization to other sub-systems. One such trend is the development from 'self-orientation' to 'other-orientation', leading to the emergence of Formulation and Query State/Attitude shortly after Suggestion and Offer on the one hand, and to Threat and Warning emerging at approximately the same stage as Challenge and Tale-tell on the other. A second trend concerns the Justification categories. Request for Justification in Control and Representational Requests for Explanation are coemergent and the emergence of types of Justification given as responses follows the same general sequence in both sub-systems and occurs at about the same time. If this is seen as a development in the direction of a greater concern with completeness of information, it may also account for the coemergence of Contingent Query: Identification with Request Justification.

4.11.7 Responding functions

The functions considered in the preceding pages have been either Initiating functions or at least Responding functions which are closely tied to specific Initiating functions, such as the Response to Content Question. There are, however, a number of other Responding functions, which are much more general in their scope. These are Acknowledge, Reject, Evasion and the Positive and Negative Response functions that are almost invariably realized by 'Yes' and 'No' or such variants as 'OK', 'uh uh', etc. Although similar in general force from one sub-sequence mode to another, the precise meaning of these functions is defined by the type of function to which they are responses. Thus, for example, 'Yes' in response to a Request has the value of Assent in the Control sub-system, whilst in response to a Yes/No Question, its value in the Representational sub-system is that of Affirm.

Given the similarity of form and of broad functional meaning, these functions might be expected to emerge at about the same time across all the sub-systems. However, this is not the case, as can be seen from table 4.6, in which the median age of emergence (in

Table 4.6 *Median age of emergence: responding function*

	Control	Expressive	Representational	Procedural
Acknowledge	21	33	21	
Assent/Agree/Affirm	18	21	18	24
Refuse/Disagree/Deny	18	27	24	
Reject	27	42	30	

months) is shown for each of the sub-systems in which they occur. (Evasion is not included in this table, as it fails to reach criterion in any of the sub-systems by the age of five years.) Why should there be these large discrepancies? Why, for example, does Refuse emerge in the Control sub-system by 18 months whilst its equivalent in the Procedural sub-system fails to reach criterion by the age of five? It hardly seems likely that children should find it so much more difficult to learn the use of 'no' as a Denial in the Procedural sub-system than to learn its use as a Refusal in the Control sub-system. The answer, therefore, is most probably one of differential perceived requirements to produce the various functions in sub-sequences in the different modes. It may also be recalled that when the total numbers of utterances occurring in the different sub-sequence modes were compared, there were between twice and three times as many utterances in both Control and Representational subsequences as in either Expressive or Procedural sub-sequences.

These results, therefore, which are unexpected from the point of view of an account of emergence which gives weight only to some such determining factor as 'linguistic complexity' or 'difficulty of learning', are relatively easily explained in terms of some such notion as 'differential frequency of requirement in discourse' with consequent differential frequency of occurrence in samples of spontaneous conversation. In the case of the Responding functions, the relative weight to give to these competing explanations of observed order of emergence is rather obvious. But presumably, although their influence is not always so clear-cut, the two determining factors, that we might broadly term 'complexity' and 'frequency' contribute to the probability of 'emergence' being observed for all the items considered in this chapter. This issue will be developed further in chapter 9.

Finally we must re-emphasize that, although data on emergence are certainly pertinent to an account of acquisition, it is not possible to make direct inferences from emergence in a child's spontaneous production to point of entry into his productive potential or to point of complete mastery. More frequent observations and a more detailed analysis of the speech data collected would be necessary to give a thorough account of the gradual process of acquisition from first use to final mastery.

5

The sequence of emergence: syntax and its relationship with other levels of analysis

In the account of sequence of emergence so far, we have concentrated on the semantic and pragmatic levels of linguistic description, and syntactic categories have only been considered, paradigmatically, as sets of alternatives at particular points in the structure of the sentence or phrase. To complete the account of sequence of emergence, therefore, we shall first describe the development of the syntagmatic organization of utterances and then, in the second part of the chapter, emergence of syntactic structures will be related to the sequence already established in chapter 4 for systems at the semantic and pragmatic levels. Since the number of individual items involved in all the systems considered is extremely large, this 'cross-system' comparison will be based on a sub-set of items selected across all three levels of linguistic analysis. Finally, the overall sequence of development will be presented in terms of a number of levels and the levels illustrated with examples drawn from the longitudinal data recorded in the observations of one child.

5.1 The method of analysis
As was explained in chapter 2, the analysis of the coded data at the level of syntax was fraught with difficulties. This was due to two factors: the very large number of occurring structural patterns and the fact that the coding had been carried out in a 'free format'. These two factors are, of course, related. At the level of clauses, for example, 12 major constituents were recognized: Subject, Object, Direct Object, Indirect Object, Complement, Adjunct, Particle, Conjunction, Lexical Verb, Copula Verb, Auxiliary Verb and Negation. Since some of these categories (e.g. Adjunct, Auxiliary Verb) could occur more than once, even in a simple clause, and since alternative positions are possible for some items (e.g. Adjunct preceding the Subject, preceding the Lexical Verb or following the Object), a system of coding which represents the sequence in which

categories are actually observed to occur gives rise to an inordinately large number of structural patterns, many of which are minor variants of essentially the same syntactic structure. The solution finally adopted was to transform the original, free format, coded data into a fixed format (cf. 2.11). For each of the main units to be analysed – sentence and noun phrase – a generalized structural description was established with the alternatives at each position in structure being given a numerical value according to principles that would facilitate subsequent grouping. Once this had been done, it was a relatively simple – although slow and laborious – matter to inspect the output of an analysis of frequency of structural patterns by age, in order to decide how to reduce them to a smaller number of related structural types.

In making these decisions about grouping, two criteria were used: theoretical significance and frequency. Clearly, structures that occur with extremely low frequency can tell us very little about the general pattern of development, particularly if the occurrences are spread over a wide age-range. However, if the pattern in question was of particular structural significance and its occurrence was limited to the last observation of the older children, even a very low total frequency might yield important developmental information. The final decision in such cases, therefore, was a matter of judgment.

Some utterance tokens were, in terms of a sentence grammar, incomplete. However not all these were ungrammatical. Some were elliptical responses and, in context, totally grammatical. Others, although technically ungrammatical, were situationally acceptable, for example, 'You ready yet?' Both these categories posed a serious dilemma. Should they be treated as if the missing (and understood) elements were present, or should they be treated as structural patterns in their own right? Neither alternative seemed satisfactory. If the first were chosen, many non-elliptical incomplete tokens would be wrongly classified, with the risk of over-estimating a child's ability. The second alternative, however, would have had two unsatisfactory outcomes: it would have unduly increased the number of structural types to be included or, where the string was a possible grammatical structure in its own right (e.g. 'Make the beds' in answer to 'What have we got to do next?' might be wrongly analysed as $V_{(imp)} + C$), it would have led to an incorrectly high estimate of the frequency of that structural type. Since all such incomplete tokens had been coded as either 'elliptical' or 'situationally acceptable but grammatically incomplete', a filter was applied which excluded them from all analyses intended to establish general developmental trends.

A further category of structural types was omitted at this stage: those that had been coded as imperative in mood. As these were likely to be very similar to declarative structures except for the omission of the subject constituent, it was decided that they would give little additional information about the development of control of syntactic structure. They were therefore omitted from all analyses concerned with order of emergence at the level of syntax.

At the end of this very lengthy operation of recoding and grouping, there remained a list of some 100 sentence-structure types and about half that number of noun phrase structures. To these was then applied the method of pairwise comparison described in chapter 4 in order to establish the sequence of emergence.

5.2 Sentence structure

Most of the sentences uttered by children in the age-range studied consist of a single clause, and so it was at this level that the greatest number of analytic distinctions was made (for the symbols used in the following discussion see table 5.1). However, from as early as 24 months, sentences consisting of more than one clause begin to occur with some frequency. The first to emerge were sentences containing experiential verbs, such as 'want', 'like', 'know' and 'think', which can take an embedded clause as complement. Since the earliest such sentences were of the form $S + V + V + (X)$ (e.g. 'I want to do (X)'), in which the embedded clause is realized by the predicate alone – the subjects of the two clauses being coreferential – a distinction was made between finite embedded clauses (those containing subject and predicate) and non-finite ones (those containing predicate only). The remaining multi-clause sentences were described in terms of combinations of four types of clause: Main, Subordinate, Embedded and Tag. Such sentences were not analysed below the level of clause. In order to simplify the task of analysis, sentence strings were sorted into five categories on the basis of an independent coding that had been made of Mood. The five categories were: Declarative and Moodless; Imperative; Polar-Interrogative; *Wh*-Interrogative; and Interrogatives realized by Intonation Only. As already explained, Imperative strings were not included in the analysis of order of emergence. The same decision was taken for Interrogatives realized by Intonation Only, and for similar reasons. Such strings are, for the most part, a sub-set of the declarative strings that children are already producing, and so little

Table 5.1 *Symbols used in constituent analysis*

Symbol	Interpretation	Symbol	Interpretation	Symbol	Interpretation
S	Subject	*O/A*	Object or Adjunct	⟨ ⟩	Encloses Embedded Clause
O	Direct Object	*aux*	Auxiliary Verb	⟨⟨ ⟩⟩	Encloses Relative Clause
IO	Indirect Object	*V*	Lexical Verb	( )	Optional Constituent
C	Complement	*cop*	Copula Verb		
IC	Intensive Complement	*neg*	Negation ('not' or 'n't')		
A	Adjunct	X	Any Nominal Constituent		

Note: In some cases, strings containing additional constituents were included with tokens of a simpler structural type, e.g. $S + V + O + A + A$ would be treated as a token of the structure $S + V + O + A$.

information about the development of structure is gained by including them. In the following three sections, therefore, only the order of emergence of declarative (including moodless) and interrogative sentences will be discussed.

5.2.1 *Declarative sentences*
The first two sentence types to emerge consist of one and two constituents. Since in the majority of these strings either *S* or *V*, but not both constituents, occur, they cannot strictly be described as declaratives. However, as they most frequently realize the functions of Ostension and – in the case of two constituent strings – Statement, they can perhaps be accorded honorary status as declaratives.

At the next stage we see the addition of a verbal constituent, either lexical or copula in addition to the subject. This allows the production of the three basic types of clause: transitive, intransitive and stative. It is interesting to note that, both in clauses containing lexical verbs and in those containing copula verbs, the Adjunct is significantly later to emerge than the Object as the third constituent.[1] Clauses containing both Object and Adjunct are not significantly ordered with respect to those containing Adjunct alone and, in the case of copula clauses, Complement + Adjunct and Adjunct alone are coemergent.

Considerably later still we find clauses containing Indirect as well as Direct Object. This is not to say, of course, that there have been no utterances before this point encoding the recipient in Change of

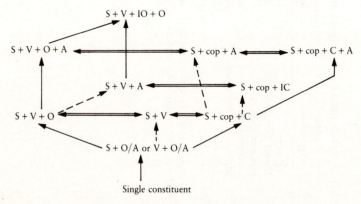

Figure 5.1 Sequence of emergence: simple active affirmative declarative sentence

Possession clauses; at first, though, the recipient is encoded as Adjunct in a full prepositional phrase and only later as Indirect Object, without a preposition. Before either of the clause types containing three nominal constituents has emerged, however, the addition of *aux* has led to the first clause type with four constituents. There is a strong trend for the first strings containing *aux* to be $S + aux + V + O/A$, but the related negative ($S + aux + neg + V + O/A$) and copula ($S + aux + cop + C/A$) strings emerge shortly afterwards ($CRIT_k < 0.02$). Coemergent with these clause types we also find clauses with *aux* and two post-verbal constituents. By this stage therefore, we have the first strings containing five constituents. At the next level, a further constituent is added to each of the clause types just discussed to give the first six constituent strings ($S + aux + neg + V + O + A$) and the first strings with two auxiliary verb constituents (e.g. '*I will have to* do it'). Finally, at the fourth level in this sub-system, we find strings with negation as well as two auxiliary verb constituents (e.g. 'We'*re not going to* be too tired').

From figure 5.2 it can be seen that there is a very strong pattern in the sequence in which items in this sub-system emerge. Items at adjacent levels are weakly ordered with respect to each other ($CRIT_k < 0.2$) whilst there is strong evidence of order ($CRIT_k < 0.08$) between items that are two levels apart. In this particular sub-system also, there is a strong suggestion that, at least for some of the items, the order of emergence is determined by the number of constituents involved, for example, $S + V + O \rightarrow S + aux + V + O/A \rightarrow S + aux + neg + V + O/A \rightarrow S + aux + neg + V + O + A \rightarrow S + aux + neg + aux + V + O/A$.

A different sort of complexity is involved in sentences containing more than one clause. As already mentioned, the first such structural pattern to emerge is the rather special case of an embedded complement to 'want', with coreference between the subjects of the two clauses (e.g. 'I want to go', 'I want to do it'). Brown (1973) and others have analysed such utterances as single clauses, with *wanna* treated as a quasi-auxiliary, similar to *gonna* = *be going to*. Two reasons led us to adopt the analysis presented here. Firstly there are sufficient children whose speech suggests the segmentation *want + to V*, for this to be considered an equally possible analysis and, secondly, as can be seen from figure 5.3, the finite embedded clause as complement to 'want' (e.g. 'I want you to read it') is only weakly ordered with respect to the non-finite form ($CRIT_k < 0.2$). Coemergent with finite embedded clause as complement are two other two-clause sentence types: Main + Tag and Main + Subordinate. The subordinate clauses involved are of two types, those introduced by the temporal conjunction *when* and those introduced by the 'logical' conjunctions *because* and *if*. In most cases, *because* encodes a relationship of 'reason' rather than one of strict causality. In this context it is interesting to note that quite a large number of children substitute '*that's why*' for '*because*' when expressing the causal relationship (e.g. 'They're crying that's why they want some', David, 42 months, referring to dolls who haven't yet been given their share of tangerine segments).

At the next level two further two-clause sentence-types emerge, both inviting some comment. First there is the coordinate structure Main + Main. At first sight it is rather surprising that this structure does not precede the one involving a subordinate clause, particularly as *and* was clearly the first conjunction to emerge. It may well be that this is a result of the coding decision to treat clauses introduced by *and* as self-contained one-clause sentences unless there was clear evidence of some logical relationship between the clauses so joined. If a weaker criterion of coordination had been used, this might well have led to this structure preceding the two-clause sentence containing subordination. Secondly, sentences containing relative clauses emerge. As will be seen below in the description of the emergence of noun-phrase structures, the first relative clauses are defining clauses introduced by ϕ or 'what' (e.g. 'I mean the one *you've got in your hand*'; '. . . the one *what I gave you*'). As noted by Limber (1973), the first relative clauses occur only as qualifiers to noun phrases functioning as object or complement or occasionally as adjunct, in the main clause. In fact, no instances at all were observed in the entire data-base of a relative clause qualifying the subject of a well-formed declarative clause containing a lexical verb. There was a total of 12 relative clauses qualifying the subject in clauses in which the subject followed a copula verb (e.g. 'There's the one what I need'). There were also eight instances of relative clauses qualifying the subject in *wh-* interrogative clauses in which the subject was not in clause-initial position (e.g. 'What's the thing what you want me to do?).

Limber offers a pragmatic explanation for this biased distribution of relative clauses, arguing that subject noun phrases are most frequently realized by proper nouns or personal pronouns and hence not susceptible to clausal qualification. The same argument also applies, of course, to pre-head modification of subject constituents. This finding can perhaps be more satisfactorily explained by reference to the distribution of 'given' and 'new' information in the clause. The unmarked option in English is for new information to be placed at the end of the clause and, although there are certainly instances of marked information focus in the data-base with the preposing of object, complement and adjunct constituents, it is the unmarked option which predominates. This is strikingly the case with respect to relative clauses.

Slightly after the emergence of the relative clause, but not significantly so, comes another syntactic structure which throws the weight of the new information to the end of the sentence: embedded clause as complement, with the structure $S + cop + \langle finite \rangle$ (e.g. 'That is what I want'). With the emergence of these two sentence types and of the clause structure $S + V + IO + O$, it can reasonably be argued that the child has reached an important landmark in his linguistic development, for each of these structures provides him with a genuine choice in relation to the organization of the information to be communicated at a particular point in discourse. In this respect each is the 'marked' alternative in contrast with the earlier-to-emerge structures $S + V + O$ (e.g. 'I want that') or $S + V + O + A$ (e.g. 'I gave it to her').

The final sentence type to emerge, the three-clause declarative, is in fact a composite category made up of structures as diverse as Main Clause + Subordinate Clause + Tag, Main Clause + 〈Embedded Clause〉 + Main Clause and Main Clause + 〈Embedded Clause + 〈Embedded Clause〉〉. None of these categories, taken singly, reached the criterion of emergence in the speech of 50% of the sample by the age of five years. But when combined, the composite category did reach criterion. This suggests that, at a certain level of delicacy, these different three-clause structures are of equivalent complexity. It also tends to confirm the general impression that the order of emergence of syntactic sentence types is largely determined by the number of constituents involved, first at the level of constituents within the main clause and then at the level of clauses functioning as constituents of the complex sentence.

5.2.2 *Interrogative sentences*
Interrogative sentences in English are, in general, marked by the inversion of the subject and the first element of the verb phrase, with the addition of 'do' when the first element of the verb phrase in the equivalent declarative sentence is a lexical verb. However not all interrogatives involve inversion: *wh-* interrogatives with 'who', 'what' and 'where' as the first constituent, followed by a copula

verb, have a structure which can be described as *wh- + cop + NP*, where the final noun phrase can be seen simply as the entity asked about. Compared with *wh-* interrogatives containing lexical verbs, or with polar interrogatives of any kind, these *wh-* interrogatives are structurally simple. So it is not surprising that *what + cop + S* is the first interrogative sentence type to emerge and that *where + cop + S* is amongst the next two. Furthermore, the specific form 'What's this/that?' is one of the utterance-types most frequently addressed to children at around the age of two years, figuring centrally as it does in the naming game (Ninio and Bruner, 1978; McShane, 1980). It is quite possible, therefore, that for some children this first *wh-* interrogative emerges initially as a rote-learned unanalysed whole (cf. Brown, 1968).

This is most unlikely to be the case, however, for the first polar interrogative type to emerge (*aux + S + V + O/A*), which is weakly ordered with respect to *what + cop + S* ($CRIT_k < 0.2$). This is the first sentence type to involve subject–auxiliary inversion and it is followed ($CRIT_k < 0.2$) by the first *wh-* interrogative with a lexical verb and inversion and by the first polar interrogative in which the copula verb is inverted with the subject. (See figure 5.4.)

Thereafter the sequence of emergence is similar to that found in declarative sentences; later items involve the addition of further constituents, either a second auxiliary or a second clause, subordinate to or embedded within the main interrogative clause. The two exceptions are 'why' interrogatives and 'who' interrogatives containing a lexical verb. The relatively late emergence of the latter structural type may be due largely to its relative infrequency, whilst the 'why' interrogative can reasonably be described as structurally more complex than other *wh-* interrogatives, in that the *wh-* word in this sentence type does not involve the interrogation of one of the constituents of the main clause but rather of a whole dependent clause (*wh- + cause/reason*).

5.2.3 *The emergence of sentence and clause structure*
When the various sub-systems of the declarative sentence are combined with the polar and *wh-* interrogatives, the overall sequence of emergence is as shown in figure 5.5. Defined in terms of clusters of coemergent items and of significant ordering between at least some members of each cluster, there appear to be seven stages in the developing control of sentence structure. In this sequence the most obvious characteristic is the increase in the number of constituents involved as the child progresses from one stage to the

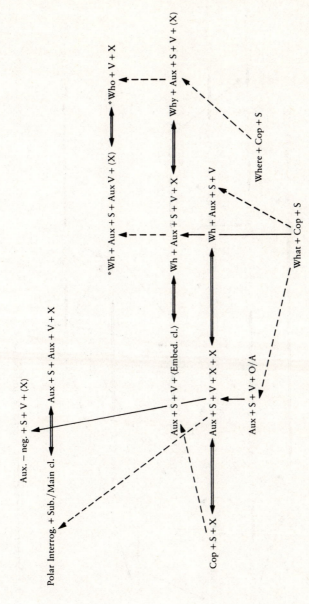

Figure 5.4 Sequence of emergence: interrogative sentences

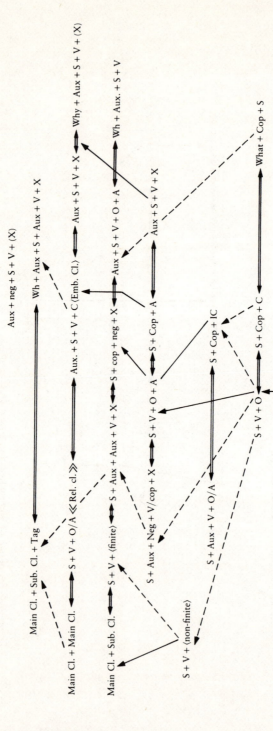

Figure 5.5 Sequence of emergence: sentence and clause

next. Generally speaking, Simple Active Affirmative Declarative sentence types of a given number of constituents emerge before the equivalent interrogative types, suggesting that the inversion of subject and auxiliary required in most interrogatives does make additional demands on the child's processing ability in the production of these sentence types. What is less expected is an apparent tendency for sentence types involving a copula to emerge later than the equivalent structure with a lexical verb (e.g. $S + V + A$ shows a tendency to emerge before $S + cop + A$ and $S + aux + neg + V + X$ emerges before $S + cop + neg + X$ ($CRIT_k < 0.2$)). One possible explanation for this is the tendency for copula verbs to be realized in a contracted, and hence unstressed, form in the input to the child (Wanner and Gleitman, 1982).

Despite these minor *décalages*, the general picture is one of increasing complexity from one stage to the next, with the majority of children showing emergence of most of the basic sentence types in English by the age of five. This sequence is, not surprisingly, very similar to that reported by other students of English. We view this result as extremely satisfactory. Where only two or three children of similar social background are observed, there remains the possibility that the sequence obtained is specific to a particular stratum of society. Given the composition of the sample in the present investigation, however, this cannot be the case. There is considerable justification, therefore, for claiming that this sequence is universal amongst children learning English as their first language.

As far as the number of ordered stages is concerned, there appears at first sight to be some conflict with the number proposed by Brown *et al.* (1969) and by Crystal *et al.* (1976). However this is entirely the result of the manner in which stages are defined. Brown *et al.*'s stages are based on MLU values, mean and upper bound, and Crystal *et al.*'s on prevalent grammatical developments. In the present study, the stages, or 'levels' as we prefer to call them,[2] emerge empirically from an analysis of the data: levels are defined as clusters of coemergent items which are at least weakly ordered with respect to other such clusters (cf. 5.4 below). Given these different approaches to the determination of stage boundaries, there is a remarkable degree of agreement between the sequence of stages proposed.

5.3 The emergence of noun phrase structures
With the enlarged definition of the noun phrase used in the present

analysis, the generalized structure of NP can be described as: (Preposition) + (Modifier) + Head + (Qualifier). Each of these positions in structure, with the exception of preposition, can be realized, however, in a variety of different ways. Head can be realized by the categories noun, pronoun, adjective or adverb, although only when the head is a noun or one of a small set of indefinite pronouns can it be preceded by a modifier. The category Modifier itself has the internal structure (Predeterminer) (Determiner) (Modifier, ... Modifier$_n$) and the category Qualifier can either be realized by a single word or by a rank-shifted phrase or clause. With all these alternatives, the number of NP structures that is theoretically possible, even limiting string-length to no more than ten words, is exceedingly large and far too numerous for analysis in the present investigation, given the relatively small number of utterances observed on each occasion.

The solution adopted, therefore, was to carry out a series of analyses with progressively coarser groupings of items at the different positions in the generalized structure. So, for example, whilst the different types of *Head* – *Nsing.*, *Npl.*, *Pers. Pron.*, *Adverb*, etc. – were separated in the analyses of the earliest strings to emerge, only the superordinate category *Head* was used in analyses of strings containing prepositions, modifiers and qualifiers. Similarly, whilst *Indef. Art.*, *Def. Art.*, *Dem. Adj.* etc. were kept separate for the earlier analyses, they were combined in the superordinate category *Det.* for analyses of structures that were relatively late to emerge.

As was seen in the description of the noun phrase in 4.7, the earliest noun phrases consist of a single word only, with *Nsing.* significantly earlier to emerge ($CRIT_k < 0.08$) than *Pers. Pron.* or *Adverb*, which are themselves coemergent. Slightly later, though not significantly so, is *Dem. Pron.* as head. This is coemergent with the first two-constituent noun phrase, *Indef. Art.* + *N. sing.* At the next level, there is a cluster of two-constituent noun phrases: *Def. Art.* + *Nsing.*, *Poss. Adj.* + *Nsing.*, *Prep* + *N/Pron.*, *Prep.* + *Adverb*. All the two-constituent strings are significantly ordered ($CRIT_k < 0.08$) with respect to their respective one-word string. In addition, *Def. Art* + *Nsing.* is significantly later to emerge than the similar string with *Indef. Art* + *Nsing.* ($CRIT_k < 0.08$). Coemergent with this cluster of two-constituent strings are the single-word noun phrases, *Npl.* and *Nnon-count*.

The next string to emerge is *Prep.* + *Det.* + *Head*. This is the first three-constituent noun-phrase and is significantly later to emerge than either *Prep.* + *N/Pron.* or *Prep* + *Adverb* ($\text{CRIT}_k < 0.08$). Only slightly later comes the next three-constituent string: *Indef. Art.* + *Mod.* + *Head.* This is coemergent with *Dem. Adj.* + *N. sing.* and with *Poss. Adj.* + *Npl.*, the latter being significantly ordered with respect to *Poss. Adj.* + *Nsing.* ($\text{CRIT}_k < 0.2$). In the next group are *Def. Art.* + *Mod.* + *Head*, *Def. Art.* + *Npl.* and *Def. Art.* + *Nnon-count.* Each of these strings is strongly ordered with respect to the related string with one constituent less (see figure 5.6). At approximately the same stage emerge *N's* + *Nsing.* and the first strings containing a Qualifier. *Head* + *Qual.* (*def. phrase*) and *Head* + *Qual.* (*word*). In both cases the head is realized by a pronoun (e.g. 'one with a handle' and 'that there').

The related strings with determiner as well as head, *Det.* + *Head* + *Qual.* (*def. phrase*) and *Det.* + *Head* + *Qual.* (*word*), are significantly later ($\text{CRIT}_k < 0.08$). In such strings the head may be realized either by a noun (e.g. 'the seat in the garden') or by an indefinite pronoun (e.g. 'the one over there'). Coemergent with these two strings is the first Qualifier realized by a full (relative) clause, *Head* + *Qual.* (*def. clause*). Once again, it first occurs with no determiner. Also at this stage emerge *Dem. Adj.* + *Mod.* + *Head* and the first four-constituent string, *Prep.* + *Det.* + *Mod.* + *Head.* Finally come *Interrog. Adj.* + *Head* and *Det.* + *Head* + *Qual.* (*def. clause*) and three four-constituent strings: *Det.* + *Mod.* + *Mod.* + *Head* (e.g. 'the big wooden car'), *Det.* + *Mod.* + *Head* + *Qual.* and *Prep.* + *Det.* + *Head* + *Qual.* In the latter two strings no distinction is made between types of qualifier, but they are more likely to be phrasal than clausal.

As with the development of clause and sentence structure, the most economical account of the development of noun-phrase structure is in terms of number of constituents. The earliest strings consist of a headword only and at successive stages additional constituents are added until finally, with phrases and clauses rank-shifted to function as qualifiers, the last strings to emerge consist of five or more constituents. There are some apparent *décalages*. Strings containing *Npl.* and *Nnon-count* are significantly later to emerge than similar strings containing *Nsing.*, and strings containing *Def. Art.* are later to emerge than strings containing *Indef. Art.* Whilst the contrasts between *Nsing.* and *Npl.* could be explained in terms of an additional morpheme in the case of *Npl.*, such an explanation cannot be invoked for the other contrasts. It may, however, be relevant that the string which is later to emerge in

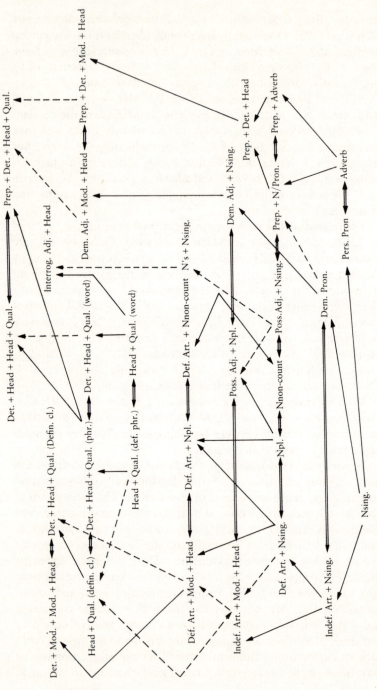

Figure 5.6 Sequence of emergence: noun phrase

each contrast also occurs less frequently even when it has emerged (see chapter 6). It may well be that such differences in frequency also occur in the input, but this possibility has not yet been investigated.

5.4 Overall sequence of emergence

As the final stage in the investigation of sequence of emergence, a similar procedure of pairwise comparisons was carried out on some 150 items selected from systems at all three levels: syntactic, semantic and pragmatic. This 'cross-system' analysis had two purposes: first, to allow the relationship between linguistic levels to be investigated and, secondly, to provide the basis for a developmental scale for use in assessment and diagnosis. Since it was anticipated that the scale might be used by clinicians and researchers who were not very familiar with all the descriptive categories used, items were selected for inclusion according to three criteria:

a) saliency: items should be easy to identify in a sample of spontaneous speech;
b) order: items chosen within any system should be strongly ordered with respect to each other and selected in such a way as to represent the full range of the sequence of emergence within that system;
c) frequency: as far as possible, items selected should occur frequently once they had emerged.

Not all items originally included in the cross-system analysis met all these criteria. A small number of items were also found to be inconsistent in their relationships with items from other systems. On these grounds some 20 items were discarded, leaving a scale of approximately 130 items. Further work is still required to produce a satisfactory assessment instrument for clinical use, but the information on which it will be based is shown in table 5.2. The most striking feature of the results of the cross-system analysis is the strong tendency for items to cluster in groups which are coemergent. This tendency was already apparent to some degree in the analysis of individual systems, but it is even more apparent when items are compared across the systems. To some extent this may be the result of the method of collecting the speech data. As explained in chapter 4, observations made at three-monthly intervals inevitably give the impression that development is saccadic. In the speech recorded from individual children there will be a number of items which appear to emerge at the same time in a

Level	Sentence/Clause Syntax	NP Syntax	NP Semantics
X	$Aux + neg + S + V + X$ $Wh\text{-} + aux + S + aux + V + X$		Head: Neg. Adverb Head: 'any'
IX	$S + cop + \langle\quad\rangle$ $Aux + S + aux + V + X$ Polar Interrog. + Sub. Clause $S + aux + neg + aux + V + (X)$	Prep. + Det. + Head + Qual. Det. + Mod. + Head + Qual.	Mod: Ordinal Qual: Adjective Head: Reflex. Pron. Head: 'where' (rel.)
VIII	'Why' Interrogative Three-Clause Declarative Any Relative Clause $S + V + IO + O$ $Aux + S + V + \langle\quad\rangle$ $Wh\text{-} + aux + S + V + X$	Interrog. Adj. + Head Det. + Head + Def. Clause	Head: 'nothing' Head: 'what'/'that' (relative) Head: 'something'/ 'anything'
VII	$Aux + S + V + X + X$ Main Clause + Sub./Main Clause $S + aux + aux + V + (X)$ $S + V + \langle finite \rangle$ Any Passive Main Clause + Tag $Cop + S + X$ $Wh\text{-} + aux + S + V$	Det. + Head + Def. Phrase Head + Def. Clause Prep + Det. + Mod. + Head Dem. Adj. + Mod. + Head/ Def. Art + Mod. + Head	Qual: Quantitative Head: 'him'
VI	$S + aux + cop + X$ $S + aux + neg + V + (X)$ $S + cop + A$ $A + aux + V + O + A$ $Aux + S + V + O/A$	Head + Def. Phrase Def. Art. + Npl.	Head: 'we'
V	$S + cop + IC$ $S + V + \langle non\text{-}finite \rangle$ $S + aux + V + (O/A)$ $S + V + O + A$ $Wh\text{-} + cop + S$	Indef. Art. + Mod. + Head Dem. Adj. + Nsing.	Head: 'he'
IV	$S + cop + C$ $S + V + (O)$	Prep. + Det. + Head Def. Art. + Nsing.	Mod: Phys. Attrib.
III	Two constituents	Prep. + Head Indef. Art. + Nsing.	Head: Interrog. Pron. Mod: Possessive Head: 'I' Head: 'it'
II			Head: Pronoun Head: Adverb
I	One constituent		Head: Noun

Modality	Time and Aspect	Conjunction	Sentence Meaning Relation	Function
Inference		'so'/'so that'	(Agent) Change Classif./ Equivalence Purposive	Condition
	Asp: Inceptive Time: Frequency	'that' (complementizer)	Possess/Benefact. + Embed. Cl. (Agent) Change Affect. Exper. Agent Cause Direct. Movement	
	Time: Extent Asp: Habitual	'when' 'if' 'but'	Temporal State/Change	Formulation
Possible		'because'	Benefactive Relation	Query State/Attitude
Obligation/ Necessity			Agent Cause + Embed. Cl.	Request Explanation/ Justification
			(Agent) Change Phys. Exper. Agent Change Existence Cogn. Exper. + Embed. Cl.	Indirect Request Suggestion
Permission/ Ability	Time: Future		Affective Experience Agent Act on Target Agent Function on Patient Cognitive Experience	Explanation/Justification Request Permission
	Asp: Perfect Asp: Contin.	'and'	Want Exper. + Embed. Cl. Evaluation Attribut. Agent Change Phys. Attrib. (Agent) Change Possession Agentive Cognitive Exper.	Intend Yes/No Question
	Time: Past		Want Experience Classification Agent Change Location	Content Question Express State/ Attitude
			Static Location	Statement Direct Request
			Operator + Nominal	Wanting Ostension Call

particular observation whereas, if a continuous record had been kept, they would actually have been observed to emerge one after another during the three-month period. However, the method subsequently used to establish order over the whole sample of children should have minimized this effect.

This clustering of items may also have resulted from the use of θ, the statistic of coemergence, equally with k, the statistic for establishing order, in interpreting the cross-system analysis. This was necessary as it was impossible to represent all the relationships of order between such a large number of items. Even when these reservations have been made, however, there is considerable evidence that the continuous process of development can also be represented as a succession of stages or levels.

For convenience of presentation, therefore, table 5.2 is set out in matrix form. On the vertical axis is the succession of levels and on the horizontal axis the major systems from which items were selected. That there are ten levels is not the result of a tidy *a priori* decision, but the outcome of the empirical analysis. The boundaries between levels are rarely absolutely clear-cut. This applies particularly to the boundaries between levels V and VI and VI and VII, where the syntactic items have a tendency to straddle the levels, which are more clearly defined in terms of the semantic and pragmatic items. Apart from these two cases, however, items allocated to any particular level are coemergent with the majority of other items at the same level ($\theta < 0.8$) and ordered, at least at the weaker level ($\mathrm{CRIT}_k < 0.2$), with respect to items in the preceding or succeeding levels. In general, the evidence for order between levels is considerably stronger for the earlier levels than for the later ones. Between levels I and II and II and III items are strongly ordered ($\mathrm{CRIT}_k < 0.8$) but, by levels V and VI, items in adjacent levels tend to be only weakly ordered ($\mathrm{CRIT}_k < 0.02$) and between levels IX and X the most that can be said is that the items at level X tend to emerge later than those at level IX.

The other very general characteristic of the sequence of development that emerges from this analysis is the tendency for development on the pragmatic and semantic levels to precede development on the syntactic level. This is the case both in general terms and in particular instances. Already by level III, the child typically expresses a substantial number of functions and by level V well over half of the SMRs have emerged, but it is not until level VII that syntactic structures in all the major moods have emerged. Two specific examples of this pragmatics-led progression can be seen in the expression of wants and in the asking of questions. The function *wanting* is one of the first three to emerge, being already present at level I. The corresponding SMRs Want Experience and Want Experience + Embedded Clause emerge at levels III and IV respectively but the full syntactic realizations of these categories do not emerge until levels IV and V. Similarly the Yes/No Question function emerges at level IV, but it is not until level VI that the well-formed syntactic realization of this function, $aux + S + V + (O/A)$ emerges. To be sure, the attribution to the semantic and pragmatic categories of utterances that lack some of the necessary syntactic features for the realization of those categories depends upon a rich interpretation of the child's communicative act in its conversational and situational context. But, where both parents and observers concur in making these interpretations, we would argue that the evidence strongly supports the claim made by Brown (1973), Slobin (1973) and others that meaning intentions are in advance of the lexico-grammatical means for their realization. It should be emphasized, however, that the child's resources extend beyond the lexico-grammatical; intonation, voice quality and gesture are all drawn upon in a relatively systematic manner to communicate his meaning intentions (Halliday, 1975; Dore, 1975; Carter, 1979). That we, like most other students of child language, have not explicitly included these supra-segmental and paralinguistic features in our description, should not be taken as an indication that they did not play an important part in the parents' interpretation of the children's utterances or in the categorizing decisions that were made in the process of coding.

5.5 The main characteristics of the sequence of levels

The following discussion of the sequence of development is illustrated from the observation of one particular child, Jonathan, who was one of the most rapid developers. At each level, each item is illustrated by an utterance from the occasion of emergence. Jonathan was one of the younger cohort, so the last observation of him was made at the age of 42 months. However, as will be seen, by that age he already had some items at level X.

In the early stages, there is a very close correspondence between level and occasion on which the constituent items emerged. However, as Jonathan progressed through the levels, this correspondence became weaker. This parallels the gradual weakening of order between items at successive levels. It seems as if, in the beginning when the child has everything to learn, the sequence of development is strongly determined by some common principle, such as the complexity or the frequency in the input of the items to be learned. And, since those that he has learned are few in number, each occurs with a sufficiently high frequency for it to be almost certain to be observed in a sample of some 100–150 utterances. As the child's repertoire increases, however, which particular new items are added becomes more dependent on chance. Furthermore, since the repertoire of items from which a choice is made in each utterance is increasing in size, there is a gradual diminution in the chance of observing any particular item in so small a sample of utterances. Although this does not seriously weaken the evidence for order from the sample of children as a whole, it does affect the picture that emerges from the data contributed by an individual child.

Level I

Item	Example	Occn
Syn.: One Constituent	'Dog' (looking at picture book)	1
NP Head: Noun	'Dog'	1
SMR: Operator + Nominal	'Doda' (points to toy rabbit, entreatingly)	1
Func.: Call	'Mummy (v)'	1
Func.: Ostension	'Dog'	1
Func.: Want	'Doda' (points to toy rabbit, entreatingly)	1

Level I is the level of the single constituent utterance. However, as many researchers have shown, such utterances can realize a variety of functions, notably: a Call for attention, either as a prelude to further communication or simply to establish or re-establish contact; Ostension, drawing attention to some object or event in the field which is potentially available for inter-subjective attention; and Wanting, which has the instrumental function of obtaining some form of goods and services. Although some single-word utterances at this stage consist of vocalizations that correspond to words which are classified as belonging to other parts of speech in adult language (cf. Nelson, 1973), it is Noun-like words which predominate. At this stage too, most children are producing some utterances which combine with the noun some indication, not necessarily verbally realized, of how the noun is to be understood – as object of desire, object of interest, object to be rejected and so on. However, as already mentioned in the earlier discussion of this item – Operator + Nominal (4.3) – these finer distinctions were not made in the present investigation and any one of them would be sufficient to credit the child with emergence of the general category. Jonathan's first observed token is 'Doda', said with appropriate entreating intonation and pointing.

Level II

Item	Example	Occn
NP Head: Pronoun	'Mummy wheel it' (asks M to push baby walker)	3
NP Head: Adverb	'Teddy . . . there'	2
SMR: Static Location	'Teddy . . . there'	2
Func.: Direct Request	'Mummy wheel it'	3
Func.: Statement	'Draw table' (has crayoned on table by mistake)	3

At level II it is still utterances consisting of a single constituent that predominate. Development is to be seen in the functions that emerge by this level, Direct Request and Statement, and in the types of word that are used to realize the repertoire of functions now available, Pronoun and Adverb. Although at level I one may have some hesitation in speaking about nouns, the words classified as pronouns and adverbs are readily recognizable members of these two classes: 'that', 'it' and 'I'; 'there' and 'here'. Not every child uses all these items at level II, but all have at least one from each class. It will be noted that, with the exception of 'I', which has a discourse function, all these items are clearly deictic in function.

With utterances limited to a single constituent, it is clear that there does not have to be a full syntactic realization for an utterance to be categorized as a Request or Statement. Direct Requests may take the form of an uninflected verb (e.g. 'push') or a particle such as 'up' or 'down' and the function Statement would be credited if an utterance clearly commented on some aspect of the situation as opposed to simply drawing attention to it (Ostension) (e.g. 'up' said of an object that has just been put on a high shelf). In Jonathan's case there were no clear cases of single constituent Requests or Statements and it can be seen that these functions did not emerge until Occasion 3. This illustrates a rather general characteristic of Jonathan's development – a tendency, when compared with the sequence found in the sample as a whole, for syntactic items to be slightly in advance, and for pragmatic items to be relatively in arrears at each stage. Some degree of departure of this kind from the norm based on the sample as a whole can be predicted from the data used to establish the sequence of emergence. If there had been no individual variation, each pair of items would have been either ordered with no counter-evidence, or coemergent. This was not the case. However the use of quite stringent criteria for claiming order or coemergence should be a guarantee that the amount of variation in individual profiles at each stage is not very great.

The final item to emerge at level II is the SMR Static Location. In the early occurrences of this SMR, the location is most frequently realized by a deictic adverb but it can also take the form of a noun naming the location of an object or person referred to in the immediately preceding conversation.

Level III

Item	Example	Occn
Syn.: Two Constituents	'Edwards out' (neighbour has gone out)	3
NP Syn.: Indef. Art. + Nsing.	'A ball'	3
NP Syn.: Prep. + Head	'Won't going in there' (=won't fit)	4
NP Head: 'it'	'Mummy wheel it'	3
NP Head: 'I'	M: 'What's in there?' J: 'I know'	3
NP Mod.: Possession	M: 'Whose pants?' J: 'Jonathan's pants'	3
NP Head: Interrog. Pron.	'Who has one of those?'	4
Time: Past	'Edwards out' (report to F later in day)	3
SMR: Classification	'Thats Brian'	2
SMR: Agent Change Location	'Mummy wheel it'	3
SMR: Want Experience	'Want Teddy'	3
Func.: Express State/Attitude	'Sorry!'	2
Func.: Content Question	'Who has one of those?' (ref. to toy in catalogue)	4

The defining characteristic of level III is the regular occurrence of utterances combining two constituents. These may be either two constituents of clause structure, typically $S + O$, $S + A$, $V + O$ or $V + A$, or two constituents of NP structure, *Indef. Art. + Nsing.* or *Prep. + Head*. At the level of clause, the combination $S + V$ is clearly later to emerge than the other combinations, though once again Jonathan is advanced in including this structure along with others such as $V + O$ (e.g. 'Draw table') on the same occasion. At the level of NP, the structure *Prep. + Head* may have three realizations: *Prep. + Noun*, *Prep + Pron.* and *Prep. + Adverb*. As Crystal *et al.* (1976) argue, there may occasionally be some difficulty in deciding whether the two constituents in particular utterances at this stage (e.g. ' Daddy car') are elements of clause or of NP structure. However, such ambiguous cases are sufficiently rare for it to be reasonable to argue for two levels of structure by level III.

The range of categories that can function as NP Head has also increased by this stage to include Interrogative Pronouns. By this stage, too, 'I' and 'it' are both present as well as 'that'. The item 'that' is not included in the list of items characteristic of this level (see table 5.2) because the cross-system analysis, on which the description of levels is based, was restricted to no more than a sub-set of items selected to be representative of the major systems investigated. A large number of items was therefore omitted from this analysis. To find out how these additional items fit into the sequence of levels presented here, it is necessary to consult the section of chapter 4 or of this chapter where the sequence of emergence of the appropriate system is described.

The first form of NP Modification, Possession, also emerges at level III. Athough the example cited here is in the structure *Mod. + Head*, the headword need not necessarily be realized for this item to be credited. In context, a noun plus possessive 's' is sufficient to mark the utterance as expressing possessive modification in the noun phrase. Also at this level we see the first reference to past time, judged, as in the example here, from the relation of the utterance to its context rather than from the marking of past tense on the verb. The SMRs to emerge at this level, Classification, Agent Change Location and Want Experience all require two clause constituents for utterances to be interpreted as expressing these categories. Although the examples of the first two SMRs each contain three constituents, this is not necessary. 'Mummy wheel' or 'Wheel it' would have been sufficient, in an appropriate context, for those utterances to have been classified as Agent Change Location. Similarly, 'That Brian' would have been treated as an instance of Classification.

Two constituents are also required for the function Content Question, although a less stringent analysis might allow the utterance of an interrogative pronoun or adverb alone to count as an instance of this category. However, even if that were granted, this item would probably still emerge at level III, as it is at this stage that interrogative pronouns and adverbs themselves emerge. Express State/Attitude would typically also be realized by two constituents (e.g. 'I tired'), but probably an expression such as 'Sorry!' is the first token of this category to occur.

Level IV

Item	Example	Occn
Syn.: $S + V + O$	'Jonathan want other one'	4
Syn.: $S + cop + C$	'That's a blue triangle'	4
NP Syn.: Def. Art. + Nsing.	'Daddy mend the wall'	4
NP Syn.: Prep. + Det. + Head	M: 'Where are you going?' J: 'To the meat shop'	4
NP Mod.: Phys. Attrib.	'Big cushion'	3
Aspect: Continuous	'Mummy's cooking chippies'	4
Aspect: Perfect	'They've gone'	4
Conjunction: 'and'	'Jonathan having chippies and beans and Daddy'	4
SMR: Agentive Cognitive Experience	'Read that one'	4
SMR: (Agent) Change Possession	'Mummy have it' (asking M to take it)	4
SMR: Agent Change Physical Attribution	'Mummy's cooking chippies'	4
SMR: Evaluate Attribute	'Cold outside'	4
SMR: Want Experience + Embedded Clause	'Jonathan want come over'	4
Func.: Yes/No Question	'Like that one?' (showing duster to M)	4
Func.: Intend	'Take shoes off'	4

Two features in particular characterize level IV: the first complete syntactic clause structures, $S + V + O$ and $S + cop + C$, and the first combination of clauses at the semantic level in Want Experience + Embedded Clause. The syntactic development requires the sequential organization of three constituents and this is also true of one of the new structures at NP level, *Prep. + Det. + Head*. The emergence of Continuous and Perfect Aspect ideally makes a similar requirement for three morphemes, although it should be noted that on the first emergence of these semantic categories, it is likely that only the bound morpheme on the verb will be realized (e.g. 'Jonathan having chippies'). As set out, it might appear that the three constituents that the child can manage at this stage would all be at one or other of the two levels of syntactic structure, clause or phrase. This is not the case, however. As some of the examples from Jonathan show, utterances can be structured at both levels, e.g. 'Read that one' which has the NP Structure *Dem. Adj. + Head* functioning as O in the clause structure $V + O$.

Other new developments at this level include a second type of NP Modification, Physical Attribute and the conjunction *and* as coordinator of clauses (e.g. 'Jonathan having chippies and beans and

Daddy' (=and so is Daddy)). There is a substantial broadening of the sentence meaning relations that are expressed to include Evaluative Attribution, (Agent Change) Physical Attribution, Change of Possession and Agentive Cognitive Experience. New functions include Intend and the other major question type, Yes/No Question. As with the Content Question at the previous level, however, this function does not receive a full syntactic realization yet, the interpretation of a questioning intention being based on intonational and context cues.

Level V

Item	Example	Occn
Syn.: *S + cop + IC*	'That's grey'	5
Syn.: *Wh- + cop + S*	'Where's my ball?'	5
Syn.: *S + V + O + A*	'When I've picked the bricks up'	5
Syn.: *S + aux + V + O/A*	'I will pull that'	5
Syn.: *S + V + ⟨non-finite⟩*	'I want to see Jonathan' (wants to look in mirror)	5
NP Syn.: Dem. Adj. + Nsing.	'What that hand?' (= what's in that hand?)	4
NP Syn.: Indef. Art + Mod. + Head	'That's a blue triangle'	4
NP Head: 'he'	'He must dive' (said in imaginary play)	8
Modality: Permission	'Can I put one in my mouth?'	5
Time: Future	'I will be a good boy'	5
SMR: Cognitive Experience	'I know'	3
SMR: Agent Function on Patient	'I will eat the big one'	5
SMR: Agent Act on Target	'I will pull that'	5
SMR: Affective Experience	'Bonny like that'	5
Func.: Request Permission	'Can I put one in my mouth?'	5
Func.: Justification	'I need water because I haven't had water for a long time'	6

Although it would be accurate to describe the syntactic development at level V as predominantly that of extending clause structure to include four constituents, this would fail to convey the diversity of the development that occurs. Starting from the basic transitive three-constituent clause of level IV, the child now branches out in three directions: (1) adding a second post-verbal constituent to produce the structure *S + V + O + A*, so that, for example, both Patient and Location can be realized in the expression of the SMR Agent Change Location; (2) introducing an auxiliary verb, in the structure *S + aux + V + O/A*, so that aspectual meanings can be realized in full and making possible the expression of the first modal meanings, Ability, Permission and Intention; (3) embedding one clause as complement to another, as in the structure $S + V + \langle V + O \rangle$. At this stage the embedded clause is non-finite, the subject being omitted as it is coreferential with the subject of the main clause.

With these developments in the syntax of the declarative clause, the child is able to make full positive statements or respond to content questions concerning almost all the SMRs in his repertoire. A similar achievement with respect to the realization of questions must wait until level VII. At level V only *wh-* Interrogatives of the form *wh-* + *cop* + *S* are possible. As already suggested, although these show an order of constituents which is the same as the result of a subject–auxiliary inversion, it seems probable that, to the child, they have a structure something like *Question word + cop + NP* (asked about).

In the structure of the noun phrase, development at level V consists in increasing the variety of two- and three-constituent NPs, rather than in extending the actual number of constituents. As in the simpler structure, *Det. + Nsing.*, it is interesting to note that in the three-constituent structure *Det. + Mod. + Head*, the indefinite article emerges before the definite article. At level V, therefore, there are still many noun phrases, both singular and plural, that lack a determiner, just as there are still sentences in which the verb is not marked for tense and in which infinitives are not preceded by 'to'.

At the semantic level, with the addition of Cognitive, Affective and Physical Experience SMRs, all the main types of experiential relations are now present. Agent Act on Target and Agent Function on Patient also both emerge together at this level, which suggests that the difference in the type of action concerned, locative in the former and functional in the latter, may be less important than was originally supposed. At this stage, too, reference to future time emerges. Although this is not dependent on an auxiliary verb for its realization, it is significant that future reference and the first auxiliaries emerge together.

The two functions to emerge at this stage, Request Permission and Justification, repeat the generally found pattern of the emergence of functional categories preceding the emergence of the syntactic categories which permit their full realization. As with other interrogative functions, the first requests for permission are often signalled by intonation rather than by full polar interrogatives. Justifications also typically first occur in elliptical responses rather than as a dependent clause in two-clause utterances. However, this was not true of the first token observed in Jonathan's data, 'I need water because I haven't had water for a long time'. Significantly, this utterance came from a later occasion than most of the examples of items emerging at level V.

Level VI

Item	Example	Occn
Syn.: $aux + S + V + O/A$	'Can I put one in my mouth?'	5
Syn.: $S + aux + V + O + A$	'When I've picked the bricks up'	5
Syn.: $S + cop + A$	'Its lights are round those'	8
Syn.: $S + aux + neg + V + (X)$	'I don't like them'	5
Syn.: $S + aux + cop + X$	'I will be a good boy'	5
NP Syn.: *Def. Art. + Npl.*	'When I've picked the bricks up'	5
NP Syn.: *Head + Def. Phrase*	'I'm going to eat the beans in there' (=in pod)	5
NP Head: 'we'	'Perhaps we'll get my anorak tomorrow'	6
SMR: Cogn. Exper. + Embed. Cl.	' I thought Bonny was taking it'	5
SMR: Agent Change Existence	'I'll show you how to make it into a finger one'	8
SMR: (Agent) Change Phys. Exper.	'My finger's not better yet'	7
Func.: Suggestion	'Perhaps we'll get my anorak tomorrow'	6
Func.: Indirect Request	'Could you bring me my cardboard books out Mummy?'	7

Level VI is very much a consolidation of level V. With respect to syntax, more declarative structures are found with an auxiliary verb, and negation is added to the declarative sentence to give $S + aux + neg + V + (X)$. The significant new development is the appearance of subject–auxiliary inversion in the simplest polar interrogative sentence: $aux + S + V + O/A$. This suggests that inversion is equivalent to the addition of negation in processing terms in the production of single-clause sentences. As above, the late emergence of $S + cop + A$ probably reflects its lower frequency in relation to other simple copula structures rather than a greater inherent complexity. At the level of NP structure, however, there is a new development: the emergence of the first qualifier, *Head + Def. Phrase*. By this stage, therefore, both pre- and post-modification of the head are now appearing in the structure of the noun phrase, but it is not until level IX that both occur together. From level VI onwards, however, almost all noun phrases have a determiner, when one is required. With the addition of *Def. Art. + Npl.*, singular, plural and non-count nouns are preceded by an article or by a demonstrative or possessive adjective.

At the semantic level, the important development is the emergence of Cognitive Experience + Embedded Clause. In spite of the fact that the subjects of the two clauses may be coreferential, this semantic relationship is typically realized by two finite clauses, one embedded within the other with the option of 'that' to introduce the embedded clause. Not surprisingly, the first occurrences of this SMR do not contain 'that', nor are they always syntactically fully well-formed (e.g. 'Think I can do it'). The other two SMRs to emerge at this stage, Agent Change Existence and (Agent) Change Physical Experience continue to fill out the main groupings, the earliest categories of which had emerged by level IV. It will be argued below (chapter 9) that Existence is a more complex concept than other types of attribute, hence the relatively late emergence of this category. Similarly, since Experiential meaning relations are inherently stative, rather than dynamic, the addition of agentively caused change makes this category more complex than the earlier-to-emerge Physical Experience.

At the pragmatic level, the functions to emerge at this stage, Indirect Request and Suggestion, are just two of a variety of control functions that depend for their differentiation on the availability of modal auxiliaries and of the sentence mood type, polar interrogative. The addition of these options to a child's verbal repertoire significantly changes the manner in which he is able, and usually expected, to negotiate collaboration and control of behaviour.

Level VII

Item	Example	Occn
Syn.: *Wh-* + *aux* + *S* + *V*	'Where did you find it?'	5
Syn.: *Cop* + *S* + *X*	'Is it Uncle Billy and Aunty Pat's trousers?'	5
Syn.: *S* + *V* + ⟨*finite*⟩	'I thought Bonny was taking it'	5
Syn.: *S* + *aux* + *aux* + *V* + (X)	'We'll have to buy a plaster for it'	7
Syn.: Main Cl. + Tag	'I'll open properly shall I?'	7
Syn.: Main Cl. + Sub. Clause	'I want my tea because I'm hungry'	6
Syn.: *Aux* + *S* + *V* + *X* + *X*	'Can I put one in my mouth?'	5
Syn.: Any Passive	'Or they'll be slapped by their mothers'	9

NP Syn.: *Dem. Adj. + Mod. + Head*	'* * with that little bit on the front'	6
NP Syn.: *Prep. + Det. + Mod. + Head*	'* * with that little bit on the front'	6
NP Syn.: *Head + Def. Cl.*	'That what you said'	8
NP Syn.: *Det. + Head + Def. Phrase*	'I'm going to eat the beans in there'	5
NP Head: 'him'	[not observed]	
NP Qual.: Quantitative	'I'll have to put a bit more in to cook'	9
Modality: Obligation/Necessity	'We'll have to buy a plaster for it'	7
Modality: Possible	'They might fall in a minute'	6
Conjunction: 'because'	'I need water because I haven't had water for a long time'	6
SMR: Agent Cause + Embed. Cl.	'Let me have that bit'	8
SMR: Benefactive	'I cut some for Mummy'	5
Func.: Request Explan./Justif.	'What are you sitting on my paper for?'	6
Func.: Query State/Attitude	'Have you got a headache coming Mummy (v)?'	7

It has already been mentioned that the boundary between levels VI and VII is less clearly defined than the boundaries between most other levels. This is partly because the cluster of syntactic structures that emerge at this stage looks in two directions. On the one hand there is the filling out of the range of interrogative structures, for example, *wh- + aux + S + V*, *cop + S + X*, and *aux + S + V + X + X*, and the addition of a second auxiliary to give the declarative structure *S + aux + aux + V + (X)*; on the other hand there are the first structures which involve two finite clauses, *S + V + ⟨finite⟩*, Main Clause + Subordinate Clause. The emergence of the subordinated clause before the coordinated clause has already been remarked on (5.2.1 above); certainly the first instances of clauses linked by 'because' (realized as /bəz/ in the case of one child) are much more clearly single utterances than the first sequences of clauses linked by 'and' or 'and then'.

The other fully realized two-clause structure to emerge at this stage is (declarative) Main Clause + Tag. As predicted by Brown and Hanlon (1970), it invariably comes later than the first well-formed polar interrogative. There is considerable individual difference, however, in the readiness with which children begin to produce tags, once the various components are available. Nor does this seem to be predicted by the frequency with which tags occur in the utterances addressed to them.

The emergence of defining clauses in the NP structure *Head + Def. Cl.* prefigures the appearance of a further two-clause structure. However, although there are clear instances of relative clauses qualifying the headword of an NP at this stage, they occur in elliptical responses or otherwise incomplete sentences. The full two-clause structure does not emerge until level VIII.

The other developments in the noun phrase involve the combining of structures already available from earlier levels to give two further three-constituent structures, *Dem. Adj. + Mod. + Head* and *Det. + Head + Def. Phrase* and the first four-constituent structure, *Prep. + Det. + Mod. + Head.* With regard to the latter, it is probably significant that at each increase in the number of constituents in the noun phrase, the first structure to emerge is one which includes a preposition. This suggests that, as is usually recognized, the preposition does not form part of the structure of the noun phrase, but is a constituent at the same level as NP in the structure of a superordinate prepositional phrase:

Prep. Phrase

Prep.   NP

Level VII also sees an important increase in the semantic options available in the system of modality: Obligation/Necessity, which encodes constraint on the agent of action, and Possible, which, either adverbially (e.g. 'perhaps') or by means of a modal verb, qualifies the probability of occurrence of a state or event. Together with the emergence of the Conjunction 'because', which encodes the logical relationship of reason or cause, these new additions indicate a significant cognitive development in the child's understanding of the complex contingency of one event upon another. The same is true to some extent of the SMR Agent Cause + Embedded Clause. A variety of verbs can occur in the main clause: 'let', 'allow', 'make', as well as 'cause'. This is a stronger variety of the constraint on the action of the agent (in the embedded clause) already noted in relation to the modal categories Obligation and Necessity. Here the source of constraint is made explicit.

The Benefactive relationship is, on the face of it, a simple one, and clearly related to Possession. Although probably more complex than Possession, the simple Benefactive relationship does not seem to be so much more so as to explain its much later emergence. The best explanation is probably one of relative frequency, therefore. The first example of any benefactive relationship to occur in the data from Jonathan is the more complex one of an action being performed for someone's benefit. This is described semantically as Benefactive + Embedded Clause, although syntactically it is realized in a single clause. Probably again because of its relatively low frequency, this SMR does not emerge until level IX.

The two functions to emerge at this stage are both related to Statement-like functions that emerged considerably earlier. The fact that Request Explanation/Justification and Query State/Attitude are relatively late to emerge is best seen in terms of the general tendency for statements and answers to emerge before questions which, in turn, can probably be explained in terms of the unequal power and status relationship between adults and children.

Level VIII

Item	Example	Occn
Syn.: *Wh-* + *aux* + *S* + *V* + *X*	'Where did you find it?'	5
Syn.: *Aux* + *S* + *V* + ⟨ ⟩	'Don't you know why it did?'	7
Syn.: Three-clause Declarative	'I ringed the bell and waked them up didn't I?'	7
Syn.: *S* + *V* + *IO* + *O*	'I'm making you one'	5
Syn.: Any Relative Clause	'You blow whichever way you want to blow it'	9
Syn.: 'Why' Interrogative	'Why do you want that?'	7
NP Syn.: *Det.* + *Head* + *Def. Clause*	'This is the bit where they go to a dog'	10
NP Syn.: *Interrog. Adj.* + *X*	'Which one would you like to-day?'	9
NP Head: 'something/anything'	'Now I draw something here'	6
NP Head: Rel. Pron. 'what/that'	'That what you said'	8
NP Head: 'nothing'	[not observed]	
Aspect: Habitual	'When it's time to get off we press that one to make it go off'	9
Time: extent	'I need water because I haven't had water for a long time'	6
Conjunction: 'but'	M: 'You want it loaded up do you?' J: 'But not with the crane'	7
Conjunction: 'if'	'If there isn't anything on TV please will you *?'	8
Conjunction: 'when'	'When it's time to get off we press that one to make it go off'	9
SMR: Temporal State/Change	'When it's time to get off we press that one to make it go off'	9
Func.: Formulation	'And then you have to turn its covers'	8

Several of the syntactic developments at level VIII have been prefigured at earlier levels: the embedding of a complement clause in a polar interrogative, *aux + S + V +* ⟨   ⟩, and the addition of a post-verbal constituent in *wh-* interrogatives, *wh- + aux + S + V + X*. The same is true of the emergence of Relative Clause in a well-formed sentence and of the related NP structure, *Det. + Head + Def. Clause* with the relative pronouns *what* and *that* as NP Head in at least some relative clauses. New developments include three-clause declaratives (including sentences in which the third clause is a Tag), '*why*' *interrogative* sentences and the structure *S + V + IO + O*, in which the recipient of action or change of possession is pronominalized and placed immediately after the verb.

With the addition of these two categories, it can reasonably be claimed that, by level VIII, the child has at his disposal all the basic declarative and interrogative sentence types of English. There is still some filling out to do, of course, in the organization of multi-clausal sentences and in the learning of the constraints that apply in the case of particular lexical items. The amount that still has to be learned should not be under-estimated (cf. Crystal *et al.* (1976): 77ff, for a detailed discussion) but we, like other writers, are impressed by how much has been acquired by this stage.

At the pragmatic level, the only new function is Formulation. This conjunctions, 'but', 'if' and 'when', and, related to the latter, the SMR Temporal State/Change. Also at this stage we find Habitual Aspect and Time: Extent.

At the pragmatic level, the only new function is Formulation. This is clearly related to the emergence of the obligation and necessity modality options at the previous level. It also has some affinity with coemergence of habitual aspect.

Level IX

Item	Example	Occn
Syn.: *S + aux + neg + aux + V + (X)*	'They shouldn't have put that purple in should they?'	9
Syn.: *Polar Interrog. + Sub. Clause*	'Shall I give you some playdoh to make his feet?'	10
Syn.: *Aux + S + aux + V + X*	'Are you going to mend Granpy's car for my Gran?'	7
Syn.: *S + cop +* ⟨ ⟩	'That's where the drawings are'	9
NP Syn.: *Det. + Mod. + Head + Qual.*	'* * with that little bit on the front'	6
NP Syn.: *Prep. + Det. + Head + Qual.*	'* * with that little bit on the front'	6

NP Head: Reflexive Pronoun	'And this one was opening itself'	8
NP Qual.: Adjective	[not observed]	
NP Mod.: Ordinal	[not observed]	
Time: Frequency	[not observed]	
Aspect: Inceptive	'It just started bleeding'	8
NP Head 'where' (rel.)	'That's where the drawings are'	9
Complementizer: 'that'	[not observed]	
SMR: Agent Cause Direct. Move.	'I'm squeezing the poorly bit out'	9
SMR: (Agent) Change Affect. Exper.	'How can they make you into a cowardy Womble?'	10
SMR: Benefactive + Embed. Cl.	'I cut some for Mummy'	5

Level X

Item	Example	Occn
Syn.: *Wh- + aux + S + aux + V + X*	[not observed]	
Syn.: *aux + neg + S + V + X*	'Don't you know why it did?'	7
NP Head: 'any'	[not observed]	
NP Head: Negative Adverb	[not observed]	
Modality: Inference	'I know the name of that one. Mister Wooden it must be'	10
Conjunction: 'so that'	'I've shut the door so that Bonny can't come in'	7
SMR: Purposive	'Is that for the clock?'	8
SMR: (Agent) Change Classification	'I'm calling it a flutterby'	9
Func.: Condition	'If it's a nice day we'll watch boats'	9

Although the empirical methods used to establish the sequence of levels produced two barely overlapping clusters of items, there is little theoretical justification for separating them. Had observations been made beyond the age of five years, there would probably have been clearer indications of order amongst the items at this stage of development. However, as for a proportion of children emergence was not observed on quite a substantial number of items, statements about these levels must remain tentative.

There are several notable additions: the realization of the complement by an embedded clause in the copula sentence, $S + cop +$ ⟨ ⟩; the addition of negation to polar interrogatives, *aux + neg + S + V + X*; the emergence of Reflexive Pronouns, with 'myself' typically the first to emerge; and the first occurrence of the Inference Modality option. However, what characterizes these two levels in general is a continuation of the filling-in that is required to complete the various linguistic systems. This is a process that will continue for several more years.

5.6 Evaluation of the observed sequence of linguistic development

The sequence of development, as reported in this and the earlier chapter, is the outcome of an empirical investigation. The question that must now be asked is whether the observed sequence can contribute to theory in this area.

In attempting to answer this question, however, it must be recognized that the use of spontaneous data alone may lead to a bias against observing the emergence of less frequently occurring items. This issue will be further discussed in chapter 6. Elicitation may possibly provide a complementary source of data in some cases, but the use of this technique has still to be investigated. Nevertheless, even without further work of this kind to check the reliability of the findings, there are a number of observations that can be made which may contribute to a clarification of theory about the sequence of development and the factors by which it is determined.

First, the data presented here give strong support to the claim that there is a universal sequence of development, at least in general outline, for British children learning English as their first language. One might therefore hypothesize that this will be true for other languages, although as Slobin (1979) has shown, there are good reasons to believe that there will be differences *between* languages in the actual sequences that occur as a result of inter-language differences in organization at all three levels of description. Secondly, there is a tendency for semantic and pragmatic distinctions to emerge before the syntactic structures through which they are eventually fully realized. This suggests that, to a large extent, and particularly in the early stages, the acquisition of language is essentially a matter of discovering the formal categories and relations through which to realize those semantic and pragmatic distinctions which have already been at least partially grasped. However, the discovery of which of the range of possible meanings that the child derives from his encounters with his social and physical environment are actually expressed in the language to which he is exposed is also an important part of the language learning process. In this and in providing the child with evidence of relationships between meanings and forms, the role of the linguistic environment is paramount. The relationship between the language learner and his linguistic environment will be further discussed in chapters 9 and 10.

Finally a word needs to be said about the segmentation of the sequence of development into levels. Whatever the number of levels or stages proposed, and whether they are arrived at *a priori* on the basis of theory or rule of thumb or, as in the present investigation, inductively on the basis of longitudinal data, any such proposal is to a large extent a matter of descriptive convenience imposed upon a continuous developmental process. Phillips (1975) puts the matter very clearly in discussing somewhat similar proposals made by Piaget concerning the sequence of cognitive development: 'Although the process is continuous, its results are discontinuous; they are qualitatively different from time to time. Because of that, Piaget has chosen to break the total course of development into units called *periods* and *stages*. Note carefully, however, that each of those cross-sections of development is described in terms of the best that the child can do at that time. Many previously acquired behaviours will occur even though he is capable of new and better ones' (p. 19). With the qualification that many linguistic 'behaviours' also remain relatively unchanged from their first emergence, this describes very well the relation of the proposed levels to the actual process of development.

The pattern of development over time

In the previous chapters, sequence of emergence was reported independently of age. This separation was quite deliberate. First, although claims about sequence are necessarily based upon observations of one event following another in time and thus on increasing age, they do not imply anything about the absolute age at which any event is observed or about the time interval between events. Secondly, since data from two cohorts, observed over different age-spans, contributed to the comparisons from which the ultimate sequences were derived, it was methodologically impossible to relate sequence to age directly.

In this chapter, by contrast, the developmental sequence already established will be mapped onto the dimension of age in terms of which the data were collected – that is to say an equal-interval scale with three months between intervals. First, linguistic systems will be considered individually, with age norms being given in terms of occasion of emergence for each item that reached the criterion of emergence by the age of five years. The relative frequency with which items occur at successive ages will also be discussed, with the full data on frequency being presented in tables A1–A19 in appendix 2. Secondly, the relationship between frequency and order of emergence will be examined and the chapter will conclude with a normative statement of the observed relationship between age and the sequence of levels derived from the preceding analysis of the longitudinal data.

6.1 Development within linguistic systems

As children develop at different rates, there is likely to be a considerable difference between the ages at which the first and the last child in the sample are observed to use a particular item for the first time. Since these are all supposedly 'normal' children, the span between the 10th and the 90th percentile provides a rough indication of the ages between which any particular item might be expected to emerge in a child developing normally, with the age of the median child providing the best estimate of the norm. It should be borne in mind, however, that because observations were made only at three-monthly intervals the data give a conservative estimate of emergence. The relatively small size of the sample of speech recorded on any occasion is likely to have had a similar effect. True age of emergence may thus be three months or more earlier than that which is reported. Errors in the opposite direction are much less likely.

A second index of development is the frequency with which items are used with increasing age. Although the relative frequency of items depends upon the structural units with which they are associated (e.g. noun phrase, clause, complete utterance) and upon whether the system to which they belong is obligatory or optional (cf. 3.8), the same base of 1000 utterances is used in calculating all frequencies. Thus a reported frequency of 57 means that 57 tokens per 1000 utterances were observed for the item in question in the total corpus of speech obtained at a particular age.

Data of this kind already exist for various corpora of adult language and it is well known that there is very wide variation in frequency between syntactic categories as well as between lexical items and that, to a considerable extent, variation in relative frequency is relatively stable across corpora collected in different contexts. Apart from those obtained in the Mount Gravatt study (Hart *et al.*, 1977),[1] however, data of this kind are not yet available for children's language. Yet they could clearly be of considerable value to clinicians as well as to researchers planning more experimental investigations. An alternative to calculating frequencies in relation to a constant base is to express the frequency with which an item occurs as a percentage of the frequency of occurrence of all members of the system to which the item belongs. The frequency with which Indirect Request is selected, for example, can be expressed as a percentage of the total number of utterances in the Control Function sub-system. When displayed graphically, relative-frequency data show very clearly how progressive additions to a system alter the pattern of use of other members of the system.

Before presenting age of emergence and frequency data for some of the major linguistic systems investigated, it will be helpful to give an indication of the size of the corpus of utterances that has been analysed at each age and of the relative proportion of those utterances that are structured. Except in the case of Inter-Personal Function, only structured utterances contribute to the data on emergence. However, in calculating frequency per 1000 utterances, the *total* number of codable utterances at each age is used as the denominator, as it was considered that the resulting frequencies would give a more accurate picture of development than those that would result from using only the total number of structured utterances as the denominator.

From table 6.1 it can be seen that there is a steady increase in the proportion of structured utterances up to about 51 months. From then on, the proportion remains steady at around 70%. The remaining 30% consist mainly of vocatives used as calls, exclamations and positive and negative one-word utterances.

6.2 Inter-Personal Purpose

Inter-Personal Purpose, it will be recalled, was described at three levels: Sequence, Sub-sequence and Function. In this section, age of emergence and frequency of functions will be described initially in relation to the sub-sequence modes in which they were considered to be options. Positive and negative responses will be omitted at this stage, but their overall frequency will be reported in the final discussion of frequencies.

Before proceeding to the individual functions, it is interesting to examine the relative frequency of the different sub-sequence modes with increasing age. These are shown graphically in figure 6.1.[2] What is striking is the trend from about 30 months onward for the

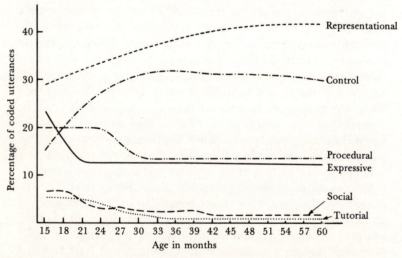

Figure 6.1 Distribution of utterances by sub-sequence mode and age

Table 6.1 *Number of utterances coded at each age*

	15	18	21	24	27	30	33	36	39	42	45	48	51	54	57	60
Number of coded utterances	1781	3007	3728	4816	5580	5404	5127	4818	12,200	12,190	6072	6506	6765	6383	6623	6387
Number of structured utterances	697	1300	2021	2715	3160	3356	3331	3235	8293	8311	4132	4519	4770	4561	4649	4481
Percentage of structured utterances	39.1	43.2	54.2	56.4	56.6	62.1	65.0	67.1	68.0	68.2	68.1	69.5	70.5	71.5	70.2	70.2

1 Except at the youngest ages, the number of coded utterances does not equal the number of interpretable utterances transcribed from 18 90-second samples. As explained in 1.8, it proved impossible to code all the transcribed speech and so a smaller number of samples was selected at random for coding where a child produced significantly more than 120 utterances in 18 samples.
2 The totals at 39 and 42 months are the combined totals of the two overlapping age-cohorts.

relative proportions of utterances in the different sub-sequence modes to remain constant. This will be seen to be repeated to a considerable extent when we examine the relative frequencies of functions within sub-sequence modes and also, indeed, when relative frequencies within other linguistic systems are considered.

6.2.1 *Control*

This is the largest group of functions, as defined in the *Coding Manual*, and includes some of the first and the last to emerge. Figure 6.2 shows the age by which the various functions had

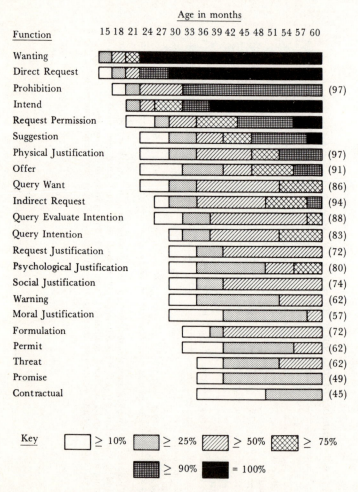

Figure 6.2 Age of emergence: Inter-personal functions: control

emerged in the speech of increasingly large percentages of the sample. As the same conventions apply to all succeeding figures of this kind, it will be convenient to mention them all at this point. First, data from the two age cohorts are combined, with precedence being given to the younger cohort. If, for example, 75% of the younger cohort has used an item by 42 months, this is assumed to apply to the older cohort as well and no change is shown until the age at which the 90% level is reached in the older cohort. (Like percentiles, these levels are cumulative and are to be read as $\geq x\%$ of the sample.) Secondly, not all items reached the 100% level (i.e. emerged in all children) by the age of 60 months, when the last observation was made. Where this is the case, the percentage reached by the last observation is shown in brackets on the extreme right. Finally, items are arranged in order of increasing age at which the 10% level was reached.

By 18 months at least 50% of the sample are expressing simple Wants and by 21 months 50% are making Direct Requests, with Prohibitions and Statements of Intention reaching the same level three months later. By 36 months a variety of interrogatively realized functions have reached the 50% level: Request Permission, Indirect Request, Suggestion, Offer, and Queries about the Wants and Intentions of others, though in their first occurrences they are not always realized by full, well-formed interrogatives. All the remaining functions – Request for Justification and the various types of Justification, Warning, Threat, Promise, Formulation, Permit and Contractual – are somewhat later to emerge. None, apart from Physical Justification, reaches the 90% level. Indeed several are still at about the 50% level at the age of 60 months.

When the development of the same functions is looked at in terms of frequency (see table A1 in appendix 2), four stand out from the rest. Wanting, which is the earliest to emerge, rises rapidly to a peak frequency of 92 (per 1000 utterances) at 21 months and then declines quite sharply to 23 at 60 months. Although never achieving the same level, Intend is to some extent the inverse, starting at a very low frequency and continuing to rise to its highest level of 36 at 60 months. It is Direct Request, however, which becomes the dominant function, rising steeply in frequency to reach 73 at 36 months and remaining near that level at all succeeding ages. By contrast, Prohibition, which reaches its highest frequency (15) at about the same age, shows a gradual decline in frequency at later ages. All the remaining functions show a similar pattern of relatively slow rise to a steady level from 45 months onwards. With the exception of Request Permission, none reaches a stable frequency which is greater than 10 per 1000.

In figure 6.3 the same frequency data are shown as proportions of all functions in the Control sub-sequence mode. Only some functions are shown as there is not space in the lower part of the graph to include the many functions which never rise above a frequency of 5 per 1000. The category Formulation can be taken as representative of these functions. The relationship between the frequency curve for Wanting and those of all other functions suggests that Wanting serves initially as an all-purpose Control function which is gradually replaced by an increasing variety of more differentiated functions. However, some of the later functions to emerge, such as Warning, Permit and Promise perform acts which, in their recognition of desires and intentions in the addressee, are quite outside the scope of the initial Wanting.

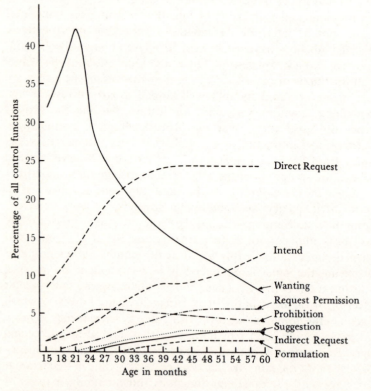

Figure 6.3 Relative frequency: Inter-personal functions: control

6.2.2 *Expressive*

As with Control, there is one function which emerges very early: Exclamation (see figure 6.4). This is being used by 75% of the sample by the first observation. The next two functions to emerge, Verbal Accompaniment to Behaviour and Express State, both reach the 50% level by 21 months. Query State, which reaches the 50% level at 39 months, is the only other Expressive function to approach the 90% level by the last observation at 60 months.

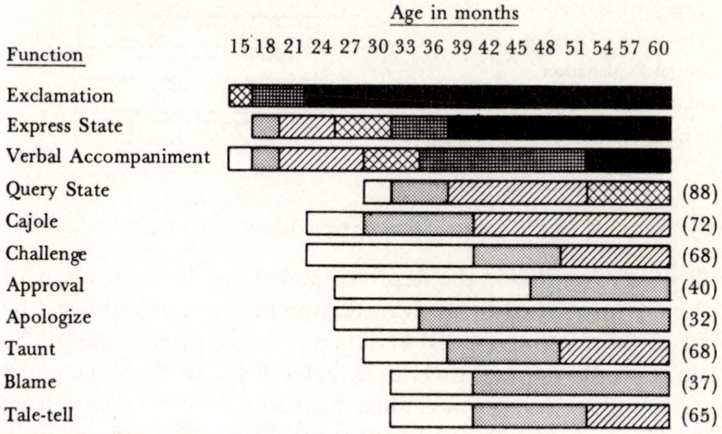

Age in months

Function	15 18 21 24 27 30 33 36 39 42 45 48 51 54 57 60	
Exclamation		
Express State		
Verbal Accompaniment		
Query State		(88)
Cajole		(72)
Challenge		(68)
Approval		(40)
Apologize		(32)
Taunt		(68)
Blame		(37)
Tale-tell		(65)

For key see Figure 6.2

Figure 6.4 Age of emergence: Inter-personal functions: expressive

As can be seen from table A2, the frequencies of the three functions Exclamation, Express State and Verbal Accompaniment to Behaviour are the only ones to rise above 10 per 1000 utterances. Of these, Exclamation is by far the most frequent initially (147), but by 60 months it has dropped to almost the same level as has been reached by Express State (36). Because frequencies are so low for all other Expressive functions, it is not feasible to represent relative frequencies graphically.

6.2.3 *Representational*

Ostension is the first function to emerge, being used by 50% of the sample at 15 months and by 100% by 24 months. Statement follows closely behind, being used by 100% at 27 months. Next follow Content Question and Content Response, both reaching the 75% level by 27 months. It is interesting that the emergence of Yes/No Question lags about six months behind Content Question

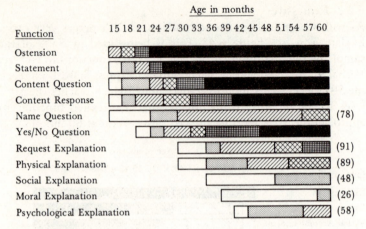

Figure 6.5 Age of emergence: Inter-personal functions: representational

and Name Question in the Representational mode (see figure 6.5). Although being used by 10% of the sample at 15 months and by 25% at 24 months, this latter function never reaches the 100% level. It would appear, therefore, that the use of this function is subject to considerable individual variation. As can be seen from table A3, after starting at a frequency of 24 per 1000 utterances, it drops rapidly to the much lower level of 4 or 5. Request for Explanation and the various categories of Explanation are all rather late to emerge. This cannot be because of any intrinsic difficulty as, in the Control mode, the equivalent categories of Justification reach the same levels on average six months earlier. A comparison of the relative frequencies of these categories in the Control and Representational modes (tables A1 and A3) shows that they are also more frequent in the Control mode, suggesting that frequency may be having an effect on age of emergence. Since this is an issue of very general significance, detailed discussion of it will be postponed until the end of the chapter.

   When the relative frequencies of the Representational functions are considered (figure 6.6), four different patterns of change are found. Ostension, which initially accounted for more than 60% of all Representational utterances shows a rapid decline after the age of 24 months. As the child becomes capable of expressing meanings in which a state or event is predicated about a topic, or in which a request for further information or for confirmation about a predication is made, the simple drawing of attention to an object or

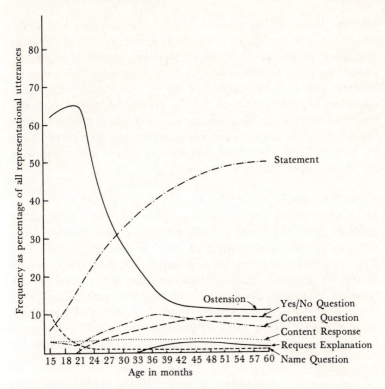

Figure 6.6 Relative frequency: Inter-personal functions: representational

event is superseded as a means of sustaining conversation. Such utterances continue to play a role in initiating sequences but, as sequences become longer, they become relatively less frequent overall. The second pattern is that demonstrated by Statement. This shows a rapid rise in frequency from 15 months onwards, such that, by 30 months, Statements are the most frequently occurring category of Representational function. Even at 60 months, their relative frequency is still increasing, though more slowly. The third pattern is to be seen in the various types of question and in the categories of explanation. (The latter occur at too low a frequency to be included on the graph.) All these functions show a more gradual increase in relative frequency until a plateau is reached in all but the case of Content Question. This category actually shows a continuing decline from the age of 36–9 months, although presumably, if observations had continued beyond 60 months, there would have been a levelling off for this category as well. As already remarked, although Content Question initially occurs more frequently than Yes/No Question, the latter category eventually becomes the more frequent. The final pattern is that of constant frequency. Response to Content Question occurs with almost exactly the same relative frequency from 15 months through to 60 months. This is clearly related to the frequency with which such questions are asked and, as will be seen in chapter 9, this too remains fairly constant over the same period. Name Question, after initially being the second most frequently occurring category, drops by 21 months to a low level, and remains almost unchanged over subsequent observations.

6.2.4 *Procedural*

Included in this sub-sequence mode (figure 6.7) are three rather different groups of function. Call, the conversation-opening function, forms one group together with its partner, Availability Response. It is interesting that although Call is the first function to emerge in this sub-sequence, reaching the 100% level by 24 months, Availability Response is much later to emerge and never rises above 68% of the sample showing evidence of use. Once again, this seems to be partly a function of the relative infrequency with which others initiate conversations with these children by

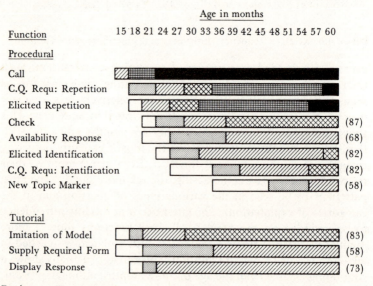

Age in months

Function	15 18 21 24 27 30 33 36 39 42 45 48 51 54 57 60

Procedural

Call
C.Q. Requ: Repetition
Elicited Repetition
Check   (87)
Availability Response   (68)
Elicited Identification   (82)
C.Q. Requ: Identification   (82)
New Topic Marker   (58)

Tutorial

Imitation of Model   (83)
Supply Required Form   (58)
Display Response   (73)

For key see Figure 6.2

Figure 6.7 Age of emergence: Inter-personal functions: procedural and tutorial

means of a Call, although there seems to be an additional dis-inclination on the part of the children to answer such Calls with an Availability Response. The second group of Procedural functions occur in 'contingent query' exchanges. As might be expected, children receive quite a large number of utterances which call for a repetition or clarification of their previous utterances and Elicited Repetition is a function which emerges quite early. They also begin to make such requests themselves, the two functions emerging almost in parallel.[3] Requests for Identification of intended referent and Elicited Identification in response to similar requests addressed to them emerge some six to 12 months later and never reach the 90% level within the period under investigation. Check, the repetition of a preceding utterance with questioning intonation, belongs to the same group and shows a pattern of emergence somewhere between the two types of contingent query.

New Topic Marker is the sole member of the third type of function to emerge in a significant proportion of the sample. This group might more aptly be described as meta-conversational functions, their role being to point up and negotiate the topic-related organization of conversation at the level of sequence. Not surprisingly, such functions occur very rarely in the children's speech; and they also show a late age of emergence.

6.2.5 *Tutorial*

Included in figure 6.7 are the few Tutorial functions that occur in the speech of a majority of the children. More than any other functions, these are dependent upon the adults' styles of interaction with their children. Whilst the majority of parents of young children engage in some sequences of conversation where the dominant purpose seems to be Tutorial, this is much less true of the parents of children aged 27 months and older. Consequently, if a child has not been observed to respond to a Request for Imitation of a Model Utterance or to a Request to Supply a Required Form or to answer a Display Question by that age, it is relatively unlikely that he will be observed to do so at a later age. Little importance, therefore, should be attached to the age-of-emergence data. However the frequency data in table A4 are still of considerable interest.

In figure 6.8 the relative frequencies of the Procedural and Tutorial functions are shown, expressed as a percentage of total frequency of the respective sub-sequence mode. In each mode, one function is seen to start with a high frequency and to show a rapid

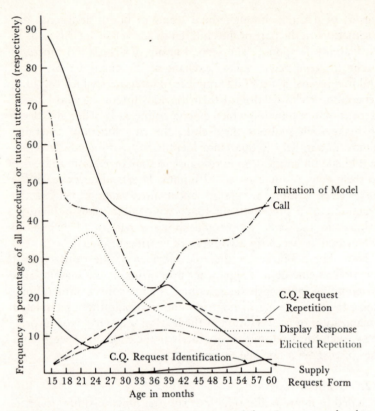

Figure 6.8 Relative frequency: Inter-personal functions: procedural and tutorial

decline: in the Procedural mode, Call then seems to settle at a steady relative frequency, whereas in the Tutorial mode Imitation of Model becomes relatively more frequent again after a trough around 36 months. Of the remaining Procedural functions, all reach a fairly steady relative frequency during the fifth year although, in the case of Elicited Repetition and Request for Repetition, this is lower than the peak reached in the fourth year. (The frequencies of Check, Availability Response, Elicited Identification and New Topic Marker are too low to be shown in figure 6.8.)

Among the Tutorial functions, Supply Required Form and Display Response show patterns that are almost inversely related in the ages at which they are relatively most and least frequent. Since the most frequently Required Forms are 'Please' and 'Thank you', it would seem that politeness is a particular focus of adult attention at about the age of three, that is to say at an age by which all children are making Direct Requests and a majority are also making Requests for Permission and using various more indirect methods of expressing their wants.

Having considered each of the sub-sequence modes in turn, it is clear that they show a similar pattern of development. In each case one relatively undifferentiated function emerges very early and is initially used with a high relative frequency. As more differentiated functions are learned, the undifferentiated one decreases in frequency and one or two of the more differentiated functions in each mode take on a greater importance. The majority of functions in all modes, however, show a much more gradual increase to a steady frequency which may still, in absolute terms, be relatively low. Expressed as frequencies per 1000 utterances, the absolute values attained are clearly governed by the number of functions recognized within the total system. With fewer distinctions, absolute values would, in general, be greater. However, the number of functional distinctions made does not affect differences in relative frequency to the same extent. Even with a much smaller number of relatively crude functional categories, there would remain substantial differences between them in the frequency with which they occurred.

Finally, before leaving Inter-Personal Purpose, it is interesting to look at the frequency of occurrence of four response categories which, realized typically by one-word utterances, have a similar meaning across all sub-sequence modes. These are Assent/Agree/Affirm (i.e. the positive response), Refuse/Disagree/Deny (i.e. the negative response), Reject (also typically realized as 'no') and Acknowledge. Figure 6.9 shows the frequency per 1000 utterances of each of these response functions for all sub-sequence modes combined. The peak in frequency of the negative response around 30 months may perhaps be seen as support for the commonly held view that many children go through a stage in their third year of asserting their independence, with this often being expressed as refusal to carry out requests and as disagreement with the statements of others. However, it is interesting to note that there is also a concurrent peak in the frequency of positive responses. On the other hand, the explanation may be simply that at this age there is a peak in the frequency with which others address questions to children which require either a positive or a negative response. This interpretation receives a considerable measure of support from the input frequency data, considered in chapter 9.

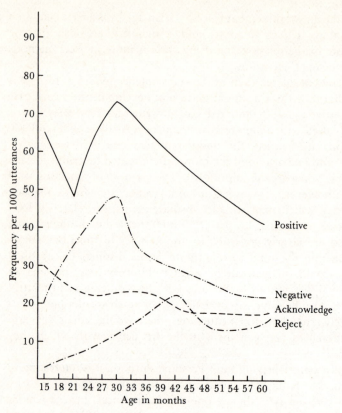

Figure 6.9 Relative frequency of response functions × age

6.3 Sentence Meaning Relations

As with Inter-Personal Purpose, it will be convenient to consider the SMRs in the groupings that were established in chapter 4. First, however, let us look (figure 6.10) at the relative frequency of the groupings themselves, as this provides a background against which the development of individual meaning relations can be better understood. As with the functions, there is one category which emerges very early and shows a dramatic decrease in frequency as other options become available. Like the early functions, it is also undifferentiated, at least in form; but, as suggested earlier, it is perhaps better seen as a portmanteau category which would repay a more differentiated analysis.

All the other groupings, with one exception, show a similar pattern of sharp increase in relative frequency until a fairly steady

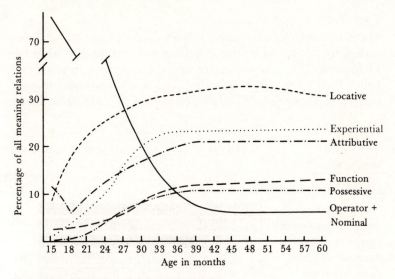

Figure 6.10 Distribution of meaning relations × age

level is reached at about the age of 36 months. The one exception, Attributive, shows an initial decrease, but this is accounted for by the high level of Classification Attributive utterances at the first observation. When the total number of structured utterances is small, as it was on this occasion, one prolonged sequence by one parent–child pair in which such responses are called for can easily produce a disproportionate effect on relative frequency. In this context, it is interesting to note that there is a similar decrease in the frequency of Supply Required Form from the first observation to the fourth (cf. figure 6.8).

Generally speaking, the rank order of the different groupings with respect to relative frequency remains very similar with increasing age. Locative continues as the most frequent group, with Possessive the least frequent. Experiential is the only group to show a significant change in rank order and its final position is reached by 27 months. What this suggests is that, despite the very substantial development that takes place between 15 and 60 months in the range of meaning relations that the child is able to express, and despite the changes that take place with maturation in the things that he is able to do and in the ways in which others relate to him, at a very basic level the areas of experience about which the child wishes, or is called upon, to communicate remain of fairly constant relative importance.

6.3.1 *Locative and Possessive*

The Locative group of meaning relations is the largest and also the earliest to emerge, with three categories reaching the 50% level by 21 months. These, however, are the only categories to reach the 100% level by the last observation and of the remainder several barely rise above the 50% level (see figure 6.11). The same figure

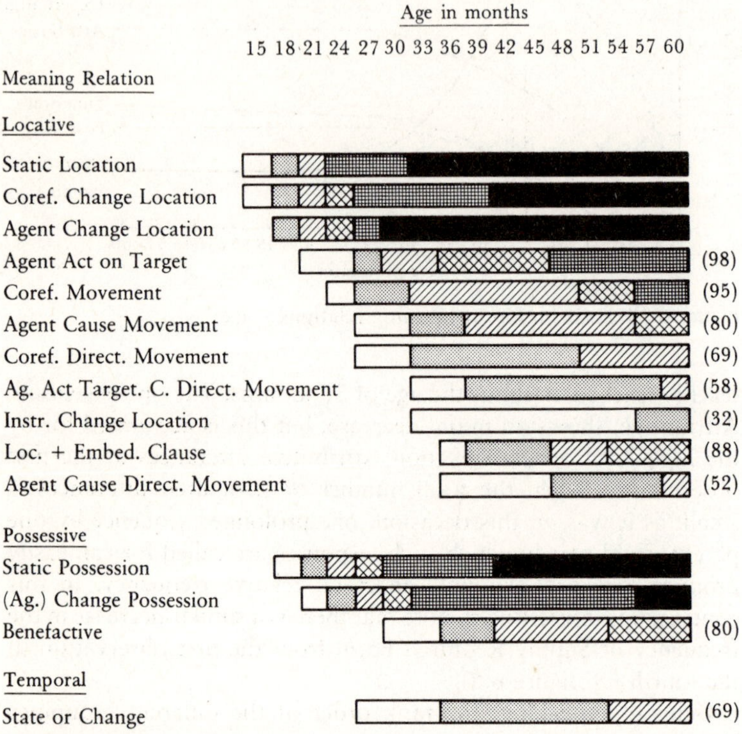

Age in months

15 18 21 24 27 30 33 36 39 42 45 48 51 54 57 60

Meaning Relation

Locative

Static Location

Coref. Change Location

Agent Change Location

Agent Act on Target   (98)

Coref. Movement   (95)

Agent Cause Movement   (80)

Coref. Direct. Movement   (69)

Ag. Act Target. C. Direct. Movement   (58)

Instr. Change Location   (32)

Loc. + Embed. Clause   (88)

Agent Cause Direct. Movement   (52)

Possessive

Static Possession

(Ag.) Change Possession

Benefactive   (80)

Temporal

State or Change   (69)

For key see Figure 6.2

Figure 6.11 Age of emergence: locative, possessive and temporal meaning relations

also contains data on age of emergence for both Possessive and Temporal relations. It shows static Possession and Change of Possession reaching the 50% level at 24 and 27 months respectively and going on to reach the 100% level well before 60 months. Benefactive and Temporal[4] relations are later to emerge and never rise above the 80% level.

Table A5 presents the frequencies of the same categories expressed as frequencies per 1000 utterances. A point to note in interpreting this and subsequent frequency tables is that, with categories whose domain is the clause rather than the utterance, the frequency per 1000 utterances may continue to rise throughout the period under investigation as a result of the continuing increase in the proportion of utterances that contain more than one clause. On the other hand, where the frequency of each meaning relation is calculated as a percentage of the total number of meaning relation tokens produced, as in figure 6.12, it is likely that some meaning relations will attain a steady relative frequency well before the last observation.

Figure 6.12 shows that among the Locative, Possessive and Temporal meaning relations, there are three broad levels of relative frequency. Static Location, Agent Cause Change of Location and Coreferential Change of Location emerge early as a group and rise

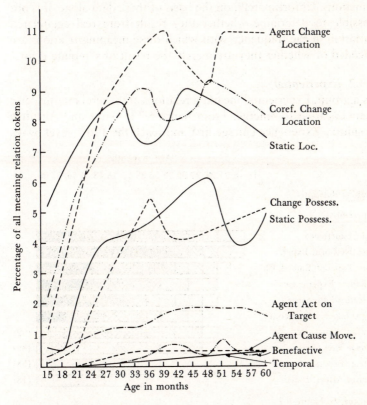

Figure 6.12 Relative frequency of locative, possessive and temporal meaning relations

rapidly in relative frequency until they reach a level of between 8% and 11%. Together, therefore, they come to account for almost 30% of all meaning relations. At the second level, Static Possession and Change of Possession, which are slightly later to emerge, rise to a relative frequency of around 5%. The third level includes all the remaining categories − Temporal, Benefactive and a variety of Locative meaning relations, which are similar in being later to emerge and in not rising above a relative frequency of 2%. Only some of these categories are included in figure 6.12, as there is not sufficient space to show them all. However, Temporal is fairly representative of those that are omitted, none reaching more than a frequency of four per 1000 utterances.

Several of the categories in these groups, far from maintaining a steady relative frequency, show quite marked oscillations which are apparently more systematic than was the case with Inter-Personal Functions. Unfortunately, on the basis of these data alone, it is not possible to determine whether they result from real age-related variation in the frequency with which these meaning relations are encoded or whether they are merely the result of sampling error.

6.3.2 *Experiential*

As a group, Experiential meaning relations are several months later than Locative to emerge. From figure 6.13, Want and Agentive Cognitive Experience emerge first and reach the 100% level by 42

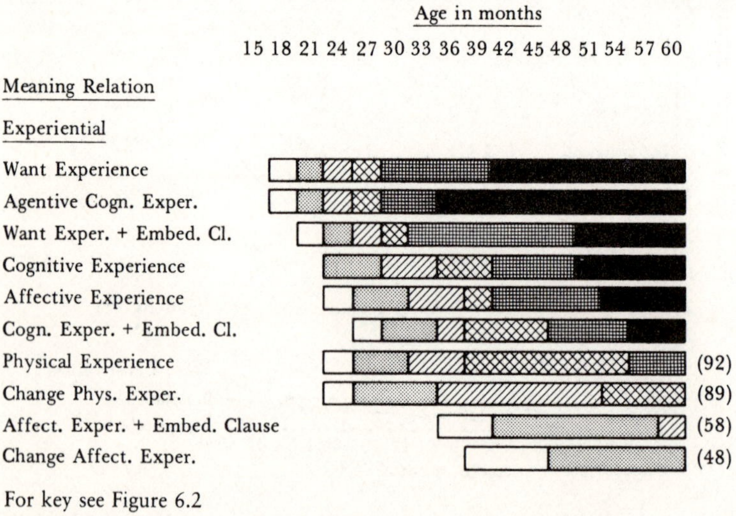

Age in months

15 18 21 24 27 30 33 36 39 42 45 48 51 54 57 60

Meaning Relation

Experiential

Want Experience
Agentive Cogn. Exper.
Want Exper. + Embed. Cl.
Cognitive Experience
Affective Experience
Cogn. Exper. + Embed. Cl.
Physical Experience (92)
Change Phys. Exper. (89)
Affect. Exper. + Embed. Clause (58)
Change Affect. Exper. (48)

For key see Figure 6.2

Figure 6.13 Age of emergence: experiential meaning relations

and 36 months respectively; the same categories with the addition of embedded clauses follow some months later, but are rather slower to reach the 100% level. Affective and Physical Experience show similar patterns of emergence, following some six months behind Agentive Cognitive Experience and being rather slower to reach the 100% level (in fact, Physical Experience only reaches 92% by the last observation at 60 months).

When we consider the group from the point of view of frequency, however, a rather different picture emerges (Table A6). Want and Agentive Cognitive Experience predictably start out with the highest frequencies but, whereas Agentive Cognitive Experience reaches a steady frequency of about 48 per 1000 utterances by 48 months, Want Experience, having reached almost the same frequency considerably earlier at 36 months, shows a marked decline over the remainder of the observations. A somewhat similar contrast is seen when we consider Want Experience + Embedded Clause and Cognitive Experience + Embedded Clause. This contrast is equally apparent when the same meaning relations are compared in terms of their relative frequencies (figure 6.14). This suggests that whilst cognitive experiences continue to increase in importance as matter for communication in the child's conversation throughout the pre-school years, particularly the experiences which require a more complex semantic structure for their expression, the direct expression of the experience of wanting declines in importance.

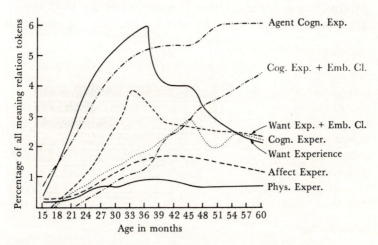

Figure 6.14 Relative frequency of experiential meaning relations

Two possible explanations suggest themselves for this development, both deriving from the child's increasing competence in areas other than the purely linguistic. On the one hand, with greater physical competence comes greater independence and a reduction in the need to communicate his wants and needs so that others may satisfy them for him. And on the other hand, increasing social competence leads to a recognition that others are free agents whose good offices – either direct action or permission – are most effectively obtained by indirect requests rather than by a bald statement of his own wants and wishes. Both these developments would lead to a decline in the overt expression of the Wanting Experience with the intention of obtaining goods and services.

Although both Affective and Physical experiences become options for expression by most children by the early part of the fourth year, they remain at a relatively low level of frequency and, in the case of Affective Experience, show a slight decline in frequency during the fifth year. Presumably the child only feels the need to communicate about these modes of experience when he is made particularly conscious of them, either when he experiences relatively extreme sensations of pain, pleasure or displeasure or when others ask him questions about his physical or affective state.

6.3.3 *Attribution*

Among the Attributive meaning relations, Classification stands out as quite different from all the other meaning relations. Although having emerged in the speech of only 10% of the sample, this category is at its highest relative frequency at the age of 15 months (see figures 6.15 and 6.16). As already suggested, this category is

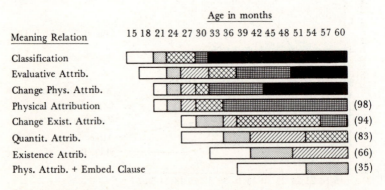

For key see Figure 6.2

Figure 6.15 Age of emergence: attributive meaning relations

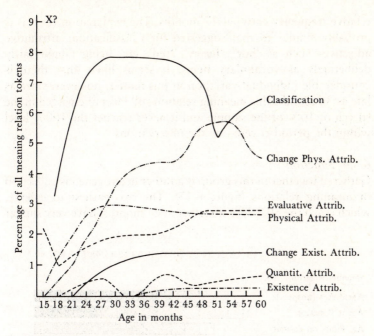

Figure 6.16 Relative frequency of attributive meanings

particularly strongly influenced by context and tokens are likely to occur in large numbers if they occur at all. It is difficult to know, therefore, whether the initial frequency is better represented by 36 per 1000 utterances at 15 months or by 14 per 1000 utterances at 18 months (see Table A7). However, there is no doubt of its very high relative frequency from 24 months onwards until the end of the fourth year. At that point it shows a sharp decline, only to rise again in the second half of the fifth year. With its close connection with vocabulary learning, it is not difficult to see why it should occur so frequently at around the age of two, but it is less obvious why there should be such a marked resurgence at the end of the pre-school period. Perhaps this results from a burst of teaching behaviour by the parents just before the children enter school.

Two other attributive meaning relations show patterns that are somewhat unusual. Evaluative Attribution, like Classification, also starts with a decline in relative frequency between 15 and 18 months (the 15 tokens on the first occasion being produced by only three children), but thereafter it follows a fairly typical pattern in rising gradually until it reaches a stable relative frequency at about 48 months. Physical Attribute is also unusual in reaching its highest relative frequency early, at 27 months. The explanation for this is probably similar to that suggested for Classification: attributive adjectives such as 'hot', 'heavy', 'red', etc. being taught fairly deliberately as vocabulary items. It seems likely that there is considerable individual variation in this matter, however, since as late as 36 months this meaning relation still has not emerged in the speech of 10% of the sample and it never reaches the 100% level within the period covered by the observations.

6.3.4 *Function*

Gathered together in this group is a rather heterogeneous collection of meaning relations (figure 6.17). The two earliest to emerge, which reach the 50% level together at 27 months, have very similar

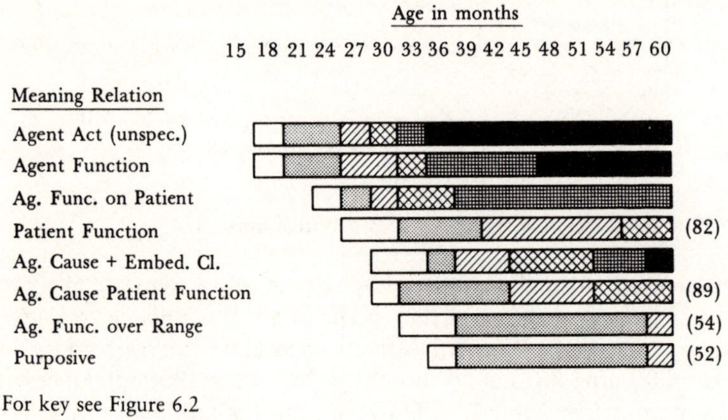

Age in months

15 18 21 24 27 30 33 36 39 42 45 48 51 54 57 60

Meaning Relation

Agent Act (unspec.)
Agent Function
Ag. Func. on Patient
Patient Function   (82)
Ag. Cause + Embed. Cl.
Ag. Cause Patient Function   (89)
Ag. Func. over Range   (54)
Purposive   (52)

For key see Figure 6.2

Figure 6.17 Age of emergence: function meaning relations

syntactic realizations. Agent Function is realized by a simple intransitive clause (e.g. 'John is playing') and Agent Act (unspecified) by the pro-verb 'do', usually in the interrogative sentence 'What are you doing?' (or more probably in its earliest realization as 'what doing?'). However, whilst Agent Function follows the regular pattern of increasing in relative frequency until a steady state is reached at about 42 months, Agent Act reaches a peak at 33 months and then shows a marked decline, before climbing to a rather higher peak at 48 months (cf. figure 6.18 and table A8). No obvious explanation suggests itself for this pattern, although it is perhaps worth noting that several categories in the Locative and Possessive group showed similar patterns of relative frequency.

The only other feature that merits comment is the relationship

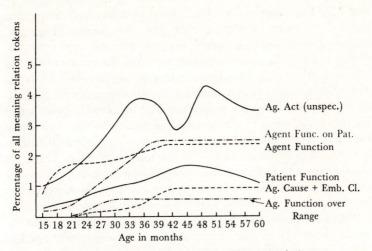

Figure 6.18 Relative frequency of function meaning relations

between Agent Function and Agent Function on Patient. The latter meaning relation differs from the former only in that it is transitive in its realization, the Patient with respect to which the function is carried out being realized as the direct object. Ultimately these two categories reach steady states of almost identical relative frequency. However Agent Function is earlier to emerge by three to six months and, as might therefore be expected, initially occurs much more frequently. These early differences in emergence and frequency may perhaps be accounted for by the difference in semantic/syntactic complexity, which, beyond a certain point in development, ceases to be important.

Having considered each of the groups of meaning relations separately, a number of general observations can be made about relative frequency in the system as a whole. Where there are many items in a system, as is the case with SMRs and Inter-Personal Functions, the frequency of occurrence of individual items must, on average, be lower than in the case of a system comprising only a small number of items. When the variation in frequency that occurs between items within any system is added to this, it is clear that the frequency of the least frequent items is likely to be very low indeed. And this is precisely what has been observed. However, if items within a system are acquired sequentially rather than simultaneously, as seems to be the case, there is a further inequality. When the first items within the system are acquired, the system is, from the learner's point of view, relatively small and so those items that have been acquired are likely to be used relatively frequently, particularly where, as in the present case, the system is obligatory, and one item has to be chosen in every structural unit to which the choice applies. As more items are acquired, the number of items from which a choice is made on each occasion increases and so it is rather unlikely that later-acquired items will ever reach the frequency levels achieved by the earlier-acquired items at the point when the number of items available was considerably smaller. Indeed the only way in which new items can be observed to occur at all is if, in a sense, they replace items that previously occurred. Thus, we should expect to find some items that show a decrease in frequency over time as new items enter the system and increase in frequency. In the meaning relations system, Operator + Nominal initially fulfils this role, decreasing regularly in relative frequency until the age of about 42 months. Thereafter the decrease is smaller and less regular and so other items must show compensating decreases to match the increasing frequency of more recently acquired items. Some items, such as Want Experience, do show such a decrease and one which can be explained in non-linguistic terms. But it may be that some of the otherwise unaccountable dips in relative frequency noticed in relation to several items can be explained as a reflex of increasing frequencies in other parts of the system.

6.4 Time, Aspect and Modality
In this section we shall consider three systems that modify the SMR in various ways, all of which can be realized through additions to the verb phrase.

6.4.1 *Time*
The description of temporal reference was made on two dimensions: whether the reference was to past, future or neutral time relative to the moment of speaking, and whether the time referred to was specified more precisely by reference to some other fixed or deictic time. In principle, these two dimensions yield a matrix of 21 categories of time reference, but in practice many of them occurred so infrequently that the distinction between past, future and neutral was collapsed for all but Point Time (e.g. 'now' v. 'when I was four') and Relative to Point (e.g. 'tomorrow' v. 'five minutes ago'). This left the 13 categories in figure 6.19 together with the unmarked Neutral category, which is not included because, being the default option, it was coded when none of the marked categories applied.

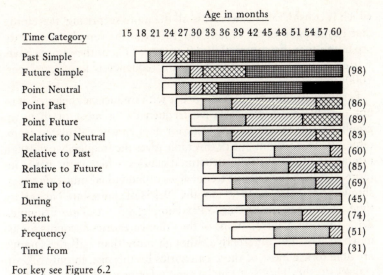

For key see Figure 6.2

Figure 6.19 Age of emergence: time

Generally speaking, where utterances make lexicalized reference to time, there is a strong tendency for Neutral time to emerge first, followed by Past and then Future, corresponding to a tendency for children to speak first about the here-and-now and then to report events that occurred in the past somewhat before entertaining possibilities about the future. However, when reference is made to a time by situating it relative to a time other than time of speaking, it is Relative to Future which emerges before Relative to Past. A second somewhat surprising feature is the contrast between the short period of time that elapses between the 10% and the 75% levels being reached for Past Simple, Future Simple and Point Neutral, and the very much longer period that elapses between the 75% and the 100% level. Although the tendency for all systems examined so far is for the age of emergence distribution to be positively skewed, this tendency is particularly pronounced for these three time categories.

When the same items are considered from the point of view of frequency, the contrasts are extreme (table A9). Past Simple starts with a frequency of 2 per 1000 utterances at the age of 15 months and reaches 94 at 60 months and is still increasing. However, with the exception of Future Simple which reaches 39 and Point Neutral which reaches 28, none of the other categories rises above the 6 per 1000 level, and the majority appear to reach a steady frequency which is considerably lower. It is all the more surprising, therefore, that Past Simple takes so long for 100% of the sample to start to use it and that, by contrast, by 60 months 74% of the sample have started to use Extent, when its mean frequency is less than 2 per 1000 utterances.

Because so many of the items occur with frequencies below 6, it is not possible to display relative frequencies of most of them in graphic form. However, the relevant data can be calculated from table A9. The bottom line of this table gives the frequency per 1000 utterances of semantically structured clauses, which is the figure in terms of which the relative frequencies of individual time categories should be calculated. At 60 months 79.1% of clauses are Neutral in time reference, 11.6% refer to Past Simple, 4.3% to Future Simple, 2.1% to Point Neutral. None of the other categories accounts for as much as 1%. Put differently, although more than half the sample are able to use most of these categories by this age, in only 5% of clauses do they choose to make time references other than to Past Simple, Future Simple and Neutral.

6.4.2 *Aspect*

All eight aspectual categories emerged in the speech of some of the children by 60 months, though only two categories, Continuous and Perfect, reached the 100% level. Interestingly, Completive and Cessive emerge some 18 months before Inceptive, and Iterative and Durative are about six months later still. Habitual lies somewhere in between, reaching the 50% level 12 months after Completive but six months before Inceptive.

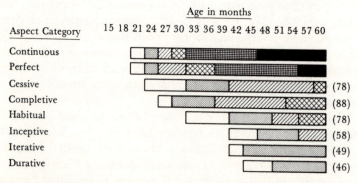

For key see Figure 6.2

Figure 6.20 Age of emergence: aspect

As with Time, relative frequency data can be calculated from table A10. Once again the majority of categories do not reach a frequency above 6 per 1000 utterances and even Continuous, the most frequent, does not rise above 41. In terms of relative frequency, therefore, even in the later observations only about 9% of clauses are marked for Aspect and, of these, 4%–5% involve Continuous Aspect and 2%–3% Perfect Aspect, with the other six categories together accounting for the remaining 1%–2%.

6.4.3 *Modal and modulation*

Finally in this section we come to the two systems of Modal and Modulation. Although semantically quite distinct in the type of modification they make to the meaning relation expressed in the clause, they are most typically realized by items selected from the auxiliary verb system and, syntactically, they have similar privileges of occurrence. Nevertheless, as figure 6.21 shows, the two systems are quite widely separated in terms of age of emergence.

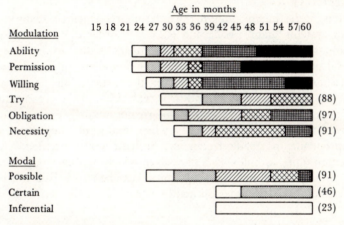

For key see Figure 6.2

Figure 6.21 Age of emergence: modal and modulation

Ability and Permission, both most typically realized by 'can', are the first categories to emerge, both reaching the 50% level by 30 months. They are closely followed by Willing, which is most typically first realized by 'will' or the contracted form ''ll'. Obligation and Necessity, realized by 'have got to', 'must', 'have to' and 'should' emerge three to six months later, so by 39 months all five categories of Modulation are likely to be present in the speech of the average child. On the other hand, Try, which is perhaps only tangentially a member of this system, takes nine months longer to reach the 50% level and fails to reach the 90% level even by the age of 60 months.

By contrast, the Modal system is much later to emerge and is much more spread out in terms of the ages at which particular levels are reached. Only Possible, realized typically by 'may' and 'might', is really firmly established by 60 months, whilst Inferential has hardly begun to appear at all. The fact that all these items are typically realized by the one class, auxiliary verb, is perhaps the best single indicator that acquisition does not depend simply on syntactic criteria.

From table A11 it can be seen that, in terms of frequency, the items in these two systems fall into three relatively distinct groups. Ability, Permission and Willing all reach fairly steady frequencies of 20–30 per 1000 utterances; Obligation and Necessity level out at around 12; whilst the remainder all remain below 6 per 1000 utterances.

It is interesting to compare the differing frequencies of items in all four systems (figures 6.22 and 6.23). (In order to allow a direct comparison to be made, frequencies are calculated to the base of 1000 utterances.) Apart from the high frequency of Past Simple, there are strong similarities between the systems. This is perhaps related to the fact that all find their realization in the organization of the verb phrase. Since the systems are not mutually exclusive, it is likely that by 36–9 months, when many of the items are approaching a steady frequency, at least some utterances will contain quite complex verb phrases in which options from several systems are combined. This expectation can be seen to be confirmed in some of the examples quoted in 5.5.

6.5 The noun phrase

Development in the noun phrase, like that in all structural units, occurs on two dimensions: increase in structural complexity and diversification of the options that occur at each position in the structure. In this section we shall consider both dimensions, starting with the options that occur at the three structural positions of Headword, Modifier and Qualifier.

6.5.1 *Headword*

Strictly speaking, the options to be considered are syntactic classes, four of which readily occur as head of the noun phrase: noun,

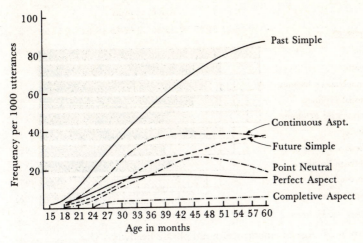

Figure 6.22 Frequency × age: time and aspect

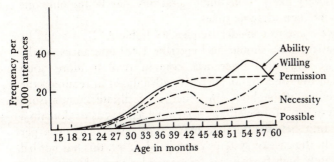

Figure 6.23 Frequency × age: modal and modulation

adjective, adverb and pronoun. Pronouns are further divided into the sub-classes, personal, demonstrative, etc., and a distinction is made within adjective (here termed modifier) between positive, on the one hand, and comparative and superlative on the other. The pattern of emergence for these various categories of Headword is shown in figure 6.24.

In interpreting these data, it is important to remember that the (appropriate) use of any member of a class is sufficient for that class to be said to have emerged in the speech of a particular child. The claim that 50% of the sample use the class Relative Pronoun by 39 months may thus mean no more than that they use a single relative pronoun, and almost invariably the first one to be used is 'what',

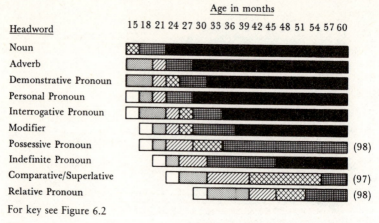

For key see Figure 6.2

Figure 6.24 Age of emergence: noun phrase headword

which is used in all syntactic contexts. Similarly, the first Possessive Pronoun is very likely to be 'mine', and this may be the only one used for some considerable time.

When we come to consider frequencies (table A12), it might be argued that the base should no longer be 1000 utterances, as the majority of structured utterances contain two or more noun phrases. On the other hand, there are advantages in retaining the same base-line throughout, in order to facilitate comparisons between systems. Moreover, any system which has as its domain a structural unit below utterance may occur more than once per utterance. In the case of systems considered so far, this has not led to inordinately high frequencies for particular items. However, as can be seen from table A12, frequencies for certain categories of Headword are extremely high and those for total number of Headwords exceed 1000 on the later occasions. Despite this inconvenience, it has been decided to retain the 1000-utterance base-line, as one of the major purposes of presenting these frequencies is to provide a basis on which estimates can be made of the size of corpus it is necessary to collect at any age in order to obtain a certain number of tokens of any particular category.

Figure 6.25 shows the relative frequency with which each syntactic class occurs as headword of the noun phrase. Although there is very considerable change over the period from 15 to 60 months, this is very largely confined to the two classes Noun and Personal Pronoun. Until 21 months more than two-thirds of all noun phrases have a noun as their head. Between 21 and 36 months

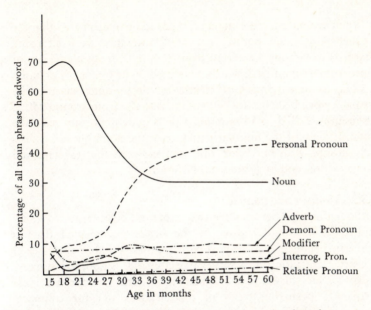

Figure 6.25 Relative frequency × age: noun phrase headword

this proportion drops rapidly, until at 39 months the steady frequency of 30% is reached. This decrease in the frequency of Nouns is almost entirely balanced by the increase in Personal Pronouns which rise rapidly between 24 and 45 months to a frequency of 40% and thereafter remain at about this level. As far as the other classes are concerned, Demonstrative and Interrogative Pronouns both start at a higher relative frequency than Personal Pronouns and then decrease quite sharply before rising again to a slight peak at around 30–3 months, after which they settle to their steady relative frequencies: just over 6% in the case of Demonstrative, and just over 3% in the case of Interrogative. Possessive Pronoun, not shown in figure 6.25, reaches its highest relative frequency at 24 months (3%) and then declines to a steady frequency of just over 1% from 39 months onward. Relative Pronoun, the last to emerge, shows a slow but steady increase from its first appearance at 27 months, reaching a relative frequency of just over 1% at 60 months. The two remaining classes, Modifier and Adverb, also fall within this same band of low relative frequencies. Modifier rises to a slight peak at 24–7 months and then settles to a steady 4%–5%; Adverb, which at about 9% has the third highest steady frequency of all the classes, is consistently at this level throughout the period under investigation.

When evaluating these changes, it has to be remembered that the frequency of noun phrases per 1000 utterances is itself rising sharply throughout the period from 356 at 18 months to 1200 or more from 48 months onwards. So although the frequency of Noun relative to other classes of Headword drops quite sharply, the frequency per 1000 utterances continues to rise from around 250 at 18 months to 375 at 54 months. This is quite important from the point of view of the internal structure of the noun phrase, as it is only groups with nouns or 'one' as headword that take the full range of pre- and post-head modification.

6.5.2 *Modifier and qualifier*

Although divided between the two structural positions of Modifier and Qualifier, modification of the headword, viewed from a semantic perspective, is neutral between these two broad classes of syntactic realization. It is this perspective that is adopted in figure 6.26, which shows age of emergence data for the ten most frequently occurring types of modification and for comparative/superlative modification, irrespective of type. Modification realized by a full clause is not included in this analysis, however. In interpreting these data, it must be recalled that modification stands in a complementary relationship to predication. The physical property of 'heaviness' may be attributed to a stone, for example, either in a predication about it, e.g. 'This stone is heavy' or by

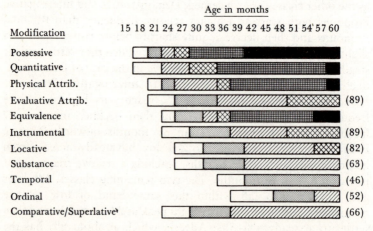

For key see Figure 6.2

Figure 6.26 Age of emergence: nominal modification

means of modification of the Patient participant, e.g. 'This is a heavy stone'. Only in the latter case would the utterance have been coded as containing Physical Attributive Modification of a nominal participant. As discussed in 4.6, a comparison of age of emergence data shows that certain types of attribution occur first in the form of predication (e.g. Evaluative) whilst others occur first as nominal modification (e.g. Quantitative and Substance). For Possession and Physical Attribution, there does not seem to be any difference, although the frequency data suggest that for both categories, there is a preference for expressing the attributive relationship by modification.

Table 6.2 *Percentage of nominal groups containing modification*

	Age in months															
	15	18	21	24	27	30	33	36	39	42	45	48	51	54	57	60
%	4	2	9	12	13	13	13	14	13	14	15	15	14	14	13	14

In considering the frequency with which modification occurs (table A13), it is informative to look at the proportion of noun phrases that contain some form of modification (excluding those cases that are clausally realized). The relevant data are shown in table 6.2.[5] Given the increasing number of types of modification that are available to children with increasing age (see figure 6.26), it is perhaps surprising that the proportion of noun phrases that contain modification approaches a steady level as early as 27 months, although the number of instances per 1000 utterances continues to rise, as does the number of noun phrases, until about the age of 48 months.

Among the types of modification, the relative frequencies with which the different types are chosen remains in very much the same order throughout. Possessive is always the most frequent, followed by Quantitative and Physical Attributive. Together, these three types account for almost 80% of tokens from 21 months onwards. Equivalence (almost exclusively accounted for by the two lexical items 'same' and 'different') is the only other type to occur at all frequently, reaching a relative frequency of about 6%. Most occurrences of nominal modification are realized syntactically by pre-nominal modifiers, but from about 24 months onwards a small proportion occur as post-nominal qualifiers. These can be divided into simple and complex, the former being realized as a single word (e.g. 'Give me that book there', 'I want it *all*'), the latter by phrases or clauses. Simple qualifiers are divided into Locative, Quantitative and Other Adjectival. Complex qualifiers are categorized according to function: Defining, Apposition, etc. Figure 6.27 presents age of emergence data for both groups. Interestingly, it is the complex qualifier with Defining function which is first to appear. The earliest examples are, of course, phrasal (e.g. 'the teddy over there'), but defining clausal qualifiers occur from 30 months onwards. One other type of complex qualifier, Apposition, reaches the 50% level by 60 months. All three types of simple qualifier do so, with Locative and Quantitative occurring from 27 months onwards. With the exception of complex defining qualifiers, none of these categories reaches the 90% level by 60 months.

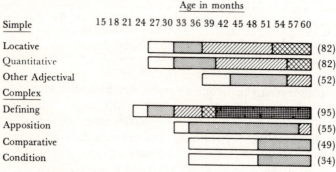

Figure 6.27 Age of emergence: nominal group qualifier

6.5.3 *Pronouns*

As already noted, pronouns take over the role of principal exponent of head of the noun phrase by 36 months. By that age, all the personal and demonstrative pronouns are in use by at least some of the children and all but 'her' and 'us' and the two plural demonstratives are being used by 90% of the sample by 60 months. Possible reasons for the observed sequence of emergence of these items will be discussed in chapter 9. What is striking about these and the other classes of pronoun is the very great differences in frequency of use. Plural pronouns, in particular, are very much rarer than their corresponding singular forms (figure 6.28, table A15).

Of the possessive pronouns, only 'mine' and 'yours' are used by more than 50% of the sample by 60 months. 'Mine' is first to

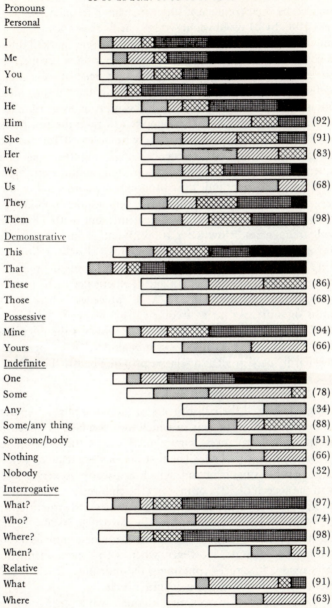

For key see Figure 6.2

Figure 6.28 Age of emergence: pronouns

emerge at around 21 months; 'yours' is significantly later, not reaching the 50% criterion until the age of 51 months. This is paralleled by their frequency: 'mine' reaches a frequency of around 10 per 1000 by 21 months but 'yours' hardly rises above 2 per 1000 at any age. These differences, which reflect a very marked differential concern with own as compared with others' property, are probably attributable in large degree to the need of some children to defend their rights against siblings close in age. Of the indefinite pronouns, only 'one' is widely used. This is probably attributable to the fact that it alone of the pronouns can take the full range of modification and qualification otherwise reserved for the noun. With a median age of emergence of 27 months, 'one' has a frequency of 25 per 1000 utterances from 33 months onwards. By comparison, the other indefinite pronouns are considerably later to emerge, with the negative pronouns 'nothing' and 'nobody' being slightly behind their positive equivalents, but with all of them having frequencies below 6 per 1000. 'What' is the first of both the interrogative and the relative pronouns, closely followed by 'where', which, although not a pronoun, has similar privileges of occurrence. Both have a median age of emergence of 27 months as interrogatives, but as relatives, 'what' precedes 'where' by nine months or more. As far as frequency is concerned, 'what' occurs almost twice as often as 'where'. 'Who', which is the next item in this system to emerge, is about a year behind 'what' as interrogative and is hardly used at all as a relative pronoun before the age of five.

6.5.4 *Noun phrase syntactic structures*

Having considered the constituents of the noun phrase separately, we can now look at the way in which they combine in increasingly more complex structures. Figure 6.29 shows the developmental sequence in relation to age. The first options are relatively early to emerge. To the singular noun, which is already occurring intelligibly in the speech of 50% or more of the children by 15 months, are added pronoun and adverb and the first two word structure, *Indef. Art. + Nsing.*, by 21 months. Initially the article is close to /ə/ in realization, which might appear to be indeterminate between indefinite and definite. However, when the phonetic distinction is clearly made, structures containing the indefinite article regularly precede those containing the definite article.

Plural nouns are also occurring on their own at the 50% level by 21 months. The fact that they are slow to reach the 90% level is probably explained by the fact that once the child has control of the generalized structure *Det. + Npl.* at about 30 months this is just as likely to occur as *Npl.* alone. This is confirmed by the frequency data (see table A16). The first structures containing a preposition, *Prep. + Adverb* and *Prep. + Nsing.*, reach the 50% level by 24

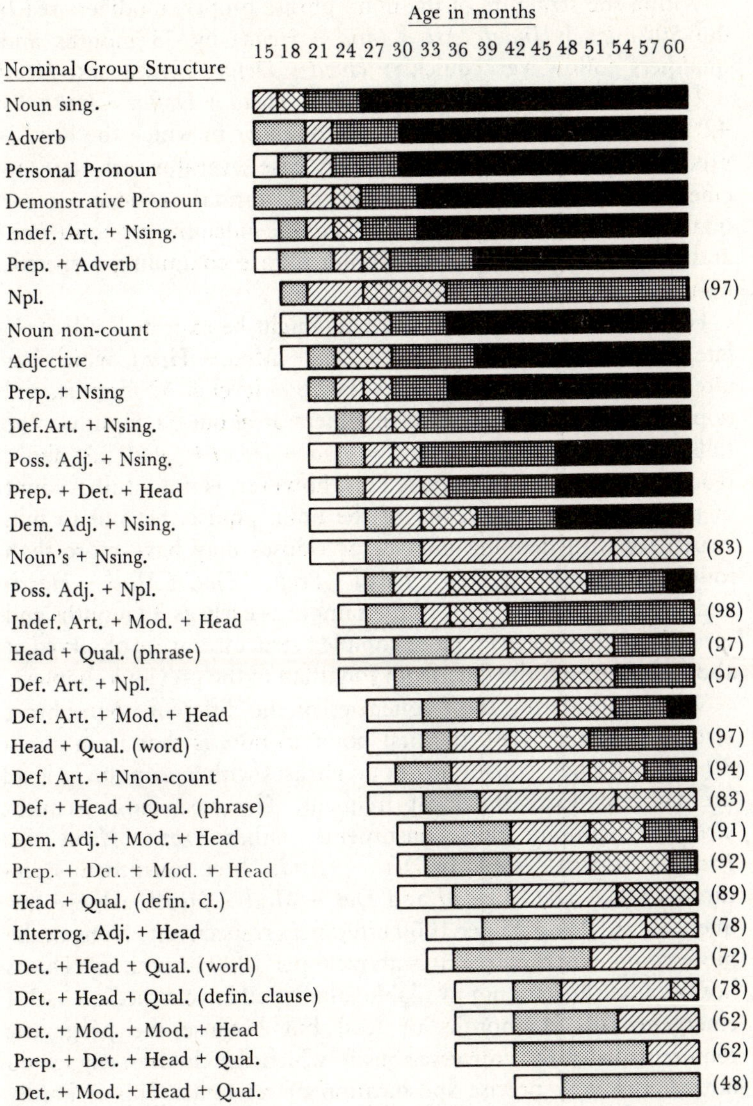

Age in months

15 18 21 24 27 30 33 36 39 42 45 48 51 54 57 60

Nominal Group Structure

Structure	Value
Noun sing.	
Adverb	
Personal Pronoun	
Demonstrative Pronoun	
Indef. Art. + Nsing.	
Prep. + Adverb	
Npl.	(97)
Noun non-count	
Adjective	
Prep. + Nsing	
Def.Art. + Nsing.	
Poss. Adj. + Nsing.	
Prep. + Det. + Head	
Dem. Adj. + Nsing.	
Noun's + Nsing.	(83)
Poss. Adj. + Npl.	
Indef. Art. + Mod. + Head	(98)
Head + Qual. (phrase)	(97)
Def. Art. + Npl.	(97)
Def. Art. + Mod. + Head	
Head + Qual. (word)	(97)
Def. Art. + Nnon-count	(94)
Def. + Head + Qual. (phrase)	(83)
Dem. Adj. + Mod. + Head	(91)
Prep. + Det. + Mod. + Head	(92)
Head + Qual. (defin. cl.)	(89)
Interrog. Adj. + Head	(78)
Det. + Head + Qual. (word)	(72)
Det. + Head + Qual. (defin. clause)	(78)
Det. + Mod. + Mod. + Head	(62)
Prep. + Det. + Head + Qual.	(62)
Det. + Mod. + Head + Qual.	(48)

For key see Figure 6.2

Figure 6.29 Age of emergence: noun phrase structures

months and prepositions are combined with internally structured noun phrases; *Prep. + Det. + Head* by 27 months, *Prep. + Det. + Mod. + Head* by 42 months and *Prep. + Det.+ Head + Qual.* by 57 months.

Within the structure of the noun phrase proper, modifiers reach the 50% level (*Indef. Art. + Mod. + Head*) by 33 months and qualifiers follow very quickly: *Head + Defin. Phrase* and *Head + Qual.* (word) by 36 months and *Head + Defin. Clause* by 42 months. Structures containing a qualifier in which the head is preceded by a determiner are in every case several months later to emerge. It appears therefore that the normal sequence is for qualification to occur first in relation to the indefinite pronoun 'one' and only later in relation to a noun phrase containing a specific noun.

Four-constituent structures are, as might be expected, relatively late to emerge. The first, *Prep. + Det. + Mod. + Head*, which has already been mentioned, reaches the 50% level at 42 months, and noun phrases containing two modifiers at about 51 months. The full-noun-phrase structure *Det. + Mod. + Head + Qual.* just about reaches criterion by five years. This, however, is not a full account of the increasing complexity of the noun phrase. Set out in full, structures with defining phrases or clauses may have more than four constituents (e.g. *Det. + Head + Prep. + Det. + Mod. + Head*) and these are used by 50% of the sample as early as 39 months and several instances of even more complex structures were observed at about this age (cf. the data from Jonathan in the previous chapter).

When considering the frequencies of the different noun-phrase structures (table A16), the first point to note is that from about 30 months, single constituent noun phrases with a pronoun as head are far and away the most frequent. The next most frequent structures contain two constituents, either *Prep. + Head* (i.e. *Prep. + Adverb/Nsing.*) or *Det. + Head*. Three-constituent structures, *Prep. + Det. + Head* and *Det. + Mod. + Head*, achieve frequencies of 50 and 25 per 1000 utterances respectively. None of the more complex structures rises above 6 per 1000 utterances. This is not because they are not available (almost all have a median age of emergence of 51 months or less) but because the pragmatic requirements of the conversations in which the children engage do not require very precise specification of referents. This is hardly surprising, since such a high proportion of conversation concerns ongoing activity or past and future events that fall within shared experience. Although no counts have been carried out on the adult input to the children, my impression is that the differential frequencies of the different noun-phrase structures are not very different from those found in the children from age four onwards. Figure 6.30 shows some of the more frequently occurring structures, expressed as frequencies per 1000 noun phrases. Compared with

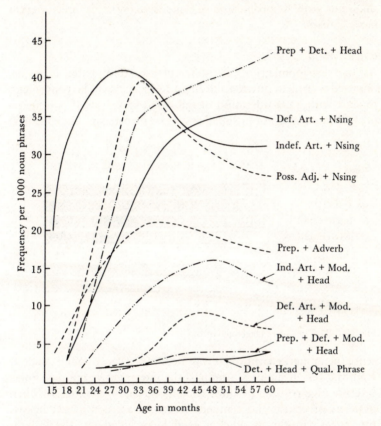

Figure 6.30 Frequency × age: selected noun phrase structures

pronominal NPs (not shown), none of these structures is very frequent. Yet even *Det. + Head + Qual. Phrase*, which never rises above 5 per 1000, has a median age of emergence as early as 39 months. Low frequency, it is clear, does not stop emergence of items being observed. However, it may distort the picture that the observer is able to construct. This is an issue that will be further discussed at the end of this chapter.

6.6 Clause and sentence structure

Finally, we arrive at the largest units of structure for which developmental data are available: the clause and the sentence. Initially, of course, all sentences consist of a single clause, but quite early, with the advent of non-finite embedded clauses, the two levels of description become necessary and, from 36 months, a small but growing proportion of sentences consist of three or even more clauses.

6.6.1 *Mood*

As the development of the different structural patterns to be reported is broken down according to mood, it will be convenient to start with a consideration of the mood system itself (see figure 6.31). Moodless is not included as a separate category as, being in a

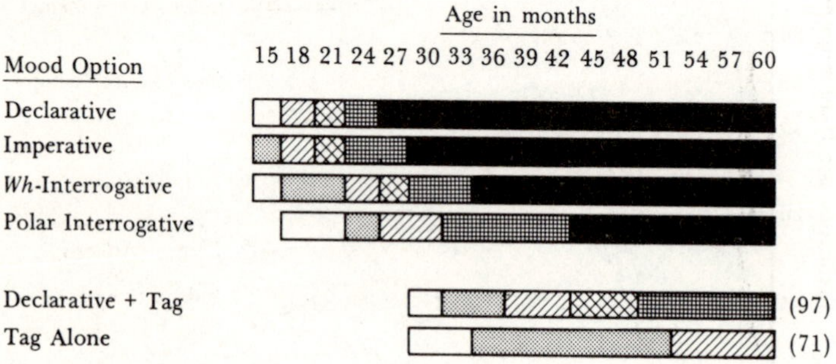

For key see Figure 6.2

Figure 6.31 Age of emergence: mood

sense the unmarked option, it is present in the speech of all children from the very beginning. Amongst the interrogative options, Polar Interrogative realized by Intonation alone is also omitted as, when patterns of clause and sentence structure are considered below, utterances with this mood choice will be included with the declaratives. The only surprise here is the early age at which Tags appear in the Declarative + Tag option. In American English, according to Brown (Brown and Hanlon, 1970), they do not appear until the age of four or later. Presumably, their earlier emergence in British English is a case of frequency of an item in the input accelerating the emergence of that item once it is within the capability of the learner. Certainly many British parents use tags quite frequently in their speech to children.

Turning to frequency (table A17 and figure 6.32), it can be seen that, leaving Moodless on one side, Declarative utterances are by far the most frequent, accounting for more than 35% of all utterances and about 60% of all mood choices. The least frequent choices, Declarative + Tag and Tag alone, together account for no more than 2% of all utterances. It is surprising, in the light of such low frequencies, that as high a proportion of the sample as 90% are using Declarative + Tag by 51 months and that Tag alone reaches the 50% level three months later. The other interesting point to note about the frequencies is that the system has virtually become stable by 45–8 months. Thereafter there is no substantial change in relative frequencies during the period up to five years of age (cf. figure 6.32).

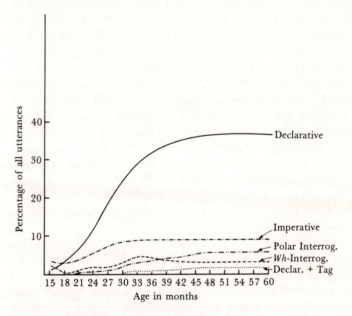

Figure 6.32 Relative frequency: mood

6.6.2 *Syntax of the sentence: declarative*

As the number of clause and sentence structural types considered is so great, it is not possible to comment on each in turn. For detailed information about the age-related pattern of emergence of particular structures see figure 6.33. However, in chapter 5 it was suggested that the simplest explanation of the observed sequence of emergence is that of increase in the number of clause constituents.

Accordingly it is in these terms that the pattern of emergence will be discussed.

Already at 15 months, 75% of the sample are producing interpretable one-word utterances. In fact, at that age no more than a minute proportion of utterances is of greater complexity and this remains true until the age of 24 months (see table A18). However, by 18 months a small proportion of the sample is producing the occasional two-constituent utterance, and this type of utterance occurs in the speech of 50% of children by 24 months. More than half of these utterances are *Noun + Noun* or *Noun + Particle/Adverb* combinations (i.e. $S + O$ or $S + A$) but $S + V$ and $V + O/A$ are not far behind, reaching the 50% level at 27 months. However, almost simultaneously with two-constituent structures, we find the first three-constituent structure, $S + V + O$, and this too has a median age of emergence of 24 months. By 27 months, there are three further three-constituent structures: $S + cop + C$, $A + S + cop$ or $A + cop + S$ and $S + cop + IC$.

The first structures containing an auxiliary verb and a non-finite embedded clause both appear between 21 and 24 months and both have a median age of emergence of 30 months. These are the first four-constituent structures, but others follow, with $S + V + O + A$, $S + cop + C + A$ and $S + aux + cop + X$ all having a median age of emergence of 33 months. Also at 33 months we find the first five-constituent structures being used by 50% of the sample: $S + aux + V + O + A$ and $S + aux + neg + V/cop + X$. Three months later the same is true of sentences containing a finite embedded clause.

Thereafter the major development is in the combination of clauses. Main Clause + Tag reaches the 50% criterion at 39 months, Main Clause + Subordinate Clause at 42 months and sentences containing a Relative Clause at 48 months. By that stage, declarative sentences containing combinations of three clauses are occurring, having reached the 50% criterion at 45 months. Between four years and the end of the observations at the age of five there are no further major developments, although individual children continue to add new structural types not listed here, particularly those involving various combinations of the principal clause types.

When we consider the relative frequencies of these sentence and clause types, many of them seem to occur with extremely low frequencies, even well after the age at which they are productive in children's repertoires. This is partly an artefact of the number of alternatives from which the four-year-old can choose and partly

Age in months

15 18 21 24 27 30 33 36 39 42 45 48 51 54 57 60

<u>Sentence/Clause Structure</u>

<u>Declarative</u>

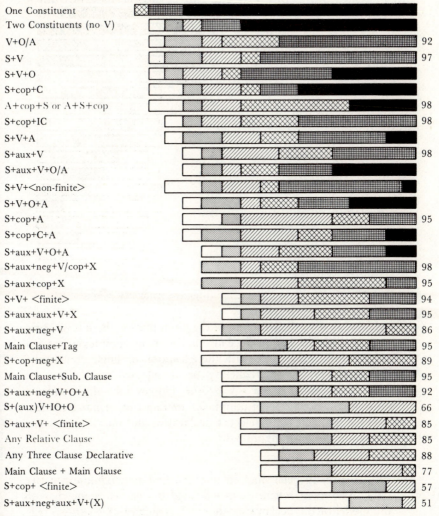

Structure	Value
One Constituent	
Two Constituents (no V)	
V+O/A	92
S+V	97
S+V+O	
S+cop+C	
A+cop+S or A+S+cop	98
S+cop+IC	98
S+V+A	
S+aux+V	98
S+aux+V+O/A	
S+V+<non-finite>	
S+V+O+A	
S+cop+A	95
S+cop+C+A	
S+aux+V+O+A	
S+aux+neg+V/cop+X	98
S+aux+cop+X	95
S+V+ <finite>	94
S+aux+aux+V+X	95
S+aux+neg+V	86
Main Clause+Tag	95
S+cop+neg+X	89
Main Clause+Sub. Clause	95
S+aux+neg+V+O+A	92
S+(aux)V+IO+O	66
S+aux+V+ <finite>	85
Any Relative Clause	85
Any Three Clause Declarative	88
Main Clause + Main Clause	77
S+cop+ <finite>	57
S+aux+neg+aux+V+(X)	51

For key see Figure 6.2

Figure 6.33 Age of emergence: declarative sentences

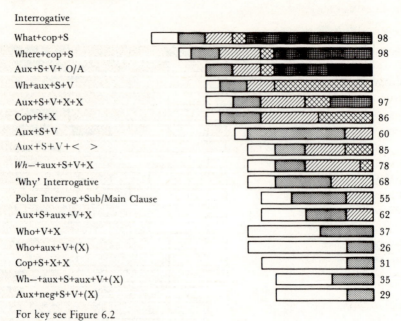

For key see Figure 6.2

Figure 6.34 Age of emergence: interrogative sentences

because, as with the structure of the noun phrase, there is in many contexts little need to produce utterances of any complexity. As can be seen from table A18, with the exception of single constituent utterances, the most frequently occurring structural types are $S + cop + C$ and $S + aux + V + O/A$. However by 48 months a substantial proportion of utterances contain two or more clauses. Relative frequencies of selected declarative and interrogative sentences are shown in figure 6.35.

6.6.3 *Interrogatives*

As has already been pointed out, the first two *wh*-interrogative structures, *what/where + cop + S*, may be learned somewhat on the model of the declarative idiomatic structure, $A + cop + S$ (e.g. 'Here is the book'). Certainly they have rather similar patterns of emergence. If the remaining interrogatives (with the exception of 'who' interrogatives) do, as many writers have argued, involve an inversion of the two constituents S and *aux*, we should not expect

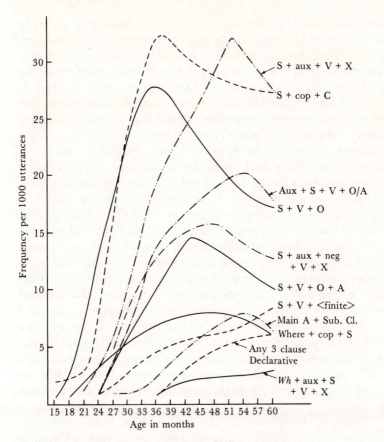

Figure 6.35 Frequency × age: sentence/clause structure

to see them emerging until declarative structures containing *aux* are firmly established at about the age of 30 months. This, in fact, proves to be the case (see figure 6.34). The first polar interrogative, *aux + S + V + O/A* reaches the 50% criterion at 33 months and the first full *wh*-interrogative, *wh- + aux + S + V*, at 36 months. Polar interrogatives with an embedded clause have a median age of emergence of 48 months and full 'why' interrogatives and two-clause polar interrogatives follow at 54 and 57 months respectively. The main surprise is the late emergence of interrogatives containing a negative. No such structure has reached the 50% criterion by the last observation at five years. It is not clear whether this should be attributed to the inherent complexity of such structures or to pragmatic factors which militate against their use. The latter seems the more likely explanation. Interrogative structures generally never achieve a high relative frequency (see table A19). As was seen in figure 6.32 above, they account at most for about 10% of choices within the mood system. Of these, by far the most frequent are the polar interrogatives, $aux + S + V + O/A$ and $aux + S + V + O + A$. As has been remarked before, what is surprising is that items that have such low relative frequencies should nevertheless occur in the speech samples of the majority of children.

Figure 6.35 shows the change in relative frequency with age of selected declarative and interrogative sentence types. What is interesting about this graph, and indeed about many of the graphs of relative frequency by age, is the shape of the growth curve of a high proportion of individual items. Starting with a frequency at or close to zero, they increase very rapidly over a number of observations and then begin a decline which, in some cases, is almost as steep as the increase. If median age of emergence is marked on each curve, it is found that, in most cases, this is located on the rising part of the curve, some months before the peak. The upward movement in the curve can therefore probably be largely attributed to the gradual increase in the proportion of children who are adding the item in question to their repertoire. However, since many of these items do not reach the 100% level of emergence, the curve might be expected to continue to rise until all children are using the item. For many of the more frequent items, however, this is clearly not the case.

A partial explanation for the downturn in many curves has already been suggested in general terms: as the range of options available increases, so the relative frequency of any particular item can be expected to decrease. But this hardly explains the sharpness of the decrease shown by many items. To account for this it seems necessary to posit a period of frequent use immediately following emergence, which may serve a 'practice' function for the learner. Certainly, in observing children's physical development, one notices how occasions seem to be sought to explore and practise new skills until they are brought to a level of proficiency where they no longer need such deliberate and conscious attention. Perhaps the frequency curves for linguistic items shown in this chapter are a reflection of a similar developmental strategy at work in language learning.

6.7 A reconsideration of frequency in relation to emergence
It is apparent from the juxtaposition of data concerning age of

emergence and relative frequency of occurrence for a wide variety of linguistic systems that there is a strong and systematic relationship between frequency and emergence. Items that are early to emerge are, by and large, those that occur most frequently and, conversely, items that have relatively low frequencies are both later to emerge and slower to enter into the speech of all children. At this point it is important to stop and ask about the nature of this relationship. Do the orders of emergence proposed in chapters 4 and 5 correspond fairly closely to order of acquisition, or are they merely an artefact of the differential frequencies with which items are observed in a corpus of spontaneous speech?

In attempting to answer this question, it may be helpful to consider an analogy. Let us suppose that we are presented with a large metal box which we know contains different coloured plastic chips, from which we are allowed randomly to take handfuls at regular intervals and, having examined them, return them to the box. Let us now suppose that five samples, each of 100 chips, yield the data in table 6.3. In evaluating these distributional data it would be important to know what had happened to the box between occasions of sampling. If we were certain that, despite the appearance of systematic change in distribution in successive samples, the contents of the box had not been tampered with between the first and the last occasions, we should treat the mean values from a few random samples as the best estimate of the proportions in which the different coloured chips would be found to be present in the box. On the other hand, if there were no guarantee that the contents of the box had remained unchanged, it would be reasonable to believe that blue and white chips had been added during the experiment and that perhaps some green and red

Table 6.3 *Results of randomly sampling from box of coloured chips*

| | Sample | | | | | |
	1	2	3	4	5	Mean
Green	82	78	79	77	75	77.8
Red	15	17	13	9	8	12.4
Yellow	3	5	6	8	6	6.0
Blue	0	0	2	5	8	3.0
White	0	0	0	1	3	0.8
Total	100	100	100	100	100	100

chips had been removed. If, in addition, one started with an expectation that change in the contents was likely to occur, the frequencies actually obtained would be seen as supporting evidence for such an expectation.

Of course the analogy is inexact and oversimplified, but it does serve to throw the problem into sharper relief. The crux is to know which of the two interpretations to put upon the observation that low frequency items tend to be late to emerge. Is this observation attributable to sampling error, that is, due to these items' low probability of occurrence in any sample of utterances? Or should it be attributed to development, that is, to relatively later acquisition of these items, which also happen to occur with low frequency once they have been acquired?

Put in these stark terms, it is clear that the first alternative taken alone must be rejected. Over the period under investigation, that is to say from 15 to 60 months, there is strong independent evidence that there is gradual development from almost no mastery of English to control of a considerable proportion of the options in most of the systems being investigated. There is also general agreement that some options enter a child's repertoire before others. The data presented in chapters 4 and 5 and in the earlier part of this chapter on order and approximate age of emergence are thus consistent with widely shared beliefs about linguistic development in general.[6] The question is: how reliable are they in detail and, in particular, are they distorted by the large differences in observed frequency of occurrence?

In order to attempt to answer this question, let us look again at the data. The first point to note is that no item has a constant frequency over the whole period from 15 to 60 months. In fact, there seem to be two rather distinct groups of items: a rather small group which occur with high frequency in the speech of almost all the younger children on the first one or two occasions and thereafter show a marked decline; and a much larger group of items which start at a frequency of zero, or close to zero, and, after their first appearance, increase in frequency at rates that are, by and large, correlated with their eventual steady frequency. Items in the first group are, clearly, earliest in the order of emergence. They are also, generally speaking, relatively undifferentiated in meaning relative to items in the second group. The Wanting function is a good example. Emerging as the first function in the Control mode, it accounts for well over two-thirds of all utterances in this mode in the early observations but is then to an increasing extent replaced by more differentiated functions, such as Direct Request, Indirect Request, Request for Permission, etc. However, even if there were not a tendency towards replacement by more differentiated options, the earliest items would inevitably decline in relative, even if not in absolute frequency. As already pointed out, in a finite universe of utterances, as the number of different linguistic types increases, the token frequency of each type must, on average, decrease; this is as true for the child's total production as it is for samples that are drawn from that total.

In the second group, the items are very much more variable in frequency, ranging, at the last observation, from more than 100 tokens per 1000 utterances to as few as 1 or 2. And it is here that the problem lies. An item that occurs with a frequency of 50 per 1000 utterances will occur on average five times in a sample of 100 utterances. An item with a frequency of only 5 per 1000 utterances, on the other hand, has only an even chance of a single occurrence being observed in a similar size sample. However, frequency at the last observation, or steady frequency if this appears to have become established before the last observation, would only be an accurate guide to the frequency with which an item would be expected to appear in the speech of any individual child who controlled that item, if it was derived from a corpus of utterances contributed by a sample of children, *all* of whom had this item in their repertoires. For many items, however, this is not the case. An inspection of the age of emergence data earlier in this chapter shows that only a minority of items reach the 100% level by the last occasion whilst there is a substantial proportion that fail even to reach the 50% level. Frequency data from the last observation are, therefore, not comparable.

In investigating the relationship between frequency and emergence, a better estimate of relative frequency can be obtained by considering the frequency of items at median age of emergence, that is to say at the age by which 50% of the sample have shown evidence of emergence. The frequencies of different items will then be more comparable, in that the frequency of each item will be based on the tokens produced on that occasion by the 50% (or slightly larger proportion) of the sample who are known to have produced the item at least once by that age. Figure 6.36 plots median age of emergence against frequency at median age for those items that both (a) increase in frequency following their first appearance, and (b) reach the 50% level by the last observation.

It may be the case that some items are restricted to rather specific

Head of Nominal Group (41 per 1000) to the function Elicited Repetition (9 per 1000). Even within the locative sub-system of the SMR, the three items that emerge at 21 months, Static Location, Coreferential Change of Location and Agent Cause Change of Location, have frequencies of 38, 28 and 18 per 1000 respectively. On the other dimension, items with a frequency of 9 per 1000 vary in median age from Elicited Repetition at 21 months to the SMR Cognitive Experience plus Embedded Clause at 36 months – a difference of 15 months. And if we go down as low as a frequency of 3 per 1000, the difference between the earliest item to emerge, the function Check at 30 months, and the latest item, Time Reference Relative to a Point in the Past at 60 months, is 30 months. With differences as great as these on both dimensions, it is clear that, whilst frequency and age of emergence are not independent, the latter is not simply a function of the former.

Below a certain frequency, however, it seems probable that error in estimating age of emergence increases quite sharply. Relatively few items are used on any one occasion by all the children who are known to be capable of so doing, and the proportion of those who can and actually do use them naturally affects the item's frequency. At any level of frequency, therefore, it is possible that the sample of speech recorded from a particular child will not contain a token of an item which has entered his repertoire since the previous observation. But the probability of this occurring becomes much greater when the expected frequency in a sample of 100 utterances for those children known to have the item in their repertoire drops below 1. This occurs when an item has a frequency of less than 10 per 1000 at median age.

If we were to draw a sample of 200 utterances, on the other hand, one token would be expected to occur of items with a frequency as low as 5 per 1000 utterances. From this point of view, two adjacent recordings can be treated as equivalent for, other things being equal, if the item was in the speaker's repertoire, one token would be expected to occur in one or other of the two halves of the combined sample. If no tokens were observed in either half it would be reasonable to infer that it was not available *at the time when the first sample was obtained*. It might, of course, have entered the repertoire by the time the second sample was obtained and still not have been observed on that occasion. By the same argument, however, it would be expected to appear at the subsequent observation. In effect, what is being suggested is that, purely on the grounds of probability, when speech samples of 100 utterances per observation are being analysed for items with a frequency at median age of between 10 and 5 tokens per 1000 utterances, emergence may show a delay as great as the time interval between adjacent observations, that is, three months in the present investigation and for items with a frequency of less than 5 per 1000, the delay may be six months or more. It is recognized, of course, that such an argument rests on the assumption that all children who have an item in their repertoire use it with equal frequency – an assumption that is very unlikely to be correct.

There are two other factors that are likely to have led to under-estimation of age of emergence. The first concerns the manner in which the data were obtained. Speech samples were obtained at three-monthly intervals from two cohorts, the younger cohort from 15 to 42 months and the older from 39 to 60 months. In the figures showing age of emergence, the age is given by which various proportions of the sample had provided evidence of emergence of the various items. These proportions are cumulative, in the sense that, once included, a child contributes to the proportion credited with having shown emergence on subsequent occasions. At 45 months, however, there is a hiatus, as the children on whom the proportions are based at that age have only been observed on two previous occasions. The proportion of this cohort showing emergence for a particular item by 45 months may thus be less than the equivalent proportion of the younger cohort at 42 months, since the latter cohort has by this age been observed on ten occasions. In practice, this is most likely to occur on items that occur with low frequency. Secondly, there is the general problem that, as the range of options increases, so does the amount of variation between individuals in their use of those options. At the lower end of the age range, development follows an almost identical sequence in all children. At the upper end, by contrast, items tend to occur as alternatives, some children using one and others another. Eventually, of course, all items will enter the repertoires of all children, but on the basis of the evidence available from spontaneous speech, it is not possible to tell whether the order of acquisition of these later emerging items is similar from child to child or whether it is as variable as observed use.

For all these reasons, confidence in the reliability of the data on order and age of emergence is greater for the earlier part of the age range studied. Looking again at figure 6.36, it can be seen that, for median ages greater than 36 months, the majority of items have a frequency at median age of 5 or less per 1000 utterances, and are therefore more likely to involve error in the estimation of age of emergence. Inspection of the relevant figures and tables in this chapter will also show that items with a median age of greater than 36 months are unlikely to reach the 90% level by the last observation of the older cohort. They are also unlikely greatly to increase in frequency beyond that observed at median age. What this suggests is that by 36 months the 'average' child has acquired a common core of relatively high frequency items that are learned in approximately the same order by all children. From that point on, order of learning may be more variable.

6.8 The overall sequence in relation to age

Having considered the empirical evidence concerning the pattern of emergence and relative frequency of individual items in relation to age, and having assessed the probable relationship between the two factors, we are finally in a position to offer some normative generalizations about the relationship of the sequence of development to age. This we shall do in relation to the sequence of levels proposed at the end of chapter 5.

As will be recalled, the ten levels identified there were the empirical outcome of an ordering analysis of items selected across all three levels of linguistic description to meet the three criteria of saliency, clear and representative ordering within systems, and frequency. These criteria, however, are not necessarily mutually compatible. In particular, some items that are both salient and clearly ordered have a relatively low frequency. This is most likely to be the case at the upper end of the sequence of emergence, since the low observed frequency of such items is contributed to by the relatively small proportion of the sample in whose speech the items have emerged. In selecting items for the 'cross-system' analysis, therefore, a balance had to be struck between the various criteria in order to obtain an overall description which would have practical usefulness for clinical or experimental application.

In assigning ages to levels, therefore, greater weight has been given to the pattern of emergence of those items at each level that occur with the greatest frequency. With such items there is less chance of over-estimating the true age of emergence. At the later levels, however, few if any of the items occur with a frequency of 10 or more per 1000 utterances, and several have a frequency of less than 5. There is thus a very real probability that the last two or three levels are reached before the ages evidenced by the data. The reader should therefore bear this in mind when reading table 6.4.

The three columns represent, from left to right, the tenth percentile, the fiftieth percentile and the ninetieth percentile. In other words, the middle column gives the age in quarter years by which the average child should have reached a particular level and the columns on either side give the ages at which the most and least advanced children will have reached the same level. There will, of course, be children who fall outside the age-range so defined for each level. Of these, the extremely advanced (e.g. Jonathan, whose data were used for exemplification in chapter 5) give no cause for concern. Children at the other extreme, however, may have problems of various kinds – physiological, psychological or environmental – that would benefit from clinical attention.

Table 6.4 *Age norms for the levels on the scale of language development*

Level	Age in years and months		
	Advanced	Average	Delayed
I	<1.3	<1.3	1.9
II	<1.3	1.9	2.0
III	1.3	2.0	2.6
IV	1.6	2.3	3.0
V	1.9	2.6	3.6
VI	2.0	3.0	4.3
VII	2.3	3.6	4.9
VIII	2.9	4.0	>5.0
IX	3.3	4.9	>5.0
X	3.9	>5.0	>5.0

It must be emphasized, however, that at this stage these age-norms should be treated as very tentative. In particular, it should be borne in mind that they are based on cumulative data obtained over a substantial number of observations of each child. When a single observation is made, the likelihood of failing to observe items that are within the child's repertoire is considerably increased, particularly with respect to the less frequently occurring items. Considerable work remains to be done, therefore, before the 'scale' and the associated age-norms presented in this and the previous chapter can be used with confidence in the assessment of individual children.

The children and their families

So far the sample has been described only in very general terms as representative of the pre-school population of Bristol. What kinds of children were they that we studied and what were the homes like in which they were growing up? In order to answer these and similar questions we interviewed all the mothers when the children were three-and-a-half years old.[1] The interview was designed with three main aims in view:

1 to find out about the children's long-term social and intellectual environment;
2 to discover what beliefs and attitudes the parents had on child-rearing, particularly in relation to their children's language development;
3 to provide measures that could be used in an investigation of possible environmental influences on language development.

In designing the interview schedule, we sought advice from Basil Bernstein, of the University of London Institute of Education, and from Peter Robinson, then at Southampton University. Both had been deeply involved in investigations of social differences in patterns of language socialization and were able to offer helpful suggestions on the sort of questions we might ask.[2] Bernstein also allowed us to use several of the instruments he had employed in studies at the Sociological Research Unit. These were, in general, incorporated without change. For the rest, questions were drafted and redrafted until a version of the complete questionnaire was ready for trial.

The questions asked were essentially of two kinds. The first asked for factual information, for example, the number and ages of siblings or how frequently the child played with other children outside the family. Since the answers to these questions could be anticipated, there was no difficulty in providing pre-coded boxes to be ticked by the interviewer as appropriate. The second kind of question was concerned with beliefs and attitudes. Coding answers to such questions is obviously much more problematic, as it is impossible to predict with the same degree of certainty the full range of answers that may be given. Two alternative strategies are available: to record answers in full, either in writing or on a tape recorder, to be coded at some later time; or to provide the interviewer with a set of pre-coded categories, the most appropriate of which is ticked at the time of the interview. The first strategy has the advantage of allowing problematic responses to be considered by more than one coder prior to a final decision being made. It also yields verbatim statements which can be used to fill out the picture constructed from the purely numerical data. However, it has the serious disadvantage of requiring substantially more time for the coding operation. The second strategy is much more economical of time. It does, however, run some risk of distorting a small minority of atypical responses to make them fit the pre-determined categories. On the other hand, where the researcher starts with hypotheses about the areas to be investigated, there is much to be said for constructing questions and alternative responses together so that the resulting data will bear as directly as possible on the hypotheses to be considered.

To claim that we had very clearly worked out hypotheses would be an over-statement, but we certainly had derived a number of expectations about significant features of the home environment from our reading of the literature. Equally importantly, the resources available for this part of the research programme were severely limited. We therefore decided to use the strategy of on-the-spot coding throughout. Two approaches were used, both illustrated by schedules taken over from the Sociological Research Unit. In the first, a 'forced choice' approach was employed. The interviewee was presented with two or more statements and asked to say which was closest to her opinion, for example, (a) Parents should insist on tidiness in children; (b) Parents should not worry too much if their children are untidy.

By presenting a number of forced choices relating to a single dichotomized attitudinal dimension, a score could be derived from the total number of answers favouring one pole of the dimension. The second approach involved asking the interviewee to rate her attitude or behaviour on a scale, for example:

When a child speaks 'badly' there are different sorts of things a mother can do. Would you read through the list and indicate for each statement what you would do.

Correct all the faults you notice in his/her speech etc. . . .	I would do this	I might do this	I would not do this

or to place a number of alternatives in the preferred rank order:

There are several different ways people think a child can learn to talk. Please rank the following statements in the order which is closest to your own view:

He just picks it up from hearing other people   _____
He learns through talking with adults   _____
He learns through talking to himself   _____
He learns through talking to other children   _____
He learns by having to ask for what he wants   _____
He learns because people teach him   _____
He learns because adults correct him when he is wrong   _____

After a preliminary analysis of the interviews for the older group of children, it was decided to add a number of further questions. Some of these merely explored in more detail areas already included in the first version. One section, however, was completely new – an attempt to explore the affective characteristics of the home and, in particular, the interaction of temperament between parents and child. Unfortunately, these additional questions were only included in the interviews for 30 of the younger children. It was therefore not possible to include the responses in any of the subsequent statistical analyses. Where appropriate, however, they will be included in the descriptive sections below.

All the interviews were carried out in the families' homes and, with a small number of exceptions, they were administered by a single researcher. Since many of the families lived several miles from the University, in places rather poorly served by public transport, it was necessary for many of the interviews to be arranged for the afternoon. This meant that in most cases the father was not present during the interview. Questions were therefore addressed to the mother in all cases but, where the father was at home, he was invited to participate. In all, 123 interviews were completed.[3] Coded responses from these were transferred to data sheets and two kinds of analysis performed. The first, which was purely descriptive, will be reported in this chapter. The second, which involved the consideration of selected variables as possible influences on variation in the children's rate of language development, will be discussed in the following chapter on variation in language development.

7.1 Family structure and social relations

It will be recalled from chapter 1 that certain categories of children were excluded from the study. Nevertheless, amongst those that were included, there was very considerable variation in the social and intellectual environments in which they were growing up, and it is this variation that will be described in this chapter.

At the beginning of the study all but one of the families consisted of mother and father and at least one child, and this remained the dominant pattern throughout. However, by the end of the study, at least eight of the families had undergone some change:[4] in seven cases, the parents had separated, leaving the children with the mother, and the one mother who had been single at the beginning of the study had remarried. Although no systematic investigation has been made of the effects of such major changes in family structure, my impression is that they did not lead to a radical alteration in the children's linguistic experience such as significantly to affect their progress in language learning. As well as the nuclear family, 31 households had included other adults at some time during the child's life. In most cases, these were grandparents, and at the time of the interview seven households had at least one grandparent resident. In most of the remaining cases, the additional adults were students or other lodgers, who had little contact with the children. The parents of one child were wardens of a children's home, and in that case there were several other resident adults as well as more than a dozen older children.

The number of children in each family varied considerably and – as was to be expected – changed during the course of the investigation. At the time of the interview, the children being studied occupied almost all possible positions in the family structure from only child to eighth in a family of 11 children. No attempt was made to control for position in the family in advance, but it is a variable of considerable interest. Table 7.1 shows the proportions of children having differing numbers of siblings, and table 7.2 shows the distribution of the sample across the following five categories, which take account of age differences between siblings as well as birth order:

A   only child or first-born with no close siblings
B   second or later born with no close siblings
C   first-born with one close sibling
D   second or later born with one close sibling
E   second or later born with two close siblings
    (close = age difference of less than three years)

Table 7.1 *Proportion of the sample having different numbers of siblings**

0	1	2	3	4	5 or more
11.4	49.6	24.4	9.8	1.6	3.3

*In this and all following tables, the values reported are percentages

Table 7.2 *Position in family (birth order + age difference)*

A	B	C	D	E
14.2	17.3	23.6	33.1	11.8

Table 7.3 *Parents' age in years at birth of child*

	18–20	21–24	25–30	30–40	40+
Mother	10.6	26.0	45.5	16.3	1.6
Father	1.6	18.7	37.4	36.6	5.7

From this table it can be seen that nearly a third of the children were either the only child in the family or the only child going through the early stages of language learning. The significance of this for rate of progress will be considered in chapter 8.

The age of the parents at the time of the child's birth was also investigated. This is obviously related to two other factors: age at marriage and the child's position in the birth order. As was to be expected, the majority of the children were born when the mothers were between 20 and 30 years of age; the fathers were, on average, a few years older (table 7.3). In all the households, the mother had given up work outside the home at the time of the birth of her first child.[5] By the time of the interview, however, quite a high proportion were undertaking some regular paid work outside the home and several more were carrying on jobs at home for which they were paid. Unfortunately, questions on this issue were only included in the revised interview. Out of the 30 respondents, ten mothers had worked part-time at some time since the child's birth.

Only one had worked full-time. In three cases, the mother had not started to work until the child was old enough to go to a nursery school; in the other cases, the child was either looked after by grandparents or by the father, who had appropriately timed shift work, or by another relative or neighbour. Although we do not have evidence from the interviews with the parents of the older children, my impression is that the proportion of mothers of pre-schoolers engaging in at least part-time work outside the home was increasing quite rapidly during the period of the investigation.

Although all the children were resident in the city of Bristol at the beginning of the study, not all had been born in Bristol. It seemed of interest, therefore, to discover more about patterns of mobility. To this end we asked questions relating to two time-scales: how many towns each of the parents had lived in and how many different homes they had lived in as a family in the preceding five years (tables 7.4 and 7.5). The number of parents who had always lived

Table 7.4 *Number of towns in which parents had lived*

	Always in Bristol	Other towns			
		1	2	3	4 or more
Mother	57.7	10.6	10.6	8.9	12.2
Father	52.8	17.1	5.7	4.1	20.3

Table 7.5 *Changes of family home in last five years*

0	1	2	3	4
56.1	26.8	12.2	2.4	2.4

in Bristol was surprisingly high: more than 50% of both mothers and fathers had never lived in any other place. Fathers were more likely to have moved around than mothers, but this is probably partly accounted for by the fact that quite a number of the fathers would have been required to do National Service. We did not ask how many of the parents were native Bristolians, but the proportion who had moved to Bristol from elsewhere was clearly quite large. It certainly included families from other parts of England, from Scotland, Wales and Ireland and one family from Jamaica. Even in the short-term, there had been a considerable degree of mobility. More than 40% of the families had moved house at least once during the preceding five years and several more moved during the remainder of the study. A high proportion of these more recent moves were within the city itself, either as a result of slum clearance and rehousing, or to larger accommodation as the family increased in size.

At the time of the interview, all but one of the families was living in a self-contained dwelling, house or flat (although as already mentioned, this was sometimes shared with grandparents or lodgers). Table 7.6 shows the number of rooms, other than kitchen and bathroom, that the families had at their disposal. All but one of the families also had access to a garden or back yard. As can be seen from table 7.6 the majority of families had four or five rooms,

Table 7.6 *Number of living rooms per family*

3	4	5	6	7 or more
6.6	34.4	38.5	10.7	9.8

either one living room and three or four bedrooms or, more frequently, two living rooms and two or three bedrooms. Whether this was adequate depended on the number of people living in the house or flat. Certainly some were over-crowded. If it is assumed that it is desirable to have no more than two people for each bedroom, at least 4% of homes were over-crowded, but the proportion was probably considerably larger, particularly amongst the families that had two small living rooms in their total of four or five rooms. From the transcripts, we have evidence of at least one family where it was necessary for two children to share a bed.

One of the consequences of frequent change of home may be a reduction in the number of social ties that the parents have with people outside the home. Where husband and wife stay in the area in which they grew up, they are likely to have a wide network of relatives and friends in the neighbourhood. By contrast, a family which moves frequently may find itself relatively isolated. A number of questions in the interview were addressed to this issue. We asked how often the child saw both sets of grandparents; how many adults there were typically in the home during the day; and

Table 7.7 *Frequency of contact with grandparents*

Every day	2–3 times a week	once a week	at least once a month	3–4 times a year	rarely	never
19.5	24.4	24.4	15.5	10.6	1.6	2.4

Table 7.8 *Frequency of adult visitors*

Less than 1 a week	1 or 2 a week	3–5 a week	more than 5 a week
17.9	26.8	21.1	34.2

how often visitors called to see the mother at home. Table 7.7 shows that more than half the children had contact with one or both sets of grandparents at least once a week and a substantial proportion (19.5%) saw at least one grandparent every day. In seven homes (5.7%) the grandparent was resident, but in the remaining cases, a visit by or to the grandparent was involved – usually the former. In many cases these visits were of such long duration that the grandparent, usually the grandmother, was treated as 'being at home with the mother during the day'. In answer to the question about how many adults there were at home during the day, 42% of the mothers reported that there were typically two or more adults.

Apart from 'resident' adults, we asked about frequency of visitors. Again about one third had a visitor almost every day (table 7.8). Taking 'resident' adults and visitors together, we get some idea of the amount of social contact the mothers had with other adults during the course of a week. Dividing the mothers into those that were alone and those who had some other adults with them most days, the picture that emerges is shown in table 7.9. In nearly 30% of homes, it would appear, there are nearly always at least two adults present and, frequently, visitors as well. At the other extreme, just over 10% of mothers are at home alone almost all the time, with visitors calling relatively rarely. Clearly, these extremes give rise to very different social environments for the growing child, with very different opportunities for conversation with mature speakers. Ironically, however, it may not be to the child's advantage to have several adults in the home for most of the time. From the transcripts it is clear that what frequently happens under such

Table 7.9 *Frequency of mothers' social contacts*

Number of adults at home	Frequency of visitors		
	Less than 1 a week	1 or 2 a week	3 or more a week
1	10.6	21.1	26.8
2 or more	7.3	5.7	28.5

Table 7.10 *Frequency of child's social contacts with peers*

Number of of children at home	Frequency of child visitors		
	Less than 1 a week	1 or 2 a week	3 or more a week
1	7.3	13.8	15.4
2 or more	10.6	16.3	36.6

circumstances is that the child has very little experience of one-to-one conversation with an adult, as the adults are too busy talking amongst themselves. From certain points of view, therefore, it may be to the child's advantage if the mother has no other adults to occupy her attention, as she is then more likely to appreciate the company her child provides. However, some mothers were certainly rather lonely and frustrated at the restriction that the child placed on their opportunities for social contacts.

We have assumed that it is to the child's advantage to have frequent opportunities for conversation with a parent or other familiar adult. And, indeed, that was one of the factors that emerged from the study of facilitating features of adult speech, to be reported below. However, it is possible that the child also benefits from opportunities to talk with other children of a similar age. We therefore asked similar questions about the number of children in the home during the day and about the frequency of visits by or to other children. Table 7.10 shows the distribution of frequency of such visits for children who were alone at home and for those who had one or more other children at home with them on a typical day. From this table it can be seen that nearly two

thirds of the children have a sibling or some other child at home
with them on a typical day and the majority of these children also
visit or are visited by other children several times each week. Of the
third who are alone at home, 80% visit or are visited by other
children once or more per week. Only 7% of the total sample had
informal contact with other children less than once a week.
However, nearly half of these attended a nursery school or play-
group several times a week. Thus, although the amount of time
spent with other children varied considerably, only four children
(3.3%) could be said to be seriously deprived of the opportunity to
interact with other children of a similar age.

From the transcripts, it is clear that the way these social contacts
occurred varied quite considerably. In some cases, the visits by
other children were planned: a friend of the mother, with one or
more pre-school children, would be invited to visit and the children
would play while the mothers drank coffee and chatted, the latter
only intervening in the children's play to settle squabbles or from
time to time to suggest activities. In other cases, the children made
their own way to a neighbour's house or were taken and left by the
mother and the children's play was totally independent of adult
supervision. The latter pattern was more frequent amongst the
older children, particularly amongst those who had one or more
siblings. The former pattern was more common amongst the
younger children, particularly amongst those who had no siblings
at home with them.

As already mentioned, some of the children attended nursery
school or play-group. Since nursery schools (though not play-
groups) generally only admit children over the age of three, few of
the children in the younger age-range were attending nursery-
school at the time of the interview. However, the proportion
increased as the children grew older. Altogether, the proportion of
children in the total sample who were attending a nursery or
play-group at the time of the interview or who had at some time
previously done so was surprisingly high, 81% having had some
nursery or play-group experience (table 7.11) (some of the children
had actually had both).

Table 7.11 *Nursery or play-group experience*

Currently attending	Previous attendance	Never attended
72.4	8.9	18.7

7.2 Family Background

Generally speaking, we have preferred to avoid using the term *social class*, since it has been defined and measured in so many different ways. We have used, instead, the term *Family Background*. As explained in chapter 1, our measure of family background was based on information about the occupation and education of both parents. As this was fully described earlier it will not be repeated, although questions on these matters were included in the interview. However, it is of interest to look in greater detail at the educational background of the parents.

During the last half century, there have been considerable changes in educational provision: raising of the school leaving age, the gradual introduction of comprehensive schools, and accompanying abandonment of selection at the age of 11 years for 'grammar' or 'secondary modern' schooling. There has also been an increase in the proportion of pupils attempting 'Ordinary' (at 15 or 16 years) and 'Advanced' (at 18 years) Level examinations for the General Certificate of Education. Equally, there has been an increasing tendency for pupils to stay on at school beyond the minimal leaving age, even though they do not take any public examinations after the Certificate of Secondary Education (CSE). These changes are reflected in the length of schooling and in the level of educational qualifications attained by the parents of the children in this study, the older parents being proportionally more likely to have left school at an earlier age and to have fewer qualifications. Few of the parents were still at school at the time of the introduction of comprehensive schools or of the CSE examination, but the majority would have been affected by the raising of the minimal school leaving age to 15 in 1948. Thus, while a small number completed their education at 14, about half stayed on until 15 or 16, chiefly at secondary modern schools, and a sizeable minority continued into the sixth form, some proceeding from there to college or university. For some of those who left school without examination qualifications, apprenticeships and professional training provided further education with a strong vocational bias. The range and diversity of educational experience in this sample of parents is summarized in table 7.12 for fathers and mothers separately. In more than half the families (58%) the parents had the same level of education and a further 19% differed only by one level. Where there was a difference in level, it was more than three times more likely that the father would be more highly qualified than the mother than the reverse.

Table 7.12 *Length and final qualification of parents' education*

	Left at 14 yrs	Left at 15 yrs	Left at 16 yrs	1 or more CSE	1 or more 'O' level	1 or more 'A' level	Left at 15/16 + 3 yrs voc. tr.	Profess. Quali.	Univ. Deg.	Degr. + 1 yr Post-graduate	Higher Degree
Mother	3.9	54.7	4.7	1.6	7.8	4.7	3.9	14.1	3.1	1.6	0
Father	7.8	46.9	1.6	0.8	6.3	1.6	6.3	14.8	5.5	4.7	3.9

It has been suggested that the grandfather's occupation and associated way of life is just as important as the parents' occupation or education in predicting the patterns of social organization within the child's home (e.g. Brandis and Henderson, 1970). Presumably this is because such patterns, being learned in childhood, are slow to change and are thus passed on from one generation to the next with little modification. In order to test this claim, we asked about the occupations of both grandfathers and classified them according to the Registrar-General's scale, I–V. Fathers' occupations were then compared with paternal grandfathers' occupations. (It did not seem appropriate to compare mothers' occupations with maternal grandfathers', as the occupations most typically taken on by young women are, on the whole, assigned lower status on the RG scale than those taken on by men.) As can be seen from table 7.13, only

Table 7.13 *Comparison of father's occupation on RG scale with that of paternal grandfather*

2 or more classes higher	1 class higher	same class	1 class lower	2 or more classes lower
15.6	25.2	40.0	12.2	7.0

40% of fathers had occupations in the same class as their own fathers. An equally large proportion had a more highly rated occupation while only 19% had a less highly rated one. These figures certainly do not suggest a static society with respect to occupation. Indeed, it appears that the general trend is in an upward direction. However, it must be remembered that, in selecting the sample, children's scores on the scale of family background were stratified and a greater representation given to the extremes than would have occurred by chance. The result is almost certainly that the degree of inter-generational occupational mobility is exaggerated in the present sample. Nevertheless, it is probably significant that in those cases where the father's occupational class is different from that of the paternal grandfather, the discrepancy is twice as likely to be in an upward direction than it is to be in a downward direction.

7.3 Beliefs and practices concerning child-rearing
Such features of family background as the occupation and education of the parents, whilst perhaps satisfactory as crude indicators

of 'social class', do not have a direct impact on the child's daily life or on the experiences from which he constructs his model of the social world (Berger and Luckmann, 1967). Of much more direct relevance are the beliefs his parents hold about child-rearing and the related practices in which they engage. Certainly, these will be influenced by the parents' own experience as children and by their education, but the relationship is not entirely deterministic: other influences, such as the beliefs and practices of friends and colleagues, ideas and values absorbed through reading and television, and the advice and example of professional workers, such as health visitors and teachers, may also be significant. It seemed important, therefore, to attempt to obtain information directly about certain beliefs and practices rather than to assume that they could be predicted from knowledge of occupation and education.

The longitudinal study of Nottingham families by John and Elizabeth Newson (1968) is probably the most thorough-going attempt to obtain information about child-rearing, and the report of the second stage had recently been published when we were designing our interview. We were not in a position to replicate their method of data-collection, but we did pay close attention to the topics on which they had solicited information. Three areas that we decided to explore with the help of schedules from the Sociological Research Unit were: (a) which activities children most preferred; (b) which actions by them were most likely to lead to disciplinary action and what form it took; and (c) parents' attitudes to toys. With respect to preferred activities, 14 common activities were listed and, for each one, the mother was asked to say how much the child enjoyed doing it. The proportion of children described as showing each of four levels of enjoyment for each activity is shown in table 7.14.

In interpreting these figures, it is useful to have some idea of the variation in the overall level of enjoyment shown by different children. Combining the two categories of 'not at all' and 'not much', the number of activities thus negatively rated ranged for individual children from 0 to 8, with 3 being the median; by way of contrast, the number of activities enjoyed 'very much' ranged from 1 to 13, with the median being 7. On the whole it appears, therefore, that the children were more positive than negative overall in their attitudes to these activities. However, it must be borne in mind that these figures are based on mothers' reports, not on direct observations. Furthermore, not all the activities occurred with equal frequency for all children and this must have affected the

Table 7.14 *Percentage of children showing different levels of enjoyment of common activities*

Activity / Child enjoyment	Not at all	Not much	Quite a lot	Very much
Getting dressed	11.1	42.7	35.0	11.1
Eating a meal	6.0	29.9	35.0	29.1
Getting washed	12.8	38.5	31.6	17.1
Having a bath	1.7	2.6	19.7	76.1
Watching TV	1.7	16.2	53.3	46.2
Playing alone	2.6	19.7	59.0	24.8
Playing with mother	0	4.3	26.5	67.5
Going shopping	5.1	12.0	40.2	42.7
Playing with other children	0.9	5.1	15.4	78.6
Visiting family friends	3.4	9.4	26.5	60.7
Going to play-group or nursery	0	3.4	19.7	59.8
Helping mother	0	6.0	32.5	59.0
Being read to	1.7	9.4	20.5	68.4
Helping father	1.7	3.4	23.1	70.1

mothers' ratings.[6] For example, not all children attended a play-group or nursery, nor were all children read to with equal frequency.

Bearing these qualifications in mind, it is interesting to look at the relative popularity of the various activities. Weighting responses from 'not at all' = 1 to 'very much' = 4, and then ranking them, it appears that *playing with other children* is the most enjoyed activity. This is followed, in order, by *having a bath* and, equal third, *playing with mother* and *helping father*. *Being read to* comes next with *helping mother* and *visiting family friends* not far behind. The least enjoyed activities are clearly *getting dressed* and *getting washed* with *having a meal* and *playing alone* the next least enjoyed. It is interesting that all the most enjoyed activities are very definitely social events with the possible exception of having a bath (although, for many children, even that may be also). They are presumably, therefore, also activities in which the child is using and extending his command of language.

When asked about forms of behaviour that they might prohibit or reprimand, mothers were asked to say, for each form of behaviour listed below,[7] whether they 'would', 'perhaps might' or 'would not' reprimand the child for doing it. The proportions giving each answer are shown in table 7.15. Some mothers noted, however, that they did not consider several of the forms of behaviour to be matters for which it was reasonable to hold children of this age responsible. Somewhat surprisingly, there are no kinds of behaviour on which mothers are in complete agreement. However, the vast majority do not prohibit *always asking questions*; on the other hand, there is almost equal agreement about the unacceptability of *pushing in front of adults, answering back* and *interrupting adults. Untidiness in general, sulking* and *failing to wash properly* find mothers almost equally divided for and against. Here again there are considerable individual differences between mothers in the number of forms of behaviour that they would or would not prohibit and also in the number with respect to which they are more flexible (or inconsistent). The number of prohibited kinds of behaviour ranged from 0 to 14 (median 8), the number not prohibited from 1 to 12 (median 5). The number about which the mothers were uncertain ranged from 0 to 10 (median 3). Conversely a surprisingly large proportion of mothers (15%) expressed no uncertainties whatsoever.

Following the question about sanctioned forms of behaviour, we asked about the forms of sanction used when children were considered to have misbehaved. Seven alternatives were offered and mothers were asked to say whether they would ever use each type of sanction or not.[8] Taking the total alternative answers for each (table 7.16), it can be seen that *explanation* is the response most frequently resorted to, with a *smack* being the second most frequent. *Threatening to call a policeman* is the type of sanction that is reported to be the one that most mothers would not use. These results are what might have been expected. However, less expected is the variation in the range of types of sanction employed. Almost half used four or more, and three mothers reported that they used all seven. On the other hand, a small number (4.4%)

Table 7.15 *Forms of behaviour that mothers might prohibit or reprimand*

Behaviour	Would	Perhaps might	Would not	No response
Leaving the bedroom untidy	35.9	21.4	42.7	0
Pushing in front of adults	84.6	8.5	6.8	0
Leaving clothes lying around	59.8	23.1	16.2	0.8
Talking at table	22.2	15.4	61.5	0.8
Not washing properly	46.2	6.0	43.6	4.3
Showing off to strangers	60.7	30.8	7.7	0.8
Always asking questions	2.6	9.4	88.0	0
Losing his/her temper	52.1	20.5	23.1	4.3
Interrupting adults	74.4	23.1	2.6	0
Leaving toys or books around	26.5	30.8	34.2	8.5
Looking miserable	17.9	17.1	60.7	4.3
Answering back	75.2	12.8	11.1	0.8
Refusing to help	17.9	17.9	58.1	6.0
Telling tales	65.0	17.9	16.2	0.8
Sulking when told off	37.6	12.0	47.0	3.4
Leaving the table before everybody has finished	39.3	7.7	47.0	6.0

reported that they used only one type: one mother only smacked, the others only used explanation.

We also asked questions about toys because, in recent years, a considerable emphasis has been given to the importance of parents providing opportunities for children to develop skills that will be of use to them at school. Without necessarily subscribing to the views of those who place such an emphasis on the instrumental value of toys, we wished to discover what were the beliefs and practices of the parents in the study. The first question offered six reasons for

Table 7.16 *Mothers' uses of sanctions for misbehaviour*

Type of sanction	Yes	No
Tell him/her that he/she is very naughty and smack him/her immediately	80.7	19.3
Tell him/her that he/she is very naughty and that his/her father will deal with him/her when he gets home	15.8	79.8
Tell him/her that this hurts mother and that she doesn't love him/her when he/she does such things	14.0	81.6
Tell him/her that if he/she does it again you will call a policeman and have him/her taken away	7.9	92.1
Send him/her to his/her room, or to bed	69.3	25.4
Tell him/her that you won't allow him to have a treat that you have promised	57.9	36.8
Explain to him/her why this is very naughty and why it makes you angry	95.6	2.6

Table 7.17 *Mothers' reasons for buying toys*

Reasons for buying toys for children	Mothers of Boys	Girls
a) To keep children amused	67.9	53.8
b) To enable children to play with their friends	10.7	18.5
c) To help children when they go to school	33.9	40.0
d) To help them find out about things	76.8	70.8
e) To free mother so she can do other things	0	12.3
f) To show that mother cares for them when she has been away	5.4	0

buying toys and asked mothers to choose the two that they considered most important.[9] In table 7.17 the responses of mothers of boys and girls are shown separately. Percentages in each cell represent the proportion of times each reason was selected as either first or second choice. The most frequently cited reason for buying toys was (d) *To help children to find out about things*. More than 70% of parents of both boys and girls selected this reason as either their first or second choice. The next most commonly selected reason was (a) *To keep children amused*.

As can be seen, there are some quite substantial sex-related differences. Mothers of boys are apparently more concerned to help them find out about things and to keep them amused. Mothers of girls, on the other hand, are somewhat less concerned about these matters. By contrast, they are more concerned about buying toys that will help their daughters when they go to school. They are also more conscious of the social function of toys in providing materials for play with their friends. The largest difference, however, is in the number of mothers of girls who see toys as a means of occupying their children while they engage in other activities. No mothers of boys selected this reason. Perhaps this difference is related to the much greater involvement shown by girls in helping with household tasks that was noted in chapter 3. At least some mothers of girls may not enjoy receiving so much 'help' and so perhaps think of toys as providing a distraction. The frequencies with which the different reasons were selected by mothers of boys and girls were subjected to a test of significance. Calculated on raw frequencies, $\chi^2 = 12.98$; for 5 df this value is significant, $p < 0.05$.[10]

Table 7.18 *Responses concerning last toy bought and favourite toy by mothers of boys and girls*

Type of toy	Last toy bought		Favourite toy	
	Boys	Girls	Boys	Girls
1 Educational toy	8.9	15.4	7.3	9.5
2 Constructional toy	14.3	6.2	18.2	4.8
3 Cuddly toy	0	4.6	9.1	28.6
4 Mechanical toy	25.0	10.8	23.6	7.9
5 Role-play toy	32.1	49.2	32.7	34.9
6 Sporting equipment	19.6	13.8	9.1	14.3

Having asked about reasons for buying toys we next asked about *the last important toy bought* for the child in the investigation, and also about the child's favourite toy. The categories into which toys were divided are shown in table 7.18, which gives the percentage distribution of responses for boys and girls separately. Responses to both questions show considerable differences between boys and girls. Parents are more likely to buy constructional and mechanical toys and sporting equipment for boys than for girls, but they are more likely to buy educational, role-play and cuddly toys for girls ($\chi^2 = 11.62$, 5 df, $p < 0.05$). The differences between boys and girls in their favourite toys are even greater, boys being more likely than girls to prefer constructional and mechanical toys and girls more

likely than boys to prefer cuddly toys. Overall the differences
between boys and girls in their preferred toys were even more
marked than the differences in the toys bought for them ($\chi^2 = 16.2$,
5 df, $p < 0.01$).

It is sometimes suggested that the differences between the sexes in
their interests and abilities are quite largely the result of 'sex-
stereotyping' by parents in childhood. One form such sex-stereo-
typing might take is the choice by parents of different kinds of toys.
Certainly in the data just presented there is evidence of sex-related
differences in the toys bought, although these are less marked than
the overall differences in the children's preferences. However, what
are particularly interesting are the patterns of congruence and lack
of congruence between parents' choices and children's preferences.
Whilst there is, in general, a fairly good fit, there are several cases
where the children seem to show rather more or less liking for a
particular type of toy than is suggested by the choices made by their
parents. Boys, for example, have a greater preference for cuddly
toys and considerably less interest in sporting equipment than
would be suggested by the toys bought for them. Girls, on the other
hand, have rather less interest in educational toys than is indicated
by the toys bought for them. Interestingly, in spite of the differences
in parents' selection of toys, the proportions of boys and girls who
were reported to prefer educational and role-play toys were almost
identical.

Clearly, no firm conclusions about the existence or the effect of
sex-role stereotyping can be drawn on the basis of such general
questions as asked in this interview. However, it is apparent that
sex-related differences do exist in children's preferences for different kinds of toy and in the reasons parents give for the choices they
make. Whilst it seems probable that some of the differences
between boys and girls in the preferences they were reported to
show are independent of the choices made on their behalf by their
parents, there is also fairly clear evidence that some parents select
toys for boys and girls differently and do so in a way that goes
beyond the differences in preference shown by the children. This is
most clearly shown in the purchase of sporting equipment for boys,
and in the purchase of educational and role-play toys for girls.
Taking the coefficient of correlation as an indication of fit between
child preference and parental choice ($r_s = 0.87$ for boys, $r_s = 0.69$
for girls) it appears that the mismatch is greater for girls than for
boys, suggesting perhaps that a greater number of parents attempt
to direct the interests of girls than do so for boys.

7.4 Beliefs and practices concerning language development

Quite a large part of the interview was devoted to questions about language development. Some questions were asked about the mothers' beliefs and attitudes with respect to language and others about their current practices. A final group of questions was concerned with literacy. The first question asked the mothers to rank seven ways people think a child can learn to talk in the order that was closest to their own point of view. In order to simplify the resulting data, the ranks have been collapsed into three groups (1 or 2; 3, 4 or 5; 6 or 7), and in table 7.19 the proportion of mothers' responses in each group is shown for each of the seven suggested ways in which children learn to talk.

Table 7.19 *Mothers' rankings of alternative explanations of ways in which children learn to talk*

	Ranks		
Ways of learning to talk	1–2	3–5	6–7
1 From hearing other people	33.3	45.8	20.8
2 Through talking with adults	67.5	30.0	2.5
3 Through talking to him/herself	5.0	32.5	62.5
4 Through talking to other children	44.2	45.0	10.8
5 By having to ask for what he/she wants	20.0	60.0	20.0
6 Because people teach him/her	27.5	47.5	25.0
7 Because adults correct him/her when he/she is wrong	15.0	40.8	44.2

The first point of note about these results is the very considerable divergence of opinion among the mothers. With the exception of alternatives (2) and (3), there was a substantial proportion of mothers at each extreme of the rank-scale for each of the explanations. However, overall, it is clear that the majority consider that children learn by *talking with other people*, most importantly *with adults*, but also *with other children*. This is distinguished by a substantial proportion from simply *hearing other people* speaking. By contrast, the majority also thought that children do not learn *through talking to themselves*. Although deliberate instruction, in the form of *teaching* or *correcting*, was considered of lesser importance by the majority, each of these explanations was ranked high by a substantial minority of mothers. A very similar result was obtained for the instrumental explanation of learning by *having to ask for what he/she wants*.

Table 7.20 *Mothers' rankings of features of children's speech that they might attend to and correct*

Features of children's speech	Ranks 1–2	3–5	6–9
1 That you can hear distinctly what he/she is saying	50.0	25.4	24.6
2 That he/she pronounces words correctly	50.8	28.0	21.2
3 That what he/she says is grammatical	8.5	27.1	64.4
4 That what he/she says is true	9.3	36.4	54.2
5 That what he/she says is relevant to the conversation	7.6	35.6	56.8
6 That he/she says things politely	11.0	44.9	52.5
7 That he/she is saying something that he/she hasn't said before	23.7	42.4	33.9
8 That he/she is saying something in a way he/she hasn't said it before	14.4	44.1	41.5
9 That he/she is making a surprising or original use of language	23.7	28.0	48.3

The second question listed a number of features of a child's speech that a mother might pay attention to and perhaps correct when considered appropriate. Mothers were asked to rank the nine features in what they considered to be their order of importance. Once again, in order to simplify the data, the ranking responses are collapsed into three rank-groupings (1 or 2; 3, 4 or 5; 6, 7, 8 or 9). The proportion of responses in each group for each of the nine features is shown in table 7.20. In the previous question the majority of mothers did not give a high rank to explanations concerning teaching or correcting, so to some extent the present question may have been forcing them to rank kinds of behaviour in which they rarely engaged. However, the responses they gave can also be seen as confirming the lack of belief in the efficacy of teaching or correction. The two features of children's speech that the majority rank high in order of meriting attention may be seen as being attended to in the interests of effective communication rather than for the purposes of teaching. This is certainly confirmed by an inspection of the recorded samples of conversation. Similarly, the second pair of features to be most often ranked first or second in importance (7 and 9) show an interest in original uses of language rather than pedagogical concern. What is perhaps more surprising, considering Brown's observation that parents are more concerned with truthfulness than grammatical accuracy (Brown *et al.*, 1969), is the small number of mothers that give a high rank to either (4) or (5). Successful, that is to say mutually intelligible, and interesting conversation is apparently of greater concern to the majority of mothers than either factual accuracy or grammaticality in their children's utterances.

Table 7.21 *Actions that mothers might take if their children were 'speaking badly'*

Type of action	Would	Might	Would not
1 Ignore it and hope it will stop	32.3	25.6	42.1
2 Correct all the faults you notice in his/her speech	52.1	25:6	22.3
3 Ask the teacher to do something about it	23.1	23.1	53.7
4 Try to get him/her to play with children who speak well	28.1	21.5	50.4
5 Leave it until he/she is older and then perhaps do something	21.5	19.0	59.5
6 Take care how you and your husband speak in front of the child	81.0	5.0	14.0
7 Ignore it because it's only a phase that children go through	25.6	31.4	43.0
8 Try to ensure that your friends and relatives always speak correctly in front of the child	19.8	16.5	63.6
9 Try to move into an area where people speak well	5.8	9.1	85.1
10 Leave it to the school to deal with	6.6	11.6	81.8

The general impression gained from this question, then, is that the mothers in this study were on the whole accepting of their children's speech. However, since we anticipated that there would be some features of their children's speech that might cause parents some concern, we asked which of several alternative courses of action they might take if they thought their child was 'speaking badly'. Table 7.21 shows the percentage of mothers who said they 'would', 'might' or 'would not' take the action specified for each of the ten alternatives. In retrospect, it is clear that the answers would have been easier to interpret if the nature of 'speaking badly' had been specified.[11] Even better would have been to ask the mothers to answer with respect to each of several types of unacceptable speech behaviour. As it is, one cannot be certain what form of unacceptable speech behaviour the mothers had in mind when they were considering the alternatives, though it seems probable that they were thinking of those forms of behaviour, if any, that they had said they would correct when answering the previous questions. If that is so, it is unclear speech or incorrect pronunciation – or using bad language – to which the answers most probably relate. Only one form of action was clearly favoured by the majority of mothers: taking care how they and their husbands spoke in front of the children. But even here, 14% said they would not do that. For the rest, it is more informative to look at what the majority would not do. They would not move house to an area where people spoke well nor would they leave it to the school to deal with; and, although they would take care about their own speech, they would not try to influence friends and relatives to speak correctly. On the other hand, more than half (59.5%) would not adopt a policy of wait and see and almost as many (52.1%) would correct all the faults that were noticed in the child's speech.

In spite of the imperfections in the questions, a fairly consistent picture emerges from the mothers' answers about their beliefs and practices concerning language development. A substantial majority believe that children learn to talk by conversing with those around them, adults in particular but also children. Teaching and correcting are seen as less important. Where unacceptable behaviour is noted, it is the parental example which is seen as most important; ignoring the problem or leaving the responsibility to the school or teacher is generally not considered appropriate. Correction of faults would or might be a strategy adopted by a majority of mothers, but in relation to pronunciation rather than grammar. The truth, relevance or politeness of their children's speech is apparently of less concern to most mothers.

When parents speak about pronunciation, it is not clear whether they are thinking of immature forms of pronunciation or of non-standard pronunciations that are characteristic of the local regional accent. To find out how many of the mothers were sensitive to the issue of standardness or otherwise of accent we asked, in the revised interview, how strongly they agreed or disagreed with a number of statements concerning this and related issues (table 7.22). Whilst for several of these statements there was a sizeable minority who gave responses indicating disapproval of the local way of speaking (in particular, the high proportion that think *Bristol speech is lazy*), it was not the same mothers from one statement to another. Scoring responses to statements 1–4 and 6, so that a score of 5 denotes a strong negative attitude to non-

Table 7.22 *Mothers' attitudes to non-standard language* ($n = 30$)

Attitudes to non-standard language	Strongly agree				Strongly disagree
1 Parents should discourage children from speaking in strong regional dialects	17.2	3.4	17.2	24.1	37.9
2 BBC (standard) English is better for getting ideas over than other forms of English	20.7	6.9	6.9	27.6	37.9
3 The dialect that a person speaks is no indication of his/her intelligence	82.8	10.3	0	3.4	3.4
4 Bristol speech is lazy	34.5	10.3	3.4	17.2	34.5
5 Parents should always pick their children's speech up if they swear	48.3	13.8	17.2	6.9	13.8
6 What you say is more important than how you say it	41.4	17.2	10.3	17.2	13.8
7 Children should be encouraged to speak about all their experiences, even if they have to struggle with words	89.7	6.9	3.4	0	0

standardness of speech and a score of 1 a tolerant attitude, only one mother had an average score as high as 4 and a further four had scores between 3 and 4. The remaining 25 had average scores of 3 or less. As might be expected, there was a tendency for mothers whose own speech contained a higher proportion of regional features to be more tolerant of such features and for mothers in professional families to be less tolerant. However, the difference was not significant.

The next two schedules were taken from a study carried out by Henderson (1973) to investigate mothers' communication (a) with other adults and (b) with their children. In the first schedule, the mothers were asked to rate how often they talked to other adults for each of twelve reasons. Three levels of frequency were set: 'hardly ever', 'sometimes' and 'often'. The proportion of mothers selecting each of the three levels of frequency for each of the twelve reasons is shown in Table 7.23. From these responses it seems that mothers most frequently talk to others to be friendly and to discuss their children, with exchanging ideas and to be understood by others coming almost equal third. By contrast, they rarely talk to find out what others think of them.

Table 7.23 *Mothers' reasons for talking to others*

Reason for talking to others	Hardly ever	Sometimes	Often
1 To be friendly	3.4	23.7	72.9
2 To exchange ideas	8.5	39.8	51.7
3 About what I have seen on TV	39.0	50.0	11.0
4 To increase the number of people I know	42.4	39.0	18.6
5 To find out what other people think of me	82.2	11.9	5.9
6 About my children	8.5	28.0	63.5
7 To question the world around me	23.7	45.8	30.5
8 To find out more about people	16.9	43.2	39.8
9 To decide what is right and wrong	20.3	50.8	28.8
10 To show my feelings to others	22.9	50.8	26.3
11 To increase my knowledge about the world	16.9	48.3	34.7
12 So that those close to me can understand me better	11.0	32.2	56.8

Henderson's main reason for asking these questions, however, was theoretical rather than merely descriptive. She was interested to discover whether there were class-related differences in mothers' reports of the frequency with which they talked to other adults for the various reasons. Drawing upon Bernstein's theoretical writings, three hypotheses were to be tested:

a) middle-class mothers would talk more frequently than working-class mothers for cognitive reasons;

b) middle-class mothers would talk more frequently than working-class mothers for inter-personal reasons;

c) working-class mothers would talk more frequently than middle-class mothers for social reasons.

In order to test these hypotheses the twelve reasons were assigned to the three broad types of discourse as follows: cognitive reasons: 2, 7, 8, 11; inter-personal reasons: 5, 9, 10, 12;[12] social reasons: 1, 3, 4, 6. The response data were then submitted to analysis of variance with repeated measures. Henderson found that there was no significant social class difference in the frequency with which mothers talked to others, nor was there a significant main effect in relation to frequency of talking in the three areas of discourse. However there was an interaction effect between social class and frequency of talking in particular areas. Middle-class mothers were more likely to talk frequently for cognitive reasons ($p < 0.01$) and working-class mothers were more likely to talk frequently for inter-personal reasons ($p < 0.01$). There was no significant difference between the classes in frequency of talking for social reasons.

Although the terminology is different, 'social class' as defined by Henderson (Brandis and Henderson, 1970) is almost identical to 'family background' as defined in the present study. It was therefore possible to analyse the responses obtained in our maternal interview in the manner described above. When this was done for the first instrument, the results of the present study entirely confirmed those obtained by Henderson.

The second instrument – the selection of alternative ways of explaining new words – was also theoretically based. With respect to the four words selected for explanation, three hypotheses were entertained:

a) middle-class mothers would choose general definitions when explaining things to children more frequently than working-class mothers;
b) middle-class mothers would choose exact, explicit concrete examples more frequently than working-class mothers;
c) working-class mothers would be more likely to choose concrete examples than middle-class mothers.

The four items in the schedule each consisted of a word and four alternative explanations, and the mothers were asked to indicate which explanations they would be likely to give as their first and second choices. Henderson states that the four statements offered for each word consisted of (a) a general definition; (b) an antonym; (c) a highly specific concrete example, and (d) a much less specific concrete example.[13]

Table 7.24 shows the four items with the statements in the order in which they were presented by Henderson. The letter preceding each statement indicates the category ((a)–(d) above) to which each statement was assigned and the figure following is the proportion of mothers in the present study who selected that statement as their first choice. Henderson looked first at the different patterns of combinations in first and second choice and found that middle-class mothers were more likely to use a larger number of combinations. As not all mothers in the present study gave two choices, this analysis could not be replicated. However, the more important comparisons concerned the first choices only. Comparing the distribution of first-choice responses across all four words within the two classes, using a 2×4 chi-square, Henderson found that the differences were not significant. We found exactly the same.[14] There

Table 7.24 *Suggested explanations for four words and proportion of mothers choosing each explanation*

1. 'Cool'	
(d) It's when something is no longer hot to touch.	47.5%
(b) It's the opposite of warm.	8.2%
(c) It's what you feel when the sun goes in.	13.1%
(a) It's a little bit warmer than cold.	31.1%
2. 'Mix'	
(a) To put things together.	36.1%
(d) When I make a stew the food is all mixed up.	27.9%
(c) It's what you do when you put different paints together to make different colours.	34.4%
(b) It's the opposite of separate.	1.6%
3. 'Dangerous'	
(a) It's when you might get hurt.	55.7%
(c) A road where there are lots of accidents.	18.0%
(d) It's dangerous to play with fire.	23.0%
(b) It's the opposite of safe.	3.3%
4. 'Flexible'	
(d) Rubber is flexible.	7.4%
(b) It's the opposite of rigid or stiff.	1.6%
(c) Your shoes are flexible.	8.2%
(a) Something that will bend without breaking.	82.8%

was a tendency for middle-class mothers to choose general definitions more often than working-class mothers and for working-class mothers to choose concrete examples more often than middle-class mothers, but the differences were not statistically significant.

Henderson next looked at differences with respect to each of the four words. Using 2×4 chi-square again, she found significant differences on all the words except 'cool'. In the case of the Bristol mothers, however, a significant difference was found only on 'dangerous'. For this word Henderson reported that middle-class mothers were more likely to choose the general definition first, whereas working-class mothers were more likely to choose the less specific concrete example ($p < 0.001$). In the case of the Bristol sample, both groups were more likely to choose the general definition first, but this tendency was more marked amongst the middle-class mothers ($\chi^2 = 12.51$, 3 df, $p < 0.01$).

On the basis of her results (including many that are not reported above) Henderson was able to argue that there were significant differences between the two social-class groups which tended to support the initial hypotheses. The Bristol data, however, offer little support for such a conclusion. One reason for this discrepancy may be in differences between the two samples in the manner in which they were constructed, the Bristol sample being less polarized towards the 'middle' and 'working' class extremes of the family background continuum than the sample studied by Henderson. This, and related issues, will be considered more fully in chapter 8.

The final group of questions concerned literacy. First we asked about the parents' own reading: how many books they owned and how many books each of them had read in the previous year. 52.8% owned 50 or more books, 21.1% between 21 and 50, 11.4% between 11 and 20 and 14.7% less than 10 books. The estimated number of books read in the preceding year is shown in table 7.25 for mothers and fathers separately. The variation is substantial. About a third of both fathers and mothers had read 20 books or more in the preceding year, but almost as high a proportion had read only one book or no books at all. Differences between the over-all distributions of mothers' and fathers' responses, on the other hand, were small. Since, in general, there was considerable similarity between the responses of the mothers and fathers of individual children, it is clear that the homes of the children differed very considerably in the value attached to reading books and this, it will be suggested in chapter 8, may be a significant influence on the children's progress in language learning.

Finally, we asked how often the mothers read to their children. The answers are shown in table 7.26. However since the interview

Table 7.25 *Number of books read by parents in previous year*

	≤1	2–3	4–8	9–20	>20
Mothers	26.7	12.1	11.2	12.9	37.1
Fathers	27.8	11.3	8.7	20.0	32.2

Table 7.26 *Frequency with which mothers read to children*

Daily	2/3 times per week	once a week	2/3 times a month	once a month or less
61.7	18.3	10.8	5.0	4.2

was administered, it has become clear that what is meant by reading varies considerably, some mothers considering looking at the pictures in a magazine or mail-order catalogue to be reading, whilst others include only reading stories in continuous prose. Furthermore, amongst those who claimed to read daily, the number of books read varied from one story at bedtime to as many as four or five spread throughout the day. The variation amongst children in their experience of stories read aloud is thus much greater than is indicated by the table.

7.5 Social class and the index of positional control

Although it has not been a major concern of the research programme as a whole to search for relationships between class of family background and variation in the development of language, such an investigation is certainly possible as a result of the manner in which the sample was constructed, and an analysis carried out in these terms will be included as part of the study of variation reported in chapter 9. In constructing the interview schedule, however, we had both the example and advice of Bernstein to draw upon and, as already mentioned, several of the schedules included in the interview were taken from the work of the Sociological Research Unit.

One of these schedules still remains to be described: the positional/personal index. Adlam and Turner (Adlam, 1977), describe this index as 'designed to measure the family's orientation towards "personal" forms of control or "positional" forms of control (Bernstein, 1971). The former indicates a loose family structure where individuals are accorded a considerable degree of discretion over their own experience and practice, the latter points to a structure where the roles are more tightly defined' (p. 208). Bernstein's (1971) hypothesis was that this index would relate on the one hand to social class and the social division of labour and, on the other, to parental modes of socialization and in particular to coding orientations adopted by mothers to their children in contexts of communication and control. It was further hypothesized that mothers' scores on this index would predict differences between children in their responses to certain language tasks administered at school. As Adlam (1977) shows, these hypotheses received substantial confirmation.

In the present investigation, the positional/personal index was included for rather different reasons. First, the maternal interview was seen as providing an opportunity to investigate the relationship between the index and family background with a different sample of mothers, and secondly, the index was considered to be a possible alternative to class of family background as a predictor of socially based differences in language development.

The schedule, as used in the present interview, consists of two parts. The first is concerned with the values and attitudes held by mothers with respect to the relationships within the family as a whole. This section consists of 16 forced-choice questions selected from the 24 in the original SRU schedule. The second section concerns the mothers' attitudes to marriage and the family, and contains all six items from the original SRU schedule. The items in both schedules varied very considerably in the pattern of responses obtained. In each item, one of the statements was considered to be 'positional' and the other 'personal'. In both sections, a few items were answered in the same way by the majority of mothers. For example in the pair

a) Parents should not encourage children to demand too much affection from them in public
b) Parents should show as much affection for their children in public as they do in private

more than 97% of mothers selected the 'personal' statement (b). On the other hand, in the pair

a) Parents should wait for children to come to them for advice
b) Parents should give advice to children when they think it is necessary

more than 87% chose (b), the 'positional' statement. The majority of items, however, yielded a more equal division of responses amongst this sample of mothers.

In order to compare the responses given by mothers in these two sections of the interview with the pattern of responses obtained in the other sections, a *positional* score was derived for each mother. This was calculated by summing the number of 'positional' choices made in both sections together. On certain items some mothers had been unable to make a choice between the two alternatives, as they considered that, depending on circumstances, both statements corresponded to attitudes that they might consider appropriate. In such cases, the response was given the value of 0.5 in summing positional responses. Calculated in this way, individual mothers' scores ranged from 1 to 16, mean score 6.6.

Before going on to consider the relationships between scores on this and other variables derived from the interview, a further development in Bernstein's theory of the relationship between class and family organization needs to be considered. Recently, in collaboration with Holland, he has developed a rather different analysis of the social divison of labour, in which a tri-partite division is adopted. This is conceptualized in terms of

> two interrelated structures, those of production and of symbolic control, and a third structure which regulates and maintains the inter and intra relationships of these basic structures. This third structure is the State, which has control of the agencies whose ultimate strength lies in the possibility of the use of force (the police and the army) and we have called it the structure of power. Each of the three structures can be conceptualised as a set of relationships based in materials, practices and institutions, and their fundamental distinguishing characteristic, we suggest, is their relationship to the material base of the society (Holland, 1980: 2).

Whilst the majority of male occupations typically considered to be working class fall clearly within the production structure, those considered to be middle class are divided between all three structures. (For a fuller account of the scheme for classifying occupations, cf. Holland, in preparation.) However, when female occupations are considered in these terms, it becomes apparent that quite a high proportion of occupations can be classified in both the production and the symbolic control structures – secretaries, are a good example. Nevertheless, although such occupations, in themselves, share some features of the structure of symbolic control, where they are carried on within an organization that, as a whole, is within the production structure, they are treated as 'low-level white collar work' within that structure (Holland and Bernstein, pers. comm.).

The attraction of this analysis of the division of labour is that it allows distinctions to be made both between and within the two broad classes, which can be hypothesized to be related to attitudes and practices that have a fairly direct bearing on language development. Similarly, predictions can be made about relationships between occupations of both parents classified in terms of the three structures, production, symbolic control and power, and scores on the positional/personal index. To test this latter group of predictions, Holland and Bernstein carried out a number of analyses on the data from the relevant sections of the maternal interview in the Bristol study. We are pleased to report their results in the following paragraphs, as they were made available to us (Bernstein, pers. comm.).

On the basis of a fairly detailed description of the work carried out in their present or most recent job, the occupations of both parents were classified as being either middle or working class and then allocated to one of the three structures. For mothers, a further distinction was made in all three structures between low-level white collar work and other occupations.[15] The first analysis tested the prediction that mothers in households where the male head had a working-class occupation would have a higher positional score than mothers in households where the male head had a middle-class occupation. The second analysis considered only middle-class households (as just defined) and tested the prediction that mothers where the male head had an occupation in the production structure would have a higher positional score than those where the male head of the household had an occupation in the structure of symbolic control. Both predictions were strongly supported (table 7.27) by the results of the analysis.

Table 7.27 *Test of difference between means on positional index: between classes and within middle-class*[16]

	Between classes		Within middle class	
	Working class	Middle class	Production	Symbolic
N	67	49	28	21
$\bar{x}$	7.37	5.20	5.96	4.19
Σx	494	255	167	88
Σx^2	4160	1613	1155	458
σ	2.8	2.4	2.4	2.1
t		4.39		2.67
df		114		47
sig. level		$p < 0.0005$ (one-tail)		$p < 0.01$ (one-tail)

Further analyses within the middle class (defined by father's occupation), taking both parents' occupations into account, were carried out to test the relation between positional score and the different combinations of fathers' and mothers' occupations. Considering first those families where both parents were in middle-class occupations, the mean scores for the different possible combinations were as shown in table 7.28. Comparing the two groups where the mothers had occupations in the structure of symbolic control (columns B and D), there is little difference between the group means, in spite of the difference in the fathers' occupations.

This suggests that, within the middle class, a low positional score (relatively speaking) associates more closely with a mother in an occupation in the structure of symbolic control than with a father's occupation in *either* structure. However the greatest *within* middle-class difference is between the means of the following two groups:

Father: middle-class production; Mother: low-level white collar
$N = 9, \bar{x} = 6.67$
Father: middle-class symbolic control; Mother: symbolic control
$N = 12, \bar{x} = 4.25$

This difference is significant at the 2.5% level (*t* test, one-tail).

Table 7.28 *Mean positional scores for different combinations of middle-class fathers' and mothers' occupation*

	A	B	C	D
Father's occupation	Prod.	Prod.	Symb. C.	Symb. C.
Mother's occupation	Prod.	Symb. C.	Prod.	Symb. C.
N	0	10	2	12
$\bar{x}$		4.20	2.50	4.25

Within the working class the only similar comparison that is possible, since all fathers had occupations in the structure of production, is that between households where the mother did low-level white collar work and those where the mother had some other occupation in the structure of production. The comparative figures are as follows:

Father: working-class production; Mother: low-level white collar work $N = 17, \bar{x} = 6.75$
Father: working-class production; Mother: production $N = 47, \bar{x} = 7.51$

Here again the trend suggests that within the working class, where the occupation of the mother is closer to the structure of symbolic control, as in the case of low-level white collar work, there will be a tendency towards a relatively lower positional score.

From these results, showing both inter- and intra-class relationships between type of occupation and degree of positional control, it seems clear that it will be worthwhile to see how both these variables are related to other types of information obtained from the maternal interview.

7.6 Relationships among mothers' answers

Wherever possible, responses to questions in the interview were scored to yield data susceptible to statistical analysis. Where appropriate, variables were then submitted to correlational analysis. With the exception of the cluster of variables centred on parental occupation and education (to be considered below), there were few relationships that reached a level of statistical significance.

As might be expected, the age of the parents was related to a number of variables in the area of family organization. The older the mother, the more likely the child was to be lower in the birth order and to have siblings close in age ($r = -0.19$, $p < 0.05$) and the less likely there were to be other adults regularly in the home ($r = -0.22$, $p < 0.02$). With increasing age both parents were less likely to have moved house in the preceding five years ($r = -0.22$, $p < 0.02$); there was also less likely to be regular contact with grandparents ($r = -0.24$, $p < 0.01$). Contact with grandparents was even more strongly negatively related to the parents' overall mobility (number of different places they had lived in) ($r = -0.47$, $p < 0.001$). Two of these variables were also significantly related to Class of Family Background: Parents' Mobility ($r = 0.53$, $p < 0.001$); and child's Position in the Family – children higher on the scale of Family Background were more likely to be first-born and less likely to have siblings close in age ($r = 0.24$, $p < 0.01$). All the remaining relationships arise rather directly out of differences in family background.

The variables concerned can be divided into two groups: those that provide indices of the formative influences on the parents, such as grandfathers' occupations, and their own education and occupations; and those that provide indices of behaviours that are hypothesized to be significant for children's learning of language. The relationships between these two sets of variables are shown in table 7.29 in the form of a correlation matrix. (Because of missing data, N is not constant but varies between 111 and 125; reported significance levels take this into account.) Not surprisingly, given the inter-relatedness amongst the 'formative' variables, there was a fairly consistent pattern of relationships between these variables and the behavioural indices. Extent of parental reading and frequency of reading to the child were both highly significantly related to all the formative variables; these forms of behaviour were also more likely to occur where the mother gave fewer positional responses, where the parents were more highly educated and

Table 7.29 *Correlation matrix: selected maternal interview variables*

	1	2	3	4	5	6	7	8	9	10	11	12	13
1 Father's Occupation	—												
2 Paternal Grand-father's Occupation	0.42***	—											
3 Maternal Grand-father's Occupation	0.39***	0.28**	—										
4 Father's Education	0.76***	0.39***	0.43***	—									
5 Mother's Education	0.62***	0.40***	0.40***	0.62***	—								
6 Class of Family Background	0.81***	0.47***	0.44***	0.85***	0.79***	—							
7 Positional Score	−0.36***	−0.33***	−0.08	−0.38***	−0.40***	−0.44***	—						

	1	2	3	4	5	6	7	8	9	10	11	12	13
8 Parental Literacy	0.50***	0.35***	0.31***	0.60***	0.47***	0.65***	−0.38***	—					
9 Frequency of Reading to Child	0.40***	0.30***	0.28**	0.32***	0.32***	0.48***	−0.29***	0.48***	—				
10 No. of Activities Sanctioned	−0.09	−0.21*	−0.07	−0.17	−0.27**	−0.17	0.42***	−0.07	0.04	—			
11 Purchase of Educational or Role-Play Toy	0.10	0.10	0.18*	0.15	0.08	0.15	−0.21*	0.13	0.16	−0.01	—		
12 Attention to Novel Features in Child's Speech	0.17	0.19	0.02	0.24**	0.38***	0.29***	−0.31***	0.17	0.09	−0.34***	−0.05	—	
13 Correction of Child's Speech	−0.10	−0.17	0.03	−0.22*	−0.30***	−0.23*	0.22*	−0.09	0.02	0.26**	−0.06	−0.61***	—

*$p < 0.05$; **$p < 0.01$; ***$p < 0.001$

themselves came from homes where the male head of the household (i.e. their own fathers) had higher occupational status.

Although weaker, the same pattern is seen for two other behavioural variables: Purchase of Educational or Role-play Toys and Attention to Novel Features in the Child's Speech; the pattern is reversed for Number of Activities Sanctioned and Correction of the Child's Speech. However, whilst the two reading variables are most strongly predicted by the composite index, Class of Family Background, the Number of Activities Sanctioned, Attention to Novel Features in Child's Speech and Correction of Child's Speech are all more strongly predicted by Mother's Education alone. More educated mothers are likely to sanction fewer activities and to be less concerned to correct their children's speech; they are also more likely to notice and value new and original forms and uses in their children's speech. As would be expected, correcting children's speech is significantly positively related to the sanctioning of activities ($r = 0.26$, $p < 0.01$) and inversely related to attending to novel features in children's speech ($r = -0.61$, $p < 0.001$).

The one behavioural variable that does not fit so neatly into the pattern just described is the one concerned with the last important toy purchased, whether it was an educational or role-play toy or some other kind of toy. The much lower correlations where this variable is involved are probably due to the fact that individual scores are dichotomized. However, it is interesting that the best predictor of what sort of toy the parents 'last bought' is the score on the positional index, mothers with low positional scores were more likely to buy educational or role-play toys ($r = 0.21$, $p < 0.05$). Such mothers were also likely to sanction fewer of the child's activities ($r = 0.42$, $p < 0.001$).

Within the formative variables, there is one particular relationship that merits further comment: that between maternal grandfather's occupation and mother's score on the positional index. A theory of cultural transmission would claim that the attitudes held by one generation are, to a very considerable extent, acquired from the previous generation in the course of socialization and would therefore expect the two variables to be related. Since a high positional score is associated with low occupational status and since it was the mothers who gave the responses for the positional index, it would be predicted that there would be a significant negative correlation between (maternal grand-) father's occupation and daughter's positional score. Although in the expected direction, the correlation was not significant. However, a significant relationship was found between (paternal grand-) father's occupation and daughter-*in-law*'s positional score. Taken together with the relatively low correlation between maternal and paternal grandfathers' occupations, this seems to suggest that, irrespective of the attitudes acquired before leaving home, a woman tends on marrying to adopt the attitudes of her husband and of her husband's family. Given the very indirect nature of the evidence, however, this interpretation can only be very tentative. It is worth noting, however, that the best single predictor of the positional score is mother's education: more highly educated mothers tend to have lower positional scores ($r = -0.40$, $p < 0.001$).

Finally, since substantial differences had emerged *within* the two social class groups in Holland and Bernstein's analysis of mothers' responses on the positional/personal dimension (see 7.5), further analyses of all the questionnaire data were made in a similar manner. The classes, it will be recalled, were defined by parents' occupations only, with a further division being made within each class between occupations involved in the structure of production and those in the structure of symbolic control. For the mothers only, an intermediate category was added for those whose occupation involved 'white-collar work', although in a context of production.

The first analysis was carried out within the working class, comparing those families where the mother's occupation was in the structure of production ($N = 47$) with families where the mother's occupation was white-collar work ($N = 20$). However, the only variables on which a significant difference was found were mother's education and mother's age at the birth of the child studied. Mothers with occupations in the structure of production tended to have less education ($t = 2.96$, $p < 0.01$) and to have been older at the time of the child's birth ($t = 2.07$, $p < 0.05$). There was also a positive trend for mothers with white-collar occupations to claim to read more frequently to their children ($t = 1.92$, $p < 0.01$).

All the other analyses were carried out within the middle class. First, comparing families in terms of fathers' occupations. Families in which the father had an occupation in the structure of symbolic control ($N = 31$) were more likely than those in which the father had an occupation in the structure of production ($N = 21$), (a) to have more children at home during the day ($t = 2.25$; $p < 0.05$) and (b) to sanction fewer of the child's activities ($t = 2.33$, $p < 0.05$). A similar analysis based on mothers' occupations produced slightly more significant differences. Families in which the mother's occupation was in the structure of symbolic control ($N = 25$) were more likely than other middle-class families ($N = 27$) (a) to have moved home more frequently ($t = 2.15$, $p < 0.05$), (b) to have less frequent contact with grandparents ($t = 2.69$, $p < 0.01$), (c) to engage in more literacy-related activities ($t = 2.25$, $p < 0.05$), (d) to sanction fewer of their children's activities ($t = 2.97$, $p < 0.01$) and (e) to correct fewer aspects of their children's speech ($t = 2.05$, $p < 0.05$). However, they were likely to talk less to their children overall ($t = 2.55$, $p < 0.05$).

Finally, a comparison was made between middle-class families where the mother's occupation was white-collar work ($N = 12$) and those where the mother's occupation was in the structure of production ($N = 13$). Mothers with white-collar occupations were more likely, (a) to be married to husbands with a higher level of education ($t = 2.82$, $p < 0.01$) and (b) to correct fewer aspects of their children's speech ($t = 2.04$, $p < 0.10$).

From these results, it can be concluded that, of the 'formative' variables, there is no single one that in all cases is the best predictor of characteristics of the home environment and of the parental behaviour investigated; Mother's Education was the best predictor of reported responses to the child's speech, Positional Score was the best predictor of the number of activities sanctioned and (negatively) of the purchase of educational or role-play toys, and Class of Family Background was the best predictor of the parents' own reading and of the frequency of their reading to their children. However, as already pointed out, all of these predictor variables are highly inter-correlated.

The final question to consider is whether these or any other of the variables derived from the maternal interview are significantly related to variation in language development. This question will be addressed in the following chapter as part of the general consideration of possible influences on variation in language development.[17]

Variation in language development

The central theme of chapters 4 and 5 was the similarity between the children studied in the sequence in which their language developed. For this sample of children, the evidence presented strongly suggests that there is a common route, at least in the early stages, and it seems probable that this will apply to other children learning English and perhaps to children learning other languages as well.

Nevertheless, a common route does not preclude some degree of variation. Indeed, as was emphasized, the evidence of order between items at adjacent levels was probabilistic rather than absolute, which means that the sequence was not identical in every case. However, most of the work still remains to be done to determine the significance of these individual differences. In this chapter, therefore, discussions will focus on those differences between individuals that can be gleaned from a consideration of the indices of development that were obtained for each cohort at the time of the last observation.

Of the existence of variation in rate of language development, however, there can be no doubt, as has already been indicated in chapter 3. There, the measure used was Mean Length of Structured Utterances (MLUS), which, because of the ease with which it can be calculated, was employed in the first phase of the analysis in order to obtain an overall impression of variability. Some reservations were expressed there about the use of this index, particularly for the later pre-school years. In this chapter, therefore, we shall explore in greater detail the relationship between MLU and other developmental indices, particularly the developmental scale which was presented at the end of chapter 5.

Whether the variation be in route or rate of language development, it remains an important matter to determine the causes. Observational studies cannot, of course, provide definitive answers to questions of causation, but they can investigate the extent to which the observed differences in language covary with other attributes of the children and of their environments and experience. This will be the topic of the final section of this chapter.

First, however, we shall return to another aspect of variation already broached in chapter 3, the relationship of language to context.

8.1 Variation according to context

During the course of a normal day, a child engages in many activities, which involve different fellow-actors and different materials. Some of these activities are familiar routines, such as getting dressed; others are more or less novel. In some activities it is the child who is the initiator, in others a parent, and in still others it may be another child. Each of these dimensions is likely to have an effect on the language that occurs – the purposes for which participants speak to each other, the content of their utterances and the actual quantity of talk, and the degree of specificity and explicitness that their communication requires.

Reviewing research on mothers' speech to young children, Snow (1977) noted that task difficulty had little effect on mothers' speech but that the kind of task engaged in had a large effect. One of the studies referred to, by Bakker-Rennes and Hoefnagel-Hohle (1974), compared six situations, half of which were categorized as caretaking (dressing, bathing and eating) and the other half as 'for fun' (playing, chatting after lunch and reading a book). The authors are reported to have found that mothers' speech was more complex in the 'fun' situations than in those designated caretaking. In a narrower comparison, Snow *et al.* (1976) found that mothers' speech was more complex in a book-reading situation than in free play.

Since conversation is a reciprocal activity, it can reasonably be assumed that if mothers' speech differs across these different activity situations there will be related differences in children's speech. What is not clear, however, is whether the children's speech varies in a way that matches their mothers' (i.e. increases in complexity when their mothers' speech does) or whether the variation is complementary (i.e. the more complex the mother's speech, the less complex the child's). Arguments could be advanced to support predictions in either direction. The reality may be even more complex, of course, involving matching in some situations and complementing in others. However, some kind of relationship is almost certain to obtain.

Unfortunately, we are not yet in a position to say anything about variation in the complexity of children's speech according to context of activity, as this work has only just begun. Nevertheless, we can amplify somewhat the account given in chapter 3 of the extent of the departure from equal distribution of the total amount of speech over the different activity contexts. There, the emphasis was on change with age in the proportion of utterances occurring in each context and on differences between boys and girls. A second analysis similarly reported the distribution of total amount of speech over the main categories of Inter-Personal Purpose. Here the focus is on the relationship between context of activity and inter-personal purpose: do the different contexts elicit different functional emphases? Only child utterances have been analysed, and the data from boys and girls have been pooled across all occasions. This must certainly have the effect of hiding important age- and sex-related differences, but it has the merit of allowing the main trends to be seen more easily, which should be useful for researchers planning to sample from a small range of contexts.

As already noted, there are several dimensions that are relevant to a description of context and, in a fine-grained analysis, it would be important to keep them distinct. However, in the present analysis only a rather gross differentiation has been made between the types of activity engaged in, with a secondary differentiation between involvement or no involvement of an adult in activities described as play or imaginary play. Participation of siblings and friends in the child's activities increases with age, although this varies considerably according to the child's position in the birth order and in the availability of playmates. However, for almost all children, in all situations except those described as play, the child's most frequent co-actor and conversational partner was an adult, usually the mother.

All child utterances were coded according to the context of activity in relation to which they occurred and according to the functions that they performed. For the purposes of the present analysis, however, some of the categories of context have been collapsed in order to reduce the number of cells, and only two of the sub-sequence modes, Representational and Control, have been examined. Nevertheless, since these two modes account for approximately two thirds of all utterances directed to others and more than three quarters of all talk on substantive topics, they should allow a fairly accurate estimate to be made of the extent to which the distribution of utterance functions is affected by context.

In each mode, one-word responses with the functions of Accept/ Confirm, Refuse/Deny, Reject and Acknowledge have been combined in one category called Other. To this category have also been added some of the rarely occurring functions in the Control mode, such as Promise and Condition, and the more frequently occurring function, Verbal Accompaniment to Behaviour (e.g. 'There we are'). One or two other categories have been combined in order to reduce the number of cells: Permit with Formulation; Query Evaluate Intention with Request Permission; and Query Want and Query Intention with Offer.

Table 8.1 shows how the total number of child utterances were distributed according to mode and context. As can be seen immediately, three contexts dominate: Play, General Activity and Talk. Given that there is this very considerable variation in the amount of speech occurring in the different contexts, the question to be addressed is whether there are also qualitative differences in the types of utterance that occur: do some functions occur proportionately more or less frequently in different contexts? First, though, is there a difference in the amount of speech in the two modes according to context of activity? The aim of the analysis is to identify contexts where more or fewer utterance tokens occur in a given mode or with a given function than would be expected by chance. The method used employs the margin totals of table 8.1 to calculate an expected frequency of occurrence for each Sequence Mode × Context cell, on the assumption that the two variables concerned are independent. Expected frequencies are shown in parentheses. (The same method is used in calculating expected frequencies for Function × Context cells below.)

It is clear from table 8.1 that there are substantial differences between observed and expected frequencies in a considerable number of Sequence Mode × Context cells, showing that the context has a considerable influence on the type of conversation that occurs. Representational speech is much more likely to occur in the contexts of Talk and Read + TV, and Control speech is more likely to occur in the contexts of Caretaking, Eating, Helping, General Activity, Play, with or without an adult, and Imaginary Play without an adult. Most of these results are what might have been expected, but two perhaps need some comment.

Meal-times are usually thought to provide a good opportunity for family conversation, and so a preponderance of Representational speech might have been expected in the context of Eating. The reason why this does not happen is that Eating cannot be

Table 8.1 *Distribution of speech by mode and context*

Mode	Context Care-taking	Eating	Helping	General Activity	Talk	Read + TV	Play	Play + Adult	Imaginary Play	Imaginary Play + Adult	Total
Representa-tional	900 (1093)	1572 (2201)	1046 (1187)	8105 (8512)	7069 (5940)	3631 (2542)	8142 (8740)	1833 (1958)	986 (1112)	284 (282)	33 568
Control	1048 (855)	2349 (1720)	1069 (928)	7059 (6652)	3513 (4642)	897 (1986)	7429 (6831)	1656 (1531)	995 (869)	219 (221)	26 234
Total	1948	3921	2115	15 164	10 582	4528	15 571	3489	1981	503	59 802

equated with meal-times. Eating was only coded if attention was being given to the activity of eating or to the food to be eaten. If the talk was about other matters, it was coded in one of the other categories, and in most cases Talk was the most appropriate. The other result that deserves comment is the different distribution of utterances across modes in the two contexts of Imaginary Play. Observed frequencies closely matches expected frequencies when an adult is involved, but Control speech is proportionately more frequent in the absence of an adult. The reason for this is the very high proportion of speech in Imaginary Play involving children only that is devoted to defining the imaginary situation and to allocating roles (e.g. 'You be the Mummy', 'Pretend you went in your space-ship').[1] With an adult involved, imaginary play is more sustained but also more dominated by the adult's exploration of the situation, as will be seen when the functions occurring most frequently are considered.

Having established that there are substantial effects of context on the mode of conversation, we can now look in more detail at the functions that utterances perform in the different contexts. The distribution of utterances across functions and contexts is shown separately for the two modes in tables 8.2 and 8.3. Here again there are very substantial differences between observed and expected frequencies, indicating that the purpose and organization of interaction varies quite considerably from one context to another. Clearly, it would be inappropriate to attempt to comment on all the cells in the tables where a 'discrepancy' is found, but some deserve particular mention.

As far as the contexts of Caretaking, Eating, Helping and General Activity are concerned, it is interesting to note that, in the Representational mode, the observed distribution is for the most part quite close to 'expected' whereas, in the control mode, there are some substantial discrepancies. The Want function occurs much more frequently than expected in Eating, Caretaking and General Activity but less in Helping; Request Permission is more frequent in Eating and Helping and, in the latter context, so is Offer. Requests occur less frequently than expected in all these contexts as do Formulations and Permission. (As might be anticipated, both these categories occur with greater than expected frequency in the contexts of Play, particularly without an adult involved.) For Talk, the interesting discrepancies are in the relatively low frequency of Ostensions but the relatively high frequencies of Yes/No and Content Questions and of Requests for Explanation and

Table 8.2 *Distribution of speech by function and context: Representational mode*

Function	Context										
Representational	Care-taking	Eating	Helping	General Activity	Talk	Read + TV	Play	Play + Adult	Imaginary Play	Imaginary Play + Adult	Total
Ostension	189 (187)	293 (326)	199 (217)	1831 (1681)	724 (1467)	1239 (754)	1874 (1690)	421 (380)	150 (205)	46 (59)	6 966
Statement	376 (378)	678 (659)	437 (439)	3183 (3400)	2997 (2965)	1081 (1523)	3957 (3415)	713 (769)	541 (414)	117 (119)	14 080
Yes/No Question	60 (68)	142 (118)	94 (79)	678 (611)	697 (533)	177 (274)	470 (613)	120 (138)	80 (74)	11 (21)	2 529
Content Question	42 (72)	116 (125)	85 (83)	730 (644)	690 (562)	282 (288)	506 (647)	142 (146)	62 (78)	12 (23)	2 667
Name Question	13 (12)	13 (21)	12 (14)	121 (106)	84 (92)	102 (47)	71 (106)	14 (24)	5 (13)	3 (4)	438
Request Explanation	10 (14)	23 (24)	19 (16)	121 (121)	189 (106)	45 (54)	72 (122)	18 (27)	4 (15)	2 (4)	503
Response to Content Question	48 (32)	46 (55)	34 (37)	283 (284)	333 (248)	123 (127)	186 (286)	70 (64)	22 (35)	33 (10)	1 178
Explanation	15 (9)	8 (16)	13 (10)	80 (81)	104 (70)	16 (36)	73 (81)	15 (18)	9 (10)	1 (3)	334
Other	147 (131)	253 (228)	153 (152)	1078 (1177)	1251 (1026)	566 (527)	933 (1181)	320 (266)	113 (143)	59 (41)	4 873
Total: Repres.	900	1572	1046	8105	7069	3631	8142	1833	986	284	33 568

Table 8.3 *Distribution of speech by function and context: Control mode*

Function	Context										
Control	Care-taking	Eating	Helping	General Activity	Talk	Read + TV	Play	Play + Adult	Imaginary Play	Imaginary Play + Adult	Total
Want	214 (176)	850 (393)	130 (176)	1370 (1182)	815 (588)	136 (150)	636 (1245)	168 (277)	50 (167)	26 (37)	4 395
Request	187 (259)	258 (582)	162 (265)	1585 (1748)	622 (870)	367 (222)	2485 (1839)	495 (410)	318 (246)	42 (54)	6 494
Prohibit	55 (46)	62 (104)	28 (47)	270 (312)	75 (156)	27 (40)	508 (329)	86 (73)	49 (44)	3 (10)	1 163
Intend	65 (97)	127 (217)	110 (99)	645 (651)	352 (324)	42 (83)	763 (685)	163 (153)	124 (92)	27 (20)	2 418
Suggest	11 (23)	19 (52)	33 (24)	87 (157)	86 (78)	16 (20)	255 (165)	37 (37)	35 (22)	4 (5)	583
Formulation and Permit	8 (15)	19 (33)	12 (15)	53 (99)	53 (49)	5 (13)	149 (104)	24 (23)	40 (14)	6 (3)	369
Request Permission	47 (60)	175 (135)	123 (62)	472 (407)	250 (202)	33 (52)	324 (428)	53 (95)	28 (57)	6 (13)	1 511
Offer and Request Intent	20 (39)	89 (87)	96 (40)	251 (262)	140 (130)	17 (33)	251 (275)	35 (61)	56 (37)	17 (8)	972
Justification	30 (37)	62 (82)	54 (37)	282 (246)	167 (122)	24 (31)	221 (259)	42 (58)	26 (35)	8 (8)	916
Other	411 (296)	688 (664)	321 (302)	2044 (1995)	953 (993)	230 (253)	1864 (2099)	553 (468)	269 (281)	80 (62)	7 413
Total: Control	1048	2349	1069	7059	3513	897	7429	1656	995	219	26 234

Explanations; and also of Responses to Content Questions. This is, *par excellence*, the context for the exchange of information – for learning through talking. It is somewhat surprising, therefore, to find that there is a greater than expected frequency of Want and Request Permission utterances in the Control mode in this context.

Attention has already been drawn to some features of conversation in the various Play contexts. Interestingly, even when an adult participates, Request Permission occurs less frequently than expected, as does Want. Instead, activity seems to be more than usually governed by Requests, Formulations and Prohibitions. In both Play and Imaginary Play without an adult there are more Statements but less Questions and Responses than expected. However the situation changes when an adult joins in: the greater than expected frequency of Response to Content Question and Other (yes/no responses) suggests that, when adults are playing, they are asking rather a lot of questions.

Perhaps the most 'discrepant' of all the contexts is Read + TV. These are, of course, quite different activities in certain respects, but both involve attending to a visual stimulus. (Read occurs most frequently in the age-range 15–30 months, when the activity mainly involves talk about pictures in books and magazines; only a minority of children are actually talking about a story that is being read to them.) The emphasis on the visual stimulus and its identification is highlighted by the much greater than expected frequency of Ostensions and Name Questions. Note, however, that there is a less than expected frequency of Statements, Yes/No Questions and Explanations, which suggests that sustained conversation does not develop to the extent that one might expect. In the Control mode, on the other hand, Request occurs more frequently than expected: presumably, children asking adults to read to them or to switch the television on.

An analysis in terms of observed and expected frequencies, therefore, certainly supports the belief that children's conversational experience varies according to context and suggests that this variation may have implications for their learning, both of and through language. However, it can do no more than point to areas that merit further investigation by other, more sophisticated methods. As indicated at the beginning of this section the functions that children perform in speaking are not independent of the functions of the utterances addressed to them. In future work, therefore, we shall need to look beyond individual utterances to the structure of the socially situated discourse in which those utterances occur.

8.2 Relationships between measures of language development

Four different types of index of language development have been employed for the analysis of within-language variation; these are outlined below. All measures were obtained at two ages: at 42 months for the complete sample (older and younger cohorts combined) and at 60 months for the older cohort only (for EPVT scores only, the ages were 39 and 57 months respectively).

As mentioned in chapter 3, the first indices to be used were global measures of Mean Length of Utterance: Mean Length of Structured Utterances (MLUS) and Mean Length of Longest Utterances (MLUL). Subsequently a number of more specific measures was derived from an analysis of the samples of spontaneous speech to represent the three descriptive levels of syntax, semantics and pragmatics. Although, as was seen in chapter 5, the general tendency was for distinctions in the functions and propositional meanings of utterances to precede the emergence of the syntactic structures required for their full realization, there were also indications that development might proceed unevenly across the three levels in individual children. For the present investigation, therefore, systems have been selected for comparison from the three levels.

Syntactic Range: the number of items in the combined systems of the structure of the sentence and clause and of the structure of the noun phrase.
Semantic Range: the number of items in the system of sentence meaning relations.
Semantic Modification: the number of items in the combined systems of time, aspect, modality and modulation.
Pragmatic Range: the number of items in the system of interpersonal functions.

In each case, the score given to an individual child is the number of items in a particular system to have emerged in his speech by the last observation.

An overall score based on the scale of language development was the third index employed. As described in chapter 5, the scale was derived from a 'cross-system' analysis of selected items from each of the major systems in which an order of emergence had been established. It can therefore be expected to be a better index of overall linguistic development, with respect to speech production, than any of the individual indices described above. Individual scores were derived as follows. As all children had, by 42 months, reached level IV or beyond, all items in levels III and below were assumed to have emerged. From level IV onwards, each item was weighted by the number of the level in which it was placed (see table 5.2) and the final score determined by summing the total number of weighted items to have emerged by the last observation. As an example, suppose a child had 14 items at level IV, 9 at level V, 3 at level VI and none at later levels, his weighted scale score would be made up as follows:[2]

14 items at level IV	56
9 items at level V	45
3 items at level VI	18
Total weighted score	119

The fourth index of language development was the English Picture Vocabulary Test. The EPVT (Brimer and Dunn, 1963) was administered to each child individually at the time of the penultimate observation (at 39 months for the younger cohort and at 39 and 57 months for the older cohort). Although described as a test of listening comprehension, this test involves only individual lexical items to which the child responds by selecting one picture from a set of four. A test involving sentence comprehension would have been preferred as an index of development in reception but, as described in chapter 1, our own sentence comprehension test proved unreliable and so the data it yielded had to be discarded. Despite its limitations as a test of comprehension, however, the EPVT does have the advantage of having been standardized on a much larger sample and so of allowing an estimate to be made of the representativeness of the Bristol sample in relation to the population of 3–5-year-old British children.

Once individual scores had been obtained for each of these indices, the data from each age cohort were submitted to a correlation analysis.[3] The results are shown in tables 8.4 and 8.5. For both age cohorts, the highest correlations between pairs of indices derived from spontaneous speech are, in every case but one, those involving the language development scale score. (The one exception is the correlation between MLUS and MLUL at 42 months.) This suggests that the scale has the potential for providing a valid index of overall language development for production. Individual indices have correlations with the scale that range from $r = 0.69$ to $r = 0.92$ at 42 months and from $r = 0.41$ to

Table 8.4 *Correlations between measures of language development at 42 months* ($n = 60$)

		1	2	3	4	5	6	7	8
1	MLUS	—							
2	MLUL	0.85	—						
3	Syntactic range	0.74	0.73	—					
4	Semantic range	0.51	0.59	0.76	—				
5	Semantic modification	0.64	0.58	0.76	0.78	—			
6	Pragmatic range	0.54	0.60	0.63	0.71	0.64	—		
7	EPVT	0.37	0.44	0.53	0.58	0.53	0.36	—	
8	Language development scale score	0.69	0.75	0.92	0.86	0.85	0.75	0.58	—

Table 8.5 *Correlations between measures of language development at 60 months* ($n = 65$)

		1	2	3	4	5	6	7	8
1	MLUS	—							
2	MLUL	0.47	—						
3	Syntactic range	0.46	0.49	—					
4	Semantic range	0.46	0.52	0.55	—				
5	Semantic modification	0.24	0.49	0.61	0.56	—			
6	Pragmatic range	0.12	0.21	0.36	0.30	0.32	—		
7	EPVT	0.15	0.14	0.27	0.29	0.36	−0.01	—	
8	Language development scale score	0.49	0.55	0.88	0.69	0.68	0.41	0.24	—

$r = 0.88$ at 60 months (all results being significant at the 1% level or better). At both ages the correlation between scale score and Pragmatic Range is lower than the correlations involving the semantic and syntactic indices and at both ages it is the index of Syntactic Range that has the highest correlation with scale score. Two rather different reasons can be suggested for this finding. First, items which contribute to the two indices, syntactic range and pragmatic range, are unequally distributed with respect to the levels in the scale: the majority of pragmatic items are found in the early stages and the majority of syntactic items in the later stages. Since even by 42 months the majority of children are scoring in the upper part of the scale, it follows that, from 42 months onwards, there will be little variation between children on the index of Pragmatic Range whereas with respect to Syntactic Range it is precisely in this age-range that one would expect to find the greatest variation.

Secondly, there is a relatively weak relationship between the range of pragmatic intentions that are realized in a child's speech and the extent of his command of the syntactic and semantic options in the language. Or, to put it differently, the same purposes can be achieved in linguistically more or less complex ways. This interpretation receives some support from the generally lower correlations with pragmatic range for each of the other variables. This is particularly striking for the older cohort.

A second general finding concerns the relationship between EPVT scores and scores on the indices derived from spontaneous speech. At both ages correlations are relatively low, some being close to a chance level at 60 months. Once again, two different kinds of explanation suggest themselves. On the one hand, the low correlations may be the result of a rather weak relationship between production and comprehension, or at least between the indices of production used here, which mainly have as their domain a complete clause or phrase, and the index of comprehension, which is concerned only with the recognition of individual lexical items. On the other hand, the result may largely reflect the distinction between the situation in which the data were obtained, the indices of production being derived from spontaneously occurring conversational interaction and the EPVT scores from a relatively formal test situation. It was noticeable that some children were ill at ease in the test situation and almost certainly performed well below their optimal level.[4]

When the two tables are compared, it is clear that there is an overall decrease in the size of the correlations with increase in age. One possible reason for this is that the indices themselves are less effective when applied to samples of speech from children who are approaching the ceiling on individual indices. This is probably an unavoidable limitation of using indices derived from the pooled data from a sample of children to measure the final level attained by individual members of the same sample. Another possible explanation for the shrinking correlations is related to the finding, reported in chapter 5, that there begins to be greater variability in the order in which particular items emerge as higher levels on the scale are reached. This may well be due to the increase in sampling error that is associated with items that have a low overall frequency of occurrence (see chapter 6). However, even if these explanations are accepted, it seems probable that there is a genuine weakening of the relationships between systems both within and between linguistic levels with increasing age. Since the same general intentions can be realized in a variety of ways, it must be expected that individual preferences will become apparent leading to unevenness in development across the various systems.

If correct, this conclusion has important implications for assessment of language development in the later pre-school years and beyond. What it implies is that no individual index taken on its own can be treated as giving an accurate estimate of overall language development. Instead, a variety of indices should be used which will allow a profile to be built up showing where development is relatively in advance and where delayed. If an overall score is required it should be based on information from a variety of linguistic systems, as is the language development scale score in the present investigation. Its greater potential reliability, when compared with the other individual indices, is indicated by the generally larger correlations that are found in relation to this measure.

What has been shown in this section is that the relationships between the various indices of linguistic development used in this study show a far from perfect fit and that they weaken with increasing age. This is certainly evidence in favour of the claim that there are individual differences in overall pattern of development, but it is not clear from these data alone whether there are distinguishable styles or patterns adopted by particular groups of children or whether the variation is much more random.

Various studies have reported differences between children that would support the existence of fairly distinct styles of learning. Nelson (1973), for example, noted a difference in the early stages between 'referential' and 'expressive' preferences in vocabulary learning and Bloom, Lightbown and Hood (1975) reported rather similar 'nominal' and 'pronominal' preferences in early multi-word utterances. One interpretation of these differences is that they are manifestations of a general dimension of difference between children in their disposition to adopt an analytic approach to language learning. Such a dimension might well also subsume the strategy shown by some children (Clark, 1974; Peters, 1983) of recalling and using, in appropriate communication contexts, 'chunks' of previously heard adult utterances that appear to have been only partially analysed.

Some writers have tended to treat these differences between children as dichotomous, implying that children are either referential/nominal or expressive/pronominal. However, this seems rather unlikely. Insofar as there are differences in learning style, these may vary within children according to context and over quite short periods of development (Wells, in press b). As Brethcr-ton *et al.* (1983) conclude, these two styles may better be thought of as strategies that most children call upon in parallel, though we should perhaps add that they may call upon them to differing degrees.

To a considerable extent, the question of how much importance to attach to such differences is a matter of emphasis, as can be seen when considering adult language. From one perspective, what is striking is that all the speakers of a particular language are to a large degree mutually intelligible, because they share a common code. From a different perspective, what may be most apparent is the extent of the differences between individuals, not only at the level of dialect, but also in their degree of fluency, their familiarity with different registers and their habitual style(s) of speaking (Fillmore, 1979). The same sort of variation can be expected to occur during the course of development. There is certainly evidence that some children make greater progress, at some stages, in mastering systems at one linguistic level of description rather than another. There is also some variation in the order of emergence of items within particular systems. At the present time, however, the weight of the evidence suggests that differences between children are better thought of in terms of minor deviations that branch off from and rejoin the main thoroughfare rather than as separate independent routes.

8.3 MLU as an index of development

It has already been suggested that it is undesirable to use a measure of one single aspect of language as an index of overall development or attainment. This applies as much to MLU as to other measures. However, as MLU has been very widely used as a general index of development, it is worth looking more closely at its relationship with other indices and particularly at its relationship with the proposed scale of development.

Since MLU is calculated on the surface form of children's utterances, it can be expected to be fairly closely related to syntactic development, at least in the early stages, but rather less closely related to development in the range of semantic distinctions that the child is able to express and even less so to developments in the types of inter-personal functions that his utterances perform. MLU is thus potentially more appropriate as a general index of syntactic development. Table 8.4 shows that at 42 months there is a relatively strong relationship between MLUS and MLUL and all the other measures based on production, but that the relationships are strongest with Syntactic Range ($r = 0.74$, $r = 0.73$). However, as table 8.5 shows, all correlations involving MLU have dropped substantially by 60 months, even those involving Syntactic Range ($r = 0.46$, $r = 0.49$). Since all the correlations between individual measures decrease between 42 and 60 months, part of the change involving MLU is probably due, as already discussed, to the increasing variability with age in the choices that are made in particular utterances from the increasingly large range of options available in each of the major linguistic systems.

More specifically, there is a slowing down of the increase in MLU from about 42 months onward (see figure 3.3) as children begin to develop various strategies for making their utterances more succinct. Ellipsis is one such strategy; others include the use of anaphoric, indefinite and reflexive pronouns. Thus, whilst it remains the case that later-to-emerge items in the syntactic systems of sentence and noun-phrase structure typically involve an increase in the number of constituents and, hence, in the number of morphemes, there are parallel developments in the management of discourse that either make no difference to utterance length or actually lead to a decrease in the number of morphemes uttered. Even in relation to syntax, therefore, there are theoretical reasons for expecting MLU to become progressively less sensitive as an index of development.

In the early stages, however, it has been assumed that MLU is a relatively sensitive index of development. This, apart from the ease with which it can be calculated, has been the main justification for its use. Brown (1973) preferred it to age as a heuristic device for grouping observations prior to the investigation of particular linguistic features and since then his MLU-based stages have come to be used very widely as a broad characterization of the sequence of development and as a means of describing the level attained by a child by a particular occasion. Brown was probably right to prefer a linguistic index, however crude, to age as a starting point for investigation, but how good is the fit between MLU and stage of language development? In order to answer this question, one needs an independent measure of development. But this is precisely what has been lacking. However, if the scale of development presented in chapter 5 is accepted as such a measure it now becomes possible to attempt to evaluate the goodness of fit between MLU and language development. MLU was not used at any stage in the construction of the scale. However, a MLU value was calculated for each observation and these were then assigned to MLU bands, corresponding to Brown's stages I–V. Observations with an MLU greater than the upper limit of stage V were assigned to a further band, band VI. As with the data on emergence of particular linguistic items, MLU was assumed to be cumulative. Once a child had reached a particular MLU band, he was assumed to remain in that band until he registered an MLU that took him into the next band: no regressions were recognized.

Given information about the occasion on which each item in the scale emerged in the speech of an individual child, it is possible to record the MLU band that the child had reached by that occasion. If this is repeated for each item in the scale and for all children in the sample, it becomes possible to investigate the relationship between MLU and sequence of development. If there is a close relationship, it can be predicted that the majority of children will have MLUs in the same band at the point of emergence of any particular item. Furthermore, since the levels that make up the scale consist of items with a high probability of coemergence, there should be a narrow distribution across MLU bands for all the items that make up a particular level.

These predictions were tested by drawing up a matrix for each level in the scale with items on one dimension and children on the other. In each cell was entered the MLU band attained by the particular child on the occasion of emergence of the particular item. Matrices were constructed for the two age-cohorts separately, as their observations spanned different parts of the scale. Analyses were then carried out on levels I to VI using data from the younger cohort and on levels VII and VIII using the data from the older cohort. No analysis was made in relation to levels IX and X as too few of the children had shown emergence of many of the items at these levels.

The first step was to identify the median MLU for each item. Substantial consistency was found amongst items at each level. All items at level I were in MLU band I; this was also true for items at levels II and III. Level IV straddled bands I and II, with 62.5% of items being in band II. At level V, 87.5% of items were in band III and the remainder in band II, and at level VI, 68.8% were in band IV and the remainder in band III. By level VII, 75% of items were in band V and the remainder in band IV, and by level VIII, all items were in band V.[5]

This seems to suggest a rather close fit between MLU and level of language development. However these results are deceptive, as they ignore the range of MLU-band values across the whole sample of children for any particular item. This was surprisingly large and, once again, there was considerable consistency across items at any level. From the earlier discussion it might have been anticipated that items from the two syntactic systems of sentence and NP structure would have shown a much narrower range, but this was not the case. With the exception of items at levels I and II, when almost all the children still registered MLU values in band I, the majority of items showed a distribution of MLU across four or more of the six bands.

In order to gain a more concise estimate of the range, the proportion of children falling into each MLU band was calculated as a percentage for each item and the average was then calculated for all items at each stage.[6] The results are shown in table 8.6 and displayed graphically in figure 8.1. As can be seen from the final column although the median MLU value shows a clear progression from band I at level I to band V at level VIII, the distribution of MLU across the five bands at each level suggests a much weaker relationship between MLU and stage of development.[7]

A closer inspection of the MLU data reveals a very uneven rate of development in MLU shown by many of the children. Quite a large number remained in the same MLU band over several consecutive observations and then jumped two or more bands between one observation and the next, only to remain at this new level for several observations. To some extent this may be an artefact of the way in which MLU values were allocated to bands. A very small

Table 8.6 *Percentage distribution of MLU value in bands by level of language development*

| Level | MLU band | | | | | | Median MLU |
	I	II	III	IV	V	VI	
I	100.0	—	—	—	—	—	I
II	92.5	4.2	2.9	0.3	—	—	I
III	79.5	13.1	6.6	0.4	0.4	—	I
IV	49.2	24.3	17.1	7.6	1.7	—	II
V	24.8	22.5	27.7	18.8	5.5	0.6	III
VI	10.7	17.9	30.1	28.0	11.7	1.6	III
VII	—	2.9	15.8	33.3	38.8	9.2	IV
VIII	—	1.5	10.2	28.6	45.4	14.3	V

Levels I–VI were calculated on the younger cohort and levels VII and VIII on the older cohort.

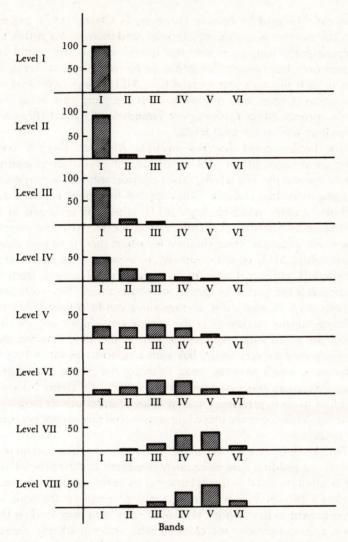

Figure 8.1 Percentage distribution of MLU values in bands by level of language development

increase could take a child over the boundary between one band and another, and then, although there was a continuing increase over the subsequent observations, it might take several observations for the child to pass the boundary of the next higher band. It must also be remembered that the corpus of utterances on which MLU was calculated at each observation was considerably smaller than the 713 used by Brown. However, as Crystal (1974) points out, this number is completely arbitrary, and there is little reason to suppose that a corpus of only one quarter of this size would be significantly less reliable. What has to be recognized, it seems, is that there is much greater variability in MLU at any given level of development than was originally supposed. And this holds for levels corresponding to the upper boundary of band I (Brown's stage I) as well as for later levels.

One further point deserves mention. Although there is very substantial variability in MLU in relation to level of development across the sample as a whole, this is considerably less with respect to most individual children. What appears to happen is that some children register relatively high MLU values for the items at a particular level whilst other children register relatively low values. There are, of course, other children for whom there is no such clear relationship. MLU is, self-evidently, an average value based on a number of individual utterances making up a corpus from a particular observation or group of observations. But there are various ways in which this average value can be attained. At one extreme, all the utterances in the corpus may cluster very closely about the mean with respect to length; at the other extreme, the majority may be very short, but with a minority of much longer utterances, which raise the mean value for the corpus as a whole. Such differences may correspond to the putative difference between children in their preference for an analytic approach to language learning discussed in the preceding section, but this has not yet been investigated.

Both kinds of observation are to be found in our data, and quite a number of children tend to be fairly consistent in their position on the continuum just described. However there does seem to be some tendency for children who make rapid progress up the scale of development to have a high MLU level relative to their level on the scale and, conversely, for children who make markedly slower progress up the scale to have a much lower MLU level.

If there are indeed different styles of speech amongst such young children, it is interesting to speculate on the causes. No doubt these will be associated to some extent with differences in temperament: some children will be laconic in speech and generally reserved in their interaction with other people, whilst others will be much more forthcoming, both in speech and in their non-verbal behaviour. But part of the explanation may well lie in the conversational opportunities that are made available by those who interact with them. If children are constantly plied with questions that demand only a 'yes' or 'no' or a minimal noun phrase in response, the majority of their utterances will be short, and their MLU will be depressed in relation to the much longer utterances that they occasionally produce when given the opportunity. By contrast, children who are encouraged to initiate both sequences of conversation and constituent exchanges are much more likely to produce a greater number of utterances approaching the upper limit of their control of the language system. There may be very little difference indeed between what these children are capable of saying – as an evaluation based on the scale of development would show – but they would appear to have very different capabilities if the measure used to assess them was based on an average, as is the case with MLU.

Of course there are likely to be longer-term consequences of habitual conversational experiences as different as those just outlined. Where opportunities are consistently restricted, rate of development may be significantly retarded. This is an issue to which we shall return in the following chapters.

8.4 Possible determinants of variation in language development

Writing on this topic some years ago (Wells, 1979b), I proposed a simple explanatory model of the influence of certain factors on variation in linguistic development. (This model is reproduced in a modified form in figure 8.2.) The behaviour that is observed in the course of naturalistic investigations is the result of a whole number of factors, of which actual linguistic ability – the availability of linguistic resources – is only one. Keeping these factors in mind, and using the language development scale score as the most satisfactory index of overall linguistic ability, we will attempt, in this section, to explain variation on this index.

One of the most important influences on the performance actually observed is the situation in which it occurs. The first section of this chapter considered the context of activity, and presented preliminary evidence of its effect on the distribution of utterance functions. The same sort of results will probably be found for systems at the semantic and syntactic levels, but these analyses have yet to be carried out. The evidence considered above was drawn from children's speech production. However investigations of the effect of context on the comprehension of these same children have already been reported by Walkerdine (1975), Walkerdine and Sinha (1978) and Bridges (1977, 1980). In all cases, the child's

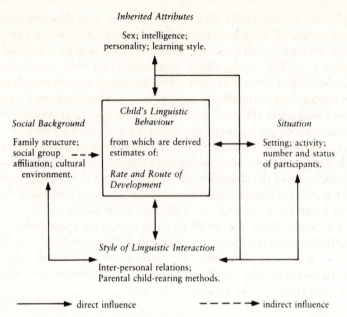

Inherited Attributes

Sex; intelligence;
personality; learning style.

Social Background

Family structure;
social group
affiliation; cultural
environment.

*Child's Linguistic
Behaviour*

from which are derived
estimates of:

*Rate and Route of
Development*

Situation

Setting; activity;
number and status
of participants.

Style of Linguistic Interaction

Inter-personal relations;
Parental child-rearing methods.

————————▶ direct influence   – – – – ▶ indirect influence

Figure 8.2 Influences on individual differences in language development
(adapted from Wells, 1979b)

perception of the task was found to affect his selection from
available strategies for demonstrating comprehension.

Evidence of the effect of the status of the participants in
conversations involving young children is somewhat sparse, as the
research to date has looked predominantly at parent–child interaction. However, in relation to comprehension, the work of Donaldson and colleagues (Donaldson, 1978) has shown that the status of
actors and questioners participating in tasks can significantly affect
children's responses and, in relation to production, there is some
evidence that children as young as four years of age are sensitive to
the differences in status and competence between adults, peers and
two year olds (Shatz and Gelman, 1973; Sachs and Devin, 1976),
with speech to younger children being modified in the same ways as
adult speech to language-learning children. However, since the age
(or presence) of siblings was free to vary in the present study, no
systematic study of the effect of ages and status of the child's
interlocutor in spontaneous conversation was possible.

8.4.1 *Inherited characteristics*
There is good reason to suppose that inherited differences between

children have a determining influence on language development. Certainly there is substantial evidence of covariation between intelligence, as measured by tests of various kinds, and indices of language development (McCarthy, 1954). However, while it is reasonable to accept a causative relationship between inherited attributes which are related to the ability to learn language and to rate of language learning, it is very much more difficult in practice to interpret correlations of the kind that McCarthy and others have reported. First, it is difficult to administer any test, even of non-verbal intelligence, without some recourse to language and, conversely, almost any form of language performance requires the application of intelligence. Intelligence and language scores, therefore, can hardly be considered to be independent. Secondly, intelligence scores, like any other scores, are based on performance measures, which are obtained in situations where success depends, at least in part, on previous experience as well as on features of the test situation. They are therefore only very indirect estimates of inherited learning ability.

The same is true of personality. Although this has received little attention in research on child language to date, there are good reasons to believe that there are differences between children at birth and throughout childhood on dimensions such as active/passive, responsive/unresponsive – just as there are differences of these kinds between parents – that will significantly affect the amount and type of linguistic interaction that the child experiences and hence the opportunities he has for learning his native language. Talking with the parents of children in the sample who had siblings, we received many unsolicited subjective judgments that this was so. However, as with intelligence, it is difficult in practice to obtain reliable measures of personality that are independent of communication style, and this is particularly true in the case of very young children.

Differences in learning style have already been discussed above and it was concluded that, at present, whilst it seems probable that there are indeed stylistic differences between children in their preferred approach to the learning task, it is not clear how many dimensions are needed to characterize these differences nor whether they persist over the whole period of development or are only relatively short-lived. Nor is it clear whether they are acquired through interactional experience or are to a large degree inherited. Despite these uncertainties, we should not ignore the possible existence of differences in learning style or the potential they may have for substantially affecting the rate, and perhaps also the route, of language learning. This is certainly what has been found in recent studies of children learning English as a second language (Wong-Fillmore, 1979).

A further problem in trying to estimate the contribution to language learning of any factors that are considered to be inherited is that, since the genetically transmitted attributes relevant to linguistic ability are likely to be similar in parents and children who are genetically related, children of above average inherited language ability are likely to experience linguistic interaction with parents who are similarly above average in linguistic ability and this' may well further accelerate their language development. Conversely, children with below average inherited ability are likely to experience linguistic interaction with parents who are similarly below average in linguistic ability with possible negative effects on their language development (Hardy-Brown, 1983).

One partial solution to these problems is to attempt to separate out the effects of heredity and environment by means of an 'adoption study' (Hardy-Brown *et al.*, 1981), in which children who are adopted at birth are compared on relevant measures with both their natural and their adoptive parents, and measures of the environment are obtained uncontaminated by the effect of shared genetic influences. Such a design was not possible in the present study. So for this and the other reasons discussed above, no attempt was made to measure either intelligence, learning style or personality and no results can be presented in relation to any of these influencing factors. However, although considered only from a theoretical point of view in the present discussion, these factors are likely in my opinion to contribute substantially to variation in rate of development.

The existence of differences between boys and girls is a much more controversial matter. When McCarthy reviewed the literature in 1954, she was able to claim that there was 'convincing proof that a real sex difference in language development exists in favor of girls' (p. 580). In most cases the differences which she reported had been seen as resulting from inherited factors associated with the physiological differences between males and females. However, since then, the size of the reported differences has diminished sharply in studies carried out in the Western world and it is now much more common to find that, when differences are observed between boys and girls, they are attributed to cultural differences in patterns of child-rearing rather than to any innate differences between the sexes (Cherry, 1975).

In the present study, after considering the spontaneous speech data in terms of a wide variety of linguistic systems, Woll (1979) concluded that there was no evidence of a consistent and significant difference between the sexes in either route or rate of development. This finding with respect to rate of development is confirmed by *t*-tests on the means for girls and boys in the data on which the correlations in tables 8.4 and 8.5 were computed. These results are all the more surprising in the light of the undoubted differences between boys and girls in their conversational experience (cf. Cherry and Lewis, 1976). In chapter 3, differences were reported in the contexts in which boys and girls tend to speak most and, to a lesser extent, in the purposes for which they speak. On the basis of these data alone, however, it is not possible to determine who is responsible for these differences, the children or the adults who interact with them.

In order to cast more light on this issue, an analysis was made of sequence initiation by context and by sex of child for a representative sub-sample of 40 children at the age of 39 months (Woll *et al.*, 1975). Overall, of the 729 sequences analysed, 72% were initiated by the children and 28% by the adults. When these were broken down by context, significant sex-related differences were found, both for the children and for the adults. The crucial differences are shown in table 8.7. As can be seen, the differences chiefly concern the contexts of Play Alone or with Adult Participation and Helping and General Activity. With either child or adult initiating, a greater proportion of sequences of conversation with boys occur when they are playing, and a greater proportion with girls when they are engaged in helping or in general activity. However this difference is

Table 8.7 *Proportional distribution of sequence initiation by children and adults according to context and sex of child*

Initiator	Context	Play Alone or with Adult Participation	Helping and General Activity	Other Contexts
Children	Boys	29.5	30.4	40.1
	Girls	22.8	35.7	41.5
Adults	Boys	26.2	28.8	45.0
	Girls	8.6	56.8	34.6

considerably greater for conversations initiated by adults than it is for conversations initiated by the children. Whether or not the difference in choice of context stems from independent differences between boys and girls in their preferred activities, there is no doubt that this difference is emphasized by the adults in their interactions with the children. Nevertheless, despite these differences in experience, boys and girls develop linguistically in similar fashion, at least until the age of entry to school.

8.4.2 *Social background*

The factors to be considered under this heading are largely those that were addressed in the maternal interview. Differences on a number of measures were reported in chapter 7 ranging from occupational status of parents and grandparents to reports of attitudes to features of children's speech. In order to establish whether any of these variables could be considered to have a determining influence on the children's rate of development, all those that it had proved possible to score were submitted to correlational analysis, with the language development scale score as the dependent variable. For this purpose, a score was calculated for every child at the age of 42 months, which was the age at which the interview was administered. Although not of the same order, four further independent variables were included in the analysis, which were derived from the recordings made at 39 and 42 months (the ages at which the cohorts overlapped). These variables concerned the total number of utterances from the two occasions combined: (1) addressed to the child by adults; (2) addressed to the child by any speaker, adult or child; (3) addressed by the child to another participant; (4) produced by the child (i.e. including Speech for Self).[8] The results of this analysis are shown in table 8.8. As the number of independent variables was large, only those showing a correlation greater than $r = \pm 0.15$ are included in the table.

Clearly, the variables that most successfully predict variation in rate of development are the group that were described in chapter 7 as characterizing the formative influences on the parents: the education of the parents and the occupational status of the parents and of the paternal grandfather. In fact, it is the formative influences on the father that appear to be the more powerful in predicting the child's rate of language development, even though it was the mother who, in almost every case, spent more time with the child. This provides further support for the suggestions made in chapter 7 that it is the characteristics of the father, rather than those

Table 8.8 *Correlations between rate of language development (language development scale score) and possible determinants*

	$r =$	$p -$
Father's Education	0.40	0.001
Mother's Education	0.26	0.05
Father's Occupation	0.35	0.001
Mother's Occupation	0.33	0.001
Paternal Grandfather's Occupation	0.30	0.001
Maternal Grandfather's Occupation	0.16	n.s.
Family Positional Score	−0.22	0.05
Parental Literacy	0.27	0.01
Parents Read to Child	0.36	0.001
Parents Correct Child's Speech	−0.16	n.s.
Child's Position in Family	0.29	0.001
Adult Speech to Child	0.20	0.05
All Speech to Child	0.23	0.01
Child Speech to Others	0.27	0.01
All Child Speech	0.22	0.05

of the mother, that set the 'tone' of the family. However, although to a lesser extent, the mother's level of education also correlates with the child's rate of language development. It should also be recalled that there was considerably less variation in the extent of mothers' education than there was in fathers' education.

The four variables of mothers' and fathers' education and occupation provided the data for the construction of the Scale of Family Background, on the basis of which children were selected for inclusion in the study. The scale, it will be recalled, was divided into four roughly equal segments (labelled classes A, B, C and D), and the children in the original random sample were allocated to one of these four classes according to their score on this scale. An equal number of children was then chosen at random from each class to make up the final sample for study.

Using each child's score on the Scale of Family Background, it is possible to calculate the correlation between this index of Family Background and rate of language development. The result is $r = 0.40$, $p < 0.001$. This is exactly the same value as achieved by fathers' education alone, which is not surprising since the inter-correlation of the two variables was found in chapter 7 to be $r = 0.85$, $p < 0.001$. Thus Family Background accounts for only 16% of the variance in language development, using the language development scale score, at the age of 42 months.

How much confidence should we place in this result? A substantial number of other researchers have reported results that point in the direction of a relatively strong relationship between 'class', whether measured in the sort of composite way used in the present investigation (e.g. Brandis and Henderson, 1970), on the basis of father's occupation only (Templin, 1957) or on the basis of such intuitive distinctions as that made by Tough (1977) between 'enabling' and 'non-enabling' homes. In almost all cases where a strong relationship has been claimed, however, the sample of children was not representative of the total population, having been selected from the two extremes, as in the case of Tough, to demonstrate a difference already assumed to exist.

To explore further the relationship found in the present investigation, the scores of the children on the two relevant variables of Family Background and the language development scale score at 42 months were plotted on a two-dimensional scatter diagram. This is reproduced as figure 8.3. Viewed as a whole, the data do seem to provide some support for the existence of a linear relationship

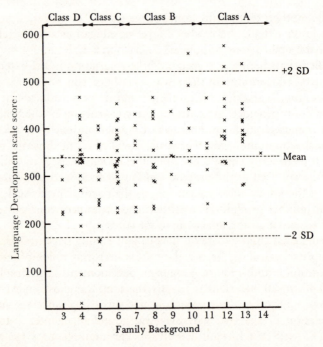

Figure 8.3 Scatter diagram of children's scores on the two indices of language development scale score and Family Background

between the two variables. However this impression is almost entirely produced by the points representing extreme scores on the language development scale score. These are contributed by some nine or so children, that is to say by less than 10% of the total sample. For the remaining 90% the evidence is distinctly less compelling, as the reader may care to verify by covering the points representing scores greater or less than two standard deviations (SD) above and below the mean on the language development scale score. It would be no exaggeration, therefore, to claim that, on the basis of the results of the present investigation, for the majority of the population, there is very little evidence of a systematic relationship between Family Background and rate of language development in the pre-school years.

It is true, however, that the extremely fast developers are significantly more likely to be found at the upper end of the Scale of Family Background, that is to say in the homes of highly educated professional or managerial parents and that, conversely, the extremely slow developers are significantly more likely to be found in the homes of minimally educated parents in semi-skilled or unskilled occupations. With respect to the two extremes, therefore, our results conform to the prevailing myth. This is what might be expected, since the myth is based on results of studies that have, for the most part, compared relatively extreme groups.

Nevertheless, even this does not take account of all the facts, for the sample we studied was not fully representative of the population from which it was drawn. In selecting the children, an approximately equal number was drawn from each of the four classes in order to facilitate statistical analysis. But the cells in the original random sample from which the study children were drawn were very far from being equal in number. An estimate, admittedly not very reliable, of the distribution of 'family background' in the population of pre-school children can be obtained from the selection interviews carried out on a random sub-set of the original sample of families of children whose names were drawn at random from the record of births (see 1.2). Table 8.9 compares the proportion in each family background class found in the random sample with the actual proportion in each class in the sample under investigation. As this comparison shows, classes A and D are substantially over-represented in the sample studied. Since extreme scorers tend to be found in the two classes that are over-represented, it can be argued that the obtained correlation almost certainly substantially over-estimates the relationship between

Table 8.9 *Distribution of children by class of family background: random sample and study sample compared*

	A	B	C	D
Random sample	15.2	28.0	41.6	15.2
Study sample	27.2	23.2	27.2	22.4

Family Background and rate of language development in the population as a whole.[9]

8.4.3 *Style of linguistic interaction*

Whatever the exact size of the correlation, it is clear that Family Background, being composed of a combination of variables that measure some of the formative influences on the parents, cannot be treated as a direct determinant of rate of language development. At most, the occupations performed by the parents and the extent of their education may have influenced their attitudes to inter-personal relations, particularly those between parents and children, and equipped them with a greater or lesser degree of knowledge relevant to making decisions on matters of child rearing. Associated with different levels of education and occupation there may also be differences in habitual styles of speaking and in the use made of the written mode of communication. However, if these differences in parental attributes are to have a direct bearing on children's language development, it will be in the more directly observable form of the parents' behaviour when actually interacting with their children.

To identify differences in styles of interaction in adult–child conversation is the aim of the work currently being carried out by the Language at Home and at School research team. In the present context, however, we shall have to rely solely on the results already discussed in the preceding section to argue the case for an interactive explanation of the observed variation in rate of language development.

We can start by drawing attention to the substantial correlation between the amount of speech addressed to the child and the amount addressed by him to other speakers ($r = 0.61$, $p < 0.001$). Here there is clearly a concurrent reciprocal relationship. If these two measures are also taken as indices of longer-term differences between families in amount of conversation, they can also be treated as potential determinants of variation in level of language development reached at 42 months, and hence of rate of development (correlations with the language development scale score: Child Speech to Others, $r = 0.27$, $p < 0.01$; All Speech to Child, $r = 0.23$, $p < 0.01$). Other features of parental behaviour, as reported in the maternal interview, that were reported to be correlated with language development scale score, were Parents Read to the Child ($r = 0.36$, $p < 0.001$) and Parental Literacy ($r = 0.24$, $p < 0.01$) and, negatively, Correcting the Child's Speech ($r = -0.16$, $p < 0.10$). Each of these might be expected to be related to the language behaviour of the children and thus, over time, to have an influence on rate of development.

To test the validity of these hypotheses, multiple regression analyses were carried out with the language development scale score as the dependent variable. Variables were entered in a pre-determined order, with Family Background being reserved to the last, in order to see how much of the total explainable variance could be accounted for without including this variable. One further independent variable was added, Child's Position in Family, which has a significant simple correlation with the language development scale score of $r = 0.29$ ($p < 0.001$). Like Family Background, this is a composite index of a variety of conditions that influence the amount and nature of linguistic interaction that the language learner experiences. For this reason, it too was reserved to the end of the analysis, being entered immediately before Family Background.

Two analyses were performed, the first with the index of the child's influence on conversation, Child Speech to Others, being entered first, followed by indices of the contribution of other speakers, the second with this order reversed. The final multiple correlation is the same in both cases, of course, but the two strategies permit some estimate to be formed of the relative contribution made by characteristics of both parties to the interaction in accounting for variance on the dependent variable. The results of these analyses are presented in tables 8.10 and 8.11.[10]

Two points may be made about these results. First, as predicted, when behavioural measures of the nature and quality of the interaction between the child and his family are entered first, these variables account for almost all of the explained variance. Family Background only contributes a residual 5%. Secondly, the alternative orders of entering the variables into the regression analyses show that, whichever order is adopted, both child and family

Table 8.10 *Multiple regression on language development scale score: child characteristics entered first*

Predictor variable	Multiple r	r^2	r^2 change	Simple r
Child Speech to Others	0.29	0.08	0.08	0.29
Parents read to Child	0.44	0.19	0.11	0.36
Correct Child Speech	0.46	0.22	0.03	−0.16
All Speech to Child	0.48	0.23	0.01	0.25
Parental Literacy	0.49	0.24	0.01	0.27
Child's Position in Family	0.53	0.29	0.05	0.29
Family Background	0.59	0.34	0.05	0.43

Table 8.11 *Multiple regression on language development scale score: other speaker characteristics entered first*

Predictor variable	Multiple r	r^2	r^2 change	Simple r
Parents read to Child	0.36	0.13	0.13	0.36
All Speech to Child	0.42	0.18	0.05	−0.25
Correct Child Speech	0.44	0.20	0.02	−0.16
Parental Literacy	0.45	0.20	0	0.27
Child Speech to Others	0.49	0.24	0.04	0.29
Child's Position in Family	0.53	0.29	0.05	0.29
Family Background	0.59	0.34	0.05	0.43

characteristics have some contribution to make to the explained variance. To this extent, the results can be seen as supporting the argument for an interactive explanation of variation in rate of development.

Regression analysis is not really suitable, however, for attempting to understand interaction, in the sense in which this term is being used here. For the moment, therefore, we must wait for more appropriate analytic methods to become available. In the meantime, we can explore alternative approaches to the subject and it is to a consideration of these that we turn in the following chapter.

The role of the input in language development

In the preceding chapters we have been mainly concerned with the development of the child's language, as evidenced by his spontaneous production, and we have charted the sequence in which that development occurs. We have also noted evidence of variation, both *within* individuals in the relationships between form, meaning and context and also *between* individuals, particularly in the rate at which development progresses.

But what about the input? What contribution does this make? All the children we studied – like children everywhere – grew up in social communities and interacted with parents and other family members in ways which included conversation. Indeed, our observations, beginning when the children were aged 15 months, consist very largely of sequences that are recognizably conversational. Since children at birth know nothing of the particular language of the community into which they enter, it is clear that, in a general way, they must learn from the speech that they hear, and particularly from their participation in conversation. But how exactly does this happen and are there any specific characteristics of the input that particularly facilitate their learning?

Unfortunately, although our data provide a rich resource for attempts to answer these questions, we have as yet made little progress in this direction. In the initial funding of the research, there were no resources for studying early conversation, even if we had been equipped to do so, and, although we now have a much clearer idea of how to set about this task (cf. Wells *et al.*, 1979, 1981), systematic analysis of the data has not yet proceeded far enough for us to be able to report any substantive findings.

However, we have carried out two small-scale investigations that have some bearing on these questions. In the first we looked at the function of the input in providing a model of the language to be learned. Does the differential frequency with which items occur in the input influence the sequence in which those items are learned?

In the second, we focussed on the more broadly conversational characteristics of the input. Do differences between adults in the manner and extent to which they adjust their speech to the immaturity of their conversational partners affect the ease with which their children master the language system?

9.1 Alternative explanations of the sequence of development

In the development of an individual child there must be an order in which particular meanings, forms and structures are learned, or at least first used appropriately. There must, that is to say, be a particular order of emergence. But there is no logical necessity for this order to be substantially the same from one child to another. Yet this is in fact the case, as the evidence presented in chapters 4 and 5 demonstrates. Such broad similarity between children in sequence of development, despite considerable variation in the rate at which development occurs, suggests that the same factors are at work in each child to determine the sequence in which learning occurs.

 One factor that immediately suggests itself is similarity amongst learners in their pre-adaptation to the task. This is what Chomsky draws attention to when he talks about the 'language faculty' (Chomsky, 1976). But pre-adaptation in learners does not predict one particular sequence of learning rather than another. To explain that we must look in more detail at what has to be learned and at the conditions under which that learning takes place.

There are doubtless many ways of characterizing these two major factors but here we shall be concerned with only two: the differential frequency with which learning opportunities are provided in the input and the relative complexity of what has to be learned. If these were to be considered as alternatives, we might propose the following hypotheses:

a) The order in which learning occurs will be determined by the relative frequency with which items within systems are heard by learners in the speech that is addressed to them.
b) The order in which learning occurs will be determined by the relative cognitive and linguistic complexity of items within systems.

Explanations corresponding to the second hypothesis have been proposed by many researchers and evidence has been adduced in support from both monolingual studies (e.g. Brown and Hanlon, 1970) and from studies involving cross-linguistic comparisons (e.g.

Slobin, 1973). The first has attracted much less support, at least in recent years, but it is not unreasonable to suppose that differential frequency of occurrence affects the relative salience of items to be learned; it certainly affects the opportunity to learn from observations of their use. Brown (1973), it is true, has argued that for the 14 English grammatical morphemes that he studied 'there is no evidence whatever that frequency of any sort is a significant determinant of order of acquisition' (p. 409), but this conclusion may be limited to the particular set of items investigated or have been affected by the way in which input frequency was calculated. Certainly, Moerk (1980) came to a different conclusion when he re-analysed the same data from Adam, Eve and Sarah. More recently, Forner (1979) has carried out a very thorough analysis of the order of acquisition of different types of *wh-* question in the learning of German by her son and found this order to be highly correlated with her own frequency of use of the same question-types in the speech that she addressed to him and, in direct contrast with Brown, she concludes that 'children produce what mothers say in the same relative order and with the same relative frequency' (p. 42).

The two hypotheses may thus seem, initially, to be in competition. Certainly, the second would be more congenial to those who emphasize the active role of the child in the learning process and to those who see language as being built upon antecedent cognitive development, whilst the first would be more favoured by those who emphasize the role of the environment and who consider modelling to be a particularly powerful form of learning. However, it is also possible to see the two hypotheses as complementary. This would lead to a third possibility for consideration:

c) The order of emergence of the items in any linguistic system will be determined by an interaction between the relative complexity of those items and their relative frequency in the speech addressed to the language learner.

The discussion so far has assumed that the same explanation will apply to all linguistic systems equally. But this need not be the case. It is perfectly possible, in principle, for the order of emergence in one system to be best accounted for by one explanation and the order in another by a different explanation. In theory, therefore, the various explanations should be evaluated with respect to all linguistic systems. This, however, would be a very lengthy and difficult procedure as the relevant input data have only been calculated for a few systems. (Utterances by other speakers were only coded when they immediately preceded an utterance by the child and, even then, they only received a coding with respect to Inter-Personal Purpose.) To investigate input frequencies for other systems would have required a hand coding specially for the purpose; in fact, only three such additional codings have been carried out and these have been confined to the recordings made of the younger sample of children (15–42 months). The three candidate hypotheses will be considered only in relation to four systems, therefore: Pronouns, Auxiliary Verbs, SMRs and Functions, and on items within those systems with a median age of emergence of 42 months or less. Although limited in number, however, the systems selected are sufficiently different from each other to allow for the possibility that the order of emergence in different systems may require a different form of explanation.

In the sections that follow, each hypothesis will be considered in turn in relation to each of the four linguistic systems. Rank orders of emergence, complexity and frequency will be determined for the items within each system and a coefficient of correlation calculated for each pair of rank orders in order to ascertain the degree of association between the sets of ranks. After evaluating the evidence from this correlational analysis, the report of the investigation will conclude with a more extended consideration of the nature and role of the input.

9.2 Order of emergence

Emergence, it will be recalled, has been defined as the first appropriate occurrence of an item in a child's speech. Order of emergence is thus the sequence in which items emerge in the course of development. Where data from many children are involved, as in the present study, some procedure has to be adopted for combining the order information from individual children and assessing the significance of the distributions found. How this was done was described in chapter 4, where it was seen that, for any pair of items, two criteria were adopted for establishing order, a strong criterion ($\text{CRIT}_k \leqslant 0.08$) and a weak criterion ($\text{CRIT}_k \leqslant 0.2$), and one criterion for establishing coemergence ($\text{CRIT}_\theta \geqslant 0.8$). Using these criteria, in every linguistic system investigated, every item was found to be ordered with respect to the majority of the other items in the same system. There were, however, some pairs which were neither significantly ordered nor coemergent.

For the present investigation, all the items in each of the four systems to be studied had to be ranked with respect to all the other items in the same system. Where any pair of items was neither coemergent nor ordered, therefore, rank assignment was based on the order for which the data provided the least disconfirmatory evidence. For example, if the 'unordered' items i and j yielded the following evidence with respect to order: i precedes j: 48%; i coemergent with j: 20%; j precedes i: 32%, i would be given the rank corresponding to earlier emergence because the proportion of cases disconfirming the order i before j (32%) is less than the proportion disconfirming the reverse order (48%).

Using the criteria for order and coemergence set out in chapter 4 and invoking the procedure just described in cases where pairs of items were unordered in terms of the criteria for order, rank orders were constructed for each of the four linguistic systems to be investigated. These rank orders are shown in the first column of each of the tables 9.1–4, below.

9.3 Complexity

Linguistic complexity is very familiar as a notion, but in practice there is no general consensus as to how it should be calculated – as Brown (1973) concluded after attempting to make a similar test of the hypothesis that complexity is a major determinant of order of acquisition. In his study of 14 grammatical morphemes, he compared a variety of approaches: cumulative semantic complexity, number of transformations in the derivation of each morpheme, and cumulative transformational complexity. Many of the predictions he was able to test involved only sub-sets of the morphemes, as cumulative complexity can only be calculated where a set of items share one or more semantic features or transformations. In the absence of a general theory, he also found it impossible to assign complexity values to morphemes that have unrelated unitary meanings.

The present investigation has been strongly influenced by Brown's general approach but, in assigning complexity values to items, somewhat different procedures were adopted in order to allow all items within any of the four systems to be scored using the same criteria. First, where Brown considered semantic and grammatical factors separately in order to compare their ability independently to predict order of acquisition, the present investigation has combined them in a single measure on the grounds that, in practice, it is very difficult to draw a sharp boundary between the two levels in their contribution to an item's relative complexity (e.g. is the gender distinction between 'him' and 'her' to be thought of as giving rise to complexity which is primarily semantic or syntactic?). Secondly, where necessary, features used in discriminating amongst items have been assigned differential weightings on the basis of theoretical considerations or, where these were lacking, on the basis of native-speaker intuitions.

The same general procedure was employed for each system. A matrix was set up in which the items in the system were marked for the presence of semantic and syntactic features which had been identified as common to at least two items in the system. These features were then given a weighting and the sum of the weighted features was taken as the complexity score for each item.

9.3.1 *Auxiliary verbs*

Of the auxiliary verbs, only the following reached the criterion of emergence in the speech of 50% of the younger children: 'do', 'be' in continuous aspect, 'have' in perfect aspect, 'have' in 'have got', 'can', 'will', 'be going to', 'have got to' and 'shall'. The features used in contrasting them were: type of auxiliary (modal *v.* non-modal); typical time reference (not-present *v.* present); for the modal auxiliaries, the type of modality involved (potential, constraint, performative); and for all auxiliaries, the syntactic form (simple *v.* complex).

In assigning weightings, each of the marked features, + modal, + non-present and + complex form was assigned a weighting of 1, with the unmarked feature in each pair being given a weighting of 0. In weighting the complexity of the three types of modality to which the most frequent first use of the four modal verbs can be assigned (cf. Wells, 1979a), it was argued that the least complex is 'potential', in which the modal qualifies the agent's involvement in the action named by the verb – that he is able or willing to perform it. 'Constraint', where an external influence impinges on the agent's performances, was considered to be intermediate in complexity. The 'performative' type, in which the modal verb is enlisted in the conventional realization of some form of indirect request or a suggestion, was considered the most complex. The weightings assigned were respectively 0, 1 and 2 (see table A1, appendix 3).

'Do' posed something of a problem. Unlike the other auxiliaries, it has no domain of meaning associated with it, and this might be considered to make it difficult to learn. On the other hand, its homophony with the pro-verb 'do', which realizes the meaning of unspecified action, may render it easy to learn on other grounds.

Since this latter use of 'do' is learned very early, it was decided to give the dummy auxiliary 'do' a complexity score of 0. Weighting the relevant features as just described, scores were assigned as shown in column 3 of table 9.1.

Table 9.1 *Emergence, complexity and input frequency of auxiliary verbs*

Order of emergence	Rank	Complexity Index	Rank	Input frequency Freq. per 1000 utts.	Rank
do	1	0	1	55.6	1
have got	2	1	3=	15.9	6
be + V-ing	4.5=	1	3=	33.0	2
have + V-en	4.5=	2	5.5=	19.6	5
can	4.5=	1	3=	19.8	4
will	4.5=	2	5.5=	30.8	3
be going to	7	3	7.5=	14.5	7
have got to	8	3	7.5=	6.3	8
shall	9	4	9	5.0	9

9.3.2 *Pronouns*

The pronouns which reached the criterion of emergence include most of the personal pronouns, the demonstratives, two interrogatives, 'what', and 'who', two indefinite pronouns, 'one' and 'some', and one relative pronoun, 'what' (the latter being used to introduce all categories of relative clause). The first distinction drawn, therefore, was between the different types of pronoun. Personal and demonstrative pronouns were given zero weighting on the grounds that deictic categories, being intimately bound up with the here-and-now of the utterance, are simpler than non-deictic categories. The remaining types of pronoun were all given a weighting of 1 for the feature 'non-deictic' plus an additional weighting for the specific type of meaning involved: Interrogative (1); Indefinite (1); Relative (4). (The weighting for the latter category reflects the very considerable syntactic complexity inevitably associated with the selection of a relative pronoun.)

A different sort of distinction can be made amongst these pronouns in terms of whether they refer to participants in the discourse ('I', 'me', 'you') or to other persons or objects. With respect to the discourse pronouns, there is the particular difficulty that they change their reference from utterance to utterance depending on who is speaking. For the first person, however, this is perhaps offset by the psychological closeness of the speaker role. So, although both first- and second-person pronouns were scored for the feature + discourse, the second feature + addressee gave an increased score only to the second-person pronoun. Amongst the pronouns that refer to third parties, some like 'they' refer to both animate and inanimate entities; others like 'he' or 'who?' are restricted to animate referents. This latter group were therefore scored for the feature + animate.

Three further distinctions that cut across those already made were taken into account: gender, number and case. For the latter two features, the marked alternative – plural or object-case – was scored; however, since there are no obvious grounds for considering one gender to give rise to greater complexity than the other, the third feature to be scored was simply + gender. The weightings applied to these features were + gender: 2; + plural: 2; + object-case: 1. Finally, the proximal/distal distinction in the demonstratives was seen as contributing to complexity; so a score of 1 was added to all demonstratives. Features and weightings are shown in table A2 and the resulting scores for all the pronouns are given in table 9.2.

9.3.3 *Sentence Meaning Relations*

Compared with auxiliaries and pronouns, the system of SMRs is much more heterogeneous. Certain broad areas of meaning can be discerned: Location, Attribution, Experience and Function, with further distinctions within each. In assigning weightings to these, reference was made to Piaget's account of stages of cognitive development (Piaget and Inhelder, 1969), in which an awareness and rudimentary understanding of the world of physical objects with attributes and locations, which may be changed through the actions of Agent, seems to precede the more inwardly turned awareness of the experiencing of those objects and events (cf. Brown, 1973; Edwards, 1973; Wells, 1974). On these grounds, Location and Attribution were given a weighting of 1, being considered, as broad areas of meaning, to be less complex than Experience, which was given a weighting of 2. Function, in which the action named by the verb typically produces no perceptible change in the environment, was also considered to be more complex than Location or Attribution, and was given a weighting of 3.

Within Location, there are two groups of additional features.

Table 9.2 *Emergence, complexity and input frequency of auxiliary pronouns*

Order of emergence	Rank	Complexity Index	Rank	Input frequency Freq. per 1000 utts.	Rank
that	2=	2	4.5=	83	4
I	2=	1	1.5=	149	3
it	2=	1	1.5=	170	2
me	4.5=	2	4.5=	28	9
you	4.5=	2	4.5=	266	1
what?	6	3	8=	69	5
one	7	3	8=	26	10
this	8	2	4.5=	12	13
he	9	4	13=	42	6
we	11=	4	13=	31	8
they	11=	3	8=	20	11
them	11=	4	13=	18	12
she	13	4	13=	33	7
who?	14	4	13=	10	15.5
him	15	5	17	11	14
these	17=	4	13=	3	17.5
those	17=	4	13=	3	17.5
what (rel.)	17=	6	18	10	15.5

First, Change of Location can be specified with respect to the type of movement, or as involving contact with the goal (Act on Target). Secondly, Location includes the more specific meaning of Possession. Because Possession is a cultural concept and not available directly to perception, this feature was counted in addition to Location, with the more complex concept of being intended for the benefit of another (Benefactive) being treated as a further additional feature.

As already mentioned, physically perceptible attributes are considered to be more easily understood than those that are culturally ascribed. Evaluative Attribute was therefore scored for the feature non-perceptible. In scoring Quantitative Attribute a specific feature, Quantity, was added on account of the known cognitive difficulty experienced by children in counting and dealing with number concepts generally. A third type of attribution that was separately distinguished was Existence. Although existence is clearly a necessary attribute of any object which is perceived, it seems probable that, for that very reason, it lacks any salience for the child (Greenfield, 1982).

Although there are clearly important distinctions between the different types of Experience – Want, Cognitive, Affective and Physical – these were not treated as features for the purposes of weighting as experiential meanings had already, as a group, been assigned a heavier weighting than Location and Attribution. In the case of the function categories, on the other hand, a distinction was drawn between animate and inanimate actors as performers of a function, with the feature of inanimate actor being scored, on the grounds that this is an exception to the general principle that actions are performed only by animate beings (Agents). In scoring meaning relations, all features that distinguish conceptually or semantically between categories within the four broad areas of meaning were given a score of 1, with the exception of the features specific to the meanings: Benefactive (2), Existence (2) and Quantitative (3).

As well as varying in the complexity of the concepts encoded, the SMRs also vary in the number of participants that are obligatorily involved (cf. chapter 2). (In this context, the predicate adjective in copula constructions is included as a participant.) Given limitations on processing capacity in the early stages of development, it seems likely that the number of separate semantic units to be related will be another factor contributing to complexity. In arriving at the complexity score for each type of meaning relation, therefore, the number of necessary participants was added to the score derived from the sum of the weighted features.

However, this was subject to two qualifications. First, where two of the participants refer to the same entity, as in the case of coreferential change of location, where agent and patient have the same referent, the coreferring arguments were treated as a single participant for the purposes of scoring, on the grounds that they require only a single nominal group for their realization. The second qualification concerns embedded clauses. Certain meaning relations frequently take a full proposition as the exponent of one of the participants. This is very common in the case of the Want and Cognitive types of experiential meaning, where what is wanted or known is itself encoded in a further meaning relation. Embedding also occurs where a proposition encoding a further meaning relation occurs as the complement of a superordinate clause realizing the Function meaning relation of Agent Cause Event (e.g. 'Mother made John wash his hands'). An addition of 1 was made to the score of all such complex meaning relations involving an embedded clause.

Complexity scores based on the two components of semantic features and semantic and structural density were assigned to the 26 meaning relations with a median age of emergence of 42 months or less (see table A3). Scores ranged from 1 for the undifferentiated category, Operator + Nominal, to 8 for Cognitive Experience + Embedded Clause. These are shown in table 9.3.

Table 9.3 *Emergence, complexity and input frequency of sentence meaning relations*

Order of emergence	Rank	Complexity Index	Complexity Rank	Input frequency Freq. per 1000 utts.	Rank
Operator + Nominal	1	1	1	38	8.5=
Static Location	2	3	3.5	70	5
Coref. Change Location	3.5=	3	3.5	101	1
Agent Change Location	3.5=	4	11.5=	97	2
Classification	5	3	3.5	78	3
Wanting Experience	6	4	11 5=	50	7
Static Possession	7.5=	4	11.5=	34	11
Agentive Cogn. Exper.	7.5=	4	11.5=	72	4
Agent Change Phys. Attrib.	9.5=	4	11.5=	38	8.5=
Static Phys. Attrib.	9.5=	3	3.5	24	15
Agent Change Possess.	11	5	20=	36	10
Agent Function	12.5=	4	11.5=	33	12
Want Exper. + Embed. Cl.	12.5=	5	20=	13	20
Evaluative Attrib.	15=	4	11.5=	57	6
Ag. Func. on Patient	15=	5	20=	33	13
Cognitive Experience	15=	4	11.5=	29	14
Agent Act on Target	17.5=	4	11.5=	24	16
Affective Experience	17.5=	4	11.5=	19	18
Physical Experience	19.5=	4	11.5=	18	19
Coref. Movement	19.5=	4	11.5=	7	23
Patient Function	21	5	20	8	22
Cogn. Exp. + Embed. Cl.	22.5=	8	26	22	17
Agent Change Exist.	22.5=	5	20=	9	21
Agent Cause + Embed. Cl.	24	7	25	4	25
Quantit. Attrib.	25.5=	6	23.5=	5	24
Benefactive Relation	25.5=	6	23.5=	2	26

9.3.4 *Inter-Personal Functions*

In attempting to assess the complexity of Inter-Personal Functions the situation is even more difficult, as there has been no work at all on the relative complexity of Functions. There are, however, certain features which serve to distinguish groups of Functions along the lines suggested by Searle (1977), and these can be assigned a notional complexity. First, then, we might make a distinction between what Searle calls Directives, Expressives and Representatives in terms of the purpose of the act and of the direction of fit between 'words' and 'world'. Whilst this way of describing the distinctions between the broad classes of Function may seem unduly elaborate with respect to the functions of children's early utterances, I would argue that it corresponds to the decisions that hearers have to make in order to interpret their utterances in any discriminating way. It is in keeping, therefore, with the strategy of 'rich interpretation' which has been adopted throughout the analysis. The purpose of Directives is to get some action carried out and the direction of fit is to bring the state of affairs in the world to match that expressed in the proposition. The purpose of Expressives is to express the psychological state of the speaker, such as surprise, approval, etc.; in this case it is not relevant to talk about the direction of fit between words and world. Representatives commit the speaker to something being the case or to discover what the hearer believes to be the case. Here the direction of fit is that the words should match the world.

To these three broad classes we might add Ostensives, the purpose of which is to get the hearer to pay attention to something. Atkinson (1979) argues that obtaining the hearer's attention is logically prior to issuing either a directive or a representative, so clearly this should have the lowest weighting. Since Expressives do not involve matching words to world, they may also be seen as less complex than Representatives. Compared with Representatives, Directives may be considered to be less complex on the grounds that, whereas the purpose of getting a hearer to do something can be achieved non-verbally as well as verbally, the purpose of Representatives can only be achieved by verbal means. On the basis of these arguments, the four classes were assigned the following weightings: Ostensives: 0; Expressives and Directives: 1; Representatives: 2. (Certain functions are treated as realizing two of these features, e.g. Formulation realizes both Directive and Representative.)

Of the major classes of function that have been distinguished, the class of Directives is rather more finely differentiated than the others with respect to the dimension of inter-personal relationships. A number of features seem to be relevant in discriminating the precise force of the different functions: who is to benefit from the action, who is to perform it, whether any recognition is shown of the fact that the hearer is an independent person whose desires and intentions should be taken into account, and whether appeal is made to some principle other than the wish of one or both of the participants as the reason for carrying out the action. Treating speaker benefit as the unmarked case (cf. the Instrumental function proposed by Halliday (1975)), all other features are considered to be marked choices and given a weighting of 1.

There are two further classes of Function not specifically considered in Searle's taxonomy, both of which share the feature of being dependent on a previous utterance, for which they seek or provide clarification. One class, labelled Contingent queries and responses by Garvey (1977), has as its ostensible function to repair communication breakdowns; the other seeks for or provides justification for preceding directives, representatives, etc. Because these functions are dependent on preceding discourse for their occurrence, they are considered to be more complex than the other classes and given a weighting of 3. Where the information requested or supplied is required to be quite specifically related to the content of the preceding discourse which is at issue (e.g. Physical Justification or Request Clarification), this places still further demands on the speaker and a further weighting of 3 is added to such functions.

In estimating complexity, it is also relevant to take into account differences in the syntactic complexity involved in the realization of functions. Some functions necessarily include a full proposition as part of the speaker's intentions (e.g. Statement, Question) whilst others do not (e.g. Exclamation, Call). Amongst those that involve a proposition, some, such as Question and Indirect Request, are typically realized by the selection of *wh-* or polar-interrogative mood, both of which are arguably more complex syntactically than declarative or imperative mood. A weighting of 1 was therefore given to functions requiring a proposition, with a further weighting of 1 for those realized by interrogative mood (see table A4, appendix 3).

Taking both pragmatic features and forms of realization into account, a complexity score was calculated for each of the 20 functions to reach criterion by 42 months. (Some functions, such as one-word positive and negative responses and those that are realized by routine formulae, were omitted from this analysis.) Scores are shown in table 9.4.

The criteria just proposed for discriminating between categories in the various systems are by no means exhaustive; others might

Table 9.4 *Emergence, complexity and input frequency of inter-personal function*

Order of emergence	Rank	Complexity Index	Rank	Input frequency Freq. per 1000 utts.	Rank
Wanting	2.5=	1	3=	5.4	19
Ostension	2.5=	1	3=	26.3	8
Exclamation	2.5=	1	3=	21.7	10
Call	2.5=	1	1	11.5	13
Direct Request	5.5=	3	6=	94.1	2
Statement	5.5=	3	6=	106.4	1
Question (Content)	7	4	9.5=	45.4	5
Express State	8	4	9.5=	33.5	6
C.Q. Repetition	9	3	6=	45.9	4
State Intention	10	4	9.5=	15.5	12
Question (Yes/No)	11	4	9.5=	57.3	3
Request Permission	12	5	13.5=	3.5	20
Indirect Request	13	5	13.5=	5.8	17
Suggestion	14	6	16.5=	18.8	11
Offer	15.5=	5	13.5=	5.7	18
Physical Justif.	15.5=	6	16.5=	21.9	9
Formulation	18.5=	7	18.5=	8.1	15
Request Justif.	18.5=	7	18.5=	6.7	16
Question (State)	18.5=	5	13.5	28.0	7
C.Q. Clarification	18.5=	8	20	11.0	14

have made a different selection or assigned different weightings. The rank orders of complexity finally adopted are therefore recognized to be no more than first approximations. Nevertheless they do have the merit of allowing the complexity explanation to be empirically evaluated in relation to all the items in each system that reached the criteria of emergence rather than in relation to isolated sub-sets of items. If these measures of complexity achieve some success in predicting order of emergence this will be a matter of empirical interest in its own right. If this also leads to further systematic work on the factors contributing to complexity, the attempt made here will have more than served its purpose.

Once complexity scores had been calculated for all items according to the procedure described above, a rank order of complexity was constructed for each system, with the lowest scoring items being assigned to the lowest ranks. Spearman rank-order correlation coefficients were then computed for the two sets of ranks, order of emergence and complexity. The resulting coefficients of correlation, corrected for tied ranks, are as shown in table 9.5.

Table 9.5 *Rank-order correlations: order of emergence ×*
complexity

Auxiliaries	Pronouns	Meaning relations	Functions
0.93	0.90	0.79	0.95

Given the strong reservations already expressed about the procedures used to arrive at the rank orderings of complexity, it would
be unwise to attach any great importance to the differing values of
the coefficients of correlation obtained for the different linguistic
systems. What is of importance, however, is the order of magnitude
of all the coefficients, which are in every case significant at the 1%
level. They clearly show that, for all four systems, there is a strong
relationship between complexity, as defined in this investigation,
and order of emergence; and this, it is suggested, can be interpreted
as providing support for an explanation of order of emergence in
terms of differential complexity.

9.4 Input frequency

The evaluation of the input frequency hypothesis is in principle
much more straightforward, as to count the frequency of items in
the speech addressed to the children is an entirely objective
procedure. However, it will be recalled that when the transcribed
speech samples were coded only child utterances were analysed in
full. Utterances addressed to the children were only coded for
inter-personal function when they immediately preceded or followed a child utterance and for SMR when they preceded an
utterance. At the beginning of the research, when the decision was
taken to limit the coding of speech addressed to the child in this
way, the chief reason for including input utterances at all was to be
able to examine the conversational context of the child's utterances.
It was not anticipated that the input might come to be investigated
in its own right and, even if this had been envisaged, there were
insufficient resources for a full coding of the input to have been
possible. Thus, when it was decided to investigate the relationship
between input and order of emergence, the necessary data on
relative frequency of items in the input were not readily available.

In the case of SMRs, frequencies were tabulated by hand from
the computer print-out of the coded data,[1] and function frequencies
were also obtained from the coded data, but by means of a LAP

tabulation analysis. In both cases, therefore, the frequencies are based on utterances which preceded utterances by the children and not on the full set of utterances addressed to them. Input utterances that would be excluded from contributing to these frequencies would be those before the final utterance in multi-utterance turns and responses which were sequence terminating. Initiating utterances to which the child failed to respond were included, however, as 'null-responses' by the child and their conversational context were included in the coding procedure. There seems little reason to suppose that the relative frequencies of SMRs would be systematically biased by these exclusions, but the effect on the function system is less easy to estimate. Sequence-terminating utterances would have a high probability of being either acknowledgements or responses realized by some variant of 'Yes' or 'No'. However, these functions have not been included in the rank order, so there is no problem of bias here. As far as non-final utterances in multi-utterance turns are concerned, the probable consequence of their omission is unknown. Frequencies of pronouns[2] and auxiliaries were tabulated by hand, direct from the transcripts, and were thus based on a larger number of utterances from each recording than the frequencies of SMRs and functions.

In order to overcome the discrepancies between systems in the size of the data-base from which frequencies were derived, all frequencies were converted to the form of frequency of occurrence per 1000 utterances. These figures, together with the associated ranks, are shown for each system in columns 5 and 6 of tables 9.1–9.4.

Rank-correlation coefficients were then computed between order of emergence and frequency in the input with correction for ties, yielding the results in table 9.6. The first three of these results are significant at the 1% level; the result for functions is non-significant. For three systems out of four, therefore, the evidence supports an explanation in terms of the frequency of items in the input determining their order of emergence. Acceptance of this explanation must be qualified, however, by the lack of support for

Table 9.6 *Rank-order correlations: order of emergence × input frequency*

Auxiliaries	Pronouns	Meaning relations	Functions
0.78	0.86	0.89	0.31

it in the case of the fourth of the major systems investigated. Indeed, this strongly discrepant result suggests that the relationships between complexity, input frequency and order of emergence are in need of further investigation.

9.5 Complexity and input frequency in interaction

The two explanations considered in the preceding sections have often been put forward as alternatives, derived from competing theories of language acquisition. The fact that both of them receive quite strong support from the same corpus of data suggests that they are not mutually exclusive alternatives. One reason for this might be that complexity and input frequency are themselves highly correlated. To discover whether this is indeed the case, the coefficients were computed for each of the four systems investigated. The results were as shown in table 9.7. As can be seen, except for functions, the correlations are high, though in no case as high as those between the stronger of the predictor variables and order of emergence. It can be concluded therefore that, for all systems but functions, both the predictor variables have a small independent contribution to make in accounting for the variance in order of emergence.

Table 9.7 *Rank-order correlations: complexity × input frequency*

Auxiliaries	Pronouns	Meaning relations	Functions
0.85	0.67	0.68	0.35

This leads to the consideration of the third hypothesis, namely that complexity and input frequency interact in determining order of emergence. It will have been noted that, for all the linguistic systems under consideration, there are several groups of items that are assigned the same complexity score. The pair of pronouns 'he' and 'she' is a very clear example, where it would be difficult to find any theoretical grounds for arguing that one member of the pair was more complex than the other. Yet the masculine pronoun is ranked higher than the feminine equivalent in order of emergence. In these circumstances, it is entirely plausible to suggest that the differential frequency with which the masculine and feminine pronouns occur in the speech addressed to the children is the factor that accounts for the difference in order of emergence. From table 9.2 it can be seen that 'he' occurs with a frequency of 42 per 1000 utterances and 'she' with a frequency of 33 and that their positions in the rank order of emergence are, respectively, 9 and 13.

The demonstratives provide what is perhaps an even clearer case. The members of the two pairs 'this'/'that' and 'these'/'those' all belong to the same class and each pair shows the proximal/distal contrast whilst the pairs are contrasted in terms of number. The prediction based on complexity would be that the singular pair would emerge before the plural pair but that there would be no within-pair difference in order of emergence. This prediction is borne out for the plural pair but not for the singular: 'that' is 2= in the rank order of emergence but 'this' is only 8. However, when we look at these items in the input, this result is fully accounted for by their differential frequency: 'that' has a frequency of 83 per 1000 utterances, 'this' a frequency of 12 and 'these' and 'those' are equal with a frequency of 3 per 1000 utterances. For this set of items, therefore, order of emergence can best be predicted by an interaction between complexity and frequency.[3]

In the other systems it is perhaps less easy to find items for which the argument for equivalence of complexity can be made with such conviction but, amongst the SMRs, Classification and Physical Attribution are similar in complexity yet widely separated in order of emergence, and the same is true for the four categories of experiential meaning. In both cases, however, the difference in input frequency may provide the explanation: Classification occurs with a frequency of 78 per 1000 utterances, whilst the frequency of Physical Attribution is only 24. Similarly, despite identical complexity scores, the four categories of experiential meaning Want, Cognitive, Affective and Physical are ranked respectively 6, 15=, 17.5= and 19.5= in order of emergence. However these ranks are quite closely matched with the ranks for frequency in the input, which are 7, 14, 18 and 19 respectively (see table 9.3).

Generalizing from these examples one might thus propose that complexity and frequency combine together to determine order of emergence. Where items of similar complexity are heard with equal frequency, they will emerge at approximately the same time in children's speech, but where they are heard with different frequencies, the more frequently heard items will be the first to emerge. The converse, however, may not be true. A frequently heard item will not emerge before less frequently heard items if it is more complex, it could be argued, because, until they are 'ready', children will not be able to benefit from the frequency with which the item is modelled in the speech that they hear. This is supported by the relationships between order of emergence, complexity and input frequency for the two meaning relations Physical Attribution and Evaluative Attribution (cf. table 9.3). Although Evaluative Attribution occurs considerably more frequently than Physical Attribution (57 tokens per 1000 utterances compared with 24), the order of emergence corresponds to the order of complexity, in which Physical Attribution is scored as less complex than Evaluative Attribution.

In order to evaluate the third hypothesis, the formula $K = \log$ (complexity $\times$ 1/frequency) was used to obtain an index of complexity adjusted for frequency. K scores were computed for each of the three systems where complexity and input frequency were both significant predictors of order of emergence and these scores were then ranked and correlated with rank order of emergence for each system. The results are shown in the bottom line of table 9.8, which also repeats the results reported for complexity and input frequency alone in order to facilitate comparisons. These results are generally positive but by no means unequivocal. For two of the three systems the interactive measure yields a higher correlation with order of emergence than either complexity or input frequency alone. However, this is not the case for the third system – auxiliaries – though it is worth noting that, for this system, complexity is an extremely powerful predictor when considered alone. Furthermore, complexity is in this case particularly highly correlated with input frequency and therefore cannot be expected to make a substantial individual contribution.

Table 9.8 *Alternative predictors of order of emergence*

| Predictor variables | Order of emergence | | |
	Auxiliaries	Pronouns	Meaning relations
Complexity	0.93	0.90	0.79
Input frequency	0.78	0.86	0.89
Complexity adjusted for input frequency	0.87	0.94	0.93

9.6 Evaluation of results

Of the three hypotheses for the observed orders of emergence of items within linguistic systems that have been empirically evaluated, it is the first that has received the most consistent support. For all systems, complexity has proved to be highly correlated with order of emergence, whereas input frequency alone or in interaction with complexity has been found to be related to order of emergence in only three of the four systems. Many previous researchers have only considered the first hypothesis and some might wish to argue that, with the results obtained here, it is unnecessary to look further. If such high correlations are obtained from ranked scores derived from indices of complexity that are both crude and somewhat insecurely grounded in theory, the lack of perfect fit, it might be argued, should be attributed to error in the measurement of complexity and in the sampling of speech from which the orders of emergence were derived.

Certainly, the evidence in favour of accepting the hypothesis of complexity as the determinant of order of emergence is strong and it may well be that with more accurate measurement it could be even stronger. However that does not mean that the high correlations between order of emergence and input frequency should be ignored. For, although on the comparative evidence one would not wish to argue that differential frequency in the input is sufficient to account for order of emergence, it cannot be dismissed as irrelevant. The problem is to know how to explain its contribution. Perhaps the place to start is with the significant correlations between complexity and frequency in all the systems except Functions. Possible reasons for the lack of significant correlation between order of emergence and input frequency in the case of this system will be considered below. Where a correlation is obtained between two variables a and b, there is always a question as to whether it is the result of direct causal relationship between a and b, or whether it occurs indirectly as a result of a and b both being caused by a third variable c. Confining ourselves to the first alternative for the moment, are there grounds for considering there to be a causal relationship in either direction between complexity and frequency?

By appeal to Zipf's law, a case could be made that, in the evolution of any language, those meanings that are most frequently expressed will have acquired the simplest realization. Zipf's law is based on an observed tendency for the most frequently used words and expressions to be shorter as a result of the operation over time of the principle of least effort (Lyons, 1968). Length is certainly one of the factors taken into account in the various indices of complexity, and the same principles may apply to other aspects of the lexico-grammatical realization of meanings. On the other hand, the meanings themselves can hardly have become simpler through frequent use; yet differences in difficulty of meaning played just as important a role as length in the ordering of items for complexity in all the systems considered. Conversely, although it may be the case that, in general, the more complex an item the less frequently it is used, it does not seem plausible to argue, for the linguistic systems under consideration, that the small differences between items in complexity can account for the large variations in the frequency with which they were used by mature speakers of the language.

There is, however, an alternative way of conceiving a causal relationship between complexity and frequency, in which the higher frequency of less complex items would be attributed to a systematic tendency on the part of adults to simplify their speech when talking with immature speakers of the language. That adults do adjust their speech when addressing young children is now well attested (cf. Snow, 1977 for a review of the evidence), and it may be that the observed correlations are the result of choices in utterance-construction by adults that are quite finely tuned to the differential difficulty, for their child addressees, of the items in the various systems. This would imply an intuitive sensitivity to small differences in linguistic complexity of a quite remarkable kind.

To date, the evidence that bears on this issue of 'fine-tuning' is somewhat contradictory. When Snow (1977) analysed the speech addressed by nine Dutch-speaking mothers to their 23–35-month-old daughters while playing and reading a book with them she found that 'of the approximately 70% of utterances that consisted of more than one term, 66% contained exclusively the prevalent semantic relations identified by Brown, and another 10% consisted of variants of "What is that?" i.e. demonstrative – entity – question' (p. 46). This she interpreted as evidence of 'very specified adjustments to the child' (p. 49). Unfortunately, the categories Snow used in her analysis do not map sufficiently closely on to the SMRs used in the present investigation for any direct comparisons to be made with respect to the relative frequencies of categories, but there is clearly a very broad similarity between her results and those reported here. Newport *et al.* (1977), on the other hand, attending chiefly to syntactic features in mothers' speech to girls between 12 and 27 months, concluded that, compared with speech to other adults, speech to young language learners is not, in general, constructionally simple and that 'whatever syntactic simplifications occur are not finely tuned to the child's developing language skills' (p. 145). More recently, however, Furrow *et al.* (1979), after studying very much the same syntactic features, reached the opposite conclusion. Cross (1977) also concluded that, for rapidly developing children at least, the input is finely tuned to the children's stage of development, although the features she attended to were pragmatic and semantic rather than syntactic.

Thus, although there is not complete agreement, the balance of the evidence supports the view that the input to language-learning children is modified to take account of their immature control of the language system. It seems reasonable to infer, therefore, that there will be a rather general bias in the frequency of items within linguistic systems towards those that are simpler, since these, we have shown, are the earliest to emerge in the children's speech. However, the claim that the input is finely tuned to the children's stage of development has a further implication, namely that the relative frequencies of items within systems will change over time in relation to the children's increasing mastery. Since none of the studies referred to above involved repeated observations of the same children, this possibility has not yet been investigated. Using the data collected in the present investigation, however, it is now possible to address this question.

9.7 The relation of the input to order of emergence

The differential frequencies of items addressed to the children, which were presented in tables 9.1–9.4, were arrived at by pooling all observations from all children between 15 and 42 months and, from the figures given, it might be supposed that frequencies remained relatively constant over the period studied. This, however, was not the case. There was a general tendency for items within the auxiliary and pronoun systems to occur with a rather low frequency on the first observation at 15 months. At around 21 months, the frequencies began to increase rather sharply until a peak was reached, after which they began a decline, though not as sharp, which continued until the end of the period under investigation at 42 months. (Figure 9.1 illustrates this trend for six of the items within the auxiliary verb system.) What makes this finding of particular interest is the relationship between the changing frequencies in the input and emergence of the same items in the speech of the children. If median age of emergence is taken as an index of emergence (marked for each item by X at the appropriate point on the relevant curve in figure 9.1 above) it can be seen that the rapid increase in the frequency of items *preceded* their emergence in the children's speech and that the peak followed by decline tended to follow shortly after the point of emergence.

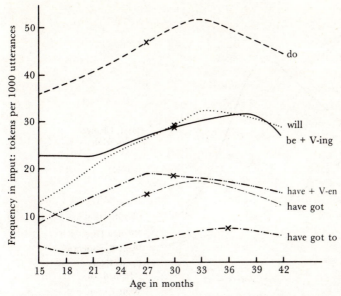

Figure 9.1 Auxiliary verbs: frequency in input in relation to median age of emergence

The situation with respect to SMRs and Functions is rather more complex. Both pronouns and auxiliaries are optional systems, in the sense that it is not necessary to select an item from either system to construct a well-formed sentence. The low frequencies in the early observations are therefore the result of a tendency on the part of adults not to include items from these systems when addressing children of this age. Since every structured utterance obligatorily encodes a function and a meaning relation, however, a speaker cannot avoid selecting some item from each of these systems. It is not possible, therefore, for *all* items from these systems to occur with low frequency in the first observations and subsequently to increase in frequency, although such a pattern is observed in the case of many of the more complex items, as can be seen in the lower part of figure 9.2, which shows the frequency curves of a selection of sentence meaning relations.

The frequency curves of the more frequently occurring – and less complex – items, on the other hand, are strikingly different. Coreferential Change of Location (e.g. 'Come here', 'I'm going downstairs')˙and Want Experience (e.g. 'Do you want a drink?') both start with high relative frequencies which decline sharply over the remainder of the period. Classification (e.g. 'What's that?',

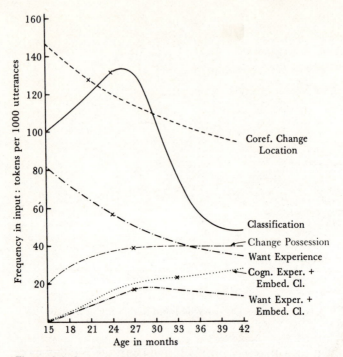

Figure 9.2 Sentence Meaning Relations: frequency in input in relation to median age of emergence

'That's a cat') starts high, climbs sharply until 24 months and then declines even more sharply to a relatively low plateau at 39 months. As with the auxiliaries, it will be noted that, for those items that show an increase in frequency during the period, whether or not this is followed by a decline, the increase precedes median age of emergence.

Data such as these certainly confirm a description of the input as finely-tuned. They also lend support to the explanation suggested above for the observed correlations between complexity and frequency in the input. Adults speaking to young children apparently do, to a considerable extent, match the frequency with which they select items to those items' relative complexity. What is more, they do so in a progressive manner which is also related to the emergence of those items in the speech of the children. But what is particularly worthy of comment is the finding that the rapid increase in the adults' frequency of use *precedes* the point of emergence in the children's speech.

Commenting on the results of her study of the input to Dutch children, Snow claims that 'the semantic content, unlike the grammar, of mothers' speech is limited to what the child can already produce himself' (1977:47). And she goes on to argue that 'Frequency of a structure in the linguistic input, even specific teaching of and practising with the structure, can have an effect on language acquisition only after the child has independently developed the cognitive basis which allows him to use that structure. At that point, the frequency and saliency of the structure in the input language can have a crucial effect on its acquisition' (p. 48). The findings of the present study lead us to question this claim about the limitation on the content of mothers' speech and to propose a somewhat different account of the significance of the input, which takes account of the progressive modification of relative frequency.

One possible reason for the discrepancy between the findings of the two investigations is that Snow made no independent study of the meanings that the children had already mastered, but relied on an assumption that the meaning relations scored in adult speech would be present in the children's speech, since this is generally the case for children of the age-range concerned. More importantly, there was no longitudinal dimension to her study, so she was not in a position to note whether there were any changes in the relative frequencies of different meanings in the input and, if so, whether such changes were related to the sequence of development in the children. Had she been able to relate change in input frequency over time to acquisition, she might have reached different conclusions.

However, a rather different explanation is also possible, which is suggested by an apparent inconsistency between the two extracts quoted above. In the second extract, Snow argues that the linguistic evidence provided by the presence of a particular structure in the input is only useful to the child when the child has the cognitive basis to use that structure. 'Use' here presumably includes comprehension just as much as production. In the first extract, on the other hand, Snow appears to refer only to production.

With Snow, we accept the arguments put forward by a number of psycholinguists (Cromer, 1974; Macnamara, 1972; Slobin, 1973) that there are cognitive prerequisites for the acquisition of linguistic distinctions. Indeed the indices of complexity referred to in this chapter are based on such an assumption. But, following arguments advanced more recently by both Cromer (1979) and Slobin (1979), we also accept that development of the cognitive basis is not in itself sufficient for production of the linguistic category. There is also a

necessary period of learning during which the child, by participating in conversations in which examples of the category are
addressed to him, first comes to comprehend the way in which
conceptual distinctions that he has grasped are mapped on to
semantic distinctions and their formal realizations in the language
to which he is exposed, and then incorporates these meanings and
their grammatical realizations in his own production. For this
learning to take place it is clearly necessary for the input to the child
to contain a sufficient frequency of examples of what has to be
learned. It may well also be particularly helpful if the frequency of
more complex items is kept low until the point where the child is
almost ready to learn them. A relatively sharp increase in frequency
at that point would then render them particularly salient and
encourage the child to pay particular attention to them. The second
extract from the paper by Snow makes this very point and she goes
on to give examples of how such learning opportunities arise
naturally during the course of conversation in relation to topics
which the child himself may well have introduced.

There are thus both theoretical and empirical grounds for
expecting the input to children to contain a greater range of
meanings than they can already produce themselves. A more
accurate statement, we believe, would be the following. A substantial proportion of the speech addressed to language-learning children matches in meaning and function – and to a lesser extent,
grammatical organization – what children themselves are able to
express. But there is also a significant proportion that is somewhat
in advance of the child's current production, and it is this which
provides the opportunity for the child to continue to extend his
mastery of the language to which he is exposed. Furthermore,
whilst this is broadly true for the whole of the period 15–42
months, the balance changes as the children mature. To begin with,
a large proportion of the adult's speech is beyond the child's current
production but, by the end of the period, this proportion is very
much smaller. Brown (1977) puts it very well when reviewing the
collection in which Snow's paper appears: 'Parents seek to communicate, I am sure, but they are not content to communicate
always the same limited set of messages. A study of detailed
mother–child interaction shows that successful communication on
one level is always the launching platform for attempts at communication on a more adult level' (p. 15). The evidence found in the
present investigation of a general tendency for items to show an
increase in relative frequency timed to occur slightly before their

emergence in the speech of the children, could be the outcome of the operation of just such a strategy by the children's interlocutors.[4]

Are the finely tuned changes in frequency, then, a deliberate attempt on the part of adults to provide an optimum learning environment for children? This seems highly unlikely. Some parents may be so conscious of their contribution to their children's development that they monitor their talk in this way, but the vast majority certainly do not. A much more plausible explanation in our view would be that the progressive modifications in adult speech occur largely in response to changes in their children. Several researchers have suggested that it is the child's comprehension that cues the selection that adults make in relation to what they choose to talk about and the forms in which they encode their meanings. Cross (1977), for example, found that the differences she observed in the speech addressed to rapidly developing children across the age-range 19–32 months were more highly correlated with the children's level of comprehension than with any measures derived from their speech production.

Cues from the child's comprehension are almost certainly one of the major determinants of the nature of the input at any stage. But there are also cues of a different kind that the child provides for the adult in the form of developments in his non-verbal behaviour. Two of the most frequently occurring SMRs illustrate this well. As was seen in figure 9.2, Coreferential Change of Location occurred with greatest frequency at 15 months. Now, although this is an age by which many children are walking well enough to be able to move around by themselves, their movements still need to be monitored to ensure that they do not get into danger. It is not surprising, therefore, that, at this age, such a high proportion of adult utterances should express meanings concerned with coming and going, nor that their frequency should decline as the children need to be monitored less and, simultaneously, are increasing the range of other meanings that they are able to comprehend. Similarly the high frequency of Want Experience utterances at the beginning of the period is probably best accounted for by the parents' attempts to check that they have understood the child's desires, which are quite largely signalled non-verbally. Once the child has linguistic means at his disposal for encoding his wants, the responsibility for communicating them can be transferred to a large extent to him, and there is consequently less requirement for the parents to ask about them.

A rather different sort of explanation seems to be called for, on the other hand, for the rapid rise to a high peak at 24 months in the frequency of Classification meanings. Whilst this high frequency may well be cued to some degree by the child's behaviour – his interest in the objects he notices and the high frequency of the utterances he produces with the function of sharing that interest with those around him (Ostension) – it seems equally likely that it is cued by a culturally shared belief amongst adults that children ought to be learning the names of objects at this stage. Certainly it is in the adults' interest that they should do so as, until they increase their lexical resources, conversation with young children is extremely restricted!

In the case of asking for or providing the names of objects it is probably appropriate to think of adults as having a fairly deliberate tutorial purpose with respect to language, and there may be other aspects of language which are occasionally deliberately 'taught'. But for most of the time the relatively finely tuned modelling of meanings and forms that the frequency data reveal occurs incidentally, as adults carry on conversations with their children for quite other purposes – to control the child's behaviour in the interests of his safety and their joint well-being, to share in and extend his interests, to maintain and enrich their inter-personal relationship and so on. Success in achieving these aims requires that the majority of the adults' contributions be pitched at a level of complexity that is not too far beyond the child's linguistic ability. However, this is achieved quite spontaneously by most adults under the control of feedback from the child's comprehension and production and does not require deliberate attention. The tuning that occurs is thus as much a response to, as a determinant of, the sequence in the child's learning.

This interpretation gains further support from the relationship between order of emergence and input frequency in the case of Inter-Personal Functions. Here, it will be recalled, there was a relatively low and non-significant correlation. This, however, should perhaps have been expected. Whilst successful conversation requires inter-subjectivity of attention leading to a convergence between speakers on the meanings intended and the lexico-grammatical forms in which they are encoded, the functions which utterances perform are reciprocal and depend upon the roles of the participants in the interaction. Children are, on the whole, the ones who request permission and adults are the ones who grant or withhold it. Children express their own needs and wants but adults ask about those of others. Children ask for explanations but it is more often adults who supply them. For Inter-Personal Functions the order of emergence seems not to be dependent on the frequency with which they occur in the input: those that emerge earliest are not those that are by and large the most frequent in adult speech nor are those that emerge later necessarily those that are heard least frequently.

It appears, therefore, that the influence of the input on the child's learning is enabling rather than determining. Once the child has the prerequisite cognitive understanding of the distinction which is encoded by a particular linguistic category, frequent appropriately contextualized occurrences of the category in the speech that is addressed to the child provide opportunities for him to make the connection between linguistic category and non-linguistic experience. However, whether this facilitation of learning actually leads to productive use of the category by the child depends on the situations in which he finds himself and on the communicative possibilities and constraints that he experiences in those situations.

In seeking to explain the observed correlations between order of emergence, complexity and relative frequency of items in the speech addressed to children in the period between 15 and 42 months, we seem, therefore, to have arrived at a complex pattern of inter-relationships. Relative linguistic complexity, we would argue, is the major determinant of order of emergence in the sense that it delimits what the child will be able to learn at each stage. Within these limits, frequency in the input plays a role in facilitating the actual learning: on the one hand, a certain minimal frequency is necessary to provide the child with a model from which to learn and, on the other, differences in relative frequency make some items more salient than others and this may lead to differences in order of emergence between items of equal complexity. The relationship between order of emergence and input frequency is thus probably best seen as one of reciprocal causality, children's learning being influenced to some extent by the relative frequency of items in the input and adults choosing to encode in their speech the meanings, functions and forms which their children are already producing or which, on the basis of a variety of cues, they believe they are able to understand and will shortly be able to produce. If this argument is correct, the relationship between complexity and input frequency is indirect, occurring largely as a by-product of the other relationships.

In the last resort, however, what both adults and children talk about is largely determined by the nature of the social and physical environment in which they live and by the cultural patterns through which the parent–child relationship is enacted. This leads to another sort of reciprocity – that of discourse – in which adjacent pairs of utterances encode complementary functions, such as request and comply, question and answer, with respect to a world of joint activities and shared perceptions. The child, therefore, does not model his speech on that of the adults who talk with him, or at least not in any simple way. Nor does the adult deliberately attempt to provide a model, except very occasionally when teaching new vocabulary or insisting on politeness routines. The more appropriate description would be to say that they attempt to communicate with each other about the matters of greatest significance – as perceived from their different points of view. That there is such a great degree of congruence results from the fact that it is the child who sets the pace and that adults, for much of the time, are happy that this should be so.

9.8 The influence of conversational characteristics of the input

The earliest studies of the input to language learners were primarily concerned to demonstrate the inaccuracy of Chomsky's (1964) characterization of the learner's primary linguistic data as a random and degenerate sample of the sentences of a language. This objective has been substantially met, as Snow (1977) demonstrates in a review of a considerable number of studies, ranging over several languages and a variety of contextual conditions. But, as Newport *et al.* (1977) point out in the same volume, it is one thing to find evidence of a cluster of modifications that together constitute a recognizable register of talk to young children and quite another to demonstrate that it has any influence on the course or rate of development. Some authors seem to be convinced that the experience of this register is both a necessary and a sufficient condition for children's learning whilst others, for example Shatz (1982), argue strongly against the sufficiency condition and appear to be sceptical even about the necessity of experiencing this specialized register as a condition for language learning. If its occurrence is universal, however, as the studies reviewed by Snow suggest it may be, it is clearly going to be difficult to obtain empirical evidence to determine the accuracy of these claims. On the other hand, if it is found that adults vary in the manner and extent to which they modify their speech when conversing with young children, it may be possible to show that such variation is systematically related to the rate at which learning takes place, even if the necessity of the experience cannot be demonstrated.

A number of studies with this objective have been carried out in recent years but, as indicated earlier in this chapter, the results have been somewhat inconclusive, not to say contradictory. As we have argued elsewhere (Barnes *et al.*, 1983), this is probably due to methodological inadequacies in most of these studies and to differences in the features of adult speech investigated. Our own attempts to address this issue are certainly not without limitations, but they have to a considerable extent overcome the problems of unrepresentativeness of the children studied and of the conversational samples obtained, and of controlling for the children's stage of development. We have also made a careful attempt adequately to measure the children's progress.

The design of the study to be reported here was similar to that used by Newport *et al.* (1977) and by Furrow *et al.* (1979). A group of the Bristol children, equated for stage of development, were recorded in naturally occurring conversations with those in their home surroundings on two occasions, T_1 and T_2, nine months apart. Progress made by the children during this interval was calculated for a variety of linguistic variables as a residual gain score, that is each child's gain was expressed in terms of its deviation from the mean gain for the sample as a whole (cf. Barnes *et al.*, 1983 for details). The adult speech addressed to the children at T_1 was then coded for a number of features which might be considered to facilitate children's language development and scores derived from these codings were finally correlated with the children's gain scores to determine which features significantly predicted variation in the amount of progress made by the children.

The 32 children studied in this investigation, which was carried out *post hoc* on observations already made as part of the larger investigation, were selected on the basis of their participation in the follow-up study, which involved following them through the first two years of compulsory schooling (cf. Wells, 1981: 9–11 for details). This sub-sample consisted of an equal number of boys and girls, with all four classes of family background represented in each sex. They also spanned the full range of linguistic attainment observed in the sample when they entered school at five years of age.

In order to equate the children for level of development at T_1, the observation of each child was selected when he or she had an MLUS value as close as possible to 1.5 morphemes. (Actual values ranged from 1.0 to 2.21, with a mean of 1.68 morphemes.) The language measures used to calculate gain scores were those described in 8.1, with the addition of two additional measures: Auxiliary Meanings, the number of semantic distinctions realized by auxiliary verbs used by the child by that point (cf. 4.5); and the mean number of lexical verbs per utterance.

The features coded for adult speech were based on the scheme devised by the research team for the analysis of adult–child conversation (Wells *et al.*, 1979, 1981). They fall into five broad groupings: Formal Features, including Mood choice; Locus of Reference; Context; Discourse Function; and Topic Incorporation. An additional feature, Amount of Speech, was included, since quantity as well as quality of input may influence rate of development. As amount of speech is likely to vary from day to day, the mean of three observations centring on the observation at T_1 was taken, as this was considered likely to give a better estimate of the amount of adult speech habitually addressed to a child than that observed on a particular occasion. For this, as for all measures of adult speech, frequencies were based on 18 90-second samples. In all, some 45 variables were derived from these codings (cf. Wells, 1980, for details).

A preliminary analysis of these data revealed a substantial number of significant correlations among the features of adult speech and between these and children's gain scores. However, as in any large-scale correlational exercise, a number of significant correlations would be expected to arise by chance. An attempt was therefore made to reduce the number of variables involved by first excluding those based on features of adult speech that were considered to be of less importance and then submitting the 31 that remained to factor analysis. The final list of variables entered into this analysis is shown in table 9.9.

With almost as many variables as cases contributing to this analysis, it would have been inappropriate to attempt to interpret the six factors that were retained (together accounting for 86% of the variance) as a structural model of adult speech. Instead, each factor was represented in the subsequent correlational analysis by the variable that had the highest loading. With the addition of Amount of Adult Speech, this yielded the following seven adult speech variables:

Mean Length of Structured Utterances
Proportion of Polar Interrogatives with Subject–Auxiliary Inversion

Table 9.9 *Adult speech variables submitted to factor analysis*

Formal features
  Mean length of structured utterances (MLUS): calculated as for child
  Difference between adult and child MLUS
  Mean number of propositions per utterance
  Mean number of lexical verbs per utterance
  Percentage of incomplete utterances
  Percentage of declaratives
  Percentage of polar interrogatives (subject–auxiliary inversion)
  Percentage of polar interrogatives (intonation only)
  Percentage of moodless utterances

Locus of reference
  Percentage of references to joint activity
  Percentage of references to non-present events

Context
  Percentage of utterances when looking at books/watching TV
  Percentage of utterances when child helping with household activities
  Percentage of utterances when adult playing with child

Discourse functions
  Direct requests in context of control
  Question: comment
  Question: display of knowledge
  Question: text-contingent
  Expressive
  Acknowledge

Topic incorporation
  Imitation of child utterance
  Expansion of child utterance
  Extend child utterance
  Extend child utterance by contrast
  Extend child current activity
  Repetition of adult utterance
  Paraphrase of adult utterance
  Develop previous adult utterance
  Unrelated: initiate new sequence

Amount of adult speech

Proportion of Polar Interrogatives realized by Intonation only
Number of Direct Requests to Control Behaviour
Number of Questions (Comment)
Number of Extensions
Amount of Adult Speech

Since the results of this correlational analysis have already been reported (Barnes *et al.*, 1983), they will not be repeated here. Instead, an attempt will be made to explore further the underlying relationships between characteristics of the input and the children's rate of progress in language learning.

First, since the study was carried out, the analysis of the children's speech at the syntactic level has been completed, allowing scores to be derived at T_1 and T_2 for each child with respect to mastery of sentence/clause structure and of noun-phrase structure.[5] Level achieved on the scale of language development has also been determined, providing in addition an overall measure of development. Residual gain scores have therefore been calculated for each of these developmental indices, thus providing a much more complete array of dependent variables.

Secondly, in the light of the significant relationships found by Hardy-Brown *et al.* (1981) between parental 'contingent' responses and children's progress, it was decided to look more closely at the three categories of Incorporation in adult speech which most clearly demonstrated contingency on the child's previous utterance. These were the categories of Imitation, Expansion and Extension, which Cross (1978) also found to be significantly more frequently addressed to accelerated than to normally developing children. Since only the last-mentioned had been included in the previous analysis, the other two were added, to give nine independent variables.

A further correlational analysis was then carried out, between the two enlarged sets of variables, yielding the results shown in table 9.10. The first three adult variables represent two aspects of the form of the input. MLU(S) was the most highly loading variable on a factor that was recognizably concerned with the length and complexity of the utterances addressed to the children. As can be seen, it is not significantly associated with any of the child gain scores, although the trend, which approaches significance in some cases, is always in the direction of a higher MLU being associated with greater gain by the children.

In evaluating this result, two things need to be borne in mind. First, the difference between mean adult MLU(S) and mean child MLU(S) was not very great, being only of the order of 2 morphemes. Secondly, the variance in adult MLU(S) was also not very great. However, even more important, as pointed out in chapter 8 in the discussion of child MLU scores, is the fact that, by definition, MLU is a measure of the *average* length of utterance. Mean and standard deviation values for this sample of adults, therefore, tell us

Table 9.10 *Correlations between adult speech variables and child residual gain scores*

	MLU(S)	% Polar Interrog. with Subj.–Aux Inversion	% Polar Interrog. Realized by Intonation Only	Direct Request to Control	Question (Comment)	Expansion of Child Utts.	Imitations of Child Utts.	Extending Utterances	Amount of Adult Speech
MLU(S)	0.29	0.26	0.22	0.48**	0.18	0.37*	0.40*	0.30	0.42*
MLU(L)	0.29	0.05	0.27	0.49**	0.09	0.38*	0.46**	0.38*	0.45**
Semantic Range	0.27	0.40*	0.21	0.27	0.12	0.11	0.13	0.20	0.19
Auxiliary Meanings	0.20	0.16	0.42*	0.34	0.18	0.34	0.33	0.21	0.29
Semantic Complexity	0.14	0.19	0.27	0.40*	0.14	0.30	0.33	0.21	0.35*
Noun-Phrase Structure	0.31	0.10	0.22	0.28	0.21	0.39*	0.45**	0.39*	0.48**
Sentence/Clause Structure	0.12	0.42*	0.07	0.35*	0.20	0.22	0.21	0.24	0.40*
Pragmatic Range	0.06	0.17	0.50**	0.27	0.27	0.21	0.25	0.08	0.25
Scale Level	0.20	0.26	0.14	0.43*	0.07	0.26	0.44*	0.39*	0.32

* $p < 0.05$ ** $p < 0.01$

nothing about the range of utterance length experienced by the individual children.

As we pointed out before (Barnes *et al.*, 1983), utterance length is not constant over a sequence of interaction, but varies according to the local demands of the conversation. Moreover, it is probable that some adults are more sensitive than others to the child's needs as a listener at different points in an unfolding conversation. If, therefore, the tuning of the length and complexity of utterances to children's immediate conversational needs could be measured, it might well be that such a measure would indeed be associated with children's progress. However, this was not done in the present study or in any other study reported to date, and so little should be read into the non-significant correlations that have generally been obtained.

The other two variables that are concerned with the structure of adult utterances are the two realizations of the polar interrogative mood choice. In the case of Polar Interrogatives Realized by Subject–Auxiliary Inversion, a significant correlation was found with gain in both Semantic Range ($r = 0.40$, $p < 0.05$) and

Sentence/Clause Structure ($r = 0.42$, $p < 0.05$). Whilst the former result would probably not have been predicted, the latter is readily interpretable. The inversion of subject and auxiliary in the polar interrogative puts the auxiliary in a salient position at the beginning of the sentence and thus singles it out for the child's attention. The value of this for the learner is shown by the fact that children who receive a higher proportion of such utterances tend to have higher scores on the measure of Sentence/Clause Structure, to which mastery of structures involving an auxiliary contributes substantially.

The Realization of Polar Interrogative by Intonation only is an alternative to the form just discussed and so it would be anticipated that, if a high proportion of such utterances were to be associated with progress in language learning, it would be another aspect of the child's language that would show the effect. This indeed proves to be the case: both the gain in auxiliary verb meanings and the gain in Pragmatic Range show significant correlations ($r = 0.42$, $p < 0.05$ and $r = 0.50$, $p < 0.01$ respectively). Whilst these results do not have an obvious explanation, the more general finding of an association between child gains and a high proportion of polar interrogatives is in agreement with the results reported by Newport *et al.* (1977) and Furrow *et al.* (1979).

The second group of variables concerns the functions for which adults speak to children. Surprisingly, in the light of what has been claimed for older children (McDonald and Pien, 1982), it is Direct Requests to Control the Child's Behaviour rather than Questions calling for Comment in reply that are associated with children's progress. In fact a high frequency of Direct Requests is associated with gains on a broad range of child variables, including scale level. However, if one of the ways in which adult speech can facilitate the child's learning task is by making it easier for him to discover the relationship between lexico-grammatical form and intended meaning, Direct Requests seem ideal for this purpose, for they are both simple in form and also often encode the next action in a sequence of activity with which the child is already familiar or prohibit an action in which the child is already engaged. Questions calling for Comment, on the other hand, may well exceed the child's capability both to attend to the information demands and to frame an appropriate answer (Shatz, 1978).

This does not, of course, mean that the relationship between these two functions as potential facilitators of the child's progress will remain the same at later stages of development. Once the child has progressed beyond a certain point, it seems likely that Direct Requests will cease to have a facilitating role (Ellis and Wells, 1980) and too high a frequency may indeed come to inhibit development, as McDonald and Pien, among others, have argued. Questions calling for Comment, on the other hand, seem likely to behave in the reverse fashion.

The third group of variables is concerned with the different ways in which adults may incorporate the child's previous utterance in their next turn. Although all three categories of incorporation are contingent on the child's utterance, they differ in the extent to which they add additional semantic content to the conversation. Imitation adds no new content; Expansion, if it correctly judges the child's intention, adds no new content to what the child intended to communicate but fills out the lexico-grammatical realization into an acceptable conversational contribution; Extension incorporates all or part of the topic of the child's utterance and adds new but related semantic content. As will be seen, all three types of contingent response are significantly associated with gains in utterance length and in noun-phrase structure. Imitation and Extension are also associated with gain on scale level. Since Imitation and Extension have very similar patterns of correlation with the child gain scores but are opposed in the addition of new content, it appears that the extent to which the adult's incorporating utterances introduce new semantic content is not what is important about them. On the other hand, in incorporating the child's utterance, all these adult utterances provide positive feedback to the child that his previous utterance is in some way of relevance or of interest to his conversational partner at this point in their interaction. The value of such utterances to the child seems, therefore, to be motivational rather than informative with respect to the organization of the language system.

Finally, Amount of Adult Speech is a purely quantitative measure that is positively correlated with all the child gain scores, and significantly so with respect to gain in length ($r = 0.45, p < 0.01$ for MLU(L)), semantic complexity ($r = 0.35, p < 0.05$), noun-phrase structure ($r = 0.48, p < 0.01$) and sentence/clause structure ($r = 0.40, p < 0.05$). There is also a clear trend towards association with gain in scale level ($r = 0.32, p < 0.10$). It appears, therefore, that the quantity as well as the quality of adult speech may have a facilitative effect on the child's rate of language learning.

But are the two independent? With the exception of the indices of length and complexity and the proportions of utterance in the different moods, all the other adult measures were based on absolute frequencies of occurrence in 27 minutes of recorded conversation. It is possible, therefore, that the observed associations between child gain scores and the measures of function and incorporation in adult speech are no more than by-products of the variation in the quantity of adult speech addressed to the child.

Two methods were used in an attempt to answer this question. First, correlations were calculated between Amount of Adult Speech and each of the other adult variables that was based on absolute frequencies. The results of this analysis were varied and of interest in their own right. Amongst the function categories, Direct Requests to Control were not significantly correlated with Amount of Speech, but Questions calling for Comment were ($r = 0.71$, $p < 0.001$), as were Expressive utterances and Acknowledgements (respectively, $r = 0.64$ and $r = 0.54$, both $p < 0.001$). What this seems to suggest is that whilst the number of Questions calling for Comment, and of Expressives and Acknowledgements tends to increase in proportion to the increase in the total amount of speech, the frequency with which Direct Requests are issued is relatively independent of the amount of speech overall. This being so, it must be concluded that, at this stage of development, a high frequency of Direct Requests is associated with progress in language learning independently of the number of utterances having other functions that are addressed to the child.

As far as incorporation is concerned, all the categories showed significant correlations with Amount of Adult Speech, ranging from $r = 0.51$, $p < 0.01$ in the case of Paraphrase, to $r = 0.69$, $p < 0.001$, in the case of Repetition. It remains possible on the basis of this analysis, therefore, that the effect of the contingency of the adult's utterances is almost completely confounded with the effect of the sheer quantity.

To resolve this question was the aim of the second analysis. For this, all the adult variables based on absolute frequencies were converted to proportional frequencies and these were then correlated with the child gain scores. If any of the adult variables still showed a significant correlation with child gain, this would indicate that there were qualitative aspects of adult speech that were independent of the absolute amount of speech. The results of this analysis were clear-cut. Only one of the adult variables showed a consistent pattern of significant association with child gain scores and that was percentage of Extending Utterances. The results for this variable are shown in table 9.11. Percentage of Direct Requests and Proportion of Questions (Comment), although positively correlated with all gain scores, only achieved a significant level with one child gain score each: the former with Sentence/Clause Structure ($r = 0.40$, $p < 0.05$) and the latter with Pragmatic Range ($r = 0.37$, $p < 0.05$).

Table 9.11 *Correlations between proportional adult variables and child residual gain-scores*

Child gain scores	% Adult Extending Utterances	%Adult Utterances in Joint Activity
MLU(S)	0.49**	0.33
MLU(L)	0.36*	0.28
Semantic Range	0.46**	0.49**
Auxiliary Meanings	0.42*	0.38*
Semantic Complexity	0.35*	0.30
Noun-Phrase Structure	0.38*	0.40*
Sentence/Clause Structure	0.58***	0.30
Pragmatic Range	0.19	0.42*
Scale Level	0.49**	0.30

* $p < 0.05$ ** $p < 0.01$ *** $p < 0.001$

The fact that percentage of Extending Utterances achieves generally higher and more consistent correlations with child gain scores than the absolute frequency of Extending Utterances suggests that what is at issue here is a stylistic dimension of adult speech. Independently of how much speech they address to their children, some adults tend to extend a greater proportion of their children's utterances than others, and it seems probable that it is this stylistic tendency which is associated with children's progress in language learning rather than the absolute frequency of such utterances. Interestingly, the same is not true for the other two types of contingent response. The percentages of Imitations and of Expansions are not significantly associated with the children's gain scores. It must be assumed, therefore, that the effect of these types of contingent utterance is much more dependent on the absolute amount of speech addressed to the child.

In carrying out this analysis, one further variable emerged as significantly associated with a number of child gain scores: percentage of Adult Utterances referring to Joint Activity (see table 9.11). The importance of joint activities of various kinds in providing a facilitative scaffolding for language learning has already been argued by Bruner in relation to the proto-language and one-word stage (Bruner, 1975; Ratner and Bruner, 1978). It appears that such joint activities continue to provide a context which facilitates language development in the stage of multi-word utterances as well.

In conclusion, therefore, it can be argued that there are certain qualitative aspects of adult speech, as well as the sheer quantity, that are associated with the rate at which children progress at this stage in their language learning.

9.9 Influences on adult behaviour

If adults vary, as they have been shown to do, in the extent to which their speech manifests the features that have just been discussed, what influences the behaviour of individual adults? To a very large extent, this question still remains to be investigated, but there are already a number of indications as to where the answer may be found.

At a very general level, there are three broad types of possible influence: long-term attributes of the adults, attributes of the children which may be either developmental or relatively stable over a time-span such as that covered by this investigation, and attributes of the interactions between particular children and adults in the contexts in which they occur. Before briefly discussing each of these, however, it must also be pointed out that in all the studies reported so far, a considerable portion of the variance on each of the measures of adult speech must be due to sampling error. When the sample of speech to be analysed is only an hour or so in duration, recorded on a single day, it is impossible to know how representative it is of the child's habitual experience of adult speech. This is all the more true when the speech sample is obtained in one or two contexts selected by the researcher.

In the present study, where no attempt was made to control for context, there were certainly differences at T_1 in the frequency with which adult–child pairs were observed to engage in different activities (see 3.3). However this would only help to explain the observed associations between features of adult speech and children's gain scores if the distribution of speech across contexts at T_1 was representative of long-term differences between adult–child pairs rather than simply the result of sampling error. While such differences in habitual contexts for interaction seem entirely plausible, this is an issue which has not yet been investigated.

As far as differences in adult attributes are concerned that might influence their characteristic manner of interacting with their children, we have little information. Some of these attributes are likely to be the result of their own experience and we investigated this in terms of the 'formative influences' on the parents that were drawn upon in constructing the Scale of Family Background. Occupational status and, even more, the education of the parents might be expected to influence habitual style of interaction and no doubt does influence certain aspects. However, with respect to the variables found to be associated with children's progress in language learning, only Amount of Adult Speech was found to be significantly correlated with Family Background: children with higher scores on the Scale of Family Background were likely to have a greater amount of speech addressed to them ($r = 0.41$, $p < 0.01$). For the qualitative aspects of adult speech, however, the correlations did not reach a level of statistical significance (Barnes *et al.*, 1983).

This is not the only source of individual differences between adults, of course, for there are other experiential factors such as friendships, reading and so on that might influence parents' attitudes to child-rearing or, more directly, their styles of interaction. There are also personality factors which, although little discussed, are likely to be an important influence. Adult behaviour is also, to an unknown extent, dependent on attributes of the child. Some of these attributes can be subsumed under the general heading 'stage of development'. This has been recognized in all the studies discussed, and attempts have been made to control for this, either statistically (Newport *et al.*, 1977) or by selecting children who are at the same stage of development. In the present study, the latter method was employed.

However, if control is exercised only with respect to a single index of development – in almost all cases MLU – there is a strong possibility, as was shown in chapter 8, that there will still remain considerable variation with respect to other aspects of development. This was certainly the case in the present study and, as was reported by Barnes *et al.* (1983), the concurrent correlations between adult and child scores at T_1 suggest that at least part of the variance on the adult measures can be accounted for as a response to differences between the children in the range and complexity of the topics that they themselves contribute and in the variety of functions that they use language to perform. So, with respect to the proportion of adult utterances that extend the topic proposed by the child, for example, it seems likely that this will depend, at least in part, on the proportion of the child's own utterances that introduce topics that the adult finds interesting and susceptible to being extended.

Such differences between children are not purely developmental, however, but relate to more stable and long-term attributes of a kind that might better be described as differences of personality. For example, some children are argumentative, whilst others readily accept what they are told; some extensively comment on and ask questions about the objects and events in their environment, whilst others use language much more frequently to secure goods and services. Some are simply more talkative than others and thus, other things being equal, are likely to receive more speech addressed to them.

In various ways, therefore, the differences observed in adult behaviour may owe as much to differences between the children with whom they converse as to inherent differences in the adults themselves. But the reverse is also true, and so, in seeking to explain the differences in adult or child behaviour we must recognize that, ultimately, they are as likely to emerge from the interaction between a particular pair of participants, as they are to be attributable to either participant considered separately. If we are to untangle the relationship between features of the input and progress in language learning, therefore, it will be necessary to develop models of multiple and reciprocal causation operating within a matrix of interaction, which, on any particular occasion, is also affected by the particular context in which it occurs. Since we are very far from having such a model, it seems for the moment safer to conclude more modestly that, although the evidence supports a belief in the potentially facilitating effect of the adult input, this facilitating input itself is the product of interaction to which both child and adult contribute to varying degrees.

Learning through interaction

At one level, the conclusions drawn from the two studies reported in chapter 9 appear to be contradictory and reminiscent of the long-standing innatist–environmentalist controversy. On the one hand, the appeal to complexity rather than to relative frequency in the input to account for the similarity in sequence of development seems to support an explanation of language development which emphasizes the autonomy of the learner and plays down the role of the input. On the other hand, the finding that rate of development was associated with specific characteristics of the adult speech addressed to the children seems to argue for a significant influence from the environment.

For many researchers, it appears, this controversy can only be resolved by the capitulation of one or other of the contending parties. This state of affairs results largely from the emphasis of the one side on the autonomy of the learner and, on the other side, from a tendency to assume that the only function that the input can perform is that of 'teaching' the child by providing primary linguistic data that are finely tuned to the child's developmental needs and emphasize the linguistic distinctions to be acquired. Both points of view, it will be argued, are unnecessarily narrow, leading to a confrontation in which both sides lose sight of the essentially interactive nature of conversation, which provides the matrix within which development takes place.

A more satisfactory explanation would be achieved, I suggest, by treating the child and the adult as of equal importance, but with roles that are complementary and interdependent. Responsibility for what is learned and for the order in which learning takes place rests almost entirely with the child. Provided that the necessary evidence is made available to him in the speech that he hears, the child will construct both a repertoire of linguistic resources and procedures for drawing upon them in interaction with others, and he will do so in a systematic manner that is largely independent of the precise nature of the input. At the same time, the provision of the primary linguistic data which are essential for the child's learning is the responsibility of the child's parents or other care-takers and the extent to which, in doing this, they also provide support and encouragement for the child in his task of constructing a functional representation of the language system of his community significantly affects the ease and speed with which he carries out his task.

The evidence from the first of the two studies reported provides support for the first part of this account. The broad similarity in sequence of development, despite quite wide variation in the characteristics of the input to individual children, strongly suggests that the locus of control over the manner and order of learning lies within the learner, or more precisely in an interaction between what the learner brings to the learning task by way of prior knowledge and information-processing strategies and the internal organization of the language to be learned.

Whether this requires us to attribute to the child an innately structured learning device of the kind proposed by Chomsky (1976), which is specific to language, is not yet clear. Some degree of genetically transmitted pre-adaptation to the learning task, which is species-specific, is almost certainly required by this account. This is necessary to explain the active nature of the child's involvement in his learning and the broad similarity in the developmental sequence of what is learned. But the knowledge and strategies that the child brings to bear on mastering the organization of the adult language may have been acquired, at least to some degree, through his interaction with the social and physical environment in the pre-linguistic and 'proto-linguistic' stages of development. As Lock (1980) puts it, 'language is "imported" into situations which have already become socially intelligible to the child' (p. 195).

But as Slobin (1981) has argued, the support that the child's understanding of 'proto-typical' situations provides for the initial task of breaking into the language system is not sufficient to account for the abstractness of the relationships that finally come to organize his representation of the grammar. Nor does the pressure to achieve successful communication adequately explain the evolutionary processes that continue to characterize language development in later childhood (Bowerman, 1982). It seems, therefore, that from the beginning, the child is disposed to treat language as 'an internal problem space *per se*' (Deutsch, 1981) and although

non-linguistic knowledge and processing strategies certainly contribute to its resolution, certain more specifically linguistic organizing
principles are required, whether these result from a developmental
specialization of more general cognitive resources or are part of the
child's original genetic endowment.

However, to emphasize the active role that the child plays in
constructing and progressively modifying his repertoire of resources for communication does not require us to devalue the
contribution made to this process by his parents and other care-
takers. The precise nature of this contribution clearly changes in
both substance and emphasis as the child progresses from the
earliest forms of intentional communication, documented by Trevarthen (1979), through the transitional phase of 'proto-language' in
which the beginnings of linguistic communication are found in the
use of phonetically consistent forms as direct realizations of unitary
functional meanings (Halliday, 1975; Dore, 1975) to the early
stages of internally structured utterances and beyond. But, throughout this progression, what is common to all stages is that, in
responding to the interpretations that they place on the children's
own behaviours, verbal and non-verbal, adults communicate with
them in ways that take account of their perceptions of the children's
current capacities, needs and endeavours. Of course, not all adults
are equally sensitive to the intentions expressed by children's
communications nor do they make an equal effort to adjust their
own behaviour to take account of the relevant attributes of their
children. Nevertheless, despite variation in the extent to which it is
finely tuned to the individual child concerned, adult behaviour is
for much of the time adapted to the needs of the novice communicator.

Putting these two strands of argument together, therefore, leads
to a view of the development of communication as fundamentally
interactional. At each stage, the child endeavours to communicate
using the resources currently available to him. The adult with
whom he is interacting interprets his behaviour in terms of her own
cultural and linguistic framework and responds in a way that both
reflects to the child the perceived significance of his behaviour and,
in the form and content of that response, provides information
about the communication system and its relation to the world that
enables the child to supplement and modify his communicative
resources.

In describing the interactional process in these terms, I have
deliberately blurred the distinction between pre-linguistic and

linguistic communication. Whilst there are marked changes in the actual form that interaction takes as the child progresses from gestural to vocal to linguistic communicative acts, it is the continuity in the nature of the interactional process that is striking. To date, however, most of the research evidence to support this account of development comes from observations of parent–child interaction in the first 18 months of life (e.g. Bruner *et al.*, 1982; Ratner and Bruner, 1978; Lock, 1980; Trevarthen, 1979; and contributors to Lock, (ed.) 1978). Studies of the stage at which children are beginning to produce linguistically structured utterances, by contrast, have provided less consistent evidence. This is partly because these studies have often had a polemical aim in the innatist–environmentalist controversy and partly because the attempt to understand the relationship of the adult's speech to the child's learning has tended to look for a unidirectional influence of adult on child. Furthermore, analysis has tended to concentrate on the formal properties of adult speech rather than looking at its functional properties for the language learner.

10.1 Potentially facilitating functions of adult speech

As a prelude to a more detailed examination of some sequences of interaction, let us reconsider the features of adult speech that have so far been investigated. But instead of looking at them in terms of the categories and levels of linguistic description, let us consider them in functional interactional terms, that is to say in terms of the intentions that may be assumed to guide a person's behaviour when they wish to succeed in communicating, particularly if their partner is a less skilled communicator.

There seem to be four broad types of intention that are relevant:

1 to secure and maintain inter-subjectivity of attention;
2 to express one's own meaning intentions in a form that one's partner will find easy to understand;
3 to ensure that one has correctly understood the meaning intentions of one's partner;
4 to provide positive responses in order to sustain the partner's desire to continue the present interaction and to engage in further interactions in the future.

There may also be a fifth intention which applies to some adults in the particular interactional situation that we are considering, namely

5 to instruct one's partner so that he or she may become a more skilled performer.

Evidence for the first of these intentions and of adjustments in adult behaviour designed to realize that intention is to be found in a study carried out by Garnica (1977). She reports that the mothers of two year olds that she observed and subsequently interviewed used generally higher pitch, exaggerated pitch movements and slower pace when talking to their children. They were also aware they were making these adjustments and believed that they were doing so in order to secure and maintain their children's attention. Subsequent studies have confirmed that these features are very prevalent in mothers' speech to children of this age.

Garnica's study was unusual in that she actually asked mothers about their motives. For the remainder of the list of intentions proposed above there is no systematically obtained evidence as to whether adults actually have and are aware of having the intentions specified. However, provided their hypothetical status is recognized, they may still serve a useful purpose in allowing an evaluation to be made of the significance of the speech adjustments that adults have been observed to make.

A number of adjustments have been noted that seem to correspond to the second aim, that of making one's meaning easy to grasp. In addition to the slowing down of rate of speaking already mentioned, these include speaking in 'simple' short, grammatically well-formed sentences; increasing semantic and pragmatic redundancy; producing repetitions and paraphrases. There is also a heightened use of non-verbal signals, such as hand and eye pointing, documented by Bridges (1977; 1979), which accompany many adult utterances. All these features, as well as increasing the probability of successful uptake of the message, provide the child with a particularly clear model of the language in use, thereby facilitating his access to the evidence that he needs in order to construct his own model of the internal organization of the language system and its systematic relationships of reference and illocutionary function to the non-linguistic environment.

Relevant to the third intention, that of ensuring correct interpretation of one's partner's utterances, are such responses as imitations and expansions, often uttered with rising intonation, which invite the listener to agree or disagree with the proposed interpretation. Contingent queries can also be thought of as a sub-type of this general category of responses: they are required when the previous utterance was too unclear or ambiguous for an interpretation to be made. More generally, all utterances which extend the topic or some other aspect of the preceding utterance implicitly inform the listener about the interpretation put upon his previous utterance. From the child's point of view, all these categories of contingent response make explicit to varying degrees the interpretations that have been put upon his own utterances and also provide him with feedback on their perceived relevance and appropriateness in context.

Feedback of a rather different kind is also provided by corrections, although a distinction must be made between corrections that concern the content of the child's utterance, seeking to bring words into line with the world, and corrections that concern the form of the utterance, where the aim is to make the child's speech conform with that of the adult community. Both types of correction, but particularly the latter, would probably be more appropriately included under the intention to instruct.

Strategies which realize the fourth intention, that of sustaining conversation, have been described by a number of researchers. Kaye and Charney (1980) use the term 'turnabouts' to describe conversational turns that both respond to the previous utterance and invite a further response, and Wells *et al.* (1981) describe in some detail the formal properties of utterances that seem designed to achieve this effect. Also likely to facilitate the child's ability and enhance his desire to participate in conversation are more general strategies, such as making reference predominantly to the child's, or even better, to joint activities, encouraging the child to initiate interactions and producing a high proportion of utterances which extend the child's meaning through semantically related questions, statements and explanations.

Although it is the short-term aim of sustaining the current conversation that has been suggested as a probable explanation of the sort of strategies just described, the adoption – or lack of adoption – of these strategies is also likely to have important longer-term consequences, whether intended or not, for the child's general motivation to engage in conversation. Children whose conversational initiatives are habitually responded to in ways that indicate that their topics are of interest and relevance are more likely to be strongly motivated to initiate conversation than those whose initiatives do not receive such contingently appropriate responses. As a result, they elicit more speech from their partners, with all the further learning opportunities that this provides (cf. the correlations reported in chapters 8 and 9 between amount of speech and children's rate of development).

Finally, we have the intention to instruct. Certainly there are specific occasions when adults seem to have quite deliberate didactic intentions. Teaching vocabulary is one very obvious example that we have observed to occur in every child's experience, and display questions in general have been found to be almost equally widespread. More variable in occurrence are elicited imitations and corrections, which, as Brown *et al.* (1969) noted, are much more likely to be concerned with the 'truth' than with the well-formedness of children's utterances. Evaluating the significance for the language learner of these didactic interventions is, however, much more difficult. Most researchers would agree on the value of playing the naming game (Ninio and Bruner, 1978; McShane, 1980) and Nelson makes strong claims for the effectiveness, under experimental conditions, of what he calls 'recasting' children's utterances in a manner which retains the meaning but alters the syntactic form (Nelson, 1977). On the other hand, many parents must have experienced the frustration of the mother, reported by McNeill (1970), whose child, after eight attempts to correct his initial utterance 'Nobody don't like me', finally produced 'Oh! Nobody don't likes me!' There is also the rather different evidence, reported in chapter 8, of the negative correlation between children's language scores at 42 months and the mothers' reports of the extent to which they corrected their children's speech.

Within the interactional framework of development that is being proposed here, however, it is possible to reconcile these conflicting results and at the same time to offer a broader evaluation of the significance of the various types of adjustment that adults make when speaking to young children. Children, it has been argued, follow a developmental sequence in first-language learning which is largely determined by an interaction between certain species-specific endowments relevant to language learning, their current knowledge and information-processing strategies, and the relative complexity of the different aspects of the language to which they are exposed. Order of learning in any particular language is substantially similar across children, but what varies is the ease and speed with which the developmental sequence is traversed. This is partly determined, no doubt, by individual differences in aptitude and in learning style, but it can also be affected by the extent to which the learning task is facilitated by experience of interaction with more mature language users, of whom the most important in terms of frequency of interactional opportunities are the parents and other caretakers.

Since the child requires evidence of how the language works, sheer quantity of conversation should, other things being equal, facilitate his task. This is confirmed by the results reported in table 9.10. But even greater facilitation should occur if, in the conversation he experiences, the utterances addressed to him are easy to process and, in general, reasonably closely matched to his current control of the language system. In practice, this seems to be the case for the vast majority of children. Where a high proportion of utterances also make transparent the relationship between form and meaning intention, as is the case in simple directives in the context of familiar activities, this too will provide valuable evidence for the learner at a certain stage of development.

Deliberate attempts to teach new linguistic forms are more problematic, and are dependent for their success on an appropriate matching of the evidence provided in corrections, in 'recasts' or in other forms of explicit modelling to what are, for the child, the areas of language of current concern to him. This seems to be a good example of what Vygotsky (1962) called 'the zone of proximal development'. If the adult is able to assess very precisely what the child can do today only with help, she may see the results in his unaided behaviour shortly afterwards. However, even if this is correct, the help the adult can give seems to be limited to the provision of particularly unambiguous and relevant evidence. Attempts to impose a form or structure on the child rarely seem to be successful.

For most children, however, such deliberate interventions do not seem to be necessary. Certainly not all children experience them. However, it remains an open question as to whether interventions such as those described by Nelson (1977) would be effective for all children in accelerating development, if they could be introduced in a more spontaneous way, or whether they would counteract other facilitative aspects of adult–child conversations. For, as well as providing evidence on the organization of the language system, adult contributions to conversations can also provide helpful feedback as to how the child's own utterances are interpreted, thus allowing him to assess their effectiveness in communicating his intentions. This is necessary in any conversation but is rarely overt. Listeners' interpretations usually match quite closely the intentions of the speaker, as is apparent in the content of the utterance produced by the listener when he takes his turn to speak. More explicit checking and negotiation of meaning intentions may be of particular value, however, for the language learner. This at least is the interpretation proposed for the significant correlations between measures of progress and frequencies of Imitations and Expansions reported in chapter 9 and by Cross (1977, 1978).

However, of the adjustments that adults make when talking with young children, perhaps the most significant in accounting for variation in rate of language learning is the extent to which they adopt strategies which sustain the child's participation and enhance his motivation to initiate further conversation. This is certainly recognized by lay-people – witness the lapel buttons distributed in some supermarkets recently which bore the appeal 'Talk to me, mum' – but has received little direct attention in the research literature (but see Howe, 1981b). It is difficult to over-emphasize the importance of strategies that increase the child's motivation to converse, since, unless he actually engages in conversation, none of the other potentially facilitating functions of talk with an adult become available to him. This evaluation is confirmed, I would argue, by the strong pattern of correlations, reported in the previous chapter, between a wide range of measures of children's progress in language learning and the proportion of adult utterances which extended the children's meanings.

10.2 Individual differences

The preceding discussion has been couched in very general terms, assuming that all children, and indeed all adults, are the same. This is clearly not the case, although the nature and extent of the differences relevant to first-language learning is very poorly understood at present. One dimension on which children differ is in general learning ability, however that is defined. But it is not clear whether this calls for any concomitant variation in the relative emphasis given to the various functions associated with the intentions attributed to adult speakers. For a small minority, however, psychological and neurological disorders of varying degrees of severity certainly elicit and perhaps require a radical difference in emphasis in the adjustments that their adult interlocutors make. Hearing impairment is one such example. Observations of hearing parents talking to hearing-impaired children show that they tend to be more concerned with modelling and directly teaching language and speech behaviour than with making contingent and interpretative responses (Gregory, 1983). Similar observations have been made of adults talking to mentally handicapped children. The motivation for this sort of adjustment is quite understandable. But in spite of claims for the success of programmes of instruction organized along these lines, it has yet to be demonstrated that, in naturalistic environments, such a strong emphasis on deliberate teaching facilitates the handicapped child's learning more than the more normal balance of the adult functions discussed above, coupled with an increased sensitivity to the child's own meaning intentions (Wood, 1983a, b).

Another dimension on which children may differ is in learning style. Although this has only recently begun to receive attention from researchers concerned with first-language learning (Nelson, 1981), differences among second-language learners on such dimensions as verbal memory, fluency and flexibility, and sensitivity to linguistic patterning and context have been identified. Evidence has been presented of the way in which these differences interact with variations in classroom organization to yield quite marked differences in ease and speed of second-language learning (Wong-Fillmore, 1979). However, with the exception of Nelson's (1973) pioneering study of the early stages of vocabulary learning in the first language, no systematic work has yet been carried out to discover whether children with different learning styles elicit or would benefit from conversational experience which emphasizes some of the functions performed by the input more than others.

10.3 The collaborative construction of meaning

To conclude this discussion of the interactional context of language learning, let us turn to some concrete examples to see how, in particular sequences of talk, adult and child communicative behaviour meshes in ways that facilitate what Lock (1980) aptly calls 'the guided reinvention of language'.

Ideally, perhaps, examples should be found that illustrate each of the proposed facilitating functions of the input one at a time. But in practice they rarely occur neatly separated in time. Parents whose conversational contributions clearly demonstrate one function are likely simultaneously to demonstrate others. Hence, no doubt, the accelerated progress that their children tend to make.

Ex. 1   Gerald (18 months) is looking at a picture book with mother.
Gerald: Lorry.
                    Mother: Lorry – yes
                                  It's a lorry isn't it?

This very simple example provides a good starting point, because it is such a clear case of the compound nature of contingent responses. Gerald produces what his mother takes to be an Ostension and she confirms the appropriateness of his utterance by repeating (Imitating) it, adding Confirmation and then offering an Expansion that also invites him to confirm her expanded interpretation. Simultaneously, of course, her expansion provides him with a model of a full clausal realization of his 'incomplete' utterance.

Because Expansions typically offer well-formed utterances in conversational contexts that allow children to register the discrepancy between their own utterance and the expanded model, many researchers have argued that they have as their primary function that of 'teaching' the child, or at least of deliberately modelling the adult form for him. Certainly, they do perform a modelling function but this is only incidental to their major function, which is that of negotiating an interpretation for the child's utterance. Conversation, to put it aphoristically, provides the means whereby two minds come to have but a single thought, or, to be more precise, come to have parallel thoughts that are, for the purposes of the interaction, functionally equivalent. In the course of most mutually satisfying conversations, a meaning structure is built up over several contributions, each speaker in turn setting his contribution more or less securely on the base constructed up to that point. If he is to make his own contribution fit, the current speaker has to judge the significance of the previous contribution for the structure that is emerging, interpreting the intentions of the previous speaker in selecting and placing it as he did.

For most of the time in conversations between mature speakers this collaborative building process proceeds smoothly, particularly when they can confidently draw on a fund of shared assumptions. This is much less true when one of the participants is still in the early stages of mastering the craft. In early conversations, therefore, there are many occasions when the child's utterance is ambiguous or even indeterminate as a realization of his meaning intention. Before responding, therefore, the adult has to check her interpretation of the intended meaning so that she can make an appropriate response. Many expansions in fact are uttered with rising intonation or with the addition of a tag, thereby explicitly inviting the child to confirm the suggested interpretation.

Interpreting the child's underlying intention on the basis of his overt behaviour is a parental practice that stretches back in the child's experience to a stage long before the acquisition of any form of conventional system of communication, and, in Newson's view, is a necessary condition of becoming a *human* being. The essential continuity of this interpretative practice is brought out if 'utterance' is substituted for 'action' in the following quotation:

> Whenever he is in the presence of another human being, the actions of a baby are not just being automatically reflected back to him in terms of their physical consequences. Instead they are being processed through a subjective filter of human interpretation, according to which, some, *but only some*, of his actions, are judged to have coherence and relevance in human terms – either as movements born of intentions, or as communications (or potential communications) addressed to another socially aware individual: subjectively filtered and then reflected back! It is thus only because mothers impute meaning to 'behaviours' elicited from infants that these eventually do come to constitute meaningful actions so far as the child himself is concerned (1978: 37).

The Expansion we see in example 1, and others like it, is thus an advanced instance of a parental strategy which has a much more profound significance than is suggested by those who interpret expansions as devices for teaching linguistic forms.

Although sequences involving expansions do not always go to full-term (cf. Ex. 1), the function of an expanding utterance is to negotiate the child's meaning intention in order to make an appropriate response. Not surprisingly, therefore, we find many instances of two-move turns in which the adult first offers an interpretative expansion and then follows – sometimes with and sometimes without a pause to allow the child the opportunity to confirm or disconfirm the interpretation – with an appropriate response:

Ex. 2   Gerald (18 months) has found teddy's bed empty.
Gerald: Teddy (calling)
                            Mother: Where's Teddy?
                                            I think Teddy's downstairs
                                            I think we took him downstairs with
                                            us

In this particular case, not only a simple response but one that contains an explanation which also paraphrases and elaborates the original answer. This, I take it, is an example of what Cross (1977) meant by the term 'synergistic sequence'.

The primacy of the interpretative function of Imitations and Expansions is supported by the continuing but much rarer occurrence of similar sequences with older children, whose utterances are completely well-formed. In both the following examples it is not the form which is initially problematic to the mother but some other aspect of the utterance.

Ex. 3   Gerald (30 months) can hear what he thinks to be an ambulance
          outside the window.
Gerald: Can I see the ambulance?

> Mother: Can I see the ambulance?
>   I don't know if it was an
>   ambulance.
>   It was just a big noise.

Ex. 4   Penny (30 months) is having difficulty in getting a pencil to write.
Penny: It won't write Ma (v)

> Mother: Won't it write? ⁓

Penny: No

> Mother: Well find another one

The rise and fall of the expansion is thus a transitional phe-
nomenon in adult–child conversation. The need to negotiate an
interpretation remains, but it is done implicitly by providing a
response which incorporates (some aspect of) the child's meaning in
the next utterance, thereby confirming its appropriateness – 'in
human terms' as Newson puts it – and extends that meaning with
topically related information.

Ex. 5   Gerald (24 months) is climbing in and out of a cardboard box.
Gerald: I am boxing with Teddy
          (= I am getting in the box with Teddy)

> Mother: (laughs)
>   You don't quite fit in – both of you in that little
>   box

By this stage in the child's development, the general force of his
intention is usually apparent, but some of the details may be
unclear. Ambiguity of reference, in particular, frequently causes
difficulty in making a precise interpretation, and so we find various
types of Contingent Query occurring which call for greater specificity of reference. It is in this context that one observes what Brown *et
al.* (1969) called 'occasional questions' and other similar forms.

Ex. 6   Mark (27 months) is talking about a broken toy.
Mark: I want Daddy take it work ⁓ mend it
          (= I want Daddy to take it to work in order to mend it)

> Mother: Daddy did?

Mark: Daddy take it away –
          take it/ə/work ⁓ mend it

> Mother: You'll have to ask him won't you?

Ex. 7   Anne (30 months) is engaging in imaginary play with her father.
          She pretends that her blanket is her elder sister, Bridget.
Anne: I've got Bridget   [she has just been to fetch her blanket]

> Father: Is that Bridget?

Anne: Now I'm going to throw it
       over to you Daddy(v)
                    Father: You're going to what?
Anne: I'm going to throw it   [she throws 'Bridget' to F]
       over to you
Anne: Bridget
                    Father: That Bridget?
Anne: Yeah (dissolves into laughter)
                    Father: I didn't know Bridget looked like that
                    . . .
                    I thought that was your blanket
Anne: No it's not
       It's Bridget

Here again, although the use of 'occasional forms' may draw the child's attention to the relationship between the *wh*- word and the required constituent, this is secondary to the main function of establishing agreement about the child's precise meaning intention in order to make an appropriate response.

In all except the first example quoted so far, the negotiation and resolution of the child's meaning intention has been followed by a relevant contingent response, often incorporating and extending the topic proposed by the child. Simultaneously, of course, the adult responses have modelled well-formed sentences, which provide evidence for the child to develop and modify his working model of the language system.

In selecting these examples, I have chosen to emphasize the negotiatory nature of the conversations and the relevance and semantic and functional relatedness of the adult's extending responses. For I am convinced that these highly motivating functions of the conversational contributions of parents who sensitively adjust their speech to ensure that conversations are mutually rewarding far outweigh in importance the efforts of other parents who make little effort to understand their children's meaning intentions or set much greater store by modelling well-formed utterances and 'correcting' their children's less-than-perfect attempts to communicate with them.

All the children I have quoted from made rapid progress in mastering English and the examples quoted are reasonably representative of their experience of conversational interaction with one or both of their parents. By way of contrast, therefore, it is worth looking at the experience of some of those who made much slower progress. They were not deprived of the evidence contained in short, simple well-formed sentences. Indeed, in some cases the evidence was deliberately imposed upon them. What was lacking was a consistent attempt to understand their meaning intentions and a willingness to make those intentions the basis for further conversation.

Ex. 8   Tony (30 months) is looking at a picture book with his mother.
        Mother: Can you see the sheep?
        See the baby sheep?
        . . .
        Well just in front of the baby sheep is a little tiny mouse
Tony: All gone Mummy(v)
        Mother: Oh God! (quietly)
        What's that?
Tony: Daddy*
Little Mummy(v)
        Mother: Can you see the baby chicken?
Tony: Uh?
        Mother: Can you see a baby chicken?
Tony: Ah!
All gone Mummy(v)
        Mother: You look for the chicken
Tony: There it is (excitedly)
        Mother: There it is
        A daddy chicken and a mummy chicken and a baby chicken

Ex. 9   Thomas (25 months) has seen some biscuits on the living room table.
Thomas: *biscuits
        Mother: Those were got specially 'cos we had visitors at the weekend
        Who came to see Tommy?
        Who came in a car?
Thomas: See Grannie Irene/ə/car
        Mother: Grannie Irene's coming next weekend
        But who came last weekend?
Thomas: Auntie Gail in /ə/ train
        Mother: Auntie Gail's coming
        They're coming on the train yes
Thomas: Colin in /ə/ train
        Mother: Colin – Colin – er – and Anne came in the car didn't they
Thomas: Colin /ə/ Anne
Colin /ə/ Anne
        Mother: Yes
Thomas: Colin /ə/ Anne
Colin /ə/ Anne
        Mother: Colin and Anne came in the train
Thomas: In /ə/ train

Thomas: Auntie train
          Mother: No not Auntie train darling(v)
                   Auntie Gail and Grannie Irene are coming
                   on the train on Friday
Thomas: Auntie Gail in /ə/ train
          Mother: That's right

Whether Thomas finally sorted out in his own mind which relations
travelled by which mode of transport on which weekend we shall
never know. But what we do know is that, in general, this sort of
conversational experience is not typical of that enjoyed by children
who learn their native language with speed and apparent ease.
However not all the slower developers were given such unhelpful
tuition. In some cases, the problem was more one of relative
neglect. Nor, on the other hand, was all tuition unhelpful.

In the final example (pp. 412–13), we return to Mark, with a
somewhat longer extract which perfectly gives the flavour of his
typical conversational experience. It starts with an observation on
his immediate sensory perception, uttered with rising intonation,
which signals to his mother that he is seeking her confirmation of
his perception – or is it of his verbal encoding of that perception?

Mark: 'Ot Mummy(v)?
          Mother: Hot? (checking)
                   [Standing by central heating radiator]
                   Yes that's the radiator
Mark: Been? . . (?=burn)
      Burn?
          Mother: Burn? (checking)
Mark: Yeh
          Mother: Yes you know it'll burn
                   don't you?

Having had his first observation confirmed and extended (with an
opportunity offered to learn an item of vocabulary, though one that
is perhaps still phonologically too complex for him to reproduce, if
not to comprehend and store in memory), he makes a second,
semantically, and no doubt experientially, related observation,
again soliciting his mother's confirmation. And again, having
checked her hearing of his message, she replies with confirmation
and extension.

In setting out a communicational account of language in volume
1 of this series (Wells, 1981) I suggested that all communication
involves a triangular relationship between speaker (I), listener
(you), and the meaning structure (it) that is built up over the course
of a sequence of interaction. The first step in creating the triangle

of communication must always be the establishment of inter-subjectivity of attention, both to each other and, together, to the 'it' that is to be built up through the ensuing interaction.

In this example, Mark's ''Ot Mummy(v)?' successfully combines the first movement outwards towards both of the other points of the triangle. His mother's checking 'Hot?' also seems to respond to both aspects of his initiation, as she looks to him and then to what he is looking at, and confirms that she is attending to him, to his intention to seek confirmation, and to the object–attribute relationship – the 'it' – that he has proposed as the topic for their joint attention. The same concern by both participants to manage both dimensions – the inter-personal and the ideational – also marks the second exchange. By the end of it, they have together constructed quite an elaborate meaning structure,

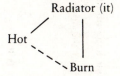

Radiator (it)

Hot

Burn

which mother enunciates in her second extending utterance and reflects back to Mark as a proposition which he knows and, she suggests, he knows that he knows. From such simple conversational exchanges develops not only the child's mastery of language, but also his awareness of language as a mode of knowing and of reflecting and operating upon what is known.

Space does not permit a similar exegesis of each and every exchange in this extract – though almost every one of them is worthy of close attention. Before returning to the topic of heat, however, a comment must be made on the two sequences in Ex. 10 in which the mother misinterpreted Mark's intention.

In both cases, Mark makes an observation on what he can see and invites his mother to share his interest. Since she has not been looking out of the window, she does not have advance knowledge of what he might have observed and so is not able to draw on contextual information to help her interpret his utterance. As in previous exchanges, she reflects back to him her interpretation – in both cases inappropriately – and asks him to confirm. But from this point on, the two sequences take very different routes.

In the first case, Mark acquiesces in her interpretation – or does he perhaps treat her checking expansion as a statement in its own right about another possible topic of interest? In the second, Mark's

Ex. 10 Mark (27 months) is in lounge with his mother.

Mark: 'Ot Mummy(v)?   [Standing by central heating
                                                              radiator]
Mother: Hot?
         Yes that's the radiator

Mark: Been? . . (?=burn)
       Burn?
Mother: Burn?

Mark: Yeh
Mother: Yes you know it'll burn don't you?
                                                         [Putting his hand on radiator]

Mark: Oh
       Ooh
Mother: Take your hand off of it

Mark: Uh?
Mother: What about the other shoe?   [Mother is asking whether he
                                                              needs his other shoelace
         .·   tied]

Mark: /ə/ all done Mummy(v)
Mother: Mm?

Mark: ⟨It⟩ done Mummy(v)
Mother: It's done is it?

Mark: Yeh
Mother: Oh
         . . . . .
         No, leave the curtain
         .·   [Trying to get up to see
                                                              out of the window]

Mark: Oh up please
Mother: Leave the curtain please

Mark: No (refusal)
Mother: Leave the curtain Mark(v)

Mark: No ..
A man
A man er dig . . . down there   [Looking out of window. Sees man digging garden]

Mother: A man walked down there? (checking)

Mark: Yeh

Mother: Oh yes

.. 6 ..

Mark: A man's fire Mummy(v)   [The man has a bonfire going]

Mother: Mm?

Mark: A man's fire

Mother: Mummy's flower? (checking)

Mark: No

Mother: What?

Mark: Mummy(v)
The MAN . FIRE (emphasizing individual words)

Mother: Man's fire? (checking)

Mark: Yeh

Mother: Oh yes the bonfire

Mark: Bonfire (imitating)

Mother: Mm

Mark: Bonfire . . .
"Oh bonfire" . . . (playing with word sound)
"Bonfire"
"Bon"
"A fire bo-bonfire" . . .
It hot Mummy(v)   [Refers to radiator]
Oh hot./ə/hot./ə/hot

Mother: Mm it will burn won't it?

Yeh

Ex. 10a

Mark: A man – er dig – down there

Mother: A man walked down there?

Mark: Yeh

Mother: Oh yes
. .

Mark: Oh yes

. . 6 . .

Mark: A man's fire Mummy(v)

Mother: Mm?

Mark: A man's fire

Mother: Mummy's flower?

Mark: No

Mother: What?

Mark: Mummy(v)
The MAN . FIRE

Mother: Man's fire?

Mark: Yeh

Mother: Oh yes the bonfire

Mark: Bonfire

Mother: Mm

own interest in his observation is sufficient to cause him to reject his mother's proffered interpretation and to reassert his original observation. But what is so interesting about this particular example is that, in order to ensure up-take of his meaning intention, Mark clearly separates the two substantive constituents of his utterance and enunciates them clearly, emphatically and with intonation contours selected for each constituent such that each is treated as a separate piece of information but a relationship between them is also indicated:

/The man/ .fire/

Only when the communicational demands are strong enough does one really discover just how much control over their linguistic resources children actually have!

The fire is actually a bonfire and, in confirming to Mark that she has finally understood what he was interested in, she expands his utterance with the more precise term. In this case, the moment was ripe for the assimilation of new information, and the process is made overt as he repeats the word, trying out its syllabic structure, in a brief episode of word-play, which certainly has no social communicative function.

In the return to 'Oh hot Mummy(v)', it is tempting to see Mark making a connection between the fire and the radiator by virtue of their common property of being hot. In any event, the topic of the hotness of the radiator returns and mother once again confirms and extends his observation.

This whole example lasts almost exactly 90 seconds: a tiny portion of just a single day. But in that short time, how many opportunities the conversational exchanges provide for him to test out, receive feedback on, modify and increase his knowledge of language, of the world and of how to bring them both together in order to communicate with another person!

10.4 Conclusion

If we now return to the question of the relative contribution of child and adult to the process of language learning, it is clear that the answer must be stated in terms of an interaction. Interaction, first, between the child's predisposition to learn to communicate and the model of language provided by those who communicate with him. Interaction, also, in the form of the specific conversations that provide the evidence from which the child learns and feedback on how his own communications are interpreted by others.

In the course of development, each child reconstructs language afresh from the evidence that is made available to him or her. Yet, because of the similarity between children in the resources and strategies they bring to bear on this task, there is considerable uniformity in the sequence in which it is achieved. Nevertheless, to recognize the child's active involvement is not to deny the important contribution of parents and other caretakers. They provide the conversational scaffolding within which this construction takes place. Nor is it to ignore the differences that exist between adults in their ability or willingness to fulfil this role. In the present investigation, all the children studied were experiencing at least the minimum parental support necessary for language learning. On the other hand, there was clearly observable variation in the quality and quantity of the conversational experience that the children enjoyed with adults and this was associated with differences in the ease and speed of their language development. Some parents more than others appeared intuitively to know how to facilitate their children's learning.

Those whose children were most successful were not concerned to give systematic linguistic instruction but rather to ensure that conversations with their children were mutually rewarding. They assumed that, when their child spoke, he or she had something to communicate, so they tried to work out what it was and, whenever possible, to provide a response that was meaningful and relevant to the child and that invited a further contribution. By employing strategies that enabled their children to participate more fully and successfully in conversation, these parents sustained their children's motivation to communicate and this, in turn, increased their opportunities to discover the means for realizing their communicative intentions more effectively.

The facilitation was not all in one direction, however. The children themselves appeared to differ in their willingness to engage in interaction and, at each stage, in the meanings and purposes that they most frequently attempted to communicate. The source of these individual differences is still to be discovered, but they, too, contribute to the forms that particular conversations take and perhaps also to the processes of language learning. Thus, whilst the adult, as the more mature communicator, has the major responsibility for sustaining and extending the child's conversational contributions, this can only be achieved within the parameters set by the child's own individual interests and inclinations. In this sense too, therefore, language learning takes place through interaction.

Appendices

Notes for transcribers on the procedure for contextualizing and transcribing language samples

Contextualization
Play through the tape with the mother, taking one sample period at a time, asking for contextual information. The following information should be obtained:

1 The names and roles of all participants in addition to the child subject.
2 The location(s) of all participants: where they were not all in the same location or there was a change of location during the sample, note this.
3 The activity(s) in which the child was engaged, described as precisely as possible: where this changed within the sample, a note should be made of the precise point at which there was a change of activity.
4 Any other relevant information that would assist the interpretation, for example what had just happened or was going to happen, details about an event under discussion, sickness, etc.
5 Elucidating information for any utterances which are not immediately intelligible: the following are some suggestions as to possible causes of unintelligibility:
   a) where there are two or more adults or two or more children it may be difficult to distinguish the individual voices: try to discover identity of speaker for each such doubtful utterance.
   b) there may be idiosyncratic words and expressions within the family, such as pet names or childish forms: make a note of the meaning of such expressions.
   c) some of the child's utterances may be indistinctly articulated: ask for mother's interpretation. (Note: where your own interpretation of the utterance differs from the mother's,

make a note of both interpretations in the transcription, indicating which is the mother's.)

6 Where a child is told to, or says he is doing, something, note should be made of whether he does so or not.

This information should be noted in such a way that it can be related to the relevant point in the sample when transcribing. Use the nearest clear, unambiguous utterance in the sample to locate the information. These notes should be sufficiently intelligible for a second person to use them when checking the transcription.

Selection of samples for transcription

The recording contains 24 90-second samples. As you play through the tape with the parents you should enter contextual notes on the sheet provided, whether there is speech in the sample or not.

At the top of the contextualization sheets is a row of 24 boxes. In the boxes at the top of the first sheet, put a cross for every sample for which the child was out of range. These samples can be identified by a hissing noise.

In normal cases only 18 samples should be transcribed. These should be selected as follows:

a) If there are 18 or fewer in-range samples, transcribe them all, giving each the code number above its box on the contextualization sheet.

b) If there are more than 18 in-range samples, you should divide the day into six periods so that at least *three in-range* samples occur in each period. The boxes at the top of the contextualization sheet are already divided into six equal periods by heavy lines. Try to make your boundaries between periods as close as possible to these heavy lines (see example below). You will now have some periods of the day containing four in-range samples. One of these four is a spare sample. To decide which to treat as spare toss a coin and use the table below:

	Spare sample
Tails + tails	1st
Tails + heads	2nd
Heads + tails	3rd
Heads + heads	4th

Mark spare samples by putting an *S* in their boxes on the contextualization sheet. You should now be left with 18 samples. Transcribe these, giving each the code number above its box on the contextualization sheet. When you have transcribed these 18, count up the number of child utterances which are not in brackets. We want to get at least 110 of these so, if there are fewer, choose the spare sample which you judge to contain most child utterances and transcribe it. If there are still not enough child utterances, repeat this process and continue repeating it until you have either run out of samples or have enough child utterances. All the spare samples which are transcribed should be given the code number above their box and this number should be preceded by an *S*.

Transcription
The transcription should be as accurate and detailed as possible. Frequently, however, it will be difficult to determine exactly what was said. If no interpretation is possible, the utterance should be indicated as unintelligible. However, an attempt should always be made to give an interpretation. In all cases where there is doubt it is important:

a) to use all the relevant contextual information in arriving at a decision;
b) to indicate which portion of the utterance is in doubt;
c) where there are two or more equally plausible possibilities to include them all and bracket them together.

Because of the limitations of ordinary typewriters, the text will be transcribed in Standard English orthography, but with a special set of conventions about punctuation (see below). Intonation is an important and integral part of speech and will frequently contribute to the decision to adopt one interpretation of an utterance rather than another. There are, however, no standard symbols for intonation, so, where the intonation is thought to be decisive in selecting one interpretation rather than another, a plain language interpretation of the utterance should be included in brackets, e.g. (expressing doubt).

Similarly, the meaning of an utterance may be quite clear although an essential part has been omitted or is inadequately articulated. In this case, an interpretation should be given in brackets following the text of the utterance as it actually occurs, e.g.

   Put em that (= I am putting them like that)

At a certain stage in development a child may produce two clauses in one intonational unit, but with a slight pause where the

Name: ....KATE.........   Recording No.: ....1........   Time at start: 9.15 am

Date of birth: 21/12/71   Date of recording 29/3/73..   Age: 15 months ....

01	02	03	04	05	06	07	08	09	10	11	12	13	14	15	16	17	18	19	20	21	22	23	24
			X	X	X										S							X	

Sample	Participants: Sharon (S), Kate, Mother	Location: Bedroom
No.: 1	Activity: Non-specific/Free play with child	/Change

- -

Ref.: 1   Speech   Behaviour
              pallets = wooden planks   Tidying up stairs
                                                     Kate had fallen and cried: just
                                                        getting better

                                                     Sharon's father works 'over the back'

                                                     Threading up beads

- -

Notes:

Sample	Participants: Kate, Mother, Sharon, Margaret (helper)	
No.: 2		Location: Bedroom
	Activity: Non-specific	Same/

- -

Ref.:   Speech   Behaviour
   18   Kate walking over mats as
                                                        Margaret tries to hoover

                                                     Vacuum cleaner!

- -

Notes:

relating word would occur in adult speech. Such cases should be treated as one utterance with a slur mark over the pause to indicate the continuation of the intonation contour. An interpretation should be given in brackets, e.g.

I wait here ⌢ Nanny comes (= I will wait here until Nanny comes)

Some of a child's utterances, although spoken aloud, are not addressed to another person. Such Speech for Self can usually be identified by a drop in volume, a lack of intonational contrast and a greater tendency to omit the subject Noun Phrase. Such utterances should be enclosed within inverted commas, e.g.

"Won't fall down" (Has put car on nearby table)

The unit to be used in the subsequent analysis is the utterance, so it is important that the transcript should clearly indicate utterance boundaries. Intonation and pausing are a good rough guide but occasionally utterances may be run together in speech. For our purposes, an utterance is defined as 'one independent clause, and any elements dependent on it'. One word, elliptical or incomplete utterances count as independent utterances, e.g.

Yes//In the morning//I thought I'd –

Thus a distinction would be made between

Yes I do (one utterance) and Yes//Shall I do it now? (two utterances)

Appendix 1B

Conventions and layout for transcription

The speech of the child being studied is set out in the left-hand column. The speech of all other participants is set out in the centre column, with identifying initials where necessary. Each new utterance starts on a new line.

Contextual information is enclosed in square brackets [ ] and set out in the right hand column.

Interpretations of utterances and descriptions of intonation where applicable, are enclosed in round brackets ( ) and included immediately after the utterance to which they apply.

Utterances, or parts of utterances, about which there is doubt are enclosed in angular brackets 〈 〉; where two interpretations are possible they are both given, separated by an oblique stroke.

Symbols of the International Phonetic Alphabet are used for utterances, or parts of utterances, which can be clearly heard, but which cannot be interpreted with certainty. Phonetic symbols are always enclosed by oblique strokes. Except where there is doubt about the speaker's intended meaning, the speech is transcribed in Standard English Orthography.

The following is a list of additional symbols used, with an explanation of their significance (stops and commas are not used as in normal punctuation).

?   A question mark is used at end of any utterance where an interrogative meaning is considered to have been intended.

!   An exclamation mark is used at the end of an utterance considered to have exclamatory intention.

'   Apostrophe: used as normal for contractions and elision of syllables.

CAPS Capitals are used where part of an utterance receives unusually heavy stress to convey emphasis or contrastive meaning.

*   Asterisks are used to indicate unintelligibility, for whatever reason. The number of asterisks corresponds as nearly as possible to the number of words judged to have been uttered.

...   Stops are used to indicate pauses. One stop is used for a very short pause. Thereafter, the number of stops used corresponds to the estimated length of the pause in seconds.

..8.. Pauses over 5 seconds in length are shown with the figure for the length of the pause.

_____ Underlining. Where utterances overlap because both speakers speak at once, the overlapping portions are underlined.

"   " Inverted commas are used to enclose utterances considered to be 'speech for self'.

⌢   A slur mark indicates unbroken intonation contour where a pause or clause boundary might otherwise indicate the end of an utterance.

–   A hyphen indicates a hiatus, either because the utterance is incomplete or because the speaker makes a fresh start at the word or utterance.

(v)   Used to indicate that the preceding word was used as a vocative, to call or hold the attention of the addressee.

Appendix 1C

Examples of transcription: the methodological experiment (chapter 1)

Version A was produced by the observer, Version B by the transcriber, who obtained contextual information later in the day, as described in chapter 1. Note: neither version was checked by another person, as the point of the experiment was to see how great the agreement would be between the two versions. Normally, however, each transcript would have been checked by an independent listener. Had this happened in the case of the two versions that follow, it is probable that the amount of disagreement between the two versions would have been considerably reduced.

Version A

Robert	D of B: 8.10.76	D of R: 7.3.79

Location: Kitchen (floor)
Participants: Robert and mother.

- -

		[Robert has complained of feeling tired. Mother suggests looking at car book together. Robert is finding toy cars which match up to the ones in the book]
	Mother: What's this?	[Mother holds up toy racing car]
Robert: Racing car		
	Mother: Good * * * * 'Cos it's just like that one isn't it?	[Places it next to car in book]
Robert: I could have one of those		
	Mother: Does it look like that? Look You put it to one side . .	
	Mother: It looks the same doesn't it?	
Robert: That's not the same as that racing car	Mother: Yes Look the lights on the front And the bar Like that It's called a ⟨St-⟩ (type of sports car)	[Mother compares features of model and picture. Points to each in turn]
Robert: There's the lights		[Robert points to lights in picture]
	Mother: Lights	[Mother corrects Robert's

[slight Bristol pronunciation of 'lights'. Has done this in earlier unrecorded conversations]

Mother: And is there a wheel on the back?
. . .
Yes

Robert: There the wheel
[Robert points to wheel on boot of car]

Mother: Yes and a hood

Robert: Yeah

Mother: And seats

Robert: (Who) the hood?

Mother: That's the hood
That bit there
[Points to it]

Robert: There's a hood
[Robert points to it]

Mother: Um
Right
. .
Look at all those cars
[Mother turns page and points to picture]

Mother: That's a factory where men make cars
Called?
What are they called?
[Mother waits for reply]

Robert: Minis

Mother: Minis
All day long

Robert: There's a Mini
[Robert points to one]

Mother: Lots and lots of Minis
Look that's how they start off
[Points to picture of production line]

Robert: There's a man
[Points to man]

Mother: Um um
. . .
[Turns over page to picture of Switzerland]

That's Switzerland

Robert: Jenny get * *

Mother: Jenny?

Robert: Yes

Mother: When?

Robert: * *
There's a Mini

Mother: Um
A Mini driving in Switzerland
(Yes) and

	In Switzerland the cows have bells round their necks Do you know why?	
Robert: Yes		
	Mother: (laughing) 'Cos their horns don't work!	[Robert does not laugh]
	...	
	Mother: Is that funny?	[Robert picks up car]
Robert: Brum! brum! (car noise)		

Version B

Robert.   D of B: 8.10.76   D of R: 7.3.79

Location: Kitchen
Participants: Robert and mother
Activity: Looking at pictures in a library book about cars with mother, and comparing his toy cars with pictures in the book.

— —

		[Robert is asking where one of his toy cars is]
	Mother: What's this?	[Mother points to picture in book]
Robert: Racing car		
	Mother: * * * * * just like that one isn't it?	
Robert: I could have one of those ⟨Can I –⟩	Mother: Does it look like that?	[Robert is holding a toy car Mother is asking if Robert's car looks like the one in book]
	Look if you put it along-side – It looks the same doesn't it?	
Robert: That looks same . a d-dat racing car (= That looks the same as that racing car)		
	Mother: Yes Look lights on	

	the front and a bar – like that It's called a Stutz	
Robert: Dere de loights (= There are the lights)		
	Mother: Lights (Mother is correcting Robert's pronunciation) And is there a wheel on the back?	
Robert: Sss		
	Mother: Yes (Mother answering her own question for Robert's benefit)	
Robert: Dere's a wheel (= There's a wheel)		
	Mother: Yes And a hood	
Robert: Ye'		
	Mother: And seats	
Robert: Where's the hood?		
	Mother: That's the hood That bit there	
Robert: Dere's the hood		
	Mm (agreeing) Right	
	Look at all those cars	[Mother points to another picture]
	Mother: That's the factory where men – men make cars	
	Mother: Called – What are they called?	
Robert: Minis		
	Mother: Minis (repeating after Robert in agreement) All day long	
Robert: Dere de Mini (= There's the Mini)		[Robert points to picture]

	Mother:	Lots and lots of Minis
		Look that's how they start off [Mother pointing to picture]
Robert: They open them	Mother:	Mm mm (in agreement)
		.. [Mother turns page of book]
	Mother:	That's Switzerland!
		.
Robert: Jenny ge-ge' me jam (= Jenny got me jam)		[A friend called Jenny brought him some jam from Switzerland]
	Mother:	Jenny? [Mother doesn't remember]
Robert: Ye' (= Yes)		
	Mother:	When?
(No response)		[Changes subject and points to picture again]
Robert: Dere's a – dere's a Mini		
	Mother:	Mm (in agreement)
		The Mini driving in Switzerland
		Look and there's Switzerland – The cows have bells round their necks
		.
		Do you know why?
Robert: Ye' (= Yes)		
	Mother:	(laughs) 'Cos their horns don't work! (laughs at her joke) That funny?
(No response)		
Robert: Broom broom (car noise)		

Appendix 2

Frequencies of linguistic items in the speech of 15 to 60-month-old children

The tables in this appendix correspond to the successive sub-sections of chapter 6. Each table presents the frequencies of the items in a particular linguistic system as they change with increasing age over the period studied: 15 to 60 months. A common base-line is adopted throughout: frequencies are expressed per 1000 utterances. Values are given to the nearest whole number, except that frequencies of less than 1 per 1000 are excluded.

Relative frequencies of items within systems can be calculated by expressing the observed frequency of a particular item as a proportion of the total frequency per 1000 utterances of the system as a whole. Note, however, that the summed frequencies of items within a system may not exactly equal the total frequency given for that system at a given age. This is because frequencies of less than 1 per 1000 are not included in the tables. In addition, not all the items that belong to a particular system are included in the tables: very rarely occurring items are omitted, as are the various one-word response categories in the systems of Inter-Personal Function.

Table A1 *Frequency per 1000 utterances × age: Inter-Personal Function: Control*

Function	Age in months															
	15	18	21	24	27	30	33	36	39	42	45	48	51	54	57	60
Wanting	40	67	92	88	65	66	63	57	41	40	36	32	30	28	21	23
Direct request	10	24	28	44	61	60	67	73	63	66	66	71	67	71	80	65
Prohibition	2	5	9	13	14	9	15	15	13	11	10	12	15	13	12	11
Intend	2	4	5	9	15	23	25	25	32	29	24	29	29	32	36	36
Request permission	—	1	3	2	6	7	11	16	13	15	11	14	16	17	16	17
Suggestion	—	—	—	1	3	7	3	3	7	8	11	7	8	11	6	7
Physical justification	—	—	—	2	3	7	3	3	4	5	5	6	7	7	5	9
Offer	—	—	—	2	2	2	3	6	6	4	5	5	8	7	5	7
Query want	—	2	—	1	1	4	3	4	6	4	6	5	4	3	3	3
Indirect request	—	—	—	—	2	4	4	8	3	3	3	4	7	7	3	5
Query evaluate intention	—	—	—	1	—	3	5	5	5	6	4	8	10	5	8	7
Query intention	—	—	—	—	2	3	3	4	4	3	4	3	3	4	4	6
Request justification	—	—	—	—	1	1	3	—	2	3	3	3	2	4	4	4
Psychological justification	—	—	—	—	—	—	1	3	3	2	3	3	4	5	4	5
Social justification	—	—	—	—	—	1	1	2	2	4	2	3	2	2	2	3
Warning	—	—	—	—	—	—	—	2	1	3	2	3	2	4	2	3
Moral justification	—	—	—	—	—	—	—	—	1	1	—	2	1	1	—	1
Formulation	—	—	—	—	—	—	2	1	3	5	5	4	2	4	5	1
Permit	—	—	—	—	—	—	—	—	1	2	2	3	2	2	2	2
Threat	—	—	—	—	—	—	—	2	2	2	2	3	3	2	2	2
Promise	—	—	—	—	—	—	—	—	1	1	—	1	1	—	1	4
Contractual	—	—	—	—	—	—	—	—	—	—	—	—	—	—	—	1
Total Control	123	211	217	253	266	291	284	318	284	299	264	263	271	290	279	272

Table A2 *Frequency per 1000 utterances × age: Inter-Personal Functions: Expressive*

Function	Age in months															
	15	18	21	24	27	30	33	36	39	42	45	48	51	54	57	60
Exclamation	147	121	67	71	62	51	48	45	37	36	33	35	35	38	41	39
Express state	6	8	20	16	23	17	27	20	32	30	33	32	23	36	26	27
Query state	0	1	1	1	0	2	3	3	5	3	3	3	5	6	4	4
Cajole	0	0	2	2	3	3	2	2	2	1	7	2	2	3	4	2
Challenge	0	0	1	0	0	1	1	0	2	3	4	4	5	3	4	1
Taunt	0	0	1	0	0	1	1	1	3	3	4	4	3	3	2	3
Tale-tell	0	0	0	2	0	1	1	1	2	2	2	3	2	2	4	3
Disapproval	0	0	1	0	1	1	1	0	1	1	1	2	1	1	3	2
Approval	0	0	0	0	0	0	0	0	1	1	1	2	0	1	1	1
Blame	0	0	0	1	0	1	2	1	1	1	3	1	0	1	1	1
Apologize	0	0	1	0	1	2	2	1	1	0	1	0	1	0	2	1
Verbal accomp.	11	6	9	6	15	9	17	13	10	6	9	17	14	16	7	12
Total Expressive	188	152	116	116	127	107	124	99	111	102	125	120	106	125	110	108

Table A3 *Frequency per 1000 utterances × age: Inter-Personal Functions: Representational*

Function	Age in months															
	15	18	21	24	27	30	33	36	39	42	45	48	51	54	57	60
Ostension	147	162	195	143	95	109	84	63	56	44	49	44	37	48	49	44
Statement	15	35	39	70	122	123	124	141	159	159	171	171	202	173	193	187
Content question	7	6	8	15	21	24	39	31	35	32	30	29	30	34	26	25
Content response	7	10	11	15	14	14	7	11	13	10	15	17	14	12	12	11
Name question	24	1	9	3	4	9	4	5	4	3	3	3	2	6	3	4
Yes/No question	2	1	3	10	12	16	17	28	28	28	39	36	36	34	38	38
Request explanation	—	—	—	—	—	1	3	6	6	8	8	10	6	8	8	5
Physical explanation	—	—	—	—	—	1	1	2	6	8	8	6	5	6	4	6
Social justification	—	—	—	—	—	—	—	—	1	3	5	1	—	2	4	1
Moral justification	—	—	—	—	—	—	—	—	—	1	—	—	1	2	—	—
Psychological justification	—	—	—	—	—	—	—	—	1	1	1	2	1	1	2	1
Total Representational	236	250	303	293	323	350	325	427	359	345	381	375	382	369	376	376

Table A4 *Frequency per 1000 utterances × age: Inter-Personal Functions: Procedural and Tutorial*

	Age in months 15	18	21	24	27	30	33	36	39	42	45	48	51	54	57	60
Function																
Procedural																
Call	141	138	116	108	68	53	50	50	45	44	52	53	54	47	58	45
C.Q. Repetition	4	10	8	20	20	17	15	15	21	21	21	17	12	15	16	16
Elicited Repetition	4	7	9	16	11	14	12	17	12	12	13	10	12	10	8	9
Check	—	1	2	2	2	3	3	2	5	4	4	5	3	4	3	3
Availability Response	4	—	2	2	2	2	2	1	5	2	4	3	2	2	3	2
Elicited Identification	—	1	1	3	2	3	4	3	3	3	3	2	3	2	3	3
C.Q. Identification	—	1	—	—	1	1	1	1	2	5	1	2	2	2	4	4
New Topic Marker	—	—	—	1	—	—	—	—	1	1	1	1	1	2	3	2
Total Procedural	160	175	172	185	149	129	119	115	114	117	128	127	121	110	120	104
Tutorial																
Imitation of Model	29	16	19	16	7	8	4	2	3	6	4	1	1	4	3	6
Supply Required Form	7	4	4	2	3	4	1	2	3	3	2	—	1	1	—	—
Display Response	4	11	16	13	5	4	4	2	3	2	1	—	3	1	2	1
Total Tutorial	42	36	45	36	18	21	19	8	13	16	12	4	10	11	8	11

Table A5 *Frequency per 1000 utterances × age: Locative, Possessive and Temporal meaning relations*

Meaning relation	Age in months															
	15	18	21	24	27	30	33	36	39	42	45	48	51	54	57	60
Locative																
Static Location	20	27	38	46	47	57	51	53	57	68	62	72	60	65	64	59
Coref. Ch. Loc.	8	23	28	31	44	54	62	65	58	64	63	73	73	72	75	59
Agent Ch. Loc.	5	16	18	52	48	57	68	69	81	75	74	71	87	89	69	88
Agent Act on Target	1	4	3	6	9	8	8	10	13	15	13	14	15	15	14	12
Coref. Movement	1	—	—	2	3	6	8	5	8	6	4	7	5	8	9	8
Agent C. Movement	—	1	—	1	1	2	7	3	4	4	4	5	2	4	5	4
Coref. Direct Mov.	—	—	—	2	1	2	2	4	1	3	2	3	3	3	3	3
Ag. Act target Cause Dir. Move.	—	—	—	—	—	—	1	1	2	2	2	2	3	2	2	1
Instrument Ch. Loc.	—	—	—	—	1	1	1	1	—	1	—	—	1	1	—	1
Locative + Embed. Cl.	—	—	—	—	—	—	1	2	2	3	4	4	3	6	3	3
Ag. Cause Direct Mov.	—	—	—	—	—	1	—	2	2	—	1	3	—	2	2	2
Total Locative MRs	36	71	88	141	156	188	210	219	230	241	232	256	255	271	251	246
Possessive																
Static Possession	2	2	10	17	25	28	36	33	38	43	38	48	38	32	33	40
(Ag.) Ch. Possession	1	1	3	10	17	21	23	39	30	34	32	35	43	39	40	42
Benefactive	—	—	—	—	1	1	3	1	5	5	3	2	7	4	3	4
Total Possessive MRs	3	4	14	28	42	49	61	73	74	83	74	85	88	75	76	87
Temporal	—	—	—	1	2	—	1	4	2	2	2	3	3	4	5	4

Table A6 *Frequency per 1000 utterances × age: Experiential meaning relations*

Meaning relation	Age in months															
	15	18	21	24	27	30	33	36	39	42	45	48	51	54	57	60
Want Experience	2	6	20	28	25	36	33	42	29	30	33	21	23	23	19	17
Agentive Cogn. Exper.	3	7	12	17	31	28	32	40	39	40	40	48	48	43	55	49
Want Exper. + Embed. Clause	—	1	3	9	10	18	26	24	20	22	19	20	21	20	19	18
Cognitive Experience	—	2	2	4	11	9	9	14	15	17	23	16	15	20	19	18
Affective Experience	1	2	2	2	9	7	10	9	13	11	13	10	12	7	11	10
Cogn. Exper. + Embed. Clause	—	—	—	1	3	6	7	9	15	18	22	27	30	31	30	38
Physical Experience	1	1	1	4	4	5	6	6	5	6	7	5	5	7	6	5
Change Phys. Exper.	—	—	1	2	3	3	5	7	4	6	3	4	3	8	6	6
Affect. Exper. + Embed. Clause	—	—	—	—	—	—	—	1	1	1	2	—	1	2	2	3
Change Affect. Exper.	—	—	—	—	—	1	—	—	—	—	2	2	—	1	2	1
Total Experiential MRs	7	20	42	67	99	113	128	154	142	153	163	155	160	163	168	165

Table A7 *Frequency per 1000 utterances × age: Attributive meaning relations*

	Age in months															
	15	18	21	24	27	30	33	36	39	42	45	48	51	54	57	60
Meaning relation																
Classification	36	14	27	45	35	50	51	54	54	46	62	53	42	47	50	51
Evaluative Attrib.	8	4	8	9	11	8	15	12	18	16	18	22	21	25	17	22
Change Phys. Attrib.	—	2	5	12	17	19	30	26	33	32	33	43	43	44	37	36
Physical Attribution	1	5	8	15	18	19	14	18	21	19	22	14	22	20	29	21
Change Exist. Attrib.	—	—	—	3	3	9	8	7	9	11	13	10	11	8	13	12
Quantit. Attrib.	—	—	2	1	3	1	—	2	5	5	3	4	2	5	3	7
Existence Attrib.	—	—	—	—	—	—	1	1	1	1	1	2	2	2	1	2
Phys. Attrib. + Emb. Cl.	—	—	—	—	—	—	—	1	—	1	1	—	1	1	1	—
Total Attributive MRs	45	25	51	86	87	108	119	121	143	132	154	149	145	153	154	154

Table A8 *Frequency per 1000 utterances × age: Function meaning relations*

Meaning relation	Age in months															
	15	18	21	24	27	30	33	36	39	42	45	48	51	54	57	60
Agent Act (unspec.)	4	7	8	9	15	20	27	26	27	21	25	33	29	31	27	29
Agent Function	3	7	9	10	10	16	14	15	17	19	15	19	17	19	20	19
Ag. Func. on Patient	1	—	3	3	7	9	9	17	18	17	19	16	20	20	20	21
Patient Function	1	2	—	1	5	6	11	9	9	12	13	9	10	11	11	8
Ag. Cause + Embed. Cl.	—	—	—	1	1	1	2	3	5	10	4	7	6	8	7	8
Ag. Cause Pat. Function	—	—	—	—	2	1	3	1	3	2	2	3	5	5	5	3
Ag. Func. over Range	—	—	—	—	1	4	4	5	3	4	3	5	8	6	5	11
Purposive	—	—	—	—	1	—	—	2	1	1	—	1	1	2	4	2
Total Function MRs	9	16	20	27	40	58	72	79	85	87	83	95	98	103	104	103

Table A9 *Frequency per 1000 utterances × age: Time*

Time category	Age in months															
	15	18	21	24	27	30	33	36	39	42	45	48	51	54	57	60
Past Simple	2	5	9	22	27	38	44	56	59	63	77	79	75	81	82	94
Future Simple	—	2	1	5	8	15	16	26	27	27	28	35	33	36	39	35
Point Neutral	—	1	2	4	8	12	14	16	22	23	27	25	22	28	22	17
Point Past	—	—	1	1	1	1	1	2	3	3	3	5	4	4	6	3
Point Future	—	—	—	—	1	1	1	3	5	2	3	3	4	6	5	3
Relative Neutral	—	—	—	1	1	1	3	4	3	2	3	3	3	4	3	3
Relative Past	—	—	—	—	—	—	—	—	1	2	—	3	1	2	1	3
Relative Future	—	—	—	—	1	1	3	2	2	2	2	3	2	3	3	3
Time up to	—	—	—	—	1	1	1	1	1	1	1	2	2	4	2	3
During	—	—	—	—	1	—	1	1	1	1	1	—	1	2	—	—
Extent	—	—	—	—	—	—	—	—	—	2	—	2	—	—	4	3
Frequency	—	—	—	—	—	—	—	1	1	1	1	2	1	1	3	2
Time from	—	—	—	—	—	—	—	1	1	—	—	—	—	1	1	—
Total Time Choices	390	435	547	578	586	642	689	720	746	759	755	783	797	809	804	813

Table A10 *Frequency per 1000 clauses × age: Aspect*

Aspect category	Age in months															
	15	18	21	24	27	30	33	36	39	42	45	48	51	54	57	60
Continuous	—	1	8	11	17	27	32	35	28	35	38	36	38	41	37	35
Perfect	—	3	5	15	14	13	15	15	19	17	15	14	13	15	25	16
Cessive	—	—	2	1	2	1	2	3	3	3	2	2	3	3	3	5
Completive	—	—	—	1	4	4	4	4	4	4	4	3	3	4	5	3
Habitual	—	—	—	1	—	1	1	1	2	1	2	2	3	6	3	4
Inceptive	—	—	—	—	—	—	—	—	1	—	1	—	2	2	1	2
Iterative	—	—	—	—	—	—	—	—	1	1	1	1	1	1	1	—
Durative	—	—	—	—	—	—	—	—	1	—	1	—	—	2	2	2
Total Aspect Choices	390	435	547	578	586	642	689	720	746	759	755	783	797	809	804	813

Table A11 *Frequency per 1000 utterances × age: Modal and Modulation*

	Age in months															
	15	18	21	24	27	30	33	36	39	42	45	48	51	54	57	60
Modulation																
Ability	—	1	2	3	5	13	19	19	25	24	20	25	29	36	26	25
Permission	—	—	2	2	6	8	12	21	22	24	20	25	24	26	22	28
Willing	—	—	—	1	3	6	11	20	14	19	13	12	14	18	23	31
Try	—	—	1	—	1	1	1	1	2	3	2	4	2	3	6	3
Obligation	—	—	—	—	1	3	3	3	3	6	8	9	12	12	9	8
Necessity	—	—	—	—	1	2	4	5	8	8	7	8	9	9	11	13
Modal																
Possible	—	—	1	—	2	2	2	4	4	4	4	3	5	6	6	4
Certain	—	—	—	—	—	—	1	—	—	1	1	1	1	1	—	2
Inferential	—	—	—	—	—	1	—	—	—	1	—	—	1	1	1	1
Total Modality	—	1	5	7	19	34	52	73	81	90	76	87	97	112	104	116

Table A12 *Frequency per 1000 utterances × age: Noun-Phrase Headword*

	Age in months															
	15	18	21	24	27	30	33	36	39	42	45	48	51	54	57	60
Headword																
Noun	248	249	348	331	306	336	322	336	343	344	348	365	375	375	361	357
Adverb	26	31	41	65	52	67	86	81	101	106	109	116	107	117	112	106
Demonstrative Pronoun	42	19	24	30	41	56	81	81	83	78	79	75	76	82	75	82
Personal Pronoun	17	34	53	97	165	257	328	374	428	458	474	482	495	523	511	528
Interrogative Pronoun	25	6	15	19	24	34	46	47	48	49	42	44	40	53	41	41
Modifier	5	11	25	35	38	33	28	42	27	43	53	51	52	59	62	55
Possessive Pronoun	3	2	13	20	17	14	20	16	14	14	13	13	16	12	15	16
Indefinite Pronoun	3	2	6	12	20	20	33	35	37	47	43	41	47	39	40	45
Comparative/Superlative	—	—	1	3	6	3	2	2	3	5	5	8	7	9	5	4
Relative Pronoun	—	—	—	—	1	1	2	2	5	6	7	11	12	13	17	16
Total Headwords	368	356	522	605	664	823	940	1012	1105	1140	1158	1198	1212	1273	1229	1237

Table A13 *Frequency per 1000 utterances × age: Nominal Modification*

Modification	Age in months															
	15	18	21	24	27	30	33	36	39	42	45	48	51	54	57	60
Possessive	4	3	21	28	42	63	65	70	63	67	66	67	62	73	63	59
Quantitative	7	2	8	17	20	16	20	32	31	37	42	49	41	44	44	53
Physical Attrib.	—	2	11	12	10	15	19	15	20	24	31	28	39	30	24	26
Evaluative Attrib.	3	1	1	3	1	2	2	5	4	4	6	6	3	6	6	5
Equivalence	1	—	1	6	6	4	9	9	9	10	7	11	8	12	14	10
Instrumental	—	1	3	3	3	2	4	3	6	9	6	6	2	8	4	7
Locative	—	1	1	1	2	1	2	2	3	3	5	5	3	5	2	4
Substance	—	—	1	2	2	2	1	2	2	2	3	2	4	2	3	3
Temporal	—	—	—	—	—	1	1	3	—	1	5	2	1	—	2	1
Ordinal	—	—	—	—	—	—	—	—	1	1	1	1	1	—	1	—
Comparative/Superlative	1	5	3	3	2	2	2	3	2	2	2	2	3	5	2	2
Total Modification	15	8	46	72	89	108	123	143	139	158	175	179	167	183	164	171

Table A14 *Frequency per 1000 utterances × age: Nominal Group Qualifier*

	Age in months															
	15	18	21	24	27	30	33	36	39	42	45	48	51	54	57	60
Simple																
Locative	—	1	1	1	1	1	2	2	3	3	3	4	2	4	2	3
Quantitative	—	—	—	—	1	1	3	4	4	3	5	3	2	4	4	6
Other Adjectival	—	—	—	3	—	—	1	—	1	1	2	1	2	—	2	—
Complex																
Defining	—	—	—	6	3	5	3	5	9	11	12	16	12	13	15	15
Apposition	—	—	—	—	—	1	1	1	1	—	1	1	1	1	2	2
Comparative	—	—	—	—	—	—	—	1	—	1	—	1	1	1	2	2
Condition	—	—	—	—	—	—	—	1	—	1	1	1	1	—	—	—
Total Qualifiers	—	1	1	10	5	8	11	17	19	22	27	29	21	25	28	30

Table A15 *Frequency per 1000 utterances × age: Pronouns*

	Age in months															
	15	18	21	24	27	30	33	36	39	42	45	48	51	54	57	60
Pronouns																
Personal																
I	4	12	17	35	73	111	144	162	163	183	174	179	179	189	180	192
Me	4	8	9	15	12	24	28	25	31	30	27	26	26	28	32	27
You	—	3	3	11	16	33	44	62	72	78	84	83	96	101	99	97
It	3	7	17	25	45	53	68	89	91	90	99	102	102	102	100	115
He	3	1	3	3	4	11	14	20	20	22	26	28	25	24	25	23
Him	—	1	—	—	1	1	4	5	4	7	4	4	6	10	8	6
She	—	—	—	2	3	5	4	6	7	8	11	9	12	14	10	17
Her	—	—	—	—	2	1	1	2	3	3	3	4	5	3	5	4
We	—	—	—	—	3	7	5	8	13	18	17	19	18	22	20	20
Us	—	—	—	—	—	1	—	1	1	1	1	1	2	2	2	2
They	—	—	3	1	4	6	6	8	10	9	17	16	14	15	16	12
Them	—	—	—	1	3	3	6	7	10	8	10	9	10	11	12	11
Demonstrative																
This	40	3	3	2	6	12	16	18	17	17	22	18	20	23	20	23
That	—	16	21	25	32	40	54	54	58	52	50	50	46	50	45	51
These	—	—	—	2	—	2	2	4	4	4	3	3	6	4	5	3
Those	—	—	—	1	3	3	3	4	2	3	3	2	4	3	2	3
Possessive																
Mine	3	2	10	11	11	6	9	8	8	10	4	7	8	5	9	9
Yours	—	—	1	—	1	2	3	2	2	2	1	1	3	2	2	2

Table A15 (cont'd)

	Age in months															
	15	18	21	24	27	30	33	36	39	42	45	48	51	54	57	60
Indefinite																
One	2	—	5	11	18	16	28	30	27	36	32	33	31	29	26	33
Some	—	—	1	—	2	3	2	3	3	3	3	2	4	2	3	3
Any	—	—	—	—	—	1	1	1	—	1	—	—	—	1	—	—
Some/anything	—	—	—	—	—	1	1	1	3	3	3	4	5	3	5	5
Someone/body	—	—	—	—	1	—	—	—	1	2	—	1	2	1	1	1
Nothing	—	—	—	—	1	—	2	1	1	1	2	1	3	1	2	2
Nobody	—	—	—	—	—	—	—	—	1	—	1	1	1	—	1	1
Interrogative																
What?	24	2	9	9	9	18	23	25	23	20	17	16	13	19	16	15
Who?	—	—	2	2	1	2	6	2	3	3	3	3	2	3	—	3
Where?	1	4	3	8	11	12	12	9	12	12	12	12	13	12	10	8
When?	—	—	—	—	—	—	—	—	1	1	1	1	1	2	1	1
Relative																
What	—	—	—	—	1	1	2	1	2	4	5	5	6	6	7	10
Where	—	—	—	—	—	—	1	1	1	1	—	1	2	4	2	1
Total Pronouns	85	59	107	165	262	275	488	559	593	632	639	641	665	691	668	710

Table A16 *Frequency per 1000 utterances × age: Noun Phrase Structures*

	Age in months															
	15	18	21	24	27	30	33	36	39	42	45	48	51	54	57	60
Noun sing.	112	116	161	118	92	81	54	40	39	27	31	30	30	21	26	22
Adverb	7	21	34	41	40	56	62	58	71	76	81	88	77	91	82	78
Personal Pronoun	16	34	53	96	163	256	320	390	418	447	464	472	483	507	495	511
Demonstrative Pronoun	42	19	24	30	41	56	79	80	81	77	77	74	76	81	72	76
Indef. Art. + Nsing.	7	11	20	23	25	36	35	39	43	38	36	45	37	40	36	40
Prep. + Adverb	19	10	7	22	11	13	20	20	26	23	22	22	24	21	22	21
Npl.	6	16	20	20	16	15	15	17	11	13	17	15	18	14	17	15
Noun non-count	7	9	28	35	20	19	19	18	15	16	15	15	15	13	16	18
Adjective	5	11	21	22	34	33	23	33	40	34	42	40	39	47	51	43
Prep. + Nsing.	—	—	3	13	15	25	25	34	35	34	42	49	50	48	50	48
Def. Art. + Nsing.	—	1	4	10	14	18	23	30	35	40	35	41	42	39	43	42
Poss. Adj. + Nsing.	3	1	9	12	24	35	38	40	35	36	35	34	32	39	39	33
Prep. + Det. + Head	—	—	3	8	14	25	33	40	43	45	44	50	49	52	56	48
Dem. Adj. + Nsing.	—	—	1	4	4	10	9	18	13	17	18	20	19	21	20	17
Noun's + Nsing.	—	—	5	4	7	4	5	2	4	3	3	3	3	3	4	2
Poss. Adj. + Npl.	—	—	1	2	4	9	11	11	10	10	9	10	12	10	7	9
Indef. Art. + Mod. + Head	—	—	1	2	4	9	10	9	15	17	14	18	18	21	12	15
Head + Qual. (phrase)	—	—	—	4	1	2	2	2	2	4	4	4	4	2	6	5

Table A16 (cont'd)

	Age in months															
	15	18	21	24	27	30	33	36	39	42	45	48	51	54	57	60
Def. Art. + Npl.	—	—	—	1	2	3	4	4	7	5	4	7	7	11	8	8
Def. Art. + Mod. + Head	—	—	—	2	1	1	2	4	6	10	11	10	9	9	10	9
Head + Qual. (word)	—	—	—	3	1	1	5	5	5	5	8	5	4	5	6	6
Def. Art. + N.non-count	—	1	—	1	1	2	4	6	5	4	5	4	6	9	6	4
Det. + Head + Qual. (phrase)	—	—	—	1	1	2	1	2	3	3	3	5	4	4	5	5
Dem. Adj. + Mod. + Head	—	—	—	—	—	1	1	—	3	3	5	3	3	4	5	3
Prep. + Det. + Mod. + Head	—	—	—	1	1	2	3	2	3	5	5	6	5	6	5	5
Head + Qual. (defin.cl.)	—	—	1	1	—	1	—	1	2	1	1	4	2	2	2	2
Interrog. Adj. + Head	—	—	—	—	1	1	1	1	1	3	3	4	3	4	5	2
Det. + Head + Qual. (defin.cl.)	—	—	—	—	—	—	—	1	1	2	4	3	3	3	3	3
Det. + Mod. + Mod. + Head	—	—	—	—	—	—	—	1	1	2	2	2	3	3	2	2
Det. + Mod. + Mod. + Head	—	—	—	—	1	1	—	—	1	2	2	2	3	3	2	2
Prep. + Det. + Head + Qual.	—	—	—	—	—	—	—	—	1	1	1	2	—	2	2	3
Det. + Mod. + Head + Qual.	—	—	—	—	—	—	—	—	1	1	2	2	1	3	2	1

Table A17 *Frequency per 1000 utterances × age: Mood*

Mood options	Age in months															
	15	18	21	24	27	30	33	36	39	42	45	48	51	54	57	60
Declarative	16	55	74	135	192	262	299	319	333	355	359	359	370	367	359	371
Imperative	35	33	42	61	80	77	90	91	92	92	97	94	96	97	103	85
Wh-Interrogative	27	5	13	18	20	30	43	37	40	67	38	33	31	39	31	35
Polar Interrogative	4	1	3	5	11	22	28	42	47	45	51	58	58	59	57	54
Polar Interrog. (Inton.)	—	4	2	2	6	8	12	16	15	10	11	8	9	9	7	14
Declarative + Tag	—	—	1	1	1	3	7	8	10	12	16	18	17	19	16	14
Tag Alone	—	—	—	—	1	1	2	1	5	2	2	4	3	2	5	4

Table A18 *Frequency per 1000 utterances × age: Declarative structures*

Sentence/clause structure	Age in months															
	15	18	21	24	27	30	33	36	39	42	45	48	51	54	57	60
Declarative																
One Constituent	291	326	385	282	206	160	115	73	83	67	67	71	65	66	52	58
Two Constituents (no V)																
V + O/A	6	10	17	24	22	24	17	12	11	9	12	11	11	12	5	6
S + V	5	5	10	14	21	17	12	9	8	8	10	8	9	8	6	4
S + V + O	2	3	4	6	10	9	7	6	7	7	9	5	7	11	7	7
S + cop + C	1	2	8	15	18	27	27	28	26	25	23	19	20	18	17	17
A + cop + S or A + S + cop	2	2	3	13	14	23	28	33	31	29	31	31	27	27	24	31
S + cop + IC	1	4	2	7	5	7	6	6	9	10	8	8	7	7	6	6
S + V + A	1	1	2	6	11	11	13	14	12	14	15	13	17	12	17	12
S + aux + V	—	2	3	6	6	11	7	8	10	9	7	9	10	9	8	15
S + aux + V + O/A	—	—	1	4	6	9	6	11	6	7	9	7	6	7	8	6
S + V + ⟨non-finite⟩	—	—	2	5	6	16	18	20	20	22	27	29	32	26	26	27
S + V + O + A	—	—	1	3	4	10	12	13	11	12	12	7	11	10	10	11
S + cop + A	—	—	—	1	4	7	6	10	12	15	14	8	11	13	12	10
S + cop + C + A	—	—	—	2	5	6	6	5	6	8	6	8	7	7	9	6
S + aux + V + O + A	—	—	—	—	3	4	6	6	8	8	7	13	10	8	8	8
S + aux + neg +	—	1	—	1	3	7	11	10	11	14	17	16	16	19	19	17
V/cop + X	—	—	—	—	5	8	11	13	15	15	15	16	14	13	11	13

Structure														
S + aux + cop + X	11	8	9	8	8	7	8	6	7	8	3	3	2	—	—
S + V + ⟨finite⟩	9	8	6	8	7	5	4	5	4	4	3	1	1	—	—
S + aux + aux + V + X	6	11	10	7	6	6	7	6	6	6	2	1	1	—	—
S + aux + neg + V	3	3	3	2	2	2	2	2	4	4	3	1	1	—	—
Main Clause + Tag	10	13	16	17	16	16	11	8	6	6	3	1	—	2	—
S + cop + neg + X	1	6	4	6	2	6	4	4	4	3	2	1	1	—	2
Main Clause + Sub. Clause	6	5	8	6	7	6	5	4	3	1	1	—	—	—	—
S + aux + neg + V + O + A	3	4	4	4	3	4	4	3	4	1	—	—	—	—	—
S + (aux) + V + IO + O	2	1	3	3	2	2	2	1	2	1	1	—	—	—	—
S + aux + V + V + ⟨finite⟩	3	4	3	5	3	3	2	2	1	2	1	—	—	—	—
Any Relative Clause	2	2	2	6	3	3	2	—	1	—	—	—	—	—	—
Any Three Clause Declarative	6	5	6	3	5	4	2	1	—	1	—	—	—	—	—
Main Clause + Main Clause	5	3	1	2	2	2	2	2	1	2	2	—	—	—	—
S + cop + ⟨finite⟩	2	2	2	1	1	1	1	—	—	—	—	—	—	—	—
S + aux + neg + V + (X)	1	2	2	1	1	—	—	—	—	—	—	—	—	—	—

Table A19 *Frequency per 1000 utterances × age: Interrogative structures*

Clause/sentence structure	Age in months															
	15	18	21	24	27	30	33	36	39	42	45	48	51	54	57	60
Interrogative																
What + cop + S	—	—	10	7	9	2	17	13	11	10	9	9	4	9	8	10
Where + cop + S	—	1	2	4	5	6	7	6	7	8	8	7	6	8	6	5
Aux + S + V + X	—	—	—	1	3	7	11	15	14	16	12	17	18	21	18	17
Wh- + aux + S + V	—	—	—	2	2	2	4	4	4	4	4	4	4	4	3	4
Aux + S + V + O + A	—	—	—	—	1	3	4	3	6	7	6	10	9	10	8	9
Cop + S + X	—	—	—	—	—	2	3	5	4	3	7	7	3	4	5	5
Aux + S + V	—	—	—	—	—	1	1	4	2	2	2	1	3	1	1	2
Aux + S + V + ⟨⟩	—	—	—	—	—	—	—	2	1	2	3	4	5	4	4	5
Wh- + aux + S + V + X	—	—	—	—	—	—	—	1	2	2	2	2	3	3	2	4
Why Interrogative	—	—	—	—	—	—	—	3	1	3	1	4	2	4	4	3
Polar Interrog. + Sub/Main Cl.	—	—	—	—	—	—	—	—	1	1	2	1	1	2	1	1
Aux + S + aux + V + X	—	—	—	—	—	—	—	2	1	1	1	2	1	3	2	2
Who + V + (X)	—	—	—	—	—	—	—	1	—	1	1	1	1	1	1	1
Who + aux + V + (X)	—	—	—	—	—	—	—	1	—	1	1	1	1	1	—	1
Cop + S + X + X	—	—	—	—	—	—	—	1	—	—	2	—	1	1	—	1
Wh- + aux + S + V + (X)	—	—	—	—	—	—	—	—	—	1	1	1	—	1	1	1
Aux + neg + S + V + (X)	—	—	—	—	—	—	—	—	—	—	1	—	1	1	—	1

Appendix 3

Tables of features and weightings used in calculating item complexity values (chapter 9).

Table A1 *Features and weightings used in calculating relative complexity of auxiliary verbs*

	Modal (1)	Non-present (1)	Complex form (1)	Potential (0)	Constraint (1)	Performative (2)	Total
do	−	−	−				0
be (V-ing)	−	−	+				1
have (V-en)	−	+	+				2
have got	−	−	+				1
can	+	−	−	+	−	−	1
will	+	+	−	+	−	−	2
be going to	+	+	+	+	−	−	3
have got to	+	−	+	−	+	−	3
shall	+	+	−	−	−	+	4

Table A2 *Features and weightings used in calculating relative complexity of pronouns*

	Personal Pron. (0)	Demonst. Pron. (0)	Interrog. Pron. (1)	Indef. Pron. (1)	Relative Pron. (4)	Non-Deictic (1)	+ Discourse (1)	+ Addressee (1)	Third Party (1)	Animate Ref. Only (1)	+ Gender (2)	+ Plural (2)	+ Object case (1)	Prox./Dist. (1)	Total
that	−	+	−	−	−	−	−	−	+	−	−	−	−	+	2
I	+	−	−	−	−	−	+	−	−	−	−	−	−	−	1
it	+	−	−	−	−	+	−	−	+	−	−	−	−	−	2
me	+	−	−	−	−	−	+	−	−	−	−	−	+	−	2
you	+	−	−	−	−	−	+	+	−	+	−	−	−	−	3
what?	−	−	+	−	−	+	−	−	+	−	−	−	−	−	3
one	−	−	−	+	−	−	−	−	+	−	−	−	−	−	2
this	−	+	−	−	−	−	−	−	+	−	−	−	−	+	2
he	+	−	−	−	−	−	−	−	+	+	+	−	−	−	4
we	+	−	−	−	−	−	+	−	−	−	−	+	−	−	3
they	+	−	−	−	−	−	−	−	+	+	−	+	−	−	4
them	+	−	−	−	−	−	−	−	+	−	−	+	+	−	4
she	+	−	−	−	−	−	−	−	+	+	+	−	−	−	4
who?	−	−	+	−	−	+	−	−	+	+	−	−	+	−	5
him	+	−	−	−	−	−	−	−	+	−	+	−	+	−	4
these	−	+	−	−	−	−	−	−	+	−	−	+	−	+	4
those	−	+	−	−	−	−	−	−	+	−	−	+	−	+	4
what (rel.)	−	−	−	−	+	+	−	−	+	−	−	−	−	−	6

Table A3 *Features and weightings used in calculating relative complexity of sentence meaning relations*

	Location (1)	Attribution (1)	Experience (2)	Function (3)	+ Movement (1)	+ Target (1)	+ Possession (1)	+ Benefactive (2)	+ Evaluative (1)	+ Quantity (3)	+ Existence (2)	+ Inan. Obj. Function (1)	No. of Nec. Partic.	+ Embed. Clause (1)	+ Coref. Agent/Patient (−1)	Total
Operator + Nominal	−	−	−	−	−	−	−	−	−	−	−	−	1	−	−	1
Static Location	+	−	−	−	−	−	−	−	−	−	−	−	2	−	−	3
Coref. Change Location	+	−	−	−	−	−	−	−	−	−	−	−	3	−	+	3
Agent Change Location	+	−	−	−	−	−	−	−	−	−	−	−	3	−	−	4
Classification	−	+	−	−	−	−	−	−	−	−	−	−	2	−	−	3
Wanting Experience	−	−	+	−	−	−	−	−	−	−	−	−	2	−	−	4
Static Possession	+	−	−	−	−	−	+	−	−	−	−	−	2	−	−	4
Agentive Cogn. Exper.	−	−	+	−	−	−	−	−	−	−	−	−	3	−	+	4
Agent Change Phys. Attrib.	−	+	−	−	−	−	−	−	−	−	−	−	3	−	−	4
Static Phys. Attrib.	−	+	−	−	−	−	−	−	−	−	−	−	2	−	−	3
Agent Change Possess.	+	−	−	−	−	−	+	−	−	−	−	−	3	−	−	5
Agent Function	−	−	−	+	−	−	−	−	−	−	−	−	1	−	−	4
Want Exper. + Embed. Cl.	−	−	+	−	−	−	−	−	−	−	−	−	3	+	+	5

Table A3 (cont'd)

	Location (1)	Attribution (1)	Experience (2)	Function (3)	+ Movement (1)	+ Target (1)	+ Possession (1)	+ Benefactive (2)	+ Evaluative (1)	+ Quantity (3)	+ Existence (2)	+ Inan. Obj. Function (1)	No. of Nec. Partic.	+ Embed. Clause (1)	+ Coref. Agent/Patient (−1)	Total
Evaluative Attrib.	−	+	−	−	−	−	−	−	+	−	−	−	2	−	−	4
Ag. Function on Patient	−	−	−	+	−	−	−	−	−	−	−	−	2	−	−	5
Cognitive Experience	−	−	+	−	−	−	−	−	−	−	−	−	2	−	−	4
Agent Act on Target	+	−	−	−	−	+	−	−	−	−	−	−	2	−	−	4
Affective Experience	−	−	+	−	−	−	−	−	−	−	−	−	2	−	−	4
Physical Experience	−	−	+	−	−	−	−	−	−	−	−	−	2	−	−	4
Coref. Movement	+	−	−	−	+	−	−	−	−	−	−	−	3	−	+	4
Patient Function	−	−	−	+	−	−	−	−	−	−	−	+	1	−	−	5
Cogn. Exper. + Emb. Cl.	−	−	+	−	−	−	−	−	−	−	−	−	5	+	−	8
Agent Change Exist.	−	+	−	−	−	−	−	−	−	−	+	−	2	−	−	5
Agent Cause + Emb. Cl.	−	−	+	−	−	−	−	−	−	−	−	−	4	+	−	7
Quantit. Attrib.	−	+	−	−	−	−	−	−	−	+	−	−	2	−	−	6
Benefactive Relation	+	−	−	−	−	−	+	+	−	−	−	−	2	−	−	6

Table A4 *Features and weightings used in calculating relative complexity of inter-personal functions*

	Attract Attention (0)	Expressive (1)	Directive (1)	Representative (2)	Text Contingent (3)	Hearer Benefit (1)	Specif. of Actor (1)	Discretion to Hearer (1)	Constraint on Hearer (1)	Proposition (1)	Interrogative (1)	Dependent. Inform. (3)	Total
Wanting	−	−	+	−	−	−	−	−	−	−	−	−	1
Ostension	−	−	+	−	−	−	−	−	−	−	−	−	1
Exclamation	−	+	−	−	−	−	−	−	−	−	−	−	1
Call	+	−	−	−	−	−	−	−	−	−	−	−	0
Direct Request	−	−	+	−	−	−	+	−	−	+	−	−	3
Statement	−	−	−	+	−	−	−	−	−	+	−	−	3
Question (content)	−	−	−	+	−	−	−	−	−	+	+	−	4
Express State	−	+	−	+	−	−	−	−	−	+	−	−	4
C.Q. Repetition	−	−	−	−	+	−	−	−	−	−	−	−	3
State Intention	−	−	−	+	−	−	+	−	−	+	−	−	4
Question (Yes/No)	−	−	−	+	−	−	−	−	−	+	+	−	4
Request Permission	−	−	+	−	−	−	+	+	−	+	+	−	5
Indirect Request	−	−	+	−	−	−	+	+	−	+	+	−	5
Suggestion	−	−	+	−	−	+	+	+	−	+	+	−	6
Offer	−	−	+	−	−	+	−	+	−	+	+	−	5
Physical Justif.	−	−	−	+	−	−	−	−	−	+	−	+	6
Formulation	−	−	+	+	−	−	+	+	+	+	−	−	7
Request Justif.	−	−	−	+	−	−	−	−	−	+	+	+	7
Question (state)	−	+	−	+	−	−	−	−	−	+	+	−	5
C.Q. Clarification	−	−	−	−	+	−	−	−	−	+	+	+	8

Notes

1 Setting up the research

   1 In the event, this proved to be an unduly pessimistic prediction. At the end of the period of data collection, 125 of the 140 children who had been recorded at least once were still left in the sample. And, as mentioned in the Introduction, ten years later the 32 children selected for the follow-up study are still all willingly participating. With hindsight, therefore, it is clear that we should have selected more children at the younger age only and followed them over the full four-year period, recording more speech on each occasion. At the time, however, we took what was probably the wisest decision.

2 Describing child speech in its conversational context

   1 To emphasize the importance that we attributed to the influence of the conversational context on the function and form of individual contributions, the coding manual was entitled *Coding Manual for the Description of Child Speech in its Conversational Context*.
   2 All page references are to the 1975 (revised) edition of the *Coding Manual*.
   3 The term Target was intended to capture the transitive nature of this locative relationship. This was the major departure from the Berkeley/Bristol agreed coding scheme.

4 The sequence of emergence of certain semantic and pragmatic systems

   1 References in this form to bodily functions in the contexts of 'eating' and 'toilet' are extremely common in our data, particularly among the younger children.
   2 The description of the relationship of functions to the sequential organization of conversation has been radically revised since the construction of the taxonomy found in the *Coding Manual* (cf. Wells *et al.*, 1979; 1981). However, in the present context, it is the original taxonomy which forms the basis of the analysis of sequence of emergence.

5 The sequence of emergence: syntax and its relationship with other levels of analysis

   1 Initially, *Particle* and *Adjunct* were treated as separate constituents. However, as the distinction itself is not always an easy one to draw, and as strings in which the two constituents were alternatives tended to be co-emergent the two categories were finally combined in the constituent henceforth labelled *Adjunct*.
   2 The choice of the term 'level' is not entirely capricious. 'Stage' carries with it the suggestion of a logically necessary sequence of discontinuous states. The evidence from the present investigation does not warrant such a claim. Further-more, by choosing a different term, we hope to avoid the assumption that might

be made that our scale is simply a filling out of the Stages I to V proposed by Brown *et al.* (1969) on the basis of MLU bands.

6 The pattern of development over time

1 The Mount Gravatt frequencies are for lexical items only, and are based on cross-sectional rather than on longitudinal sampling.
2 Throughout this section, curves have been smoothed in order to render the figures more readable. Data points are, of course, less neatly distributed. They can be reconstructed from the frequency data in the relevant tables in Appendix 2.
3 As Garvey (1977) and Homewood (1983) have pointed out, such contingent queries do not always occur in the context of a breakdown in communication. Adults quite frequently also use contingent queries to evade requests or to express surprise, and some children routinely use them in the early stages as a way of acknowledging a previous utterance.
4 It should be made clear that the category Temporal relation is restricted to clauses in which a specification of time occurs as the predicate, that is, as an obligatory participant (e.g. 'It's tea-time'). Where an utterance contains an optional specification of time (e.g. 'We got back before it began to rain') this is accounted for in the Time system. If this specification is realized by a full clause, as in the above example, this clause is treated as being embedded within the meaning relation which it qualifies. Thus the example above would be coded as Locative + Embedded clause. Reference to figure 6.11 and table A5 shows that by five years of age 88% of the sample are producing locative meaning relations that contain embedded clauses, including temporal qualification, and that such utterances occur with a frequency of three per 1000 utterances.
5 The unexpectedly high proportion at 15 months should probably be disregarded. The majority of tokens are instances of quantitative attribution contributed by just three children, and are probably unanalysed expressions.
6 Brown and Hanlon (1970) also discuss the relationship between order of emergence and frequency, and reach similar conclusions. The appearance at a certain point and subsequent (relatively) frequent use of an item that had previously not occurred in the speech of that child or of any other child at a comparable stage of development can only reasonably be interpreted in terms of the entry of that item into the child's productive system at about that time.

7 The children and their families

1 For the older children, this took place at about the time of the second observation; for the younger children it took place at the time of the last observation, although in the case of a small number of children it was several months later.
2 In acknowledging the help gratefully received, we must exonerate them from any responsibility for the final form of the interview schedule.
3 Not all questions were answered in full. The number of mothers responding to specific questions thus varied between 114 and 123. In reporting the results, proportions are based on the number of mothers actually answering the item in question.
4 This may slightly under-estimate the amount of change. Except at the times of formal interviews, we did not ask questions about such private matters. It should be added, however, that at least two children were withdrawn from the original sample of 140 (128 + reserves) following a break-up of the family.
5 In this respect the sample is probably atypical. Those mothers who continued to work may have refused to participate or their children may have been excluded because they attended a day-nursery or other form of child-care throughout the

day. However there were two or three children whose mothers were working again by the time the study started but who had made arrangements for their children to be cared for at home.

6 For some activities, percentages do not sum to 100. This is because the mothers did not always make a response, usually because the activity did not occur for the child in question.

7 A somewhat longer list was used in the SRU schedule; the results are as yet unpublished (Bernstein and Young, 1967).

8 The original intention was for the mothers to rank the two sanctions they would be most likely to apply and to indicate which one they would be least likely to apply. In practice, most gave yes/no answers, unranked, for all of the alternatives. As both types of response occurred, it is only possible to say which two types of sanction were most used and which least.

9 This schedule was first used by the SRU and the results are reported in Bernstein and Young (1967). In their schedule, the six reasons had to be ranked 1–6.

10 Considering that many of the mothers responding to this question had children of both sexes and that the question was posed in general terms, these differences are rather surprising. It can only be assumed that, in selecting their reasons, many mothers were thinking about a particular child.

11 In the SRU version of the schedule, mothers were asked 'What do you mean by "badly"?' *after* the schedule had been completed. In the light of the wealth of information obtained, it was decided not to proceed with the analysis of the answers previously given (Bernstein, pers. comm.).

12 Henderson found that item 5, 'to find out what other people think of me' was answered negatively. It was therefore dropped from the subsequent analysis.

13 Unfortunately, in classifying the alternatives, Henderson changed the definition of the contrast between (c) and (d) to *explicit* v *implicit* – which is not the same as *highly specific* v *less specific*. In the present study, however, the results are not affected by this change.

14 For this and subsequent analyses, where comparisons are made between 'middle' and 'working' class groups, 'middle class' = class A and class B and 'working class' = class C and class D. The number of parents in occupations in the power structure was so small that they were omitted from the analyses to be reported.

15 The number of parents in occupations in the power structure was so small that they were omitted from the analyses to be reported.

16 In calculating positional scores, Holland and Bernstein gave a score of zero on items where the mother refused to choose one of the two alternative statements. This would have the effect of slightly depressing mean scores in all groups.

17 Despite the differences just reported within the two social classes with respect to mothers' responses in the interview, none of the comparisons between groups, where the groups are defined in terms of Holland and Bernstein's categorization of occupations, were systematically associated with differences in the children's rate of language development.

8 Variation in language development

1 A particularly striking feature of the speech of many of the children in this context is the use of the past tense. It is tempting to see this as marking the imaginary or hypothetical status of these descriptions in the 'pretend' mode.

2 In order to facilitate scoring, the number of items at each level above level III was equalized to 16. This involved one or two minor adjustments to the version of the scale presented in chapter 5, as follows:
Level IV The sentence meaning relation *Physical Attribution* was added.
Level V The Modality category *Permission* was omitted.
Level VI The Function category *Suggestion* was omitted and the following categories transferred from level VII: Clause Syntax: *Cop* + *S* + *X*, *Wh* + *aux*

+ *S* + *V*; NP syntax; ·*Dem. Adj.* + *Mod.* + *Head* or *Def. Art.* + *Mod.* + *Head*;
Modality; *Obligation* or *Necessity*.

Level VII In addition to the items transferred to level VI, the NP Syntax category
Det + *Head* + *Def. Phrase* was omitted.

Level VIII The following categories were omitted: Sentence Syntax *Any Relative
Clause* and Time *Extent*.

No changes were made to levels IX and X.

It must be emphasized that this method of scoring was adopted on a trial basis
for the present investigation and weightings assigned in such a way as to
discriminate between children of the same age but at different levels. It should
not be treated as the definitive scoring system. This will only be arrived at after
extensive clinical application.

3 The programs used for all the statistical analyses reported in this chapter were
those contained in the Statistical Package for the Social Sciences (SPSS).

4 The second explanation is particularly relevant in attempting to account for the
considerably higher correlation found between EPVT and family background
($r = 0.45$, $p < 0.01$) than between family background and any of the indices of
language production. It was certainly our impression that children from the
lower part of the family background range were more likely to be ill at ease in
the test setting.

5 Not all items had emerged in the speech of all children. In calculating median
MLU, however, this fact was ignored and it was assumed that $N = 60$ for all
items at levels I–VI and $N = 65$ for items at levels VII–VIII.

6 As non-emerging items in the data from individual children contribute no
information with respect to MLU at point of emergence, the percentage of
children having an MLU in each band was calculated for each item on only those
children for whom the item had emerged by the last observation.

7 A further qualification must be made with respect to these distributions. Since
those at levels VII and VIII were calculated on the older cohort, there is a strong
probability that they are discontinuous with those at levels I–VI. Since very few
of the children in the older cohort were at a lower MLU band than band III at the
time of the first observation, there was no possibility for these children to register
an MLU value of less than band III, even though the actual emergence of some of
the items at levels VII and VIII may have occurred at an earlier age and,
therefore, probably at a lower level of MLU than that recorded at the first
observation. It is likely, therefore, that the distribution across MLU bands for
levels VI and VII under-represents the actual spread.

8 The mean of the two occasions was taken as this was considered to provide a
more reliable estimate of amount of speech than the value obtained from a single
occasion.

9 Similar results emerged from an inspection of scatter diagrams for the individual
indices of language production described earlier in the chapter.

10 The reported simple correlations with Weighted Scale Score in the regression
analysis tables are slightly different from those reported in table 8.8. This is due
to a difference in *N*. Not all mothers gave an answer to the question about
correcting children's speech, so all these cases were omitted from the regression
analyses. For these only, therefore, $N = 119$.

9 The role of the input in language development

1 This operation was carried out at a time when we were unable to perform
analyses using the computer for the reasons explained in the Introduction.

2 Frequencies of pronouns were tabulated by Sally Davis from the input to 32 only
of the younger children as part of an investigation carried out for the degree of
M.Ed. (Davis, 1980). We are grateful for her assistance in carrying out this
work.

3 Lyons (personal communication) has pointed out that in the case of both these pairs of pronouns, the earlier to be acquired is the unmarked member of the pair. However, in Lyons (1977) he makes an important distinction between pairs of items that are formally marked, for example, 'host' v. 'hostess', and those that are only distributionally marked, for example, 'long' v. 'short', and goes on to argue that distributional marking correlates with, and in many cases can be plausibly explained as being determined by, semantic marking (p. 307). Now it is true that 'he' is semantically marked with respect to 'she', given that 'he' can correspond to the generic use of 'man', for example, 'Man believes he is the only animal to have a language in the true sense of the term', but it is highly unlikely that young children hear 'he' used in this generic way and so it is doubtful whether 'he' is semantically marked at that point in development. The same sort of arguments can, I think, be advanced in the case of the marked status of 'that'. If this is so, the only marking that is relevant to the earlier emergence of 'he' and 'that' is distributional as far as the child is concerned and that is precisely what is accounted for by input frequency. It is perhaps of interest that, for a number of children in the study, 'he' (or ' 'e') is heard in what appears to be free variation with 'it', for example, 'Shut the door. You've left 'e open'.

4 It must be remembered that the age at which particular items emerge in the speech of individual children ranges from several months before to several months after the median age. The related change in frequency in the pooled input to all the children (figures 9.1 and 9.2) can thus be expected to show a continuous rather than an abrupt increase.

5 These two new variables were substituted for the original Syntactic Complexity variable and Number of Lexical Verbs per Utterance was also deleted from subsequent analyses.

References and citation index

Adlam, D. S. (ed.) (1977) *Code in Context*. London: Routledge and Kegan Paul. **310**

Adlam, D. S. and Turner, G. (1977) Code in context. In Adlam, D. S. (ed.), *Code in Context*. **310**

Anderson, J. M. (1971) *The Grammar of Case*. Cambridge: Cambridge University Press. **59**

Atkinson, R. M. (1979) Prerequisites for reference. In Ochs, E. and Schieffelin, B. B. (eds.), *Developmental Pragmatics*. New York: Academic Press. **364**

Atkinson, R. M. (1982) *Explanations in the Study of Child Language Development*. Cambridge: Cambridge University Press. **146**

Austin, J. L. (1962) *How to do Things with Words*. Oxford: Oxford University Press. **59, 64**

Bakker-Rennes, H. and Hoefnagel-Hohle, M. (1974) Situatie verschillen in taalgebruik (Situation differences in language use). Unpublished Master's thesis, University of Amsterdam. Summarized in Snow, C. (1977). **322**

Barnes, S. B., Gutfreund, M., Satterly, D. J. and Wells, C. G. (1983) Characteristics of adult speech which predict children's language development. *Journal of Child Language, 10:* 65–84. **383, 386, 387, 393**

Bart, W. M. and Krus, D. J. (1973) An ordering-theoretic method to determine hierarchies among items. *Educational and Psychological Measurements, 33:* 291–300. **138, 139, 140**

Bates, E., Camaioni, L. and Volterra, V. (1975) The acquisition of performatives prior to speech. *Merrill–Palmer Quarterly, 21* (3): 205–26. **180**

Bates, E., Benigni, L., Bretherton, I., Camaioni, L. and Volterra, V. (1976) From gesture to the first word: on cognitive and social prerequisites. In Lewis, M. and Rosenblum, L. (eds.), *Origins of Behaviour: Communication and Language*. New York: Wiley. **3**

Berger, P. L. and Luckmann, T. (1967) *The Social Construction of Reality*. Harmondsworth: Penguin. **294**

Bernstein, B. (1971) *Class, Codes and Control*, vol. I. London: Routledge and Kegan Paul. **20, 310**

Bernstein, B. and Young (1967) Social class of differences in conceptions of the users of toys. *Sociology, 1:* 131–40. **458**

Bever, T. G. (1970) The cognitive basis for linguistic structures. In J. R. Hayes (ed.), *Cognition and the Development of Language*. New York: Wiley. **39**

Bloom, Lois, M. (1970) *Language Development: Form and Function in Emerging Grammars*. Cambridge, Mass.: M.I.T. Press. **88**

Bloom, L. (1974) Talking, understanding, thinking. In Schiefelbusch, R. L. and Lloyd, L. L. (eds.), *Language Perspectives – Acquisition, Retardation and Intervention*. Baltimore: University Park Press. **127**

Bloom, L., Capatides, J. B. and Tackeff, J. (1981) Further remarks on interpretive analysis: in response to Christine Howe. *Journal of Child Language, 8:* 403–11. **89**

Bloom, L., Lightbown, P. and Hood, L. (1975) *Structure and Variation in Child Language*. Monographs of the Society for Research In Child Development Monographs, 40, 1. Chicago: University of Chicago Press. **334**

Blount, B. G. (1977) Ethnography and caretaker–child interaction. In Snow, C. E. and Ferguson, C. (eds.), *Talking to Children: Language Input and Acquisition*. Cambridge: Cambridge University Press. **57**

Bowerman, M. (1982) Reorganizational processes in language development. In Wanner, E. and Gleitman, L. R. (eds.), *Language Acquisition: the State of the Art*. **396**

Brandis, W. and Henderson, D. (1970) *Social Class, Language and Communication*. London: Routledge and Kegan Paul. **21, 293, 307, 348**

Bretherton, I., McNew, S., Snyder, L. and Bates, E. (1983) Individual differences at 20 months: analytic and holistic strategies in language acquisition. *Journal of Child Language, 10:* 293–320. **335**

Bridges, Allayne (1977) The role of context and linguistic cues in language comprehension of pre-school children. Unpublished Ph.D. thesis, Bristol University, School of Education. **39, 399**

Bridges, A. (1979) Directing two-year-old's attention; some clues to understanding. *Journal of Child Language, 6:* 211–26. **39, 341, 399**

Bridges, A. (1980) SVO comprehension strategies reconsidered: the evidence of individual patterns of response. *Journal of Child Language, 7:* 89–104. **39, 341**

Bridges, A., Sinha, C. and Walkerdine, V. (1981) The development of comprehension. In Wells, C. G., *Learning through Interaction*. **39**

Brimer, M. A. and Dunn, L. (1963) English Picture Vocabulary Test. Windsor: NFER. **40, 331**

Brown, R. (1968) The development of WH questions in child speech. *Journal of Verbal Learning and Verbal Behaviour, 7:* 279–90. **198**

Brown, R. (1973) *A First Language: the Early Stages*. London: G. Allen and Unwin. **2, 56, 57, 88, 93, 120, 121, 122, 130, 147, 150, 193, 209, 336, 357, 360**

Brown, R. (1977) Introduction to 'Talking to Children'. In Snow, C. E. and

Ferguson, C. (eds.), *Talking to Children: Language Input and Acquisition*. Cambridge: Cambridge University Press. 378

Brown, R., Cazden, C. and Bellugi, U. (1969) The child's grammar from I to III. In Hill, J. P. (ed.), *The 1967 Minnesota Symposium on Child Psychology, vol. 2*. Minneapolis: University Minn. Press. **2, 20, 59, 120, 201, 302, 401, 407, 456**

Brown, R. and Hanlon, C. (1970) Derivational complexity and order of acquisition in child speech. In Brown, R. (ed.), *Psycholinguistics*. New York: Free Press. **2, 174, 219, 266, 354, 457**

Bruner, J. S. (1975) The ontogenesis of speech acts. *Journal of Child Language, 2, 1:* 1–20. **392**

Bruner, J. S., Roy, C. and Ratner, N. (1982) The beginnings of request. In Nelson, K. E. (ed.), *Children's Language, vol. 3*. Hillsdale, N.J.: Lawrence Erlbaum. **398**

Carter, A. (1974) The development of communication in the sensori-motor period: a case study. Unpublished Ph.D. dissertation, University of California, Berkeley. **180**

Carter, A. (1979) Pre-speech meaning relations: an outline of one infant's sensori-motor morpheme development. In Fletcher, P. and Garman, M. (eds.), *Language Acquisition*. Cambridge: Cambridge University Press. **3, 209**

Chafe, W. L. (1970) *Meaning and the Structure of Language*. Chicago: University of Chicago Press. **59, 69**

Cherry, Louise, J. (1975) Sex differences in child speech: McCarthy revisited. Research Bulletin. Educational Testing Service, Princetown, New Jersey. **345**

Cherry, L. J. and Lewis, M. (1976) Mothers and two-year-olds: a study of sex-differentiated aspects of verbal interaction. *Developmental Psychology, 12:* 278–82. **345**

Chomsky, N. A. (1964) Discussion of Miller and Ervin's paper. In Bellugi, U. and Brown, R. (eds.), *The Acquisition of Language*. Monographs of the Society for Research in Child Development, 29, no. 1. **37, 382**

Chomsky, N. A. (1965) *Aspects of the Theory of Syntax*. Cambridge, Mass.: M.I.T. Press. **19, 58, 165**

Chomsky, N. A. (1976) *Reflections on Language*. London: Temple Smith. **354, 396**

Clark, H. H. and Haviland, S. E. (1977) Comprehension and the given-new contract. In Freedle, R. O. (ed.), *Discourse Production and Comprehension*. Norwood, N.J.: Ablex. **164**

Clark, Ruth (1974) Performing without competence. *Journal of Child Language, 1:* 1–10. **334**

Cromer, R. F. (1974) The development of language and cognition: the cognition hypothesis. In Foss, B. M. (ed.), *New Perspectives in Child Development*. Harmondsworth: Penguin. **377**

Cromer, R. F. (1979) The strengths of the weak form of the cognition hypothesis for language acquisition. In Lee, V. (ed.), *Language Development*. London: Croom Helm. 56, 377

Cross, T. G. (1977) Mother's speech adjustments: the contribution of selected child listener variables. In Snow, C. E. and Ferguson, C. (eds.), *Talking to Children: Language Input and Acquisition*. Cambridge: Cambridge University Press. 374, 379, 403, 406

Cross, T. G. (1978) Mother's speech and its association with rate of linguistic development in young children. In Snow, C. and Waterson, N. (eds.), *The Development of Communication*. Chichester: Wiley. 386, 403

Crystal, D. (1974) Review of Brown, R. 'A First Language'. *Journal of Child Language*, 1: 289–306. 121, 340

Crystal, D., Fletcher, P. and Garman, M. (1976) *The Grammatical Analysis of Language Disability: A Procedure for Assessment and Remediation*. London: Edward Arnold. 201, 222

Davies, E. C. (1979) *On the Semantics of Syntax*. London: Croom Helm. 86, 87

Davis, S. M. (1980) Children's Acquisition of the Pronoun System. Unpublished M.Ed. Dissertation, University of Bristol. 459

Deutsch, M. (1965) The role of social class in language development and cognition. *American Journal of Orthopsychiatry, 35:* 78–88. 20

Deutsch, W. (1981) Introduction. In Deutsch, W. (ed.), *The Child's Construction of Language*. London: Academic Press. 396

Donaldson, M. (1978) *Children's Minds*. London: Fontana. 342

Dore, J. (1974) A pragmatic description of early language development. *Journal of Psycholinguistic Research, 3:* 343–50. 120

Dore, J. (1975) Holophrases, speech acts and language universals. *Journal of Child Language, 2:* 21–40. 120, 180, 209, 397

Edwards, D. (1973) Sensory-motor intelligence and semantic relations in early child grammar. *Cognition, 2:* 395–434. 360

Ellis, R. and Wells, C. G. (1980) Enabling factors in adult–child discourse. *First Language, 1:* 46–62. 389

Ervin-Tripp, S. M. (1980) Speech acts, social meaning and social learning. In Giles, H., Robinson, W. P. and Smith, P. M. (eds.), *Language: Social Psychological Perspectives*. Oxford: Pergamon. 179

Fillmore, C. J. (1968) The case for case. In Bach, E. and Harms, R. T. (eds.), *Universals in Linguistic Theory*. New York: Holt, Rinehart and Winston. 59, 68

Fillmore, C. J. (1979) On fluency. In Fillmore, C. J., Kempler, D. and Wang, W. S.-Y. (eds.), *Individual Differences in Language Ability and Language Behavior*. New York: Academic Press. 335

Fletcher, P. (1981) Description and explanation in the acquisition of verb-forms. *Journal of Child Language, 8:* 93–108. 132, 158

Forner, M. (1979). The mother as LAD: interaction between order and frequency of parental input and child production. In Eckman, F. R. and

Hastings, A. J. (eds.), *Studies in First and Second Language Acquisition*. Rowley, Mass.: Newbury House. 355

Fraser, C., Bellugi, U. and Brown, R. (1963) Control of grammar in imitation, comprehension and production. *Journal of Verbal Learning and Verbal Behavior, 2:* 121–35. 39

Furrow, D., Nelson, K. and Benedict, H. (1979) Mother's speech to children and syntactic development: some simple relationships. *Journal of Child Language, 6:* 423–42. 373, 383, 388

Garnica, O. K. (1977) Some prosodic and paralinguistic features of speech in young children. In Snow, C. E. and Ferguson, C. (eds.) *Talking to Children: Language Input and Acquisition*. Cambridge: Cambridge University Press. 182, 399

Garman, M. (1979) Early grammatical development. In Fletcher, P. and Garman, M. (eds.), *Language Acquisition*. Cambridge: Cambridge University Press. 121

Garvey, C. (1977) The contingent query: a dependent act in conversation. In Lewis, M. and Rosenblum, L. A. (eds.), *Interaction, Conversation and the Development of Language*. New York: Wiley. 182, 365, 457

Greenfield, P. M. (1982) The role of perceived variability in the transition to language. *Journal of Child Language, 9:* 1–12. 361

Gregory, S. (1983) Language development in deaf children: delayed or different? Paper presented at Child Language Seminar, University of Strathclyde, March. 403

Griffiths, P. (1979) Speech acts and early sentences. In Fletcher, P. and Garman, M. (eds.), *Language Acquisition*. Cambridge: Cambridge University Press. 120, 180

Guilford, J. P. and Fruchter, B. (1978) *Fundamental Statistics in Psychology and Education* (sixth edition). New York: McGraw Hill. 138

Halliday, M. A. K. (1961) Categories of the theory of grammar. *Word, 17:* 3. 80

Halliday, M. A. K. (1964) *Syntax and the consumer*. Monograph Series on Language and Linguistics, 17 (ed. Stuart, C. I. J. M.). Washington: Georgetown University Press. 59

Halliday, M. A. K. (1967a) Notes on transitivity and theme in English, Part 1 and 2. *Journal of Linguistics, 3:* 37–82. 59

Halliday, M. A. K. (1967b) Notes on transitivity and theme in English, Part 2. *Journal of Linguistics, 3:* 199–244. 59, 164

Halliday, M. A. K. (1968) Notes on transitivity and theme in English, Part 3. *Journal of Linguistics, 4:* 179–216. 59

Halliday, M. A. K. (1970) Language structure and language function. In Lyons, J. (ed.), *New Horizons in Linguistics*. Harmondsworth: Penguin. 78, 159

Halliday, M. A. K. (1975) *Learning How to Mean*. London: Arnold. 3, 120, 177, 179, 180, 181, 209, 365, 397

Halliday, M. A. K. (1977) Language as code and language as behaviour: a systemic–functional interpretation of the nature and ontogenesis of dialogue. To appear in Lamb, S. M. and Makkai, A. (eds.), *Semiotics of Culture and Language*. 59

Halliday, M. A. K. and Hasan, R. (1976) *Cohesion in English*. London: Longman. 80

Hardy-Brown, K. (1983) Universals and individual differences: disentangling two approaches to the study of language acquisition. *Developmental Psychology, 19:* 610–24. 344

Hardy-Brown, K., Plomin, R. and De Fries, J. C. (1981) Genetic and environmental influences on the rate of communicative development in the first year of life. *Developmental Psychology, 17:* 704–17. **344, 386**

Hart, N. W. M., Walker, R. F. and Gray, B. (1977) *The Language of Children: A Key to Literacy*. Reading, Mass.: Addison–Wesley. 227

Heath, S. B. (1983) *Ways with Words*. Cambridge: Cambridge University Press. 57

Henderson, D. (1970) Contextual specificity, discretion and cognitive socialization with special reference to language. *Sociology, 4:* 311–38. **305–9**

Holland, J. (1980) Social class and changes in orientations to meanings. *Sociology, 15:* 1–18. **312**

Holland, J. (in preparation) Gender and class. Adolescent conceptions of aspects of the division of labour. Thesis to be submitted for the degree of Ph.D., University of London Institute of Education. **312**

Homewood, J. R. (1983) Contingent queries and the development of language. Unpublished Ph.D. Thesis, University of Bristol. **182, 457**

Howe, C. J. (1981a) Interpretive analysis and role semantics: a ten-year mesalliance? *Journal of Child Language, 8:* 439–56. 88

Howe, C. (1981b) *Acquiring Language in a Conversational Context*. London: Academic Press. **88, 403**

Huttenlocher, J. (1974) The origins of language comprehension. In Solso, R. L. (ed.), *Theories in Cognitive Psychology*. Hillsdale, N. J.: Lawrence Erlbaum Associates. 127

Ingram, E. (1969) Language development in children. In Fraser, H. and O'Donnell, W. R. (eds.), *Applied Linguistics and the Teaching of English*. London: Longmans. **37, 126**

Kaye, K. and Charney, R. (1980) How mothers maintain dialogue with two-year olds. In Olson, D. (ed.), *The Social Foundations of Language and Thought*. New York: Norton. **400**

Klima, E. S. and Bellugi, U. (1966) Syntactic regularities in the speech of children. In Lyons, J. and Wales, R. J. (eds.), *Psycholinguistics Papers*. Edinburgh: Edinburgh University Press. **2, 59**

Labov, W. (1970) The logic of non-standard English. In Williams, F. (ed.), *Language and Poverty*. Chicago: Markham Publishing Co. 20

Labov, W. (1972a) *Sociolinguistic Patterns*. Philadelphia: University of Pennsylvania Press. **5, 126**

Labov, W. (1972b) *Language in the Inner City.* Philadelphia: University of Pennsylvania Press. **158**

Labov, W. and Fanshel, D. (1977) *Therapeutic Discourse: Psychotherapy as Conversation.* New York: Academic Press. **87**

Lenneberg, E. H. (1967) *Biological Foundations of Language.* New York: Wiley. **19**

Limber, J. (1973) The genesis of complex sentences. In Moore, T. E. (ed.), *Cognitive Development and the Acquisition of Language.* New York: Academic Press. **195**

Lock, A. (1978) *Action, Gesture and Symbol – The Emergence of Language.* London: Academic Press. **398**

Lock, A. (1980) *The Guided Reinvention of Language.* London: Academic Press. **396, 398, 404**

Lyons, J. (1968) *Introduction to Theoretical Linguistics.* Cambridge: Cambridge University Press. **154, 156, 372**

Lyons, J. (1977) *Semantics.* Cambridge: Cambridge University Press. **460**

McCarthy, D. (1930) *The Language Development of the Pre-school Child.* Institute of Child Welfare Monograph Series, 4. Minneapolis: University of Minnesota Press. **4**

McCarthy, D. (1954) Language development in children. In Carmichael, L. (ed.), *Manual of Child Psychology.* New York: Wiley. **20, 29, 40, 342, 344**

McDonald, L. and Pien, D. (1982) Mother conversational behaviour as a function of interactional intent. *Journal of Child Language,* 9: 337–58. **388, 389**

Macnamara, J. (1972) Cognitive basis of language learning in infants. *Psychological Review,* 79: 1–13. **377**

McNeill, D. (1970) *The Acquisition of Language: The Study of Developmental Psycholinguistics.* New York: Harper and Row. **401**

McShane, J. (1980) *Learning to Talk.* Cambridge: Cambridge University Press. **58, 117, 198, 401**

McTear, M. (1981) Towards a model for analysing conversations involving children. In French, P. and MacLure, M. (eds.), *Adult–Child Conversation.* London: Croom Helm. **87**

Miller, G. A. (1977) *Spontaneous Apprentices: Children and Language.* New York, The Seabury Press. **1**

Miller, G. A., Galanter, E. and Pribram, K. (1960) *Plans and the Structure of Behavior.* New York: Holt, Rinehart and Winston. **61**

Moerk, E. L. (1980) Relationships between parental input frequencies and children's language acquisition: a reanalysis of Brown's data. *Journal of Child Language,* 7: 105–18. **355**

Morrisby, J. R. (1955) *Compound Series Test.* Hemel Hempstead: Educational and Industrial Test Services. **40**

Nelson, K. (1973) *Structure and strategy in learning to talk.* Monographs of the Society for Research in Child Development, 38, 1–2, Series 149. Chicago: University of Chicago Press. **57, 210, 334, 404**

Nelson, K. (1981) Individual differences in language development: implications for development and language. *Developmental Psychology, 17:* 170–87. **57, 404**

Nelson, K. E. (1977) Aspects of language acquisition and use from age two to age twenty. *Journal of the American Academy of Child Psychiatry, 16:* 584–607. **401, 402**

Newport, E. L., Gleitman, H. and Gleitman, L. R. (1977) Mother I'd rather do it myself: some effects and non-effects of maternal speech style. In Snow, C. E. and Ferguson, C. A. (eds.), *Talking to Children: Language Input and Acquisition.* Cambridge: Cambridge University Press. **373, 382, 383, 388, 393**

Newson, J. (1978) Dialogue and development. In Lock, A. (ed.), *Action, Gesture and Symbol – The Emergence of Language.* 405–6, **407**

Newson, J. and Newson, E. (1968) *Four Years Old in an Urban Community.* London: Allen and Unwin. **294**

Ninio, A. and Bruner, J. S. (1978) The achievement and antecedents of labelling. *Journal of Child Language, 5:* 1–16. **117, 198, 401**

Peters, A. M. (1983) *The Units of Language Acquisition.* Cambridge: Cambridge University Press. **334**

Phillips, J. L. (1975) *The Origins of Intellect: Piaget's Theory* (second edition). San Francisco: W. H. Freeman. **225**

Piaget, J. and Inhelder, B. (1969) *The Psychology of the Child.* London: Routledge and Kegan Paul. **360**

Quirk, R., Greenbaum, S., Leech, G. and Svartvik, J. (1973) *A University Grammar of English.* London: Longman. **82**

Ratner, N. and Bruner, J. S. (1978) Games, social exchange and the acquisition of language. *Journal of Child Language, 5:* 391–402. **3, 392, 398**

Sachs, J. and Devin, J. (1976) Young children's use of age-appropriate speech styles in social interaction and role-playing. *Journal of Child Language, 3:* 81–98. **342**

Searle, J. R. (1969) *Speech Acts: An Essay in the Philosophy of Language.* Cambridge: Cambridge University Press. **64**

Searle, J. R. (1977) A classification of illocutionary acts. *Language in Society, 5:* 1–23. **59, 364, 365**

Shatz, M. (1978) Children's comprehension of their mothers' question–directives. *Journal of Child Language, 5:* 39–46. **388**

Shatz, M. (1982) On mechanisms of language acquisition: Can features of the communicative environment account for development? In Wanner, E. and Gleitman, L. R. (eds.), *Language Acquisition: the State of the Art.* **382**

Shatz, M. and Gelman, R. (1973) *Development of communication skills.* Monographs of the Society for Research in Child Development, 152. Chicago: University of Chicago Press. **342**

Sinclair, J. McH. (1972) *A Course in Spoken English: Grammar.* London: Oxford University Press. **82**

Sinclair, J. McH. (1975) Discourse in relation to language structure and semiotics. Paper presented to Burg Wartenstein Symposium 66: Semiotics of Culture and Language, Vienna, August 1975 (mimeo).

Sinclair, J. McH. and Coulthard, M. (1975) *Towards and Analysis of Discourse: the English Used by Teachers and Pupils*. London: Oxford University Press. 59

Sinha, C. and Walkerdine, V. (1978) Conservation: a problem in language, culture and thought. In Waterson, N. and Snow, C. (eds.), *The Development of Communication*. Chichester: Wiley. 39

Slobin, D. I. (1967) A Field Manual for Cross-Cultural Study of the Acquisition of Communicative Competence (second draft), University of California, Berkeley. 93

Slobin, D. I. (1973) Cognitive prerequisites for the development of grammar. In Ferguson, C. and Slobin, D. I. (eds.), *Studies of Child Language Development*. New York: Holt, Rinehart. 56, 134, 209, 355, 377

Slobin, D. I. (1979) The role of language in language acquisition. (Mimeo.) University of California, Berkeley. 57, 224, 377

Slobin, D. I. (1981) The origin of grammatical encoding of events. In Deutsch, W. (ed.), *The Child's Construction of Language*. London: Academic Press. 396

Slobin, D. I. (1982) Universal and particular in the acquisition of language. In Wanner, E. and Gleitman, L. R. (eds.) *Language Acquisition: the State of the Art*. 57

Slobin, D. I. and Welsh, C. A. (1973) Elicited imitation as a research tool in developmental psycholinguistics. In Ferguson, C. A. and Slobin, D. I. (eds.), *Studies of Child Language Development*. New York: Holt, Rinehart. 39

Snow, C. (1977) Mother's speech research: from input to acquisition. In Snow, C. and Ferguson, C. (eds.) *Talking to Children: Language Input and Acquisition*. 3, 322, 373, 377, 382

Snow, C., Arlman-Rupp, A., Hassing, Y., Jobse, J., Joosten, J. and Vorster, J. (1976) Mother's speech in three social classes. *Journal of Psycholinguistic Research*, 5: 1–20. 322

Templin, M. C. (1957) *Certain Language Skills in Children*. Minneapolis: University of Minnesota Press. 4, 20, 40, 348

Tough, J. (1977) *The Development of Meaning*. London: Allen and Unwin. 348

Trevarthen, C. (1974) Conversations with a two-month-old. *New Scientist, 2 May 1974*, p. 230. 56

Trevarthen, C. (1979) Communication and cooperation in early infancy: a description of primary intersubjectivity. In Bullowa, M. (ed.) *Before Speech: The Beginning of Interpersonal Communication*. Cambridge: Cambridge University Press. 398

Trevarthen, C. and Hubley, P. (1978) Secondary intersubjectivity: confidence, confiding and acts of meaning in the first year. In A. Lock (ed.) *Action, Gesture and Symbol – The Emergence of Language*. 56

Vygotsky, L. S. (1962) *Thought and Language.* Cambridge, Mass.: M.I.T. Press. **56, 67, 402**

Walkerdine, V. (1975) Spatial and Temporal Relations in the Linguistic and Cognitive Development of Young Children. Unpublished Ph.D. Thesis, University of Bristol, School of Education. **39, 341**

Walkerdine, V. and Sinha, C. (1978) The internal triangle: language reasoning and the social context. In Markova, I. (ed.), *Language and the Social Context.* Chichester: Wiley. **127, 341**

Walkerdine, V. and Sinha, C. (1981) Developing linguistic strategies in young school children. In Wells, C. G., *Learning through Interaction.* **39**

Wanner, E. and Gleitman, L. R. (eds.) (1982) *Language Acquisition: the State of the Art.* Cambridge: Cambridge University Press. **201**

Weir, R. (1962) *Language in the Crib.* The Hague: Mouton. **146**

Wells, C. G. (1974) Learning to code experience through language. *Journal of Child Language, 1:* 243–69. **360**

Wells, C. G. (1975) *Coding Manual for the Description of Child Speech in its Conversational Context.* University of Bristol School of Education. Revised edition. **58, 60, 98, 133**

Wells, C. G. (1978) What makes for successful language development? In Campbell, R. and Smith, P. (eds.) *Recent Advances in the Psychology of Language.* New York: Plenum. **126**

Wells, C. G. (1979a) Learning and using the auxiliary verb in English. In Lee, V. (ed.), *Language Development.* London: Croom Helm. **159, 160, 162, 358**

Wells, C. G. (1979b) Variation in child language. In Fletcher, P. and Garman, M. (eds.) *Language Acquisition* Cambridge: Cambridge University Press. Reprinted in Lee, V. (ed.) *Language Development.* London: Croom Helm. **341, 342**

Wells, C. G. (1980) Adjustments in adult–child conversation: some effects of interaction. In Giles, H., Robinson, W. P. and Smith, P. M. (eds.), *Language: Social-Psychological Perspectives.* Oxford: Pergamon. **384**

Wells, C. G. (1981) *Learning through Interaction: the Study of Language Development.* Cambridge: Cambridge University Press. **18, 57, 84, 383, 410**

Wells, C. G. (1982) Influences of the home on language development. In Davies, A. (ed.), *Language and Learning at School and Home.* London: SSRC/Heinemann. **128**

Wells, C. G. (in press a) Pre-school literacy-related activities and success in school. In Olson, D., Torrance, N. and Hildyard, A. (eds.), *Literacy, Language, and Learning.* Cambridge: Cambridge University Press. **117**

Wells, C. G. (in press b) Variation in child language. In Fletcher, P. and Garman, M. (eds.) *Language Acquisition* (revised edition). Cambridge: Cambridge University Press. **335**

Wells, C. G., MacLure, M. and Montgomery, M. M. (1981) Some

strategies for sustaining conversation. In Werth, P. (ed.), *Conversation, Speech and Discourse*. London: Croom Helm. **174, 353, 384, 400, 456**

Wells, C. G., Montgomery, M. M. and MacLure, M. (1979) Adult–child discourse: outline of a model of analysis. *Journal of Pragmatics, 3:* 337–80. **353, 384, 456**

Wells, C. G. and Robinson, W. P. (1982) The role of adult speech in language development. In Fraser, C. and Scherer, K. (eds.) *The Social Psychology of Language*. Cambridge University Press. **23**

Woll, B. (1979) Sex as a variable in child language development. *Bristol Working Papers in Language, 1:* 71–86. **345**

Woll, B., Ferrier, L. and Wells, C. G. (1975) Children and their parents: who starts the talking, why and when? Paper presented at the 'Language and the Social Context' Conference, Stirling, January 1975. **345**

Wong-Fillmore, L. (1979) Individual differences in second language acquisition. In Fillmore, C. J., Kempler, D. and Wang, W. S.-Y. (eds.), *Individual Differences in Language Ability and Language Behavior*. New York: Academic Press. **344, 404**

Wood, D. (1983a) Talking to deaf children. In *Proceedings of the 8th National Conference of the Australian Association for Special Education*. **404**

Wood, D. (1983b) Teaching: natural and contrived. *Child Development Society Newsletter, 31:* 2–7. London: University of London Institute of Education. **404**

Subject index